The Nervous

•

PROPAGANDA ANXIETIES FROM
WORLD WAR I TO THE COLD WAR

Columbia Studies in Contemporary American History
William E. Leuchtenburg and Alan Brinkley, General Editors

The Nervous Liberals

•

PROPAGANDA ANXIETIES FROM
WORLD WAR I TO THE COLD WAR

Brett Gary

COLUMBIA UNIVERSITY PRESS
New York

COLUMBIA UNIVERSITY PRESS

Publishers Since 1893

New York   Chichester, West Sussex

Copyright © 1999 Columbia University Press

All rights reserved

Library of Congress Cataloging-in-Publication Data

Gary, Brett

The nervous liberals : propaganda anxieties

from World War I to the Cold War / Brett Gary.

p.   cm.   — (Columbia studies in contemporary American history)

Includes bibliographical references and index.

ISBN 0-231-11364-1 (cloth). — ISBN 0-231-11365-X (pbk.)

1. United States—Politics and government—1919–1933. 2. United

States—Politics and government—1933–1945 3. Liberalism—United

States—History—20th century. 4. Propaganda, American—

History—20th century. 5. World War, 1914–1918—Propaganda.

6. World War, 1939–1945—Propaganda.

I. Title. II. Series.

E743.G35   1999

303.3′75′097309041—DC21   99-31171

CIP

∞

Designed by Ben Farber

Casebound editions of Columbia University Press books are

printed on permanent and durable acid-free paper.

Printed in the United States of America

c 10 9 8 7 6 5 4 3 2 1

p 10 9 8 7 6 5 4 3 2 1

This book is dedicated with love and thanks to Peg and Joe Gary
to Joey and Annabel
and to Amy

CONTENTS

ACKNOWLEDGMENTS

Like most scholars completing books that have taken years and dominated several phases of their lives, I am indebted to teachers, friends, and colleagues from a variety of institutions. I began this project as my dissertation in the Department of American Civilization at the University of Pennsylvania, where I had the good fortune to work with Professors Murray G. Murphey and Bruce Kuklick. Murray was an indefatigable teacher who taught me much of what I know about American history. Bruce was an exemplary dissertation adviser who not only turned around my chapters with stunning speed but taught me that an ethos of complexity is far more intellectually honest and interesting than a view that divides the world into good and evil forces. As I have moved this project from a thesis to book, he continued to engage my work, reminding me of the complexity imperative, and I know my book is much stronger because of it. I am grateful to both.

While at Penn, I was lucky to encounter many other gifted people who offered their ideas, encouragement, and, when possible, their financial support. Janice Radway provided stimulating early support for this study. Peshe Kuriloff helped me keep bread on my table, as did John Noakes, a fellow student of the national security state who shared ideas, wrangled funds for other graduate students, and organized dissertation reading groups and then speaking engagements in the world beyond Penn. John was an invaluable colleague for many Penn students in a variety of disciplines. Others generously shared their bread, spare futon couches, and encouragement—Stan Schmidt, Phil Kronebush and Kim Hallier, Lauren Turner, Janice and Bob Benedict, Deborah Franklin, Elizabeth Wilson, Lisa Null, and Jim Vogele— or their analytical and editorial services, including Doctor Ed O'Reilly (who spotted every mixed metaphor), Saul Cornell, Pam Sankar, Nancy Bercaw, and especially Nancy Bernhard. Nancy knows this book nearly as well as I, sees it with clearer eyes, and from the day years ago in Van Pelt Library when she told me to go home and start writing to her incisive reading of this book's conclusion several months ago, she has been a model colleague whose good humor, intelligence, knowledge, and supportive friendship have been keenly felt and deeply appreciated. She and David Margolin were generous hosts many times in this book's gestation.

Colleagues in the predoctoral fellows program at the Smithsonian Institution's National Museum of American History were similarly stimulating, including John Cheng, Ian Gordon, Carolyn Goldstein, and generous with their spare sleeping quarters, especially Ruth Oldenziel and Ed and Lucy Russell. Ed, in a moment of typically clear thinking, illuminated the central tension that drives this narrative. To Pete Daniel, Charlie McGovern, Larry Bird, and Mary Dwyer, I offer thanks for giving me a year to write my dissertation in the Smithsonian's truly supportive atmosphere. Likewise, I would like to thank the Rockefeller Archive Center at Pocantico Hills, and its excellent archivists, for their financial support and access to their valuable facilities. Archivist Thomas Rosenbaum was especially valuable in helping me understand the treasures housed in the Rockefeller Foundation's archives, and my memories of our Chinese dinners when we talked over my research remain vivid. I would also like to thank the staff of Yale University's Manuscripts and Archives for making Harold D. Lasswell's papers available. To Mary Ronan and other archivists in the Civil Reference Division of the National Archives and Records Administration, thank you for expediting the declassification of the Justice Department's Special War Policies Unit files, and for attending to my many requests. To Jim Roan and the National Museum of American History library, and the librarians in the Justice Department Library's archives, thank you for your help. And to the Library of Congress archivists, thank you for your help with the records of the Special Division of the Study of Wartime Communications, as well as with Archibald MacLeish's papers from his stint as Librarian of Congress.

American Studies colleagues at the University of Colorado offered friendship, astute commentaries on my manuscript chapters, and more good bread. Erika Doss gave me opportunities to try my ideas in public, Rickie Solinger helped me think about framing my ideas and making their consequences clearer, Mark Pittenger gave me careful, exceptionally helpful suggestions on several chapters. Nancy Mann performed top-notch editorial work on part of the manuscript. Linda Kerr-Saville made my life much happier and easier as our administrative assistant at Colorado's Sewall Academic Program. She also helped me find two excellent research assistants, Joyce Mizrahi and Erin Hicks. Chris Lewis was an endless source of bibliographic information, and Willian Wei did his best to make our working conditions at CU better. My good friend Len Ackland helped me work through my ideas on our countless and sorely missed hikes in the Flatirons and on the mesas, always doing so by mixing humor and outrage at the antidemocratic manifestations of the national security state; he also applied his journalist's editorial eye to my introduction, forcing me to think and write more clearly. And he and Carol Stutzman were invariably the warmest of hosts. Fellow hiker and dear friend Gary Ferrini helped me think past my manuscript and reminded me how important generosity of time and energy are in the cultivation of enduring friendships. And John Remo Gennari, graduate school crony and colleague at Colorado, provided delicious garlic-infused meals, passion for music, love of athletic grace, and astute commentary on my prose style and argument. He has also taught me much about dignity. I humbly thank them all.

Beyond Philadelphia and Boulder, others have been gracious in their generosity and helpful in their support of my academic career. Alberic Culhane, OSB, long ago noticed that I had an affinity for books and ideas. Bob Rydell saw this as well when he was just starting out as a young professor at Montana State University and encouraged me to pursue my academic interests. Since then he has stayed involved in my career, giving me much-needed teaching opportunities, reading the entire manuscript several times, and encouraging others to hear me out. He and his wife, Kiki, have been gracious hosts and friends. Richard Polenberg read portions of the book at earlier stages, as did Garth Jowett, K. R. M. Short, Harvey Kaye, and Elliot Gorn. John Durham Peters helped me publish several chapters in article form. All made this a better work. Alan Brinkley gave me insightful criticism on several chapters and ultimately helped me find a home for this book in his series with Columbia University Press. For his generous readings and for directing my manuscript to editor-in-chief Kate Wittenberg and her highly capable staff at Columbia University Press, I offer special thanks. I also thank Sarah St. Onge, copy-editor extraordinaire, who has paid such exceptional attention to my manuscript. To Columbia's outside reviewers, thank you for your suggestions.

Neil Postman, Terry Moran, and Ted Magder of the Department of Culture and Communication at New York University gave me a place to ply my trade while finishing this manuscript. I thank them for the teaching opportunities and for the chance to give full airing to my argument at one of their annual Media Ecology conferences. Ted and Julie Jakolat both offered me immensely useful suggestions for my conclusion as I was trying to meet crucial deadlines. More important, my brief stint at NYU gave me the chance to get to know Jonathan Zimmerman. Jon lent me his office and computer whenever he could, is an unending source of energy and enthusiasm and ideas, and reminded me by example of the great value of laughter as psychic balm. I doubt I could have finished this book with anything resembling humor or grace without his generous friendship.

Mara Sandoval, Pac Pao Gibson, Tamara Rowe, Megan Matzinger, Gabrielle Taylor, Cristina Melfi and Kathy Williams deserve my deepest thanks for being such great daycare providers and teachers, and tendering my children such love.

To my new colleagues in the Drew University History Department and the Graduate Program in Modern History and Literature, thank you for giving me such a fine place to hang my shingle at last.

To Craig, T.K., Zilla, Huntcakes, Billy, Hiney, Beardy, Jenner, and Brigand, thanks for your friendship, shared passions, and high expectations for one another. I've tried to do my best.

Finally, to my family. My parents, Peg and Joe Gary, have been unstintingly optimistic about all I do, and that has paid off, as they always prayed it would. They have been model citizens and parents, showering their children, grandchildren, and friends with unceasing affection and support, contributing to a more just and civilized community where they live. Their fifty-plus years of marriage are a monument to teamwork and laughter. I thank my siblings, Marie, Joan, Brian, and Mark, and their families for their humor and forbearance and want them to know that I have tried to write this book with them as my ideal readers, although I do recommend a stiff cup of coffee and a bright lamp as accessories. My wife's parents, Joe and Barbara Bentley, have been truly generous supporters of my work and my need for cold fresh water and starry skies, as have her sisters and their families. Their affection and indulgence are gratefully received.

My greatest thanks go to Amy Bentley, my wife, colleague, and partner. Amy has been an unflagging champion of my work since graduate school, has endured far too many drafts of each chapter and invariably made each clearer and shorter, and has kept reminding me all along that I did have something worth saying. Her creativity, intelligence, fair-mindedness, and success as a scholar nourish and delight me. Her care of our beautiful children, Joey and Annabel, reassures me daily. And her persistent optimism, grace, tenderness, and dazzling ability to juggle the world's demands seem so natural that I do not acknowledge nearly often enough how lucky I am and how special she is. I hereby acknowledge it and thank her for helping me see this through. It would have been wrecked on the shoals of Harold Lasswell's ghastly prose long ago were it not for Amy.

To my parents, my children, and especially to Amy, I dedicate this book.

New York City

The Nervous Liberals

•

PROPAGANDA ANXIETIES FROM WORLD WAR I TO THE COLD WAR

INTRODUCTION

Histories about the modern uses of propaganda almost invariably point to the First World War and its immediate aftermath as the period when people became acutely aware that campaigns and techniques of mass persuasion were an ineluctable condition of modern existence. Though propaganda was widely employed prior to the twentieth century for purposes of empire and crown, nation building and revolution, religious consolidation and reformation, and, of course, for the demonization of all varieties of enemies, its extensive use by all World War I belligerents created a new consciousness about the relationship between modern communications technologies and public manipulation. Never before, contemporaries noted, had warring parties relied so heavily on mass propaganda campaigns as part of their war efforts, and never before had citizens been so aware of the extent to which they were being actively manipulated by governments, both foreign and their own.[1]

The concept (or label) "propaganda"—with all its negative connotations of orchestrated deception—helped observers and critics understand the patriotic hysteria in all countries and the repressive domestic climates those passions provoked. In subsequent years, as postwar disillusionment led to widespread reassessment of the war's causes and consequences, the propaganda campaigns conducted by all warring nations became explanations for the high hopes and dashed expectations that characterized nations' moods and, especially, for the vicious hatreds that produced vindictive, doomed postwar settlements. Although its uses were ancient, post-WWI critics conceived of propaganda as an industrial-era, even a distinctly twentieth-century problem: it combined the aggressive passions of nationalism and revolution with machine-age scales of mass production and distribution (employing powerful new communications technologies), targeted uprooted, dislocated, and allegedly volatile mass publics, was buttressed by the increasingly widespread perception that irrational impulses govern human behavior, and was practiced by an emerging coterie of professionalized experts who understood (and celebrated) the commercial or political efficacy of manipulating those irrational forces for concealed purposes.[2]

In the aftermath of the Great War, "propaganda consciousness" contributed significantly to the chastened democratic faith of an entire generation of U.S. liberal intellectuals.[3] Indeed, liberal faith in democratic theory would never recover from what one writer calls the American "discovery of propaganda,"[4] a discovery marked by an outpouring of popular and scholarly literature by political and social critics, historians, journalists, novelists, philosophers, and others aghast (though a few were delighted) by this technologically enhanced capacity of nation-states, revolutionaries, and interest groups to direct attention and emotion by bombarding apparently susceptible "mass" audiences with persuasive images and ideas. As political scientist Harold D. Lasswell wrote in his 1927 study *Propaganda Technique in the World War*, "A word has appeared, which has come to have an ominous clang in many minds—Propaganda. We live among more people than ever, who are puzzled, uneasy, or vexed at the unknown cunning which seems to have duped and degraded them."[5] A bibliography Lasswell and colleagues compiled in 1935 reflects this fear and fascination, listing over fifteen hundred articles, pamphlets, and books written on the topic between 1919 and 1934; updating the bibliography in 1946, the same bibliographers identified an additional fifteen hundred titles published between 1935 and 1945.[6] Barry Alan Marks, in a penetrating mid-1950s study, summarized this explosion of interest and provided a framework for understanding the common assumptions among Western intellectuals in an era some dubbed "the Age of Propaganda":

> Writers took pains to demonstrate that, however much evidence of propaganda could be found in the past, the propaganda during the Great War was significantly different from all that had gone before and was, in effect, something new. Some asserted that the distinctive quality of modern propaganda was that it had become an official activity of the state and was, therefore, buttressed by large amounts of money and great organizational skill; some spoke . . . of a new intensity or a new scale and effectiveness.

Most of these postwar writers conceived of propaganda as a "new and powerful threat to America," based on a litany of its presumably destructive powers: it was a force almost "unlimited in its power to capture the minds and hearts of men (usually for purposes of evil)"; it was "unbelievable in its capacity to deceive"; and it "made obsolete the traditional canons of truth and logic."[7] These assumptions led, I argue, to deep and fundamental divisions within modern American liberalism, especially over questions of public versus expert responsibility and over matters of individual liberty versus collective security.

Taken together, the ubiquitous wartime campaigns, the postwar dismay, the blame placed on propaganda for unleashing repressive forces, and the perception that human reason and intellect could not withstand the onslaught of mass-mediated images and slogans shattered important nineteenth-century liberal faiths, especially in the ideas of informed discourse, a rational public, the eventual triumph of truth, and good government. The pessimistic conclusions resulting from the encounter with propaganda on a mass scale were exemplified by the postwar writings of one the most influential public intellectuals of the WWI generation, Walter Lippmann.[8] Lippmann's withering attack on the irrationality of the public was a powerful culmination in the U.S. sphere of a several-decade-long trend among European and American intellectuals warning about the dangers of the "crowd psychology" (driven by its "unconscious substratum"), the rising tide of "barbarism" attendant to mass democracy, the "fallacy" of human intellectualism, and the "instincts of the herd."[9] Although committed to representative democracy, Lippmann demolished democratic orthodoxy, promoting instead the need for government managed by responsible experts who could run the public's affairs (and, in times of crisis, effectively channel and mobilize public opinion so that the symbolic functions of democratic rituals would still gratify public sensibilities). Lippmann's ideas, which play a significant role in this study, did not go unchallenged by stalwarts of democratic theory such as John Dewey. But as Stuart Ewen and J. Michael Sproule and others have recently shown, this negative perception of public irrationality was rife in intellectual circles and coincided with the rise of a formidable public relations industry that identified WWI as a convincing case study of how exceedingly well public relations counselors, advertisers, and publicity agents could manage the public mind.[10] This evidence of the powerful art of mass persuasion was grist for the critics, but for "democratic realists" like Lippmann and political scientist Harold Lasswell it justified revising traditional democratic theory by removing the idea of a competent public from its center, replacing it with technocratic experts, including symbols specialists.[11] Reflecting the contempt for traditional notions of democratic theory based on public opinion, Lasswell wrote, "The public has not led with benignity and restraint. The good life is not in the mighty rushing wind of public sentiment. It is no organic secretion of the horde, but the tedious achievement of the few. . . . Thus argues the despondent democrat."[12] Like his fellow despondent progressive Lippmann, Lasswell claimed that the future of democratic governments was safer in the hands of the few than the benighted many. Their perception of public manipulability, shared by many social scientists of the post-WWI generation, reinforced the idea that social and political institutions should be rationalized and made more efficient through scientific and engineering-based models and techniques.[13]

For critics of this refashioned, top-down version of democratic theory—such as Dewey, the Rockefeller Foundation's John Marshall (director of the foundation's communications research projects), First Amendment scholar Zechariah Chafee Jr., and poet Archibald MacLeish—the relentless authority of the combined thesis of propaganda's power and public susceptibility was formidable, difficult even for its critics to escape. The foundational debate between Lippmann and Dewey was situated within the framework of a pessimistic mass society thesis. And although their images and metaphors were "colored by apocalyptic assumptions," to use Patrick Brantlinger's phrase for describing mass society theses in general, the Lippmann-Dewey colloquy was also shaped by distinctively U.S. concerns about propaganda's challenge to the viability of democratic theory and republican forms of government.[14] As I show, the ongoing debates between Lippmann-styled technocratic realists and Deweyan idealists emerged as a central tension within liberal intellectual circles. As liberals tried to work out an understanding of the relationship among public capacity, expert responsibility, and democratic theory in an age of propaganda, the realists consistently were able to define the debate's terms by stressing the problem of public incompetence and posing opinion management as the solution. They were challenged, however, by those idealists who bristled at the undemocratic assumptions of this logic.

The other central tension in modern liberalism that this study explores was closely related, growing out of concerns about the effects of mass communications that were shaped in no small part by the rise of totalitarian systems in Italy, Germany, and the Soviet Union.[15] By the mid-1930s, U.S. propaganda anxieties were made concrete and ominous by fears of foreign subversion in the United States, resulting in the perception that the state and polis needed protection from totalitarian propaganda. The debates about how best to protect democratic society from Fascist and Communist propaganda laid bare, as they had in the WWI era, the tensions between liberal civil libertarians (exemplified by Chafee and MacLeish) and the security-oriented liberals (embodied by Lasswell and the Justice Department's Special Defense Unit). To a significant extent, the fears of propaganda leading up to World War II echoed those from the previous war, and the civil libertarians drew on the experience of WWI to fashion their critique and to promote a speech-protective, hysteria-proof approach to propaganda control. It is crucial, however, to note that they too found it absolutely necessary to fashion a propaganda-control strategy, largely because of their fear of

Nazi propaganda. As in WWI and the first Red Scare, WWII-era propaganda anxieties resulted in another variation on democracy-constricting, expert-centered politics, this time in the guise of national security liberalism.

What I want to suggest, then, is that two main problems of propaganda bedeviled liberal intellectuals and government officials in the period from WWI to the beginning of the cold war. The first revolved around the question of how to resuscitate democratic theory in an age of propaganda; the second focused on the more concrete security-based problem of protecting U.S. society from antidemocratic ideas and activities. Both sets of problems were defined and debated within the frameworks of the expert versus public-centered conflict and the liberty versus security conflict. Conceptually and chronologically, the first problem (the crisis of democratic theory) establishes the intellectual context for the second (the totalitarian propaganda scare). While this book is driven by debates and conflicts over ideas among intellectuals—a traditional approach to intellectual history—it is also driven by archival research and a narrative that focuses on the institutional response to the threat of totalitarian propaganda and the creation of what Justice Department officials called a "preventive and protective" barrier between the American people and presumably dangerous ideas. It tells two stories: how liberal intellectuals thought about propaganda, and how they and government officials created a propaganda "prophylaxis," as I call it, in response.

The main story is about how liberal intellectuals, government officials, and key cultural and educational institutions mobilized for a war against Nazi propaganda. Although I am interested in the genealogy of ideas about propaganda, my larger purpose is to use the tensions and conflicts generated by those ideas to clarify the culture of U.S. intellectual and political liberalism from WWI to the early cold war. While arguing that propaganda anxieties shed light on some of the central tensions and paradoxes of early to midcentury liberalism, there were many strains within liberalism and significant conflict over other issues that this study does not address. As historians Alan Dawley, Gary Gerstle, Robert Westbrook, and Alan Brinkley have recently argued, quite different strains of liberalism emerged in the 1920s and 1930s, especially over the role of the state as an instrument of social and economic justice.[16] Gerstle thus refers to the "protean character" of American liberalism, and Brinkley suggests the difficulty of defining U.S. liberalism with any precision: "All liberals claim to believe in personal liberty, human progress, and the pursuit of rational self-interest by individuals as the basis of a free society. But there is considerable, often intense, disagreement among them over what those ideas mean." He goes on to say that "in the twentieth century alone, the word 'liberalism' has designated at least three very different concepts of progress and freedom," which he labels laissez-faire liberalism, reform liberalism, and rights-based liberalism. The last strain focused "on increasing the rights and freedoms of individuals and social groups" and "attempted to expand the notion of personal liberty and individual freedom for everyone," but, as I show, these intentions ran headlong into other imperatives, especially the state's continually expanding national security function.[17] By the end of WWII it was not clear which menagerie of liberal beliefs could coexist in a world thought to be imperiled by totalitarianism.[18]

For the most part, interwar liberalism was capacious. So was intellectual culture, although the primacy of science-based research was rapidly leading to rigid disciplinary boundaries, especially between the social sciences and the humanities. But propaganda anxieties transcended those boundaries, to some extent, because they produced similar fears across academic fields and institutions. In fact, propaganda studies were broadly interdisciplinary, with expertise and problem-solving strategies in one discipline invariably influencing the questions and strategies developed in adjacent fields. As in most areas of interdisciplinary research, however, science-based models for propaganda studies received the available funding (primarily from foundations) and attracted government attention.[19] While these trends are important to the intellectual history of propaganda research—and to this story—the more relevant issue is that the key players came from diverse fields and institutions, including journalism, philosophy, the social sciences, mass communications research, philanthropy, law, literature, and government service. Sharing a broad set of concerns about the power and effects of mass communications and the need to preserve and protect U.S. democracy, the main cast of characters stepped easily and frequently across disciplines and from one institution to another. As Nazi power threatened global security and the United States moved toward war, the fluidity of ideas and personnel through institutions became especially noteworthy, leading to a remarkable degree of intellectual cross-fertilization and, just as noteworthy, ideological consolidation. For the main actors in this study, two primary questions generated common goals and produced a unique and fascinating institutional and intellectual collaboration.

Answering the questions "How is the United States threatened by Nazi propaganda?" and "What is to be done about it?" demanded an integration of thought and action, a mobilization of intellect. Thus, while illuminating competing imperatives and ideas within U.S. liberalism, this study also provides a different way to think about the emergence and construction of the national security state. My archival and institutional research reveals that the U.S. war against Nazi propaganda grew out of a significant collaborative effort among the nation's premier educational, philanthropic, and cultural institutions, in eventual collaboration with the state.[20] In looking at the interinstitutional, interdisciplinary mobilization, I also trace the ideological and ethical tightropes walked by this study's action-oriented "nervous liberals"—to use Archibald MacLeish's apt phrase—who sought to protect civil liberties but were also the architects of the propaganda prophylaxis and the state's own propaganda efforts as war broke out.[21] MacLeish, who figures prominently in the narrative, wore many hats and fully embodied the era's tensions and ironies. An ardent antifascist interventionist and civil libertarian, he blasted the "nervous liberals" who in the late 1930s hoped to control antidemocratic propaganda through speech and organization-restrictive legislation. Yet by the onset of U.S. involvement in WWII, he had himself become quite nervous, using his offices as Librarian of Congress and director of the Office of Facts and Figures to coordinate the federal government's war against propaganda and to enjoin his fellow writers and artists to suspend their critical voices and become instruments in the war of words and ideas. Let me be clear: I do not question the good faith and intentions of MacLeish, the Rockefeller Foundation's John Marshall, and others in their cohort. They were early and principled interventionists in a necessary war against Fascism, and they mobilized intellectual and institutional resources at a critical juncture, well before an isolationist U.S. Congress and public would have permitted the Roosevelt administration to do so. They also hoped that democratic strategies for controlling propaganda could be achieved and strove to ensure that they would. Their dual commitments to liberty and security are emblematic of the conflict-laden struggle to fight a democratic war against invidious forces and ideas. But their struggles show how fragile the commitment to civil liberties, a free flow of information, and ideological tolerance became when the war against totalitarian propaganda reached full throttle and could not be demobilized when Communists reemerged as the great propaganda menace threatening the nation. By war's end, expert-centered national security liberalism triumphed, and public-centered free-speech liberalism had few platforms in the academy, the press, or the state from which it could be heard.

While this is not a declensionist narrative as such, I want to suggest that the propaganda anxieties that beset U.S. culture in the era from WWI to the cold war might not have resulted in such ideological constriction had the nation's political and intellectual classes perceived the U.S. public as being capable, rational, and responsible. The pessimistic assumptions about public incompetence and susceptibility that pervaded much liberal intellectual culture for most of the twentieth century deepened as the totalitarian powers—with their dictatorship cults, international fifth columns, and mass followings—grew as national security threats.[22] If leading liberal thinkers and policy makers had had a higher estimation of public capacity would they have offered a more principled defense of democratic institutions? Would they have contributed to the national security state's enormous growth had they been less fearful of the supposed machine-age power of propaganda?

Before turning to an overview of the chapters, some definitional matters are in order, especially about the book's key word. Today, curiously few political analysts employ the term "propaganda" to describe political communication within U.S. culture, despite what often seems like the self-evidently propagandistic nature of those materials. While questions about the power of mass communications to shape public tastes, interests, and behaviors are routinely asked in numerous books, university-level media studies courses, Sunday op-ed pieces, and the ubiquitous commentary about popular culture's immense effects on our culture and consciousness, the term "propaganda" has a much diminished role in our daily political lexicon, leading to the question, What happened to the idea of propaganda? I offer several preliminary suggestions. First, propaganda as a label suffered (and suffers) from a certain imprecision; it is not unlike Justice Potter Stewart's fabled nondefinition of pornography: "I don't know how to define it, but I know it when I see it." Communications theorist Jacques Ellul's study *Propaganda: The Formation of Men's Attitudes* speaks to this ambiguity in an unintended way. From his perspective, propaganda is so much a part of the "technological society" that virtually everything fits under the rubric. He writes: "Propaganda is a good deal less the political weapon of a regime (it is that also) than the effect of a technological society that embraces the entire man and tends to be a completely integrated society."[23] Useful for its global view and insights into the bureaucratic, communications-mediated world we inhabit, Ellul's technologically deterministic formulation that propaganda completely envelops us does not lead to particularly precise labeling. Others, like communications historians Garth Jowett and Victoria O'Donnell, do not really distinguish propaganda from advertising, seeing the two as essentially the same processes and indicating the extent to which the different "arts" of mass persuasion have become ubiquitous and inseparable in late-twentieth-century culture.[24] For my part, I try to maintain that distinction by defining propaganda as the organized manipulation of key cultural symbols and images (and biases) for the purposes of persuading a mass audience to take a position, or move to action, or remain inactive *on a controversial matter.*[25]

Understanding why the term is infrequently used to describe contemporary forms of political persuasion was part of the genesis of this project, begun long ago after a brief stint as a legislative aide on Capitol Hill. My historical investigation suggests it would have puzzled journalists, government lawyers, social scientists, and media critics in the period under study, for they were beset with anxieties about propaganda and its influences. At the same time, their obsession also offers clues to why the term lost its utility in everyday political analysis. In the end, that has largely to do with the fact that the label became a form of geopolitical name-calling used to marginalize and discredit highly ideological and controversial speech and activity. The term became heavily laden with the baggage of Nazi Germany's and the Soviet Union's total control of all forms of mass communication and their organized activities abroad. As a result, in U.S. culture, at least, propaganda came to be understood almost exclusively as a technique for the dissemination of antidemocratic ideas. Only totalitarians and their extremist dupes used this inherently undemocratic form of political persuasion; in democracies, competing interest groups and political parties, even the state, used "information" and publicity. Thus the term itself became a prisoner of WWII-era propaganda and was used as a label to warn against and dismiss both the legitimacy and provenance of unpopular and "foreign" ideas.[26]

These assumptions were built into the very laws used to control propaganda materials in the United States and remained dominant within mainstream political culture through the cold war. The McCormack-Dickstein Committee, formed with the intention of reporting on and developing laws aimed at controlling both Communist and Fascist materials in the United States, argued in 1935 that Nazi propaganda was widespread, diffuse in form, deceptive in practice, and aimed at promoting dangerous hatreds at home and loyalties to foreign causes. It found significant evidence of Communist activities in the United States as well. Both ideologies were deemed to be foreign; neither was "a national political party"; and neither "operate[d] on American principles."[27]

The committee's fear was grounded in the generally unquestioned assumption that propaganda as a technique was demonstrably effective for spreading dangerous ideas and provoking violent action; when connected to foreign ideologies, it was particularly threatening. The committee's "ultimate object" therefore was to protect the United States from the unchecked dissemination of foreign ideologies through propaganda channels. It reported that such activities should be "exposed, forbidden, and prevented if necessary." The committee even called for the enactment of a new sedition act aimed at outlawing the Communist and Nazi parties and recommended that their propaganda agents in the United States—such as booksellers, newspaper publishers, publicity agents, youth organizations, and others—be required to register with the U.S. government as agents of foreign principles.[28] Congress did not make the parties illegal (although the Smith Act prosecutions in the late 1940s had that de facto effect on the American Communist Party) but did pass the Foreign Agents Registration Act (1938) and the Voorhis Act (1940) as specific propaganda control laws that quickly became the main tools of enforcement for the Justice Department's Special Defense Unit. These two registration and disclosure laws were premised on the idea that anyone conducting political activities on behalf of foreign governments should register with the federal government and that their materials should be labeled for public consumption as the propaganda of a foreign entity.[29]

Throughout this study I use the term "propaganda" according to the definitions explicitly proffered or implicitly understood by those who examined the problem within their specific settings and note that those who did not define propaganda as being essentially undemocratic and threatening to democratic processes were the exception.[30] As the overall narrative trajectory shows, the label became so implicated by fears of Nazi and Communist subversion that the legal definition of propaganda as an instrument or form of sedition came increasingly into play, which brought WWI-era espionage laws, seditious conspiracy laws, and the Smith Act's sedition provisions to bear on the legal treatment of propaganda.[31] In brief, the definitions, laws, and organized efforts to study, expose, and punish foreign propaganda activities in the United States consolidated the victory of national security liberalism over a civil liberties–focused liberalism. The same fears about the power of propaganda and the same language about subversion and—by contrast, Americanism—that legitimized a crackdown on WWI-era dissenters and radicals resulted in the silencing of domestic Fascists at the onset of WWII and justified an even more extensive assault on U.S. Communists in the early cold war. Because of fears about political propaganda—narrowly and punitively defined—some forms of association and communication were deemed unacceptably dangerous and beyond the pale of First Amendment protections. Even the most speech-protective federal jurists balked at protecting propagandistic—or seditious—speech forms.

The tensions between public-centered versus expert-centered politics and free speech versus national security versions of liberalism reveal ironies and contradictions that cannot be extracted from the specific historical context of first preparing for war against Nazi words and images and then immediately shifting to a cold war struggle against Communist ideas. A heightened and constant attention to and anxiety about the power of

words as instruments of subversion made the transition from mass society anxieties to an all-out war on totalitarian propaganda more seamless
than it should have been. This study provides a window into just how
deep those fears were and how highly sophisticated people came to believe
that powerful propagandas combined with public naïveté might well undermine U.S. institutions. Such beliefs shrank the democratic faith, seriously threatened democratic processes, and resulted in a much diminished
belief in public capabilities.

Beginning with the excesses of WWI, chapter 1 establishes the intellectual and political framework for subsequent chapters by setting up the two
main discourses about propaganda—as a problem for democratic theory
and as a problem for national security—and the tensions they produced
within liberal culture. Establishing the contours of the debate between
Lippmann and Dewey as the central framework for subsequent intellectual inquiry about mass communications and democratic theory, this chapter looks at how these liberal pragmatists turned their queries to the issue
of revitalizing democratic theory in an age of propaganda, setting the stage
for an ongoing debate about the necessity (or desirability) of an expert-
centered reorientation of democratic theory. From the standpoint of the
legal control of propaganda, it examines how modern civil libertarians, especially Zechariah Chafee Jr., tried to resolve the conflict between national security and First Amendment protections by drawing on the negative
and positive lessons of WWI, lessons that Chafee thought could be instructive to all who wished to preserve a democracy-renewing marketplace
of ideas, even in moments of national emergency.

Both sets of problems became central questions in U.S. political science
and the emerging field of mass communication research, and chapter 2
takes up the work of political scientist Harold Lasswell, whose efforts to
make propaganda studies a key concern in political science made him one
of the most influential students of political communications by WWII.[32]
Lasswell's ideas and activities embodied the competing imperatives in U.S.
liberalism: he managed to embrace simultaneously Lippmann's penchant
for expertism and opinion control, Dewey's emphasis on expert facilita-
tion of public debate, and both their faiths in scientific technique as the
solution to problems posed by propaganda. He also conceived of propaganda as a value-neutral tool that all interest groups should learn to master but on war's eve became a key figure in the state's efforts to eliminate
Nazi and Communist propaganda from the U.S. sphere. Together with
the Rockefeller Foundation's John Marshall, Lasswell helped bring together the leading scholars in the incipient field of mass communications to

orchestrate foundation, university, and government-based propaganda research. In fact, Lasswell's war-era work provides the main thread running through this book's institutional narrative, as his affiliations connect the Rockefeller Foundation, the Library of Congress, the Justice Department, and many other public and private entities.

Chapter 3 shows how the broader cultural anxieties about propaganda and the impulse to find scientific strategies for understanding it were most fully realized in the Rockefeller Foundation–sponsored Communications Research projects. This chapter argues that preparing for war against fascist propaganda was the crystallizing moment for the new field of communications research and that the first generation—the so-called founding fathers, including Lasswell, Paul Lazarsfeld, Hadley Cantril, and others—defined their research questions and strategies and developed their techniques in the course of enhancing the state's surveillance capacities.[33] The Rockefeller Foundation's crucial role in simultaneously developing the academic field and enhancing the nation's propaganda defenses made John Marshall a key figure. By 1940 the projects he orchestrated included the Princeton Radio Research Project; the Princeton Public Opinion Research Project; the Princeton Shortwave Listening Center; the Office of Radio Research at Columbia; the Graduate Library Reading Project at the University of Chicago; the Film Library of the Museum of Modern Art; the Library of Congress Film Project; the American Film Center; the Totalitarian Communications Research Project at the New School of Social Research; and the Experimental Division for the Study of Wartime Communications at the Library of Congress. By war's eve—well before the state had mobilized its own research sites—each project was involved in war-related research, most working collaboratively on propaganda defense matters.

Chapter 4 is one of three chapters examining how the federal government conceived, developed, and, in this instance, hid its propaganda defense activities. Focusing on Archibald MacLeish's role as rhetorician of democracy and principal builder of the propaganda prophylaxis, this chapter begins with his compelling but controversial Manichaean pronouncements about the need for an all-out intellectual and spiritual battle against fascism and then turns to his work utilizing the Library of Congress as a national security intelligence site. The chapter illustrates the national security imperatives that came to dominate the wartime state: although MacLeish strove to engineer a war against Fascist ideas that would not traduce civil liberties in the United States, MacLeishean rhetoric about the all-out war between the spirit of the West and totalitarianism became the rallying cry of national security (especially cold war) liberalism. Carrying his belief in the search for truth into his wartime work as the Librarian of Congress and director of the Office of Facts and Figures, he inevitably encountered security imperatives and logic that consistently thwarted his civil libertarian ambitions. Ironically, that logic became manifest in the Library of Congress itself, which housed Lasswell's Experimental Division for the Study of Wartime Communications, an operation most useful in the Justice Department's successful legal efforts to punish propaganda activities.

Chapters 5 and 6, based on the records of the Justice Department's Special Defense Unit (later known as the Special War Policies Unit), look at the development of strategies for the legal control of Fascist propaganda. Assigned the dual roles of simultaneously protecting civil liberties and ensuring internal security by preventing the dissemination of disunifying, morale-sapping materials, the Special Defense Unit embodies all the competing tensions within modern liberalism. Chapter 5 examines the formation of this special propaganda control division, its internal debates, the strategies its Chafee-inspired legal theorists developed on the war's eve, and their attention to the symbolic politics of censorship in a wartime democracy. Chapter 6 shows what happened when war broke out and how Special Defense Unit lawyers reinvigorated the "clear and present danger" test as a speech-restrictive rather than a speech-protective standard for the control of so-called seditious speech. Illustrating the wartime liberal retreat to a security-based restriction of speech and association rights, this chapter examines the Justice Department's federal court prosecutions of the domestic Fascist press using the Foreign Agents Registration Act, the WWI-era seditious conspiracy provisions of the Espionage Act, and the recently enacted Smith Act. The FARA and sedition prosecutions, enhanced by Lasswell's expert testimony about the nature of enemy propaganda, were based in the profound fear of the power of Nazi propaganda, a fear that seemed warranted by Nazi military and political successes. They also immobilized free speech liberalism.

The brief conclusion shows the consequences of this immobilization in the early cold war, when equally profound fears of Communist propaganda converged with national security liberalism, resulting in another war on invidious propaganda and renewed calls for unified public opinion.

By the end of WWII the optimistic promises of social justice and free speech liberalism were defeated by a culture-wide fear of internal subversion through propaganda, by a definition of propaganda as an especially dangerous (and un-American) form of speech, and by the rapid (and continuous) growth of a national security state mentality that made the protection of security a far greater good than the protection of extremist speech. The consequences for dissent, debate, and even the exploration of political alternatives in the postwar freeze were profound as the crusade for ideological consensus and the perceived need to ferret out dangerous fifth-column propagandists continued to run roughshod over other liberal values and commitments.

CHAPTER ONE

Dangerous Words and Images: Propaganda's Threat to Democracy

By the end of the 1930s, as World War II was breaking out in Europe, Americans anxious about propaganda's threat to U.S. democracy focused on the totalitarian Fascist and Communist movements, especially their supposedly effective techniques of fifth-column subversion through propaganda.[1] Journalists of all stripes and congressional investigative entities such as the House Un-American Activities Committee identified propaganda as an effective instrument of political manipulation in the United States, focusing their attention on the pamphlets, speeches, insignia, rallies, leadership, and foreign influences over the different supposedly un-American organizations operating in the United States. Dozens upon dozens of military disaffection, alien control, repatriation, registration and disclosure, and sedition bills were introduced by an increasingly suspicious and edgy Congress. And numerous ad hoc organizations formed to monitor and report on all manner of propaganda activities. Within liberal political and intellectual culture on the eve of WWII, the prevailing perception of propaganda was that it was a dangerous antidemocratic weapon that needed to be combated, but without destroying democratic processes along the way. The excesses of World War I loomed too large in liberals' memories to allow speech and association-restrictive measures and policies to go unchallenged.

Chief among the stalwarts of the speech-tolerant civil libertarian strain in pre-WWII U.S. culture was the noted First Amendment authority and Harvard law professor Zechariah Chafee Jr. Chafee, who earned his stature and his battle scars as a critic of WWI-era state repression, saw clearly the dilemma facing liberal policy makers, jurists, and others confronting the problem of developing democratic strategies for the control of undemocratic activities. Offering a guidepost to fellow liberals, he framed his landmark 1941 study *Free Speech in the United States* around this conundrum. For Chafee, the problem had two main components: In what ways does propagandistic, even "seditious" speech threaten U.S. democracy? And how could the liberal guardians of that democracy deal with such a threat without diminishing or destroying democratic protections?[2] Chafee's questions were emblematic of the liberal problem with propaganda, and they frame the discussion in this chapter and, indeed, in the entire book. No one who thought seriously about the relationship between propaganda and democracy, or about the problem of controlling propaganda, could ignore Chafee's landmark work, either in the form of his 1920 volume, *Freedom of Speech*, or his 1941 study, *Free Speech in the United States*, a work begun on the eve of WWII and published just as the United States was entering the war. Free speech liberals looked to him for guidance, and national security liberals (or ardent anti-Fascist liberals more concerned about the Fascist threat than about protecting the First Amendment) tried to find the holes in his analysis. Either way, Chafee framed the questions and dilemmas in ways that could not be ignored by those who were concerned about protecting democratic processes while also protecting U.S. society.

Chafee provided an important intellectual and historical bridge from WWI to WWII as well. His questions and recommendations reveal how profoundly the use of propaganda during WWI had affected Americans. As a central figure in framing the historical conscience of interwar civil libertarians, he was adamant that the near-hysterical fear of German spies and propaganda during WWI—and of all varieties of leftists during the war and the Red Scare—should not revisit the United States with the coming of WWII. He looked about with anxiety as he saw a fearful Congress pass potentially dangerous laws, including the Hatch Act and especially the Alien Registration Act of 1940, with its peacetime sedition measure, known as the Smith Act. He was also worried about the power of totalitarian propaganda, however, so his concerns about how a democracy should combat propaganda were inseparable from both specific worries about fifth columnists in the United States on the eve of WWII and from the painful experience of WWI, when U.S. attacks on and uses of propaganda proved so destructive of democratic procedures and ideals.

Thus Chafee exemplified interwar liberals not only in his civil libertarian–driven worries that the efforts to control propaganda would harm democratic processes but also in another important concern about propaganda: like his fellow liberal optimist John Dewey, he was concerned about the effects of propaganda on the public and its political practices. He worried that words and images used in emotional and reckless ways weakened public discourse and public-opinion-centered democratic practices, and, like other pragmatists in his generation, he too offered the counsel of "scientific" solutions to the many-faceted problem of propaganda. As against democratic realists like Walter Lippmann, E. L. Bernays, and Harold Lasswell, who offered scientific techniques coupled with expert-centered, top-down politics as the solution to stabilizing democracy in an age of propaganda, Chafee sided with thinkers like Dewey, the semanticists Stuart Chase and H. I. Hayakawa, and the adult educators at the Institute for Propaganda Analysis who argued that scientific techniques (loosely construed) should be employed and taught to the public in order for it to defend itself. While Chafee framed his discussion about the relationship between First Amendment protections and national security interests in legislative and juridical questions, larger questions informing the liberal dilemma with propaganda guided this inquiry: How powerful are words and images? How susceptible is the public? How much faith should one invest in the public's capacity to distinguish between sense and nonsense? And at what point should experts or authorities intervene in the unruly democratic search for truth to ensure order?

These questions and tensions about language, public capacities, and the role of experts in the mass-mediated modern age defined Chafee's efforts to locate and make concrete speech-protective and democracy-enhancing guidelines for the control of propaganda speech, and those same questions also ran through the four main themes or discourses in the interwar discussion about propaganda and democracy. The first and most enduring theme is the idea that propaganda is dangerous to U.S. democracy because it is implicitly deceptive, usually foreign, and potentially subversive. The second theme—crystallized in the debate between Lippmann and Dewey—emerged from the post-WWI "discovery" of propaganda and combined suspicions about traditional democratic theory with the perception that the already suspect "masses" were even more easily manipulated in an age of mass communications. The third, quicksand-of-language theme grew out of the widely held idea that propaganda destroys the intelligible language necessary for rational discussion, reflecting an obsession with the power of words and widespread pessimism about modern men and women's ability to communicate meaningfully and rationally in an age when hucksters and propagandists had become ubiquitous. The fourth thread, inextricable from the others, centered on the question of how a democratic state should achieve a balance between political liberty and national security, and, as Chafee's ruminations suggest, this concern was continuous from WWI to WWII.

There was no unified response to the problem of propaganda because it posed many problems. But within U.S. liberal culture, the discussion about propaganda kept returning to the same fundamental questions framed by Chafee: How does propaganda threaten democracy? And what should be done about it? The debates about these questions reveal fundamental tensions within U.S. intellectual culture in the first half of the twentieth century, fissures that were continually revisited as the nation moved from the end of one total war to the beginning of another.

World War I and the Age of Propaganda

One reason that U.S. intellectuals have paid so much attention to the use of propaganda in WWI and afterward was that that war was, in many respects, about words and their meanings.[3] In the American arena, where U.S. interests were neither concrete nor agreed upon, words and symbols carried great burdens. This was true from the beginning of the European war in 1914, long before the United States was involved. And when the United States finally entered the war in Europe in the late spring of 1917, even after several years' debates among congresspeople and leading intellectuals, it was still not at all clear to many Americans what the nation's interests were nor why the United States was getting involved.

According to historian David Kennedy, the fractious debates about U.S. entry into the war, even regarding President Woodrow Wilson's April 1917 war resolution, "reflected the persistent confusion about America's stake in the fighting, and about the precise causes and purposes of America's entry."[4] Wilson presented the war aims in abstract and highly idealized terms: it was a war "to make the world safe for democracy" and was going to be a war "to end all wars." Antiwar spokesmen knew the significance of this battle of words for defining the war's meanings and, according to Kennedy, "saw only hypocrisy in the demand for war in the name of democracy." The apparent emptiness of Wilsonian rhetoric was of great import in the war's aftermath, when overblown wartime rhetoric gave way to intense scrutiny of the semantic duplicities of propaganda.[5]

Several components of the vast wartime propaganda campaigns conducted by all belligerents help explain the contemporary confusion about the war and its purposes and illuminate as well the widespread postwar reaction against propaganda: all the warring nations tried to shape U.S. opinion; the Wilson administration had to sell the war to a diverse, ethnically heterogeneous population, many of whom opposed U.S. involvement; and the need to sell the war, combined with considerable opposition to it (some of which was externally influenced), produced intense repression against those who interfered with the official meanings proffered by the Wilson administration and the Committee on Public Information (CPI).

Led by the progressive publicist George Creel, the CPI (known as the Creel Committee), promoted the war and Wilsonian idealism as a crusade to preserve liberal democracy and to "redeem barbarous Europe."[6] Creel and his lieutenants did this with righteous zeal. They closely monitored purity of thought and opinion, defined patriotism in narrow, bombastic terms, utilized all instruments of communication, made all public gathering places sites of indoctrination, and defined all dissent as treason. From the very outset, Wilson and Creel, the Justice Department, and the post office vilified war opponents and energetically used all available means to silence opposition.[7] According to historians critical of Creel's work, CPI propaganda "frequently wore a benign face, and . . . its creators genuinely believed it to be in the service of an altruistic cause," but on the whole it showed an "overbearing concern for 'correct' opinion, for expression, for language itself."[8] Creel's agency promoted jingoism, intolerance, and vigilantism, an assessment that quickly became the reigning interpretation both of Creel's legacy and, at war's end, of the power of propaganda.

The CPI's much-celebrated Four-Minute Men—of which there were several million—used atrocity stories in their four-minute public speeches, promoted hate films, urged Americans to keep track of one another and report on suspect utterances, and employed patriotic singing "to keep patriotism 'at white heat,'" to use Creel's words (quoted on p. 62).

The Creel Committee explained opposition to the war as a product of German propaganda and tried to define a mainstream view of propaganda as something decidedly foreign and not-American. By contrast, Creel and his defenders regularly claimed that the U.S. government engaged only in the production of "publicity" and "information."[9] Indeed, Creel's self-aggrandizing postwar volume, *How We Advertised America* (1920), bragged that his foreign activities had helped destroy the morale of the German army by stimulating a collapse of morale on the German homefront and generally claimed that the highly orchestrated foreign propaganda campaigns "had been of crucial importance in bringing about victory."[10] But in the postwar atmosphere of viewing all propaganda-related matters suspiciously, these claims became part of the evidence of propaganda's enormous power, on the one hand, and of Creel's responsibility for the war-era assault on civil liberties, on the other. Indeed, postwar civil libertarians held the Creel Committee largely responsible for the climate of intolerance during the war and the subsequent Red Scare.[11] Yet while the CPI's xenophobia certainly contributed to wartime intolerance, it was nothing new in American culture.

The polyglot makeup of early-twentieth-century U.S. society exacerbated the wartime phobias, drawing on anxieties and fears of domestic subversion that had long been used to mount attacks on dissent within immigrant populations. John Morton Blum suggests that the foreign is often conflated with the radical, and in the period before WWI these anxieties were exacerbated by a hypernationalism illustrated by statements such as Theodore Roosevelt's claim that "There is no room for the hyphen in our citizenship." Such sentiments became commonplace with the wartime "100 percent Americanism" campaigns.[12] As Blum explains, during the war, "exploiting latent prejudices against the radical and the foreign, and identifying these two, organizers of public opinion . . . translated passive dislike into truculent hysteria" (p. 114). Kennedy seconds this, suggesting that xenophobia was not new in the United States in 1917, "but the war opened a wider field for its excesses."[13] Fears of subversion and disloyalty among the hyphenated Americans may have been legitimate, given real acts of industrial espionage and the existence of German spy rings.[14] But assertions like Wilson's that foreigners had "poisoned . . . the very arteries of our national life" also made foreigners responsible for introducing the poison, or "germ," of propaganda into the American bloodstream.[15] "German propagandist" was a widely used epithet, one that also signified more than just words, referring also to propaganda of the deed, manifested in strikes, occasional violence, and spy activity. Marks explains that "this early association of propaganda with conspiracy, with espionage, and with sabotage is particularly important in view of the pejorative connotations which the concept of propaganda has had ever since."[16] In this linkage, words and actions were seen as being synonymous, an implication of the meaning of the word "propaganda" that had a powerful and punitive resonance in the nation's wartime courtrooms, at both the state and federal levels, where decisions about so-called bad speech were premised on the assumption of direct and causal connections between propagandistic language and dangerous, violent, and subversive antiwar acts.[17]

Americans tended to believe in the "cleverness, ubiquity, and effectiveness of German propaganda," and the nation perceived itself as being susceptible to—a "fertile field" for—propaganda in general.[18] As war hysteria deepened, fueled by the CPI's truculence, the tendency to confuse mere words with overt acts, and antiwar sentiment with foreign subversion, meant that any opposition to or criticism of the war became highly suspicious. This was especially true when such opposition was uttered from within labors' ranks, by the unemployed, by radical political organizations such the Socialists, the I.W.W., or anarchists, or among immigrant groups culturally tied to the Central Powers or to that newly formed revolutionary state, the Soviet Union. Within this climate, law enforcement officials and the state and federal courts interpreted even harmless statements uttered far from military bases or industrial plants as interfering with the war effort. Because would-be soldiers and wartime laborers were presumably the most susceptible to antiwar propaganda disseminated by antiwar Germans, pacifists, socialists, anarchists, and radical unions, they were the ones most assiduously protected by the WWI propaganda control legislation.

As early as June 1916 (a year before President Wilson's war declaration), U.S. Attorney General Thomas Gregory called for federal legislation to punish espionage and curtail freedom of speech and press. Congress twice refused to pass such bills prior to American entrance in the war, but on the evening Wilson declared war and called for a "firm hand" to be used against the "disloyal," Congress reintroduced legislation that provided for censorship of the press, punishment for interference with the armed services, and control of the mails to prevent their use for the dissemination of allegedly treasonable propaganda. The press-censorship measures provoked outrage among the nation's newspaper editors, who invoked democratic principles and the need for responsible criticism, so they were removed from the emergency legislation. But Congress quickly passed the Espionage Act of 1917 and soon amended and expanded the law's provisions with a sweeping sedition amendment in 1918.[19] The war's proponents intended to prevent antiwar sentiments from infecting the wartime spirit by punishing any speech, printed or verbal, that might have any possibility—even the remotest "bad tendency"—of interfering with the nation's war efforts, especially efforts at military recruitment and preparedness.[20] And the CPI urged vigilance on the part of the American public.

According to the attorney general's 1917 report to Congress, the Justice Department specifically targeted the "persistent propaganda" attacking the Selective Service Act by passage of the Espionage Act.[21] The Espionage Act, enacted in June 1917, established three new wartime offenses, including "willfully making or conveying false reports, willfully causing or attempting to cause insubordination, disloyalty, mutiny, or refusal of duty, in the military or naval forces of the United States, or willfully obstructing the recruiting or enlistment service of the United States."[22] Although the attorney general argued that the Espionage Act "had proved an effective instrumentality against deliberate or organized disloyal propaganda," he said it "did not go far enough in some respects," especially in reaching "the individual casual or impulsive disloyal utterances" (quoted on p. 40). Therefore eleven months later Congress greatly expanded the reach of the Espionage Act with the 1918 sedition amendment that expressly protected the recruitment of a militia by targeting antidraft and antiwar propaganda. The new law inserted the far more restrictive language "attempt to obstruct" and added nine more offenses, including "uttering, printing, writing, or publishing any disloyal, profane, scurrilous, or abusive language, or language intended to cause contempt, scorn, contumely or disrepute as regards the form of government of the United States." This new law also made punishable any "words or acts supporting or favoring the cause of any country at war with us, or opposing the cause of the United States" (quoted on p. 41).[23] Attempting to "stamp out all utterances of a disloyal character" (quoted on p. 40), Congress thus passed broad laws that made words and deeds equivalent.

As Chafee explained, federal and state officials were guided by the total-war notion that "wars are no longer won by armies in the field, but by the *morale* of the whole people" and thereby interpreted all "attacks upon our cause . . . as dangerous and unjustified as if made among the soldiers in rear trenches" (p. 8). By passing such laws explicitly aimed at controlling anti-war and antidraft speech, Congress affected wartime freedom of speech much more than if it had used the extant—and sufficiently harsh—conspiracy and treason statutes that punished only "direct and dangerous interference with the war" (p. 36).[24]

The laws also gave the Department of the Post Office and the postmaster general wide latitude to remove antiwar materials from the mails. Postmaster General Burleson wielded this power enthusiastically and injudiciously, using it to strip the mailing privileges from radical, pacifist, and foreign-born groups whose antiwar opinions he and Attorney General Gregory especially feared.[25] As Chafee remarked, state and federal officials were not "overly inconvenienced" by the First Amendment and the rest of the Bill of Rights when confronted with wartime speech they opposed. Indeed, the war-era record is astounding. According to Chafee, "over nineteen hundred prosecutions and other judicial proceedings during the war, involving speeches, newspaper articles, pamphlets and books were followed after the armistice by a widespread legislative consideration of bills punishing the advocacy of extreme radicalism."[26]

Leading civil libertarians of the WWI period denounced the governmental excesses but also indirectly accepted the same assumptions about the power of propaganda. Chafee, Felix Frankfurter, Ernst Freund, Roscoe Pound, R. G. Brown, and others, writing under the auspices of the National Popular Government League, produced a prominent and controversial catalog of the U.S. Justice Department's abusive practices during the war and the Red Scare entitled "Report Upon the Illegal Practices of the United States Department of Justice." This 1920 report laid the blame for the civil liberties violations squarely within the Justice Department, but it also blamed the Creel Committee's propaganda for creating a vigilante climate. Among other things, it even excoriated the attorney general for operating outside the scope of his duties by making the Justice Department itself "a propaganda bureau" by sending out to the nation's newspapers and magazines "quantities of material designed to excite public opinion against radicals, all at the expense of the government."[27] The report's signatories agreed that the Justice Department's efforts to control all manner of speech activities had been a civil liberties embarrassment, one that undermined the nation's democratic promises. This basic narrative of federal abuses during the war and the first Red Scare became the received story line among civil libertarians.[28]

To the chagrin of interwar civil libertarians, the U.S. Supreme Court also legitimated the state's wartime repression of antiwar and antidraft speech activities. In a series of landmark First Amendment decisions handed down after the Armistice, the Court gave its seal of approval to federal prosecutors' broadly construed and punitive interpretations of the Espionage Act and the sedition amendment in the *Schenck, Frohwerk, Debs,* and *Abrams* cases. Overall, the WWI-era fear of propaganda led to the creation of a reckless legislative and legal machinery that quickly and zealously crushed all forms of dissent. All this proved to postwar commentators that propaganda in any form must be immensely powerful if it could produce such hysteria.

The Postwar Recognition of Propaganda

According to Barry Alan Marks, "As writers for popular magazines reevaluated the nation's experience with war propaganda, there was more shock and concern about precisely this aspect of propaganda than any other: the fact that propaganda appeared to be a force of boundless power."[29] As Marks explains, in trying to understand the immense gap between wartime rhetoric and postwar realities, U.S. writers hit upon propaganda—or official lies—as at least one explanation of their disillusionment. This framework, for instance, provided a propaganda-centered interpretation of the harshness of the Versailles Treaty: wartime atrocity propaganda directly contributed to the severe peace following the war by generating a lust for vengeance in Europe.[30] It had also created unrealistic expectations of international comity at home.

Marks provides a useful narrative of this angry reexamination of wartime propaganda in the United States, suggesting that when British writers published gloating accounts of how British propagandists had manipulated both U.S. opinion leaders and the public, Americans became aware of just how extensively the British interpretations of the war penetrated both U.S. universities and popular consciousness through film, pamphlets, and interviews.[31] Others published widely read accounts of British efforts to shape U.S. public opinion, including Sir Campbell Stuart's *Secrets of Crewe House: The Story of a Famous Campaign* (1920) and Arthur Ponsoby's 1928 volume *Falsehood in Wartime, Containing an Assortment of Lies Circulated Throughout the Nations During the Great War.* One of the most important components of Ponsoby's work was its detailed refutation of wartime atrocity stories, showing many of them to be propagandists' concoctions. Assessing the significance of this work, Marks says that "in the long run, the atrocity tale became a piece of evidence in the belief that 'propaganda' was synonymous with 'lies,' a further evidence that the American public had been terribly deceived, as well as an explanation of how and why Allied propaganda had been so shockingly effective."[32] Writing almost two decades after the war, historian Walter Millis, in *The Road to War: America, 1914–1917* (1935), concluded that British information control and lies had made the Americans vulnerable to a one-sided view of the war.[33] Millis resented both the manipulation and its apparent effectiveness.

In 1927 Hartley Grattan published an article for the *American Mercury* entitled "The Historians Cut Loose," in which he wrote: "Bang! went Princip's pistol at Sarajevo, and bang! went all the professors. By the end of July they were restive and fuming; by the end of August they were in violent eruption. And thereafter for five long years, the word objectivity was abolished from their vocabularies. They harangued Kiwanis, they wrote letters to the newspapers, they preached in churches, they invaded the movie-parlors, they roared like lions."[34] Marks says that the discovery of the role intellectuals played in wartime propagandizing "was one of the sources of greatest shock as Americans discovered the 'new' force that had been loosed upon the world," and recent historians such as Carol Gruber, David Kennedy, and Peter Novick have continued developing this line of inquiry into U.S. intellectuals'—especially historians'—involvement in the propaganda efforts, reinforcing the earlier discoveries of the extent to which academics became wartime publicists instead of scholars.[35]

As Creel's critics then and now have noted, U.S. public schools at all levels became indoctrination centers. The educational materials the historians produced were among the most widely read forms of CPI propaganda, distributed to over 800,000 secondary school teachers. The war study courses prepared by professional historians for the National Board for Historical Service (under CPI aegis) and the war issues courses taught throughout the nation's wartime universities developed the same themes. Rewriting history to make Germany seem decidedly more barbaric than the rest of Europe, the study guides omitted background discussions beyond simple black-and-white explanations about the war's cause. Loath to sully "the bright cause of Allied unity," they offered "neither negative notes nor ambiguities," Kennedy writes. "Nothing could be allowed to obscure the theme" of the "life-and-death struggle between democracy and autocracy, upon whose outcome the future of civilization depended."[36]

Critics consistently noted that the "emotion-stirring potential of words" was the most important characteristic of propaganda. Others fixed on the idea of propaganda as deception and lies and argued that propaganda was the enemy of informed debate and rational discussion, thereby impeding the search for truth and undermining a critical tenet of the liberal faith in the "marketplace of ideas." Propaganda was thus doubly insidious. If putatively democratic governments were capable of undermining democratic processes by tainting the very information necessary to the effective functioning of democracy and if propaganda was so powerful in its ability to deceive and capture the emotive and violent side of humans, then surely democratic theory was endangered. And, if intellectuals had been taken in, then surely the public was easy prey. For if scholars had turned their tools to propagandistic purposes, then who could be trusted? What information was trustworthy? The idea that propaganda threatened democratic procedures therefore became a powerful fixture in the postwar debates about democratic theory in an age of mass communications.

Theoretically, this is where the propaganda critique converged with the mass society thesis, an essentially antimodernist, antidemocratic framework articulated by intellectuals in the modern era in response to the historical conjuncture of industrialization, urbanization, the communications revolution, and the apparent susceptibility of modern publics to the power of propaganda.[37] As Tony Bennett argues, the mass society thesis should be viewed "as a loosely defined 'outlook' consisting of a number of intersecting themes—the decline of the 'organic community,' the rise of mass culture, the social atomization of 'mass man.' " These themes, he argues, "articulated a polyphony of negative and pessimistic reactions to the related processes of industrialization, urbanization, the development of political democracy . . . and the emergence of contemporary forms of 'mass communication.'"[38] The idea that "urbanized man" had become "relatively defenseless, an easy prey" to mass communications because of being sundered from more stable social networks and more traditional social and values hierarchies "encouraged," James Curran writes, "a relatively uncomplicated view of the media as all-powerful propaganda agencies brainwashing a susceptible and defenseless public. The media propelled 'word bullets' that penetrated deep into its inert and passive victims"[39] Although communications historian J. Michael Sproule argues that most serious students of communications quickly rejected the "magic bullet" thesis of propaganda's power, anxieties about that power worked in tandem with a whole cluster of negative assumptions about public capabilities. Stuart Ewen addresses this conjuncture of the mass society thesis with U.S. anxieties about public irrationality and malleability in his study of the history of public relations; tracing the influence of European thinkers such as LeBon, Tarde, Trotter, Wallas, and Freud in American intellectual life, he shows how influential U.S. thinkers such as Robert E. Park, Walter Lippmann, and the so-called father of American public relations, E. L. Bernays, picked up on variations of their theses to fashion a view of the modern, mass public as incapable, irrational, emotional, and remarkably susceptible to those who could master the instruments of mass communications.[40]

The most important dimension of this amalgamation of the mass society thesis with the propaganda critique in the U.S. arena was its concern about political man and his rationality (the nouns were invariably masculine, although the attributes of passivity, irrationality, etc., were feminized). The American propaganda–mass society critique shared important assumptions with the European framework, including the view that humans are essentially "non-rational creatures of emotion, instinct, impulse, sentiment, prejudice, and habit," a cluster of assumptions that helped explain propaganda's apparent power.[41] Unlike most of the European theorists who were more concerned about mass influence on cultural tastes and values, however, U.S. critics saw the problem in more explicitly political ways. That is, the conjunction of the propaganda critique with the mass society thesis had dire ramifications for traditional democratic theory. For U.S. liberal intellectuals, propaganda's assault on democratic theory required solutions within the realm of theory and politics. Two of the United States' premier public intellectuals, the journalist Walter Lippmann and the philosopher John Dewey, explored the relationship between propaganda and democratic theory, developing, alongside Chafee, one of the most significant frameworks for thinking about the problem in interwar intellectual culture. Both proffered solutions born of a generation's faith in scientific methods and the promise of scientific expertise, and while the assumptions they drew from the mass society thesis might have been the same, the differences in the solutions they offered were considerable, variances that speak to a central tension within U.S. liberalism over the role of the public versus experts in a mass-mediated age.

Lippmann, Dewey, and the Crisis of Democratic Theory

When Walter Lippmann wrote *Public Opinion* (1922) and his follow-up volume *The Phantom Public* (1925) and John Dewey published *The Public and Its Problems* (1927), both knew that nineteenth-century optimism about democracy and social progress was being severely tested by the technological incursions of the "machine age."[42] Indebted to British philosopher Graham Wallas's social criticism, both Lippmann and Dewey accepted Wallas's observations in *The Great Society* (1914) that the forces of mechanized mass production, cable and telegraph communications, cheap printing, and railway and steam transportation had produced a "great"—or "mass"—society that few people were either prepared for or capable of comprehending.[43] Although Wallas influenced Lippmann more than Dewey, both used the term "Great Society" as descriptive of the myriad complexities and volatility produced by the communications revolutions. They worried that the modern public had been cast adrift and knew that modernity's disruptive forces were weakly countered by lagging political and social institutions still oriented to a pre-machine-age view of the world. William Ogburn's concept of cultural lag helped them explain the failure of political and social institutions to meet the challenges of changing circumstances and to understand, as Dewey wrote, that "men feel that they are caught in the sweep of forces too vast to understand or master."[44]

Propaganda was among these forces. Indeed, both Lippmann and Dewey drew the powerful lesson from WWI that the masses—a term each employed—were more susceptible than ever before to manipulation on a mass scale. Dewey, the more optimistic of the two, declared that democracy "calls for adverse criticism in abundance." The public had been "eclipsed," he opined, admitting that "optimism about democracy to-day is under a cloud."[45] Lippmann's own forecast for democratic theory in the age of propaganda was even darker.

The linkage between the power of technology and the creation of a mass public was crucial to Lippmann's and Dewey's versions of the U.S. mass society thesis. Dewey, for example, used the terms "machine age" and "new age of human relationships" interchangeably, but he also ascribed causality: the machine age created the new age of human relationships, which were still local in experience but increasingly dependent on mass media for entertainment and knowledge about worldly affairs (pp. 140–41). And a rudderless modern society was a grave threat to functioning democracy because publics were increasingly uninvolved and uninterested even in the political matters of their local communities. Thus both Dewey and Lippmann were preoccupied by the problem of achieving a democratic politics whose guardians were a coherent, self-interested, and responsible public.[46] Although their vocabularies derived from the Europeanist mass culture critique—and both relied on negative "bread and circuses" metaphors—the Arnoldian fears of high culture laid low by anarchy were not the salient issues for these post-WWI American pragmatists. They were far less concerned about the leveling of cultural tastes than the problem of democratic theory in an age of mass communications.

Despite shared assumptions and concerns, however, the crisis of democratic theory had a much different meaning for Dewey than for Lippmann. Dewey believed a nineteenth-century conception of democratic politics as being public-centered could be salvaged for the twentieth century (by mobilizing the symbols of democracy and stimulating participation in local affairs), with help from applied scientific knowledge.[47] Lippmann was not so sure a public-centered theory of democracy should even be imagined (and if so, mobilized only for symbolic purposes) and envisioned an expert-centered polity guided by scientifically trained opinion makers.[48] More suspicious of the state and more skeptical of experts as replacements for a self-governing public than Lippmann, Dewey in his public-centered idealism embodied an optimistic and progressive strain in interwar U.S. liberalism, especially compared to Lippmann's boldly skeptical "democratic realism."[49] Together, Dewey's cautiously hopeful restatement of the philosophy of democracy and Lippmann's scathing critique of the modern mass public provide two of the most influential arguments about mass society, democratic theory, and the problem of propaganda.[50]

The tension between the two positions informed and structured for decades the mass society–democratic theory colloquy in American social thought, and most social scientific discussions about the relationship of propaganda to public opinion and democratic theory would be situated—and contested—within frameworks articulated by Lippmann and Dewey.[51] Lippmann's was more influential in large part because it was written in an age when propaganda's apparent power produced great skepticism about public capacities. His instrumentalist and expert-centered approach to the harnessing of mass communications was reassuring to a postwar generation interested in learning how to understand and utilize these new instruments for social reform and rational politics. Indeed, Lippmann's administrative model for social science communications research would long dominate the field of communications studies, as it would the political communications subfield of political science, in large part because it offered the idea of mastery to an intellectual class. Dewey, on the other hand, attempted to articulate a coherent philosophy of democracy in an age of mass communications, explicitly trying to counter Lippmann's essentially undemocratic prescriptions for using knowledge to manufacture consent.[52]

Both Lippmann and Dewey embraced the rhetoric of science, or scientism, but Lippmann posited expertise as a stabilizing factor in mass politics threatened by propaganda's growing influence. In this way, Lippmann was very much in harmony with others of his generation who applied science metaphors and efficiency motifs in their assertions about the reform possibilities of the modern social sciences.[53] Machine-age politics became more expert-driven, historian John M. Jordan contends, because social reformers, journalists, managers, and politicians drew on a science-based epistemological framework that expressed its intellectual certitude through the language of control and mastery. While Lippmann drew on, and mightily contributed to, this scientistic discourse of power, his argument also crystallized the highly influential line of thinking about the power of the media and the basic (in)competence of the public. Thus he also appealed to experts trained in social science who were interested in controlling the flow of information to obtain desired social and political results. Lippmann's two-part thesis about expertise and incompetence fit snugly and persuasively into an expanding social engineering impetus within U.S. liberalism. As historian Mark C. Smith suggests, however, the intellectual hegemony of the science-as-mastery position within the social sciences was much contested by Lippmann's more progressive contemporaries, including Dewey, who offered a different perspective on the relationship among scientific methods, social knowledge, and democratic practice.[54]

The Dominant Paradigm:
Lippmann's Critique of Democratic Theory

The tension between propaganda's danger and its utility is crucial to Lippmann's understanding of the relationship between outmoded democratic theory and modern mass society. While he was anxious about the distracting and manipulative power of propaganda in a public-centered polis, he thought that propaganda could be useful to policy experts and administrators who were striving to gain control over the social and economic world, much as their engineering cohorts were doing in the physical world. He developed his expert-centered, applied social engineering theory of modern democracy in both *Public Opinion* and *The Phantom Public*. Although *Public Opinion* generally indicted propaganda, advertising, and popular entertainment as destructive forces, these were superficial problems compared to the limitations of human intelligence in combination with a theory of democracy premised on human rationality. For Lippmann, people's emotional and distracted responses to mass communications were just surface manifestations of a larger epistemological problem of which democratic theory did not take account.

Lippmann expressed this dark outlook in *Public Opinion* and *The Phantom Public* by employing metaphors of incapacity. Beginning *Public Opinion* by quoting the cave allegory from book seven of Plato's *Republic*,

Lippmann announced his primary argument and established his central metaphor: people think they live in the world and see it for what it is, but in reality they occupy a world of shadows and live in an environment they do not see and cannot therefore comprehend. Herein lies the source of most human folly: "Whatever we believe to be a true picture, we treat as if it were the environment itself." People believe in and are victims of the "pictures in their heads," which are almost invariably mistaken perceptions of reality. Lippmann's whole argument is grounded in this epistemological claim: most people, he said, live in fictional mental landscapes that he called "pseudo-environments." "We know the environment in which . . . we live [only] indirectly," he wrote. The "substance" of his argument grew from this observation: "Democracy in its original form never seriously faced the problem . . . [that] the pictures inside people's heads do not automatically correspond with the world outside."[55] In *The Phantom Public* he expanded the metaphor of visual inadequacy to depict the citizen as even more disabled: "The private citizen today has come to feel rather like a deaf spectator in the back row, who ought to keep his mind on the mystery off there, but cannot quite manage to keep awake." Deaf and nearly blind, Lippmann's "disenchanted man"—his version of "mass man"—"lives in a world which he cannot see, does not understand and is unable to direct." Declaring that the public's "sovereignty is a fiction," Lippmann labeled the public a "phantom," an intangible, evanescent specter haunting democratic theory. For Lippmann, by 1925 there was no substantive, healthy public in the body politic. It was only a figment of democratic theory's imagination.[56] The public had been replaced by an incapable mass.

Lippmann believed that the average citizen "is asked to practice an unattainable idea" and pointedly stated that he had not met anyone, including President Woodrow Wilson (a trained political scientist), "who came anywhere near to embodying the accepted ideal of the sovereign and omnicompetent citizen."[57] As he made clear in an utterly pessimistic passage, a democratic theory that assumed everyone is fit to participate and should participate fully in modern politics was simply wrong: "The mass of absolutely illiterate, of feeble-minded, grossly neurotic, undernourished and frustrated individuals, is . . . much more considerable there is reason to think than we generally suppose," he argued; as a result, "the stream of public opinion is stopped by them in little eddies of misunderstanding, where it is discolored with prejudice and far-fetched analogy" (p. 75). Lippmann therefore had no faith in the assumptions of the democratic theorists, whom he called "Jeffersonian" democrats. Their conception of the "omnicompetent" democratic citizen was mostly a residue of cultural lag and a product of pre-twentieth-century circumstances in which a local, "partial experience of public affairs" was sufficient to school the citizen for responsible participation in the larger environment (pp. 273–74). But in the machine age, the public could only "meddle ignorantly or tyrannically" with the problems of a "complicated civilization."[58]

The bulk of *Public Opinion* deepens this two-pronged thesis through a series of arguments showing how "cultural lag" and "stereotypes" render the modern citizen inadequate for the responsibilities of democracy. The notion of the stereotype is probably the idea for which *Public Opinion* is best known, and Lippmann used it to explain the internal mental patterns through which incoming information and images are interpreted, filtered, and distorted into false pictures. Stereotypes, he suggested, are virtually inescapable: culture, language, religion, ethnicity, and other forms of human communication and organization produce them, shaping people's culturally and experientially bound pseudo-environments, creating virtually insuperable barriers to rational, informed politics. "We are told about the world before we see it. We imagine most things before we experience them. And those preconceptions, unless education has made us acutely aware, govern deeply the whole process of perception."[59]

Lippmann's faith in scientific modes of inquiry, however, provided an exception to the apparent totality of his theory. Education and experience, cultural refinement and cosmopolitanism, and, most of all, the use of the scientific method could provide an escape from narrow and limiting stereotypes (p. 90). The scientific method, he averred, offered mastery over stereotypes, and knowledge about how the mind tends to work was fundamental to social scientists' task of re-forming the world along more rational lines. Like the semanticists who thought they identified a solution to social problems in the relationship among thought, language, and the world, Lippmann contended that the concept of pseudo-environments was the starting point for a scientific politics. If the problem was that perception determines action, then the solution was to change how the world is imagined (p. 17).[60] And while Lippmann understood propaganda as an obstacle to clarity and rationality and worried about its capacities to compound stereotypes and obscure reality, he also viewed it as a potential tool for the efficient engineering of consent. The solution to propaganda's threat to democracy lay in science, Lippmann believed, especially in the "technic" employed by scientifically trained and disciplined policy experts. The industrial scientists' abilities to yield "a working image of reality" could be, he argued, replicated in the policy-making arena; with social scientists applying scientific methods to the arena of social life, they could offer up hard facts and careful analysis to political leaders, thereby eliminating mere opinion as the basis for political decisions. Science would close the distance between the pseudo-environment and the real environment, and Lippmann's technocratic priesthood would work in concert with the policy makers. Together they would form an alliance of "insiders" driving the wheels of society forward by conquering drift and adding mastery (pp. 376–77).

This vision of propaganda's possibilities in conjunction with an alliance of experts and policy makers grew out of Lippmann's wartime experience and shaped his impressions of its negative and positive powers. During World War I, Lippmann himself performed propaganda-related work in several capacities, first for Colonel House with the Inter-Allied Propaganda Board and then for George Creel's CPI. As Lippmann biographer Ronald Steel writes, "the war and his propaganda work" showed Lippmann "how easily public opinion could be molded."[61] He was astonished, instructed, and dismayed by what he saw. While he admired the potential for propaganda to mobilize public sentiment efficiently, the war also deeply disturbed him because he saw the failures of human intellect at work and learned how inadequate the channels of mass communication were for presenting the public the news it needed. At the Paris Peace Conference, for instance, Lippmann witnessed how "reporters grasped at scraps of news and fed one another with rumors that were then pumped into front-page dispatches" (p. 152). The calamity, from Lippmann's perspective, was that elites—reporters and political aides—were just as susceptible to planted rumors and hysteria as were the people who read their dispatches, and thus journalists, the putative providers of democracy's essential information, not only failed themselves to overcome propagandists' deceptions but passed those deceptions on to their audiences as fact.

When Lippmann returned from Europe, he initially argued that the problem of modern democracy lay in journalism itself, and he wrote three articles about the relationship between a free press and democracy, published in book form in 1920 as *Liberty and the News*.[62] In this work, Lippmann said the need for a free, objective, professional press was absolutely essential for the preservation of democracy, opining that if all encumbrances on the activities of the press were removed and stricter professional standards imposed, the democratic discussion would in fact be enhanced (pp. 171–72).[63] By 1922, however, when *Public Opinion* was published, Lippmann's pessimism about the capacity for objectivity and the problems of journalism had deepened.[64] He essentially abandoned his earlier belief that journalism would be the instrument for salvaging democracy, primarily because he came to believe that the typical journalist "knows that he is seeing the world through subjective lenses" but "lacks that sustaining conviction of a certain technic which finally freed the physical sciences from theological control."[65] Inadequate journalism was only emblematic of a larger problem, he argued, and the limits of a public-centered theory of democracy lay not in the flow of information but rather in the problem of epistemology. Therefore in *Public Opinion* his real concern about propaganda's capacity to deceive was rooted in the threat it posed to the technocratic elite on whom an expert-centered democracy would depend.

Lippmann did not arrive at this idealized union of scientifically trained experts and policy makers by speculation. His vision was a product of another of his wartime jobs, a true insider position in a top secret project, called the Inquiry, where he worked with a group of specialists—geographers, historians, political scientists, economists, psychologists, archaeologists, and others—whose job it was to draw up plans for the frontiers of postwar Europe in preparation for the Paris Peace Conference. It was a formative experience for the young Lippmann, and it certainly helped him identify the features of the massive applied research bureau he proposed in *Public Opinion*.[66] He learned that among the experts who should be aligned with policy makers were political scientists specially trained in "intelligence work," by which he meant opinion analysis and formation. Fortunately, he argued, the "very old . . . art" of creating consent did not "die out with the appearance of democracy" but "has, in fact, improved enormously in technic, because it is now based on analysis rather than on rule of thumb. And so, as a result of psychological research, coupled with the modern means of communication, the practice of democracy has turned a corner" (pp. 248–49). Democracy in an age of mass communications could be made more stable, predictable, and efficient through scientific persuasion. And propaganda could be a most useful tool for making governance more efficient, especially in moments of crisis. As he said, "When quick results are imperative, the manipulation of masses through symbols may be the only quick way of having a critical thing done" (p. 236).

This was a powerful and profoundly elitist idea, one that argued for expert-driven politics, a politics of manipulation, a politics of empty symbols, a politics bereft of an active and self-interested public. It was also an idea amenable to the social sciences in a period in which social scientists were clamoring for respectability by claiming the mantle of science. As subsequent chapters will show, Lippmann was not the only American liberal who advocated the necessity of making propaganda an efficient weapon for the manufacturing of consent. Indeed, Lippmann's democratic realist position profoundly shaped an emerging paradigm in the interwar social sciences, posing a significant theoretical and conceptual challenge to democratic orthodoxy. But it did not go unchallenged by reformers from a previous generation nor by members of his own generation who were committed to revitalizing traditional democratic theory and public-centered politics to meet the demands of the machine age. They well understood the deeply undemocratic implications of Lippmann's instrumentalist perception of expertism and propaganda.

Dewey's Counterargument

When John Dewey reviewed Lippmann's *Public Opinion* in 1922 in the *New Republic*, he remarked that "one finishes the book almost without realizing that it is perhaps the most effective indictment of democracy . . . ever penned." However, he also complained that Lippmann had laid too much stress on the "enlightenment" of administrators and executives and not enough on enlightening the public. He said that democracy "demands a more thoroughgoing education than the education of officials, administrators and directors of industry" that Lippmann had urged. Lippmann "sidetracked" the debate about modern democracy and "missed the challenge" of it.[67] In his 1925 review of *The Phantom Public*, Dewey said Lippmann laid too much blame on the theory of democracy itself and failed to see that the problems of democracy were symptoms, not causes, of the larger problems of the modern polity.[68]

Dewey's rebuttal was a vital thread in the interwar liberal discussions about public opinion, the role of the social sciences, the challenge presented by propaganda, and the strengths and weaknesses of democratic theory. In comparison to Lippmann, Dewey was a veritable champion of the public and of participatory democracy whose solution to the crisis of faith in democratic theory was to pull the public back into the center of political decision making. Where Lippmann wanted to use the symbols of political life to manipulate the public, Dewey saw the need to make those symbols part of a reinvigorated political community. Lippmann turned to experts and elites to shape a more rational politics. Dewey rejected this argument as business as usual, declaring: "The world has suffered more from leaders and authorities than from the masses. The essential need . . . is the improvement of the methods and conditions of debate, discussion and persuasion. That is *the* problem of the public."[69]

Dewey responded to Lippmann and other democratic realists at length in a series of lectures in 1926 on the philosophy of democracy.[70] Published in 1927 as *The Public and Its Problems*, Dewey's commentary offers an interesting paradox that illustrates the extent to which interwar liberals were made nervous by the combination of mass society conditions and propaganda. Dewey relied extensively on the standard outline of the mass society critique and even acknowledged his indebtedness to Lippmann for the "ideas involved in [his] entire discussion."[71] Yet he recoiled at what he perceived as the antidemocratic implications of Lippmann's critique. The crisis of democracy was not for Dewey a problem of public incapacity. Nor was it a failed or outmoded theory of democracy. Rather, it was the absence of a coherent public as a starting point for democratically oriented political behavior and ideas. "How," Dewey asked, "can a public be organized . . . when literally it does not stay in place?"[72] Certainly not by scientifically trained experts artificially creating unified public opinion through propaganda.

Unlike Lippmann, Dewey was careful not to rely too much on expertise and the judgments of intellectuals, yet he maintained faith in scientific methods to advance social progress. In his 1946 introduction to a reissue of *The Public and Its Problems,* Dewey restated his longtime faith in scientific inquiry as a vehicle for progressive reform: "Some of us have been insisting for some time that science bears exactly the same relation to the progress of culture as do the affairs acknowledged to be technological." He added that social problems could be most directly and effectively resolved by the application of "that effective intelligence named scientific method." Dewey, James Carey notes, wanted a science "that would clarify our purposes, advance our mutual understanding, and permit cooperative action."[73]

Dewey argued against Lippmann's model of rule by experts by noting that if "the masses are as intellectually irredeemable as the premise implies . . . the very ignorance, bias, frivolity, jealousy, instability, which are alleged to incapacitate them . . . unfit them still more for passive submission to rule by intellectuals."[74] He delineated a different kind of role for experts. They would help provide the public with the information necessary to perform its functions. They would ensure more accurate and adequate public discussion about its interests. They would facilitate the democratic dialogue and thereby create a shared political consciousness and a shared set of interests. The "problem of the public," he reiterated, was that the conditions for public debate and discussion needed improvement (pp. 177–78). As for the manufacturing of opinion and consent to achieve presumably desirable outcomes, he wrote: "Opinion casually formed and formed under the direction of those having something at stake in having a lie believed can be public opinion only in name" (p. 178). In the absence of a public rooted in, aware of, and capable of expressing its "common interests," democracy was endangered (pp. 34–35). This was what frightened him the most about propaganda: it made it difficult for the public to be certain of its own interests, further increasing its vulnerabilities to organized manipulation.

The wartime and postwar proliferation of propagandists in the guise of public relations agents and advertising men represented a fundamental threat to the processes of democracy. "We seem to be approaching a state of government by hired promoters of opinion called publicity agents" who had "developed an extraordinary facility in enlisting upon their side the inertia, prejudices and emotional partisanship of the masses by use of a technique [propaganda] which impedes free inquiry and expression" (p. 169). Where Lippmann appraised this as a given, even an efficiency-enhancing development for taking the messiness out of modern politics, Dewey called it "a social pathology" that worked against public inquiry into its own affairs and circumstances and contributed to an "increase in the amount of errors and half-truths which have got into circulation" (p. 170).

For Dewey, an informed and rational political culture was threatened by mass-produced ideas, consumerism, and a declining interest in political affairs. Pointing to the diversions offered by movies, radio, pulp fiction, and automobile culture, he invoked the same kind of "bread and circuses" argument made by Lippmann, complaining that citizens were being replaced by consumers. Such distraction from politics made it easier for political elites to manipulate symbols and ideas and generate artificial, even destructive, political "unities," as he called them. In the absence of stable local communities, organic political associations were too easily replaced by national party politics and expanding statism. These expressions of nonlocal, nonorganic political association were negatively enhanced by powerful communications technologies that, when used for entertainment purposes, had a great capacity to distract and "crowd to one side" the "political elements" in humans; when used for political purposes, they enhanced the capacity of publicity men and propagandists to create artificial unities (p. 139).

Although Dewey was optimistic that communications technologies might ensure public-centered democracy, he recognized that there were abundant obstacles to achieving a clear perception of common interests and to creating political language with agreed-upon meanings, meanings born of common experience. He therefore looked to the revitalizing power of shared rituals and the associated symbols of public-oriented experiences as vehicles for political renewal. He was convinced it was possible for the public to organize itself into "effective political action" by transforming itself through changes in "ideas and ideals" (p. 126). Full participation in the symbolically powerful rituals of democratic life (rituals Lippmann would trivialize through orchestration and manufactured consent) would begin the process of public regeneration (pp. 142–44). Experts would have a beneficial role here. "It is not necessary that the many should have the knowledge and skill to carry on the needed investigations," he wrote, explaining that the public could not expect omnicompetence. The public could and should be competent, however, and therefore it was the obligation of experts—social scientists, journalists, and public officials among them—to make certain that it had "the ability to judge of the bearing of the knowledge supplied by others upon common concerns" (p. 209).

For Dewey, propaganda as a technique defeated these purposes, because it was necessarily interested in "putting ideas over" on people or in creating what he called false "unities" instead of engaging people in productive exchange. In order to revive democracy, Dewey said, the idea of it must also be "clarified" and more deeply "apprehended." Like Justice Louis Brandeis, who argued that the cure for bad speech was more speech, Dewey argued that "the cure for the ailments of democracy is more democracy." The "bewildered" public would not be able to find itself unless local, communal life were restored, and through this process an "instrumentality" of shared and "communicated experience" would develop. Out of those shared "signs and symbols" of democratic participation a common language of democracy would emerge, making possible a broader and even more invigorating common conversation (pp. 143, 144).

While both Lippmann's "realist" and Dewey's "idealist" positions were immensely influential within U.S. liberal culture between the wars (and, indeed, until today), the sophisticated, extensive propaganda technologies emerging in the interwar-era made Dewey's goal of revitalized public-centered communication seem utopian, especially given the language of control and mastery dominating the interwar social science lexicon. As John Jordan writes, "engineering's inevitably hierarchical logic threatened the delicate balance of democratic politics" because advocates of applied science, especially those in the Lippmann vein, tried to avoid the hurly-burly of democratic processes by assuming (and claiming) that "the methods and logic of applied science apparently guaranteed correct answers to every problem."[75] While I disagree with Jordan's contention that Dewey shared the same predilections, his observations are useful, especially those noting that U.S. social sciences and U.S. liberalism were rooted in a hierarchical scientism whose lexicon and metaphors of efficiency, rationality, and control precluded a commitment to the uncertain outcomes of bottom-up politics. This interpretation is especially applicable to the interwar critique of propaganda, as well as to Lippmann, who responded to the uncertainties of mass-mediated democracy by championing the "science" of manufacturing consent.

The Quicksand of Language in the Age of Propaganda

Dewey, of course, was not the only interwar commentator who worried about how the forces of mass communications technologies and propaganda were affecting the common language of democracy. For poets and novelists of the WWI generation, meaningless language had been one of most devastating consequences of the war. Writers from all nations mocked the discordance between the high-blown justifications for war and the lived experience of war as carnage, rot, and waste. For U.S. writers, Wilsonian language promising that American ideals could make the rest of the world orderly, safe, and democratic seemed patently false. In the postwar era, literary modernists became transfixed by the need for a new language, one purged of obfuscation and certainties. While John Dos Passos filled his fractured *U.S.A.* novel with newsreel scenes to convey the sense of war as orchestrated words and images, expatriate writers such as Ernest Hemingway and Archibald MacLeish juxtaposed useless patriotic platitudes with the idea that the war's real meaning was ambiguous at best and that maybe there was no meaning but loss. Hemingway contemptuously rejected the reassuring language of officialdom as his antiheroic narrator in *A Farewell to Arms*, the American lieutenant "Tenente," recoiled in silent anger when told by a more gullible man how to think about the war. Refusing the flowery language of patriotic injunction, Hemingway's self-modeled Tenente insisted that only concrete details, and not abstractions, could ever capture the realities of war:

> I was always embarrassed by the words sacred, glorious, and sacrifice, and the expression in vain. We had heard them, sometimes standing in the rain almost out of earshot, so that only the shouted words came through, and had read them, on proclamations that were slapped up by billposters over other proclamations, now for a long time, and I had seen nothing sacred, and the things that were glorious had no glory. . . . Abstract words such as glory, honor, courage, or hallow were obscene behind the concrete names of villages, the numbers of roads, the names of rivers, the numbers of regiments and the dates.[76]

For MacLeish, who lost a brother in the war and fought in it himself, the war marked the end of innocence, "The End of the World" even. Using the metaphor of a circus tent to describe the playful naïveté of the prewar world, he described the cataclysm the war had brought: "Quite unexpectedly the top blew off," he wrote, leaving "those thousands of white faces, those dazed eyes. . . . There in the sudden blackness the black pall / Of nothing, nothing, nothing—nothing at all."[77] Perhaps most famously, the British poet Wilfred Owen captured the empty rhetoric of patriotic duty in his haunting poem "Dulce Et Decorum Est," in which he mocked the inherited certitude that "it is sweet and becoming to die for one's country." He used mustard gas metaphors to capture the poison of such promises on "innocent tongues":

> If you could hear, at every jolt, the blood
> Come gargling from the froth-corrupted lungs
> Bitter as the cud
> Of vile, incurable sores on innocent tongues,—
> My friend, you would not tell with such high zest
> To children ardent for some desperate glory,
> The old lie: *Dulce et decorum est*
> *Pro patria mori.*[78]

Wilfred Owen died fighting for England mere days before the Armistice.

German novelist Erich Marie Remarque haunted his postwar audience with his depiction of the distance between official German (and by extension, all belligerents') reports that things were "all quiet on the western front" when the reality lay in the accumulating death tolls and the putrid, exhausting existence of life, and then death, on the front. Taken together, the concerns of all these writers are aptly summarized by historian Richard Pells, who expressed the idea that in an age of words without meaning, civilization seemed on the verge of total disorder: "The loss of individual control, the irrelevance of rational interpretation, the failure of political or religious or philosophical language to make personal catastrophe intelligible became the primary experience of modern warfare."[79]

As with postwar poets and novelists, the 1920s and 1930s found scholars and writers from many disciplines—linguistics, philosophy, mathematics, psychology, among others—obsessed with the idea of language gone awry. The U.S. practitioners of the general semantics, a more scientific and decidedly less poetic approach to language, were very much beset by the idea that propagandistic language, machine-age conditions, and human susceptibility to magical ways of thinking had made human language increasingly useless as a problem-solving tool. For the semanticists, the experience of mass manipulation in WWI, combined with pessimism about human rationality, the rise of ballyhoo culture in the 1920s, and political demagogues leading the world back to the brink of war in the 1930s, provided evidence that however utopian their possibilities, mass communications technologies were more likely to be used to harangue and manipulate modern mass publics than to solve collective problems and increase human understanding.

By the mid-1930s—a decade after Dewey's response to Lippmann—propaganda's assault on emotion, reason, and language as a useful tool for the search for truth was once again very much on the mind of U.S. intellectuals. The startling successes of the Nazi party in Germany had revalidated post-WWI anxieties and renewed interest in the subject. To students of human languages and communications, the Nazi mastery of all forms of propaganda techniques suggested that a perilous problem beset the modern era: language, the most necessary tool for human problem solving, was under siege by deception and lies on a mass scale, and presumably rational people were being taken in by it.

The two primary U.S. popularizers of the general semantics, journalist Stuart Chase and linguist H. I. Hayakawa, made especially clear these connections between superstitious beliefs in words and late-1930s fears that propaganda, especially of the Nazi strain, threatened civilization. For both, the concept "word-magic" explained how people can be swayed by emotional, as opposed to reportorial, language, a tendency that gives language its awful power to provoke instinctive and violent responses. Like Lippmann, both Chase and Hayakawa pointed to the gap between the words people use to describe the world and the world itself and believed that if we could correct our epistemologies, we could fix the problem of irrationality or at least have less muddled discussions about social problems. Like Dewey, they were anxious about propagandists' abilities to exploit those gaps and were exasperated at how easily emotional or "affective" language could be used for exploitative purposes. And like many in their generation, Chase and Hayakawa had an abiding faith in scientific method as the solution to social and political problems and promised that a more scientific understanding of language combined with applied techniques might provide the public with a weapon against propaganda's assault on modern consciousness.

Chase's *The Tyranny of Words* (1938) and H. I. Hayakawa's *Language in Action* (1941) drew principally on three intellectual sources: *The Meaning of Meaning* (1923), by I. A. Richards and C. K. Ogden; the Polish mathematician Alfred Korzybski's *Science and Sanity: An Introduction to Non-Aristotelian Systems and General Semantics* (1933); and physicist Paul W. Bridgman's discussion of scientific methods in *The Logic of Modern Physics*.[80] Along with these ur-texts of the field of general semantics, Chase and Hayakawa drew on an emerging literature about language in a range of academic disciplines, from anthropology and psychology, to physics and mathematics, to linguistics and philosophy.[81] And both explicitly situated their discussion of language gone amiss within the context of late-1930s anxieties that propaganda was once again exciting war passions.

Chase and Hayakawa popularized Ogden and Richard's concept of word-magic and the idea that language should be studied as the science of symbolism. As Ogden and Richards suggested in 1923, the superstition that words correspond to the things for which they stand is a "potent instinctive belief," one that allows words to be used as "part of the mechanism of deceit."[82] A deeply conservative force, word-magic gives occult powers to words, reinforces the powers of superstition, and maintains culturally bound linguistic habits that "grip us with the habits of thought which have grown up with their use" (p. 29). Thus individual words structure the thoughts of each generation, influence both memory and imagination, and thereby create cognitive patterns that inhibit our capacity to understand and address modern complexities. In fact, Ogden and Richards argued, the twentieth century "suffers more grievously than any previous age from the ravages of such verbal superstitions" (p. 29). What was needed, they wrote shortly after WWI, was a science of language that would "throw light on the primitive idea that Words and Things are related by some magic bond" (p. 47). Their main point—and the one that Chase and Hayakawa popularized—is that there is only an imputed relation between words and things, between the symbols we use to reflect on and describe the world and the world we actually encounter. For speech to have meaning, for it to be as thoroughly scientific as possible, the word (symbol) must point to a concrete object (referent); otherwise it is an abstraction and risks meaninglessness. This is positivism applied to language. From Korzybski, Chase and Hayakawa borrowed essentially the same positivistic idea: that finding the concrete referent for words was absolutely necessary to uttering language with meaning. From Bridgman, they learned the importance of subjecting concepts to scientific operations in order to demonstrate their truth.

Both Chase and Hayakawa pointed to Depression-era political concerns to illustrate the insights of the general semantics, and both explicitly addressed the connections between propaganda as a threat to reliable communications and political order and the need for scientific methods applied to language. Both were convinced that a science of semantics was necessary as an instrument for modern living and that it could provide a critical role for intellectuals as guides for leading the public through the verbal minefields of modern propaganda. Scientific language, rooted in concrete referents and subject to verification, was the only truly dependable language, and scientific methods applied to language might stave off the social and political consequences of words misused and misunderstood, possibly saving a world poised on the brink of disorder and violence. Because words had so much influence in constructing the world and our reactions to it, language itself needed greater attention, especially in an age when the instruments of mass communications could make propaganda and its dangerous "two-valued orientation" so influential.[83]

Chase and Hayakawa used tones, word choices, and examples familiar from Lippmann and Dewey. Invoking their machine-age framework of anxieties, Chase outlined the connections among bad language, human rootlessness, mass communication technologies, political and commercial propaganda, and susceptibility to all these forces: "Power Age communities have grown far beyond the check of individual experience. They rely increasingly on printed matter, radio, communication at a distance. This has operated to enlarge the field for words, absolutely and relatively, and has created a paradise for fakirs."[84] In short, Chase reiterated Lippmann's and Dewey's litany of machine-age problems but made language the central explanation. Bad language was at issue because the mass scale of the modern era made individual experience inadequate as a means of checking either the truthfulness or the motives of those using modern instruments of communications to further their own purposes. And because we do not habitually employ semantic tests to protect ourselves from these ill-motivated fakirs, we are as susceptible to them as we are to three-legged calves and other sideshows: "A community of semantic illiterates, of persons unable to perceive the meaning of what they read and hear, is one of perilous equilibrium," Chase wrote. "Advertisers, as well as demagogues, thrive on this illiteracy. . . . Without ability to translate words into verifiable meanings, most people are the inevitable victims of both commercial and literary fraud. Their mental life is increasingly corrupted" (p. 27). Indeed here was another instance of the propaganda-based mass society critique, this time embedded in the idea of language gone awry.

For Chase and Hayakawa, inadequate understanding of how language works made bad thinking possible, and bad thinking made dangerous language more destructive. Bad thinking in an age of propaganda was potentially catastrophic because it allowed propaganda to fuel raging political fires. Alluding to the "already blazing war between 'fascism' and 'communism,'" for instance, Chase acknowledged that this conflict was more than just a battle of words, but "the words themselves, and the dialectic which accompanies them, have kindled emotional fires which far transcend the differences in fact" (p. 20). "In modern times" Chase wrote, violence "comes *after* the conflict has been set in motion by propaganda. Bad language is now the mightiest weapon in the arsenal of despots and demagogues. Witness Dr. Goebbels" (p. 21).

Hayakawa, like Chase, argued that while despots might exploit our linguistic naïveté, each individual needed to be responsible for her or his own susceptibilities. Echoing Chase, he said that "to the extent that we too think like savages and babble like idiots, we all share the guilt for the mess in which human society finds itself. To cure these evils, we must first go to work on ourselves."[85] Both reported that a semantic approach to language provided the method necessary to save language from meaninglessness and to protect the public from propaganda. "The goal of semantics," Chase wrote, "might be stated as 'Find the referent.' "[86] To this insight he added Bridgman's understanding that scientific methods provide verification in the laboratory and thus verifiability to scientific language. These two insights—finding the referent and using verifiable language—gave Chase the idea for an method that could be applied by everyone to daily language.

Chase argued that if only people would disabuse themselves of word-magic, find the concrete referents for the words they were using, use language that can be verified, avoid abstractions and absolutes, and apply the test of "semantic blanks" to speech that seems to have no concrete referents or relies too greatly on abstraction, then political sanity might be restored. "Indeed, it is doubtful if a people learned in semantics would tolerate any sort of supreme political dictator," he earnestly wrote. "A typical speech by an aspiring Hitler would be translated into its intrinsic meaning, if any. Abstract words and phrases without discoverable referents would register a semantic blank, noises without meaning" (p. 21). Quoting a typical Hitler speech, he showed how the method of employing semantic blanks would work. First the speech: "The Aryan Fatherland, which has nursed the souls of heroes, calls upon you for the supreme sacrifice which you, in whom flows heroic blood, will not fail, and which will echo forever down the corridors of history." Then, using the semantic blank to replace every abstraction or word without a concrete referent, Chase translated the same passage as: "The blab blab, which has nursed the blabs of blabs, calls upon you for the blab blab which you, in whom flows blab blood, will not fail, and which will echo blab down the blabs of blab" (p. 21).

The "blab," he wrote, "is not an attempt to be funny; it is a semantic blank. Nothing comes through. The hearer, versed in reducing high-order abstractions to either nil or a series of roughly similar events in the real world of experience, and protected from emotive associations with such words, simply hears nothing comprehensible" (p. 21). Indeed, Chase's example, while it might be humorous, was meant to be taken entirely seriously as a strategy for self-defense against propaganda. As he suggested, "We are in sight of a technique which will let us take a political speech, a dictator's ukase . . . a plan to sell the world . . . analyze it, and tell specifically what is wrong with it, down to counting the blabs" (p. 169). For

Chase, the semantic method offered some hope for avoiding an ever-escalating war of words.

For Hayakawa, who was neither as optimistic as Chase that a science of semantics would stop the Hitlers of the world nor as afraid of emotional speech (which he called affective speech), the value of semantics was also in the insights it provided about how language works and in the techniques it suggested for making speech better. Hayakawa's work was more original and more deeply comprehensive in its understanding of human language and its variations. And although he and Chase shared many similar themes, his work was a scholar's synthesis, while Chase's was a popularizer's synthesis. Like Chase, however, he offered scientific techniques to resolve the problem of language, demanded that we look to concrete language (he called it extensional language) to find meaning, and offered his own version (or Korzybski's version) of the semantic blank, which he called the "verbal index." And he too warned against the "two-valued orientation" used by propagandists to seduce people into a linguistically induced "mob spirit" (pp. 138–39).

Hayakawa explained that the "verbal index" was "a simple technique" for preventing abstract, emotional, value-laden, and motive-driven speech "from having their harmful effect on our thinking." Instead of using the label Englishmen, or Jews, or Frenchmen, for example, Hayakawa suggested that one should say or write: "Englishman$_1$, Englishman$_2$ . . . Frenchman$_1$, Frenchman$_2$, Frenchman$_3$." Explaining, he said that the "terms of the classification tell us what the individuals in that class have in common" and the index numbers "remind us of the characteristics left out." Such a technique would therefore allow us to formulate a rule to guide "all our thinking and reading: Cow$_1$ is NOT cow$_2$; Jew$_1$ is NOT Jew$_2$." This rule, "if remembered, prevents us from confusing levels of abstractions and forces us to consider the facts on those occasions when we might otherwise find ourselves leaping to conclusions which we may later have cause to regret."[87] Such a strategy, he suggested, would defuse fascists' appeals to stereotyping and race-based classifications.

Finally, Hayakawa directed his readers to be especially wary of the Fascist use of the "two-valued orientation," a propaganda device Chase also warned against. The two-valued orientation, Hayakawa explained, was the clearest evidence of someone's intention to persuade or cajole. It was the most common technique used by those selfishly interested in dividing the world into false categories, a fallacious way of thinking that suggests things can be seen in two values only, affirmative and negative, good and bad, hot and cold, and so forth. To Hayakawa, the Nazi use of the two-valued orientation was the prime example of its pernicious effectiveness:

Here, as even a cursory examination of official Nazi party propaganda shows, the two-valued orientation is relied upon almost exclusively. Hunger, famine, unemployment, crooked capitalism, defeat in the first World War, bad smells, immorality, treachery, selfishness, and all things offensive are lined up on the "bad" side with "Jewish-dominated plutocracy." Anyone or anything that stands in the way of Hitler's wishes is "Jewish" . . . and, as a crowning insult, "non-Aryan." On the other hand, everything that Hitler chooses to call "Aryan" is noble, virtuous, heroic, and altogether glorious. Courage, self-discipline, honor, beauty, health, and joy are "Aryan." (p. 130)

For Hayakawa, the most frightening consequence of this powerful strategy was that it leads to violence and mob rule. Indeed, he argued that there was an intrinsic connection between two-valued orientations and violence, because the two-valued orientation is based on the assumption that *"there is no middle ground"* (p. 131). In a section called the "Two-Valued Orientation and the Mob Spirit," Hayakawa explained that this orientation "is used by all spread-eagle orators and demagogues" as their principle argumentative technique: "As in Germany, it produces here the results of intoxication, fanaticism, and brutality. . . . Listeners who uncritically permit themselves to be carried away by such oratory week after week almost invariably find their pulses rising, their fists clenching, and the desire to act violently accumulating within them." To continue, he noted that "the two-valued orientation produces the combative spirit, *but nothing else*" (pp. 138–39).

Science, by contrast, requires an infinite-valued orientation, and, as Hayakawa suggested, democratic life requires, at the least, the use of multivalued orientation, because then shades of difference will be recognized and embraced. Ultimately, this scientific approach to all forms of evidence was the great contribution scientific methodology could make to democracy because, he argued, scientific operations are nonjudgmental and based on an open-ended search for truth. For Hayakawa, then, the language and methods of science and the methods and spirit of democracy ultimately rested on similar principles, with democracy having much to learn from science and potentially even being saved by application of scientific methods to the world of political language (pp. 133–35).

Chase and Hayakawa were not, of course, the only voices warning against two-valued orientations and the use of word-magic by the end of the 1930s. For First Amendment theorist Zechariah Chafee Jr., writing on the very eve of U.S. involvement in WWII, legal liberalism also required a more democratic approach to thinking about words and their effects, especially if the legal establishment was going to avoid the trap of word-magic and the confusion of the mere word with the deed. Without using the same terms as the semanticists, Chafee also looked at the problem of language and offered his own supposedly objective measuring rod for thinking about the problem of bad speech and its limits. Like Hayakawa, he knew a multivalued orientation would be necessary if democracy were to survive the powerful, primitive tendency to think in terms of two-valued orientations, thinking that could easily lead to the same civil liberties disasters in WWII as it had in WWI. And like Dewey, he knew that if the democratic spirit was to survive the war, then a faith in the public's capacities to discern its own interests needed to be promoted, and the public right to engage in the vital discussions necessary for determining those interests needed to be protected. This meant that the public had a right to engage in the search for truth, and democracy as a way of life, as opposed to a set of symbols, could not afford the two-valued orientation that had produced so much intolerance and repression in World War I.

Zechariah Chafee and the Limits of Free Speech

In 1940–41, as the nation's mood darkened and anxieties about the Nazi menace deepened, the national security state continued its expansion for a war on fascist propaganda. Zechariah Chafee Jr. offered a cautionary tale to readers of legal treatises. Updating and expanding his 1920 landmark volume *Freedom of Speech*, Chafee amplified his arguments for a new and larger audience in *Free Speech in the United States* (1941), and both works became central texts for legal liberals concerned about speech matters in the WWII era. His earlier work was a highly critical response to reactionary American policies during and just after WWI, one that had long influenced modern First Amendment thinking, and he wrote the expanded version in hopes of staving off such policies as U.S. involvement in WWII became imminent. Both works cataloged the frenzied WWI-era suppression of political speech and association at the local, state, and federal levels, and both provided free speech advocates with an authoritative argument about the misguided legal thinking that permitted a nationwide failure to protect First Amendment freedoms.

Chafee warned that the same patterns might be repeated: vigilantism at the local level; patriotic fervor translated into punitive legislation at the state and national levels; unchecked prosecutorial zeal among federal attorneys; and failure at the federal court and Supreme Court levels to protect all but the most truly dangerous forms of political speech. Anticipating that dissent from official doctrine would "arouse resentment and fears and vigorous demands for prosecutions and other forms of suppression," Chafee hoped to allay the tendency among increasingly nervous liberals to capitulate to those demands and calmly reminded his readers that it was "necessary for thoughtful Americans to remember the national tradition of free speech" (*Free Speech*, p. vii). Beyond that, he offered what he understood as the closest approximation to an objective test for measuring the dangerousness of words, a test that would be altogether necessary as anxiety about dissenting language and dangerous words and images grew.

A Harvard law professor, Chafee—perhaps even more than Oliver Wendell Holmes Jr., Louis Brandeis, Roscoe Pound, and Learned Hand— defined free speech liberalism's main tenets in the interwar period and greatly influenced several generations of jurists, scholars, law students, and government lawyers through his writing and teaching. Chafee argued that democratic governments needed to maintain faith in the public's capacity to make discerning and rational judgments about political ideas. His argument for a speech-protective balance between internal security and individual liberty was premised on the theory that democracy is almost always strengthened by a plurality of ideas and voices expressed in open discussion, that the real aim of unfettered speech is social wisdom and the pursuit of collective truth, and that democracy is actually more endangered when people are afraid of expressing their ideas: "I have pointed out that the imprisonment of 'half-baked' agitators for 'foolish talk' may often discourage wise men from publishing valuable criticism of governmental policies," he wrote. "Consequently, what might be well said is not said at all" (p. xiii). For Chafee, this endangered democracy, and public faith in democracy, far more than did almost all forms of extremist expression, because it limited the range of ideas that might be debated, and it made the desire for security greater than the interest in truth. As he explained, "unremitting regard for the First Amendment benefits the nation even more than it protects the individuals who are prosecuted. The real value of freedom of speech is not to the minority that wants to talk, but to the majority that does not want to listen." True security, he said, is not produced by a machinery of surveillance and punishment, but "in the tolerance of private citizens" (p. xiv).

Chafee knew that widespread fears about the dangerous powers of political propaganda had only grown between the wars. Like other civil libertarians, he worried about the dangers of Nazi propaganda at two levels: He believed it had been a successful tool of subversion throughout Europe and that it could also harm American morale and the war effort. But, more importantly, he feared that the state's own antisubversive activities would lead to such restrictions on liberty that the state itself would become a greater threat to democracy than the extreme ideas it suppressed. Thus his treatment of the free speech tradition's historical evolution was unequivocally a product of contemporary concerns. His survey ranged from the alien and sedition acts of the early republic, to WWI and the Red Scare, up through the 1940 passage of the Smith Act, the first peacetime sedition act passed since the late eighteenth century. But WWI was his real focal point and the object lesson he wished to hold up for display. He feared that the same propaganda anxieties that earlier beclouded the legal imagination would once again obviate the necessary distinctions between words and acts. He had good reason to worry, for there was plenty of evidence by spring 1941, when he completed his book, that this would be the case: the widely used Espionage Act of 1917 was still in force to punish propaganda activities, and the legal arsenal had expanded to include the Foreign Agents Registration Act of 1938, the Voorhis Act of 1940, and the Alien Registration Act of 1940, which included the seditious conspiracy amendment known as the Smith Act. Chafee did not doubt that much of the antidemocratic, generally fascistic propaganda targeted by these laws was odious and acknowledged that some of it was probably dangerous enough to require suppression. But as a civil libertarian invested in strengthening the tenuous liberal commitment to civil liberties, he worried that the laws old and new would likely be turned to the punishment of merely crackpot speech, as he called it. For Chafee, crackpot speech was not necessarily dangerous, and the public was generally wise enough to see it as such. Therefore he tried to draw his tests of dangerous speech carefully and precisely, and he urged his fellow citizens to do so as well, lest the democratic principles and wisdom embedded in the First Amendment be sacrificed in the zeal for wartime security and uniformity of opinion.

In offering up a usable past, Chafee examined both obvious mistakes and missed opportunities where enlightened judgment and sound legal decisions had been available but not utilized. In looking to the WWI examples, he held up the opinions by Justices Holmes and Brandeis in the famous *Schenck* and *Abrams* cases to find the most useful language for defining free speech principles. But, more important, he focused on Judge Learned Hand's reversed federal court decision in the case of *Masses vs. Patten* for the best framework for defining the limits on the state's authority to curb speech. Hand, Chafee asserted, helped provided a framework and language for ensuring that the delicate balance between the competing interests of individual liberty and national security would not be thrown off by the quest for safety.

Like Hand, Chafee knew that a responsible liberalism needed to have a model for drawing careful distinctions between words as mere utterances and words as triggers to action. It also needed to assess carefully the differences between critical but "fruitful" (pp. viii–ix) speech that aided the search for truth and truly irresponsible or seditious speech that endangered the state's security and necessary functions. While he knew that finding a truly objective test was nigh impossible when dealing with the subjective realm of words and their interpretations, he believed that finding the point at which the state could legitimately distinguish between protected and punishable speech was an utterly necessary task for wartime American democracy.

Chafee's theory of free speech was grounded on balancing a series of competing interests, those of individuals, the society, and the state. At a time of war those competing interests tilted toward the need for public safety, but in general society had a compelling interest in individual free speech not just for the liberty of individuals but because the search for truth was a collective process. Chafee feared the state's coercive influence over free speech because "once force is thrown into the argument, it becomes a matter of chance whether it is thrown on the false side or the true, and truth loses all its natural advantage in the contest." At the same time, and in the same passage, he also noted that "unlimited discussion sometimes interferes with [the] purposes" of order and security, especially military training and defense, and therefore social interest diluted the claim for "absolutely unlimited discussion." But the "principle of political wisdom" given "binding force" by the First Amendment argued that in the search for a balance between collective security and individual and group liberty, "freedom of speech ought to weigh very heavily in the scale" (p. 31).

Chafee cautioned his readers that "the great interest in free speech should be sacrificed only when the interest in public safety is really imperiled, and not, as most men believe, when it is barely conceivable that it may be slightly affected." And laying down his standard for determining dangerousness, he said that "in war time . . . speech should be unrestricted by the censorship or by punishment, unless it is clearly liable to *cause direct and dangerous* interference with the conduct of the war" (p. 35; emphasis added). For Chafee, then, questions of causality, directness, and dangerousness defined the objective criteria for determining when the state's security interests outweighed the individual and social interest in unfettered speech. Restriction short of these speech-protective limits would be premature and obstructive of the greater social interest in protecting individual liberty. This was both the wisdom and the legal principle he drew from Learned Hand's reasoning in the *Masses* decision.

Chafee interpreted the First Amendment as being primarily interested in protecting political speech that contributed to "an informative and informed public opinion." Other kinds of speech—obscene speech, for instance—did not rate the same degree of protection as political speech. He also argued that, far short of state action, individuals had a duty to police their own speech. He suggested that the idea of "fruitful" speech should help them be clear about the social value of their speech. Unfruitful speech neither contributes to public discussion nor to the spirit of tolerance necessary to keeping public discussion open and productive. This is what made sectarian propaganda potentially triply dangerous to the democratic process (pp. vii–viii). Because it encouraged intolerance among its adherents, it failed to contribute to the search for truth; because it provoked majoritarian ire, it potentially impinged on others' civil liberties; and besides diminishing the democratic spirit, it also potentially brought in the state's force, a force not necessarily interested in the truth. Individuals therefore had a responsibility to speak fruitfully, lest they unleash repressive forces. As he warned, "It is not going to be an easy task during the next few years to maintain freedom of speech unimpaired. There will be hard times ahead . . . during which many devoted citizens will readily believe that the safety of the nation demands the suppression of all criticism against those in authority" (p. viii). The tendency toward suppression, he added, "will be immensely strengthened if speakers and writers use their privilege of free discussion carelessly or maliciously, so as to further their own ambitions or the immediate self interests of their particular minority. By abusing liberty of speech, they may easily further its abolition" (p. ix). He argued therefore that the emergency called for speech uttered in good faith.

Drawing on the experience of WWI, Chafee knew that the greatest threat to political liberty would not come from dissenters. Rather, he feared the legal framework of laws and precedents that was already in place to enforce majoritarian intolerance and state repression. During WWI the federal district courts and the Supreme Court (by its very inaction) had essentially given prosecutors wide latitude under the Espionage Act to punish speech with bad tendencies. The almost vindictive use of the Blackstonian bad tendency test for assaying wartime speech was, according to Chafee, a consequence of the fear of propaganda and the idea that words carried with them their intended effects. No one anticipated that the 1917 Espionage Act "would be rapidly turned into a law under which opinions hostile to the war had practically no protection," he wrote. But "the tremendous wave of popular feeling against pacifists and pro-Germans during the war . . . due to the hysterical fear of spies and other German propaganda" resulted in a blanket application of the highly restrictive bad tendency doctrine in case after case (p. 64). He worried that the "sweeping judicial interpretation of [the Espionage Act] which the government lawyers obtained from the Supreme Court, and wider still from the District Courts, will be constantly cited as precedents for punishing expressions of opinion about the merits and conduct of the next war" (p. 103). Chafee worried about this legal arsenal far more than he worried about the "unfruitful" speech uttered by politically marginal dissenters.

The problems of the WWI-era use of the Espionage Act were extensive: The courts failed to acknowledge the social interest in individual speech and defined social interest only in terms of national security. They also failed to use the much more objective and speech-protective tests proffered by Judge Learned Hand in the *Masses* case. Instead, they relied on the bad tendency standard, which was arbitrary, gave too much room to judicial bias, and failed to provide strict guidelines for defining the limits of government control of speech. Coupled with the doctrine of presumed intent (the assumption that speakers intend the consequences of their words), it allowed juries and judges wide latitude to punish words with which they disagreed without requiring any evidence of the actual danger or effects of those words.

The failures of the federal judiciary in the WWI speech cases (especially the Supreme Court's waiting to hand down a speech case decision until after the war was over) and the absence of a "well-considered standard of criminality" made Chafee keen to identify a more objective standard for determining the limits of free speech (p. 34). Finding the point at which the most dangerous words could be distinguished from other utterances seemed to him the job of defining an interpretation of the First Amendment that balanced society's interest in free speech with its interest in safety. The bad tendency test along with presumed intent did not aid this task because both were unscientific in their understanding of cause and effect as applied to utterances and acts. They had no standing in the common law, where intention could not be the crucial test of guilt. And they failed to offer a uniform standard that would diminish the role of jury or judicial bias.

Learned Hand had understood these problems and had given "the fullest attention to the meaning of free speech" by applying the proximity and dangerousness tests to wartime speech. Hand insisted that a plausible causal relationship, fixed in time, needed to be demonstrated with respect to words and actions. And he argued that the test of dangerousness required "the strong danger that [an utterance] will cause injurious acts" (p. 44). Hand did not discount the power of words to prompt action or change opinions and argued that those words that "counsel the violation of law cannot by any latitude of interpretation be a part of that public opinion which is the final source of government in a democratic state" (quoted on p. 44). But he gave the state much less authority to punish speech using the Espionage Act than had the rest of the federal judiciary in subsequent WWI speech cases.

Unfortunately, Chafee argued, Hand's tests did not become the prevailing wartime interpretation of words and their danger under the authority of the Espionage Act. Postmaster General Burleson and the Circuit Court of Appeals had considered Hand's proximity to danger test in the *Masses* case "unsound," and consequently the postmaster general had reversed Hand's ruling, and the Appeals Court had upheld the reversal, thereby legitimizing the more speech-restrictive bad tendency and presumptive intent doctrines in the first major Espionage Act case of WWI (p. 49). They argued instead that speech was punishable under the Espionage Act "if the natural and reasonable effect of what is said is to encourage resistance to law, and the words are used in an endeavor to persuade to resistance" (Circuit Court of Appeals, quoted on p. 49). According to Chafee, "the undoubted effect of the final decision in *Masses vs. Patten* was to establish the old-time doctrine of remote bad tendency in the minds of district judges throughout the country. . . . As a result of this and similar decisions, the district judges ignored entirely the first element of criminal attempt and solicitation, that the effort, though unsuccessful, must approach dangerously near success. . . . Intention thus became the crucial test of guilt in any prosecution of opposition to the government's war policies." Intention was subsequently inferred from "the existence of the indirect injurious effect," not direct and proximate effects (p. 50). The decision left judges and juries with "nothing but speculation upon the remote political and economic effect of words and the probable condition of mind of a person whose ideas were entirely different from their own" (p. 63).

Hand's interpretation of the Espionage Act's provisions was right, Chafee argued, and anyone not seized by war fever could see this. He was also correct in his understanding of the relationship between utterance and act and of the legal protection that should be accorded utterances when they are not directly connected to acts. By ruling that proximity to success should be the legal standard for treating wartime propaganda, Hand successfully fixed the "boundary line of punishable speech . . . at the point where words come close to injurious conduct" (p. 43). As Chafee said, Hand's decision "was the only sort of rule about war-time utterances which should have been permitted . . . it was the only workable assumption. His rule gave the jury something definite to consider—the actual nature of the words and the danger of interference with the armed forces" (p. 63). For Chafee, this was as close to science as the law could get in matters having to do with the interpretation of words and their effects. Chafee did not want to see this interpretative framework passed up again.

As Chafee knew, the issues raised by the problem of controlling undesirable political propaganda spoke of deep conflicts within modern U.S. liberalism, and as I will show in later chapters, for the Justice Department lawyers preparing for a war against Nazi propaganda, Chafee's blueprint for protecting the First Amendment tradition became the benchmark by which they judged their own work. But those chapters also show that the national security anxieties—powerful propaganda coupled with public susceptibility—had an important effect on those federal officials responsible for erecting a propaganda defense.

Thus, while the tensions between free speech liberalism and national security liberalism shaped the debates and strategies over the question of what do about propaganda, they also informed the debates about the effects of propaganda on U.S. democracy. The competing versions of public competence versus mass susceptibility and public-centered versus expert-driven democracy that emerged in the interwar discovery of propaganda were all influential in the ideas, language, and career of political scientist Harold Lasswell, the interwar generation's foremost authority on propaganda, a scholar who claimed allegiance to both Lippmann and Dewey, who referred to his own "scientific" school of propaganda analysis as the "quantitative semantics" and who became a key figure in nation's defensive war on propaganda.

CHAPTER TWO

Harold D. Lasswell and the Scientific Study of Propaganda

Harold Lasswell embodies the central tensions and divisions defining U.S. intellectual culture in the interwar era, especially within the social sciences. Lasswell claimed that John Dewey had more intellectual influence over him than any other thinker, especially in his belief in science as a tool for democracy. But in the split between the democratic realists and idealists, Lasswell's thought and language—including his metaphors of mastery and control—bear much greater resemblance to Walter Lippmann's. Indeed, one can argue that Lasswell became the veritable fulfillment of Lippmann's image of the social science technocrat, armed with "technic" and ready to serve rationality and power. His abundant writings from the mid-1920s through the early 1940s express the confidence of an unabashed social engineer making governance more efficient and scientific. His defenders contend, however, that his interests in the relationship between science and power and the role of expertise in that equation had primarily to do with the question of how experts could best serve democracy; he was, they argue, thoroughly committed to the Deweyan idea that the people were capable of good decision making, as long as they had access to adequate materials, providing which was the job of the highly skilled.[1]

One can identify in Lasswell's thinking and career trajectory a shift away from a sustained critique of democratic theory's weaknesses to a tough-minded appraisal of democracy's moral strength and U.S. society's weaknesses during the wartime emergency. Political scientist Ronald Brunner argues that Lasswell began with the assumption that morals preceded science and as the nation moved toward war in the early 1940s, he understood that his job, as Brunner quotes him, "was to be ruled by the truth," especially the moral truths of democratic theory and practice. Brunner reports that his mentor's main purpose was "preserving human dignity," especially against totalitarianism.[2]

Lasswell's unquenchable desire for new approaches to the scientific study of politics and society made him both a pathbreaking thinker and a prolific but often cumbersome writer. Mastering a range of literatures and drawing extensively on different technical vocabularies gave Lasswell's prose style an extremely opaque quality, especially later in his career.[3] His friend Leo Rosten accused him of "blithely scramb[ling] together technical terms" in his passion for omniscience.[4] But his contemporaries followed where he led, and according to political scientist Gabriel Almond, Lasswell ranked "among the half dozen creative innovators in the social sciences in the twentieth century. Few would question that he was the most original and productive political scientist of his time."[5] Members of the American Political Science Association certainly recognized his stature, naming him in 1955 one of the three most important American political scientists in the history of the discipline. Lasswell's critic Bernard Crick notes that by the late 1950s, Lasswell had become the most well known of contemporary American political scientists, the "acknowledged master of the specifically scientific school" of political thought. Lasswell's prolific writings, Crick said, had "achieved an imminence, in their size and complexity, somewhere between a Skyscraper and a Maze."[6]

An empiricist, a behaviorist, a Freudian, a systems theorist, a quantifier, the developer of the scientific method of content analysis, one of the "founding fathers" of the scientific school of mass communications, and cofounder of the policy sciences, Lasswell aimed to develop an interdisciplinary political science that could contribute to the prevention of political violence by understanding those factors—especially insecurity—that create upheaval. Yet Lasswell never articulated the anxiety or anger about public relations and propaganda that exercised most intellectuals who angrily remembered World War I. Instead, he saw another dimension of propaganda: that it was rational and could be used to divert political tensions and diminish the threat of political violence. Indeed, even by the late 1930s, when anxious critics were chronicling propaganda's many offenses (at home and abroad), he was arguing that students of politics and communications needed to use their knowledge of how political symbols could be employed to serve the ends of a more stable and predictable democratic politics, thereby making the values of democracy clearer and more widely apprehended by modern publics.[7] He also developed an interest in propaganda analysis as a protective strategy against destabilizing and revolutionary political movements emanating from what he called the "garrison states,"[8] promoting the notion of a democratic propaganda offensive against antidemocratic forces. Both views were inextricable from his vision of the relationship among social science expertise, the need for thorough understanding of individual and collective insecurities and their relationships to core political and cultural symbols, and the interests of the state in an age of mass communications. For him, propaganda was a technology of control, one that could either induce or inhibit violence, and he much preferred the latter.

Like others who spoke of the efficiency of employing modern techniques of persuasion and opinion control (Edward Bernays, for instance), Lasswell's corollary position through the 1920s and 1930s was that democratic theory was not rational: The " 'omnicompetent' theory of democracy seems more and more absurd," he wrote in 1935 in a special *Annals* issue on "Pressure Groups and Propaganda."[8] For Lasswell, there was no contradiction in employing the term "democratic propaganda" within democratic politics. For his harshest critics, however, like Bernard Crick, Lasswell's conflation of science with control and politics with the exercise of power implicated him as an authoritarian, one whose expert-centered, consent-manufacturing approach to politics represented the fruition of Lippmann's technocratic utopianism. By moving the study of the techniques of opinion control to the center of his vision of political science, Lasswell created a reputation for himself as one who debased public-centered democratic theory and justified the uses of social science as a tool of information and opinion management on behalf of established institutions.[10] More recent students of Lasswell's legacy argue that he was a complicated thinker and writer whose work is still not well enough understood (partly because of his "nearly incomprehensible prose") and whose real agenda was urging social scientists toward an active role in the creation of a more human society, what Lasswell described as the "advancement of the good life." As historian Mark C. Smith writes, Lasswell's "ultimate goal for empirical social research was a politics of prevention in which social scientists . . . would forestall the outbreak of wars and social violence through the alleviation of personal and collective insecurities."[11]

As this chapter will show, Lasswell's concern with the power of propaganda as an instrument of upheaval did become a significant component of his analysis of world political instability on the eve of World War II, and because of his intensive study of propaganda (accompanied by several "career reversals," to use Mark Smith's phrase) Lasswell was thus positioned to help organize key intellectual resources for the defense against antidemocratic propaganda activities at that time.[12] After examining Lasswell's intellectual project and the development of his social scientific approach to propaganda, the chapter establishes the context for understanding Lasswell's role in creating a protective propaganda prophylaxis. Set within the context of the late-1930s Brown Scare and the seemingly inexorable march to WWII, it reveals how the pervasive anxiety about propaganda, especially of the Nazi variety, produced imperatives for Lasswell and other leading social scientists to combine private monies and public institutions to create an extensive network of private, academic, and governmental communications intelligence activities that ultimately served both to defend and to restrict U.S. democracy.

Throughout, this chapter explores the always contested relationships between knowledge and power, expertise and democracy, political action and social control. Lasswell's work was invariably caught within the period's debates about the purposes of social knowledge. Mark C. Smith establishes a useful framework when he explains that a "central question" (actually a cluster of related questions) divided U.S. intellectuals, especially social scientists, and drove their larger debates: "What is the proper role of the social scientist in relation to his or her knowledge of society?":

> Should the correct role of the social scientist be that of a technical expert who provides information and advice to whomever requests it? Or should the social scientist go beyond understanding and analyzing society and use scientifically derived information consciously and personally to help create a better society more suited to humankind's basic needs and desires? How can one reconcile either the delivery of information exclusively to political and economic elites or the determination of social and political goals by a self-determined elite of social scientists within a democracy? (p. 6)

As Lasswell's ideas and activities make clear, those questions were not easily resolved, especially as political and economic elites geared the nation for war.

Lasswell's Post-WWI Skepticism

Born in 1902 in Donnellson, Illinois, to a bookish family, Harold Dwight Lasswell was something of a prodigy. His father was a Presbyterian minister and his mother a schoolteacher. When Lasswell entered the University of Chicago in 1918, at the age of sixteen, he had already been inspired by his family and an especially dedicated teacher to explore the writings of great thinkers, including Karl Marx and Sigmund Freud, and before he left high school he had also enjoyed the pleasure of an afternoon's conversation with John Dewey.[13] At the university, he was deeply influenced by the energetic and innovative social scientists in all disciplines, including Chicago's renowned sociologist Robert E. Park, anthropologist George Herbert Mead, philosopher John Dewey, and economist Thorstein Veblen. He read across the social sciences while majoring in political science and economics and stayed at Chicago after completing his bachelor's degree to begin graduate work in political science under his politically active reform-minded mentor, the political scientist Charles E. Merriam.[14]

Merriam had worked for George Creel's CPI during WWI, and the experience sparked his interests in propaganda, collective psychology, and the sociology of nationalism as fields of study.[15] These lines of inquiry seemed to merge with Merriam's hopes of reforming political science by making it more scientific and quantitative, and he therefore challenged his "brilliant and ambitious" student to take up these particular academic concerns.[16] Lasswell later wrote that Merriam was "particularly active at this time in the general field of civic training and the sources of civic loyalty, [and] focused my own interest on political propaganda of which the origin, effects and (particularly) the psychology were to become the subject matter of my life work."[17] Bernard Crick notes that Lasswell developed a commitment "to fulfil his master's hopes for scientific method in political studies," and he "patiently set out to construct various 'conceptual frameworks' by which society might be understood and then, possibly, controlled more scientifically."[18]

Lasswell's first major effort to develop these conceptual frameworks emerged in his dissertation and the book based on it, *Propaganda Technique in the World War*, a study that set the stage for four decades of scholarship on propaganda, political psychology, social science methodologies, the symbols of nationalism, and the study of power.[19] Lasswell researched and wrote this book, published in 1927, at a time when many Americans were extremely anxious—even paranoid—about the influence of propaganda in modern social and political life.[20] Lasswell did not share this anguish. His study of wartime propaganda reflected no shock, horror, or disillusionment with the extensive propaganda campaigns undertaken by all the belligerent governments during the war. Nor did his other writings from the period. In fact, he boldly pronounced in a 1926 review of Walter Lippmann's *The Phantom Public* that Lippmann had not gone quite far enough in his recognition of just how important mass persuasion had become in modern politics.

Rehearsing Lippmann's argument about public incapacity, the failures of orthodox democratic theory, and the need to restrain the public from meddling in affairs best left to experts, Lasswell notes that Lippmann "seems to flinch from drawing the conclusions to which the logic of his own brilliant studies into the nature of opinion seems to lead": that modern politics demands mass persuasion. Quoting Lippmann, he elaborated: "Inasmuch as the public verdict is 'made to depend on who has the loudest or the most-entrancing voice, the most skilful or the most brazen publicity man, the best access to the most space in the newspapers,' . . . it would seem that those who would control the public in the interest of what they conceive to be sound policy ought to outbrazen the rest." Acknowledging that voicing such an argument about public "infirmity" was a "taboo," Lasswell concluded the review by saying that it was true nonetheless. "Sign systems and intelligence bureaus" such as Lippmann recommended "may help the few to make up their own minds . . . but the mobilization of the many depends upon other means," namely, propaganda.[21]

Another essay from the same period reinforced this idea by turning to the various social sciences for insights into more effective mass persuasion, which Lasswell defined as the manipulation of "significant symbols" in order to adjust "collective attitudes" and values. Entitled "The Theory of Political Persuasion," this 1927 piece illustrated the many forms mass persuasion could take, from selling products to selling political candidates. Lasswell illustrated this by speculating how the different disciplines of political science, anthropology, psychology, and even biology might provide terminologies and frameworks for understanding the processes of manipulating collective responses. Informing his reader about the surfeit of choices and the need to choose one's techniques with care, he wrote: "Whatever form of words helps to ignite the imagination of the practical manipulator of attitudes is the most valuable one." And what constraints might be imposed by democratic theory or a respect for a genuinely developed pubic opinion? None at all: "Democracy has proclaimed the dictatorship of palaver, and the technique of dictating to the dictator is named propaganda."[22]

Propaganda Technique in the World War elaborates these assumptions. It has been identified primarily as a muckraking account of official propaganda campaigns during the Great War, and Lasswell certainly enumerated the uses of atrocity campaigns and other official efforts to manipulate public consciousness in order to harden alliances, generate hatred and fear, maintain domestic morale, and destroy enemy morale (which he described as propaganda's main purposes).[23] But his account raised technical and administrative questions about the successful uses of propaganda, not ethical or moral ones. Lasswell wanted to know which techniques failed, which worked, and how propaganda could be made more efficient and predictably successful. As Gabriel Almond notes, Lasswell's rigorously scholarly work set out to specify "the conditions which limit or facilitate" the effectiveness of propaganda techniques.[24] Lasswell undertook this project, he announced, "to evolve an explicit theory of how international war propaganda may be conducted with success."[25]

At the descriptive level, *Propaganda Technique* examined how the U.S., British, French, and German governments tried to solve the "persistent organizational struggles" over propaganda strategies among their foreign offices, their militaries, and their political leaders. For Lasswell, the notable problems the Germans and other nations encountered producing coordinated campaigns were not just interesting historical details; these failures provided useful organizational lessons. Any effective propaganda strategy had to be integrated at all levels, Lasswell learned. And the most efficiently run were headed up by professional propagandists, who were generally newspapermen. In this study and elsewhere, Lasswell did not see propaganda "as some foreign matter, some intrusion into the body politic, but rather as a generic aspect of the political system," noted his student, the political sociologist Morris Janowitz. For Lasswell, "the process of persuasion [was] a generic aspect of social control." Janowitz, who worked closely with Lasswell as a propaganda analyst during WWII, called *Propaganda Technique* a "brilliant classic" and declared that the historical importance of the study was that it was the first to incorporate the "management of violence" into the mainstream of political science.[26]

The work was also Lasswell's first stab at content analysis, a technique he would develop more rigorously during WWII. Janowitz explained that this interest in content analysis, "with its concern for the molecular dissection of communication content," began when Lasswell was a student at the University of Chicago, when he was privy to conversations among faculty members of the English Department about how they had used their textual analysis skills during WWI to aid the development of cryptography. According to Janowitz, "this intellectual exercise stimulated his thinking and provided the background for his application of content analysis to political communication." He argued that Lasswell's incipient interest in content analysis moved him toward "a more systematic conceptualization of the symbolic environment," with a focus on the institutions involved in "creating, disseminating, and utilizing symbol systems." Lasswell also developed "standards of performance for judging and evaluating the content and practices of 'symbol manipulators' " and monitoring their influences on political and social processes.[27]

Given Lasswell's career-long concern with the role of communications experts in the modern polity—especially those he called symbol manipulators—and his fascination with the use of propaganda as an instrument of ideological mobilization and control, it makes sense to read *Propaganda Technique in the World War* as a blueprint for improving propaganda techniques. It was not a "progressive critique," as some claim. Aside from the telling details, the work's most distinctive feature was Lasswell's insistent distancing of his objective analysis from the war generation's moral outrage about propaganda. Moreover he had a tendency to use the imperative voice when discussing the necessity of understanding how propaganda works; in fact, his use of the imperative marks virtually all his writings about propaganda.

In this first major work, Lasswell offered an unflinchingly realistic appraisal of mass manipulation as a condition of modern politics. He immediately established his skepticism about orthodox democratic theory when, alluding to his contemporaries' postwar disillusionment and anxieties, he acknowledged the widespread perception that something had gone terribly wrong because of the word with the "ominous clang"—propaganda—but he dismissed these vexations as the concerns of "earnest souls" chagrined by their own "credulous utopianism."[28] Eschewing their "traditional species of democratic romanticism," he announced that, in fact, "familiarity with the ruling public has bred contempt" (p. 4). Lasswell identified neither the deluded democrats nor those contemptuous of the public but clearly implied that a scientific, mass persuasion–based politics was more realistic than a nineteenth-century public-centered one.

Like Lippmann, Lasswell championed the social scientist as the mediator between the many and the few or, perhaps more accurately, the facilitator of the few to the many. In virtually all his future discussions about propaganda, Lasswell reiterated *Propaganda Technique*'s confidence in social scientists' value for the manufacturing of consent. But while Lippmann rhapsodized about scientists and their "technic," young Lasswell was not so sanguine in 1927 that social scientists had yet put their analytical and methodological houses in order: "The people who probe the mysteries of public opinion in politics must, for the present, at least, rely upon something other than exact measurement, to confirm or discredit their speculations," he wrote. "Generalizations about public opinion stick because they are plausible and not because they are experimentally established." Thus the war and its propaganda campaigns provided the lesson that hypotheses about the manipulation of public opinion needed scientific modeling and testing. Because Lasswell and his contemporaries saw themselves "witnessing . . . the growth of a world public . . . agitated and organized" by mass persuasion (pp. 5–6), the study of public-opinion formation and propaganda processes needed to become a central concern of the social sciences, he argued. Optimistic about the promise of the still undeveloped social sciences, Lasswell was confident that propaganda as a tool and process of mass persuasion could and should be commandeered to good purposes, especially in wartime. Skepticism, he averred, should not be directed at the use of propaganda techniques but rather at unproven assertions about their power and effectiveness.

Focusing on ideological states and not military or material conditions, Lasswell defined propaganda as a technique for controlling "the mental environment." Ideological control of populations in or out of war would not be achieved by "changing such objective conditions as the supply of cigarettes or the chemical composition of food," Lasswell said, but through "the control of opinion by significant symbols" or through the use of "stories, rumours, reports, pictures and other forms of social communication," in other words, "the management of opinions and attitudes by the direct manipulation of social suggestion" (pp. 8–9). A decade later he used essentially the same terms in what had become his standard definition of the word "propaganda." Describing it as the use of words or symbols for the "transmission of attitudes that are recognized as *controversial* within a given community," he said the goal of the propagandist was always "the manipulation of collective attitudes." It is "not the purpose but the method," he said, that "distinguishes propaganda from the management of men by violence, boycott, bribery, and similar means of social control."[29] The questions it raised were not about ethics or morality but about efficiency: "How may hate be mobilized against an enemy? How may the enemy be demoralized by astute manipulation? How is it possible to cement the friendship of neutral and allied peoples?"[30] Total warfare "necessitated the mobilization of the civilian mind," and "no government could have a united nation behind it unless it controlled the minds of its people." Domestic unity could not be "achieved by the regimentation of muscles," he said. "It is achieved by a repetition of ideas rather than movements. The civilian mind is standardized by news and not by drills" (pp. 10–11).

For Lasswell, the goal of "standardizing the civilian mind" was a given for those in power or those seeking power in modern politics. In a period of growing nationalism and ideological conflict, political science should be committed to making the powerful instrument of propaganda more effective. "Propaganda . . . is developing its practitioners, its professors, its teachers and its theories," he said, and "governments will rely increasingly upon the professional propagandists for advice and aid" (p. 34). Politicians certainly needed these new communications experts, for "policies are not safely formulated without expert information on the state of that opinion upon which they rely for success," he wrote (p. 28).

The perspective Lasswell developed in his 1927 study remained consistent over time and paralleled other realists of his era who understood the necessity and efficacy of manufacturing consent, especially the most well-known popularizer of this "pro-propaganda" strain, the public relations theorist and practitioner E. L. Bernays, whose 1928 volume *Propaganda* was essentially a popularization of Lippmann's critique of democratic theory and a celebration of the miracles the modern public relations agent could perform.[31]

The consistency among Lippmann, Lasswell, and Bernays is very clear in virtually all Bernays's writings. One piece, entitled "Molding Public Opinion," crystallizes his themes. Submitted as part of a special *Annals* issue on "Pressure Groups and Propaganda," this essay was a typically self-promoting, boldly undemocratic piece about publicity men and propagandists. Writing for the "leadership class," Bernays said that he was presenting a "dispassionate outline of the techniques and the media involved in the molding of public opinion by any group."[32] For Bernays, as for Lasswell, a chief lesson of WWI was not that it demonstrated the negative influences of propaganda but rather that it showed the possibility of molding public opinion toward desired ends. Like Lasswell, he suggested that propaganda could be either good or bad: "Certainly," he said, "forces for the public good should use the weapon" (p. 82). He too saw the necessity of understanding how the public's "psychological raw materials" could be used by "every leader . . . in his endeavours to win the public to his point of view" (p. 83); likewise, Bernays also knew that the communications revolution had provided new and exciting opportunities to connect leaders to the public and to mobilize public emotions.

While Lasswell was not so cheeky as Bernays and was a serious scholar not a paid promoter, an essay Lasswell published in 1928 in the *International Journal of Ethics*, entitled "The Function of the Propagandist," developed Bernays-like arguments about interest group politics and the necessity of drawing attention to one's claims and interests as persuasively as possible. Acknowledging the inexhaustible postwar public anguish about wartime propaganda, he responded by essentially providing an ethical rehabilitation of agents of mass persuasion, arguing that they were, in fact, socially and ethically valuable participants in circumstances in which "the few . . . would rule the many under democratic conditions." In the era of modern interest group politics, he insisted, "The propagandist is a species of advocate, and there are many ways to justify the function of advocacy." He did so by averring that advocacy actually contributes to social harmony, nonviolence, and political stability because it enables all groups to have their say, thereby avoiding the frustration that results in group violence when some groups are not afforded such opportunities. (Whether interest group advocates contributed to the truth was not really the issue, because social harmony was a more important goal and truth nearly impossible to distinguish in a world of competing claims.) Thus the use of propaganda was not a moral issue, except insofar as it fostered the positive morality of staving off individual and collective violence. As a technique for "controlling attitudes by the manipulation of significant symbols," propaganda is "no more moral or immoral than a pump handle," he famously wrote.

"Whether specialization in the technique can be justified in one's mind depends upon the conviction that the long-run interest of society in social harmony will be served by expert mobilization of opinion" (pp. 260–261).

For Lasswell, this matter of helping different groups achieve social harmony was the real ethical—or moral—question about propaganda. He predicted (wrongly) that over time people would come to accept the role of the propagandist—as they had come to accept lawyers as advocates—when they learned more about "his function of advocacy" (p. 259). Additionally, in his iconoclastic way, Lasswell also suggested that the propagandist might well serve the valuable function of getting rid of the sacred "aura" and the "sanctimonious taboo" surrounding the idea of the "will of the people," which, he argued, should be "reduced to the matter of fact" that the public will is mutable (pp. 262, 264).

For Lasswell, then, propaganda was at least a value-neutral tool, one that potentially had highly ethical social uses, especially when used for the purposes of avoiding violence and reducing conflict. He carried this understanding of propaganda with him into his energetic and far-reaching search for a comprehensive social scientific system and for universal human values and needs. Identifying these human universals would be the most important step in preventing violence and helping people achieve "the good life." At the same time, the search was premised on the inadequacy of democratic theory and a perception of the public as "spasmodic, superficial, and ignorant."[33]

Lasswell's Search for a Comprehensive Scientific Politics

On receiving his doctorate and publishing *Propaganda Technique in the World War*, Lasswell stayed at the University of Chicago in Professor Merriam's Political Science Department, teaching courses on propaganda and political psychology and exploring his interests in what he called the "psychological aspects of [his] chosen field."[34] His early research convinced him that traditional political scientists were theoretically and methodologically outdated. His search for an understanding of individual and collective psychology led him to sociology, psychology, and, most important, to psychiatric research and training. As he became more compelled by Freud's understanding of the unconscious and the tug of the irrational on the individual and collective psyche, his discipline's traditional concerns about theories of the state and constitutionalism and its faith in resolution of conflict through rational self-interest seemed to Lasswell quite beside the point. Pointing to Lasswell's Freudian turn, his frequent collaborator Bruce Lannes Smith explained that Lasswell discovered that "human motives are generated in the nursery, the bedroom, in childhood excretory experiences and reveries" and therefore political science had to be reconceived as the study of the ways in which "private motives" become more or less "unconsciously or irrationally displaced onto 'public causes.'"[35] Such interests would take Lasswell and political science in new directions and required an extended excursion into literatures and hands-on research that might explain the impact of society on the individual psyche.

By the late 1920s Lasswell took up these new lines of inquiry with zeal, describing them as bringing "the techniques of modern psychology and psychoanalysis to bear upon a study of political personalities."[36] He spent time in 1926–27 with the Australian émigré Elton Mayo studying Mayo's depth interviewing and recording techniques, apparently undergoing some counseling with Mayo, and working with him in various clinical settings, all the while learning psychoanalytic techniques and the value of clinical experience for understanding how social environments affect individual personalities.[37] According to Mark Smith, Lasswell's work with Mayo led Lasswell to accept "two key ideas that would permeate and redirect his purposive social science." The first was Mayo's "emphasis on adjustment," especially his interest "in the cure, which, he thought, lay in the reestablishment of strong social bonds" (p. 225). (Smith argues that this emphasis on adjustment by Merriam, Mayo, and Lasswell, resulted in a deradicalized acceptance of industrial society and its institutions and therefore an "acceptance of the status quo" [p. 226].) Additionally, Mayo deepened Lasswell's understanding of the Freudian "belief that a very thin line separates the abnormal from the normal and that pathological examples are excellent case studies for ordinary behavior." From Smith's perspective, this helped Lasswell develop his individualistic political psychology, but it was one based on an "overemphasis on irrational behavior in normal individuals," a framework that reinforced Lasswell's undemocratic assumptions, particularly about the irrationality of collective political behavior and belief (p. 226).

In 1928 Lasswell obtained a fellowship from the Social Science Research Council to do research at mental hospitals. Working in two of the most innovative clinical settings for psychological research—with William Alanson White at St. Elizabeth's Hospital in Washington, D.C., and with Harry Stack Sullivan at Sheppard and Pratt Hospital outside Baltimore—Lasswell began the next phase of connecting the world of psychoanalysis to the world of politics. Interested in classifying different political personalities according to psychoanalytic categories, Lasswell worked with White's and Sullivan's patients conducting depth interviews and reading their case histories. He also gained access to psychiatric patients and their records at the Pennsylvania State Hospital in Philadelphia, the Bloomingdale Hospital of White Plains,

New York, and the Boston Psychiatric Hospital.[38] As Bruce Lannes Smith noted, it "was observation in the mental hospital and participant observation on the psychoanalytic couch that produced the real 'data'" that sparked Lasswell's interests and provided the impetus for his major studies in the 1930s on personality, psychopathology, and politics.[39] In 1928–29 Lasswell further immersed himself in the world of clinical psychology and psychoanalytic theory and became a more orthodox Freudian while living in Vienna and then Berlin, where he studied psychiatry and psychoanalysis, underwent psychoanalysis at the hands of Theodor Reik, and received training to qualify as a lay analyst.[40]

From the standpoint of understanding Lasswell's total theory of politics—and the place of psychoanalysis, masses and elites, and the social sciences within that theory—it is useful to consider his major works from the 1930s. By 1930 Lasswell had published a variety of short articles about the value of psychiatric records and interviews for political science.[41] In 1930 he published *Psychopathology and Politics*, a work Gabriel Almond termed "the first relatively systematic, empirical study of the psychological aspects of political behavior."[42] Here Lasswell first attempted to describe a science of politics aimed at both methodological and social reform. In one major section of the work, he drew on clinical materials and his own depth interviews to present case histories of, and explain in Freudian terms, three political personalities he labeled as the "agitators," the "administrators," and the "theorists." (Based on his case studies, his book focused on the agitators and administrators.) The rest of the book constituted a methodological and theoretical statement about what he had attempted in this work and included discussions on the uses of life histories in political science, the depth interview as a mode of research (which Gabriel Almond called "the technique of free association as a method of getting data on politically relevant feelings and attitudes"), and the utility of studying deviant or abnormal personality types to understand political behavior. The issues Lasswell addressed in this study became the core of his research program for the next several decades.

Parts of *Psychopathology and Politics* were "hastily, even incoherently, drafted," according to Smith.[43] Like most of Lasswell's work, it was laborious, jargon-ridden, and ponderous. A brief sample of Lasswell's summary argument suffices to reveal his belief in the importance of a psychoanalytic framework to explain how politics embody irrational social forces and to illustrate his infamous prose style.

> Political movements derive their vitality from the displacement of private affects upon public objects. Political crises are complicated

by the concurrent reactivation of specific primitive motives which were organized in the early experience of the individuals concerned. Political symbols are particularly adapted to serve as targets for displaced affect because of their ambiguity of reference, in relation to individual experience, and because of their general circulation. Although the dynamic of politics is the tension level of all individuals, all tension does not produce political acts. Nor do all emotional bonds lead to political action. Political acts depend upon the symbolization of the discontent of the individual in terms of a more inclusive self which champions a set of demands for social action.[44]

Ever in search of formulae to encapsulate his arguments, Lasswell compressed his overall argument about the displacement of oedipal and libidinal motives and frustrations onto the political stage into a single equation. Displaced motives, he explained, are rationalized in terms of ideologies and actions. His formula, he confidently said, "expresses the developmental facts about the fully developed political man": "$p \} d \} r = P$, where p equals private motive; d equals displacement onto a public object; r equals rationalization in terms of public interest; P equals the political man; and $\}$ equals transformed onto" (pp. 75–76). Apparently it was a matter of some contention among Lasswell's students as to whether this equation was intended literally or was a rhetorical exaggeration designed to draw attention to the importance of psychological motivations and frustrations as the grounding of political phenomena.[45] Rhetorical or not, this formula illustrates Lasswell's bedrock assumptions about unconscious and displaced personal motives being acted out in the arena of politics.

Because the political manifestations of displaced frustrations were often unpredictable and violent, Lasswell argued that it was the job of political science to develop strategies for intervention, through therapy and opinion control. If political science was going to ameliorate the kinds of individual and group frustrations that often resulted in eruptions of violence, Lasswell contended, it needed to develop both a theory and method of prevention. For Lasswell, then, identifying unconscious projections into the realm of belief and action was only part of his agenda for political science; the other was ensuring that professional political science develop what he called a "preventive politics" and a "preventive mental hygiene."[46] This meant that political science needed deeper grounding in the literature of social psychology and psychoanalysis and individual political scientists needed training in therapeutic techniques. He wrote that "the achievement of the ideal of preventive politics depends less upon changes in social organization than upon improving the methods and the education of social administrators and social scientists" (p. 203). By using psychoanalytical techniques in his clinically based studies of political agitators and administrators, Lasswell added an innovative research strategy to the incipient behaviorist movement in U.S. political science. Indeed, his students and contemporaries contend that Lasswell fundamentally challenged conventional political science with his distinctive uses of behavioralism and Freudian theory. According to Bruce Smith, Lasswell embraced Freudian theory because it offered the possibility for developing a "total theory" of political behavior and because it provided a framework for thinking about, and perhaps mitigating, the effects of the irrational in politics. Taking his metaphor from the clinic, Lasswell contended that society was the patient and psychoanalytically trained social scientists should be practitioners of preventive politics.

In *Psychopathology and Politics* Lasswell defined the "central problem" of the politics of prevention as reducing "the level of strain and maladaptation in society." "Our thinking has too long been led by the threadbare terminology of democracy versus dictatorship, of democracy versus aristocracy," he wrote. These categories for describing the bases of conflict and violence were not enough. There were too many significant conflicts within democracy itself, especially over the social distribution of wealth, safety, and respect. Recognizing from his work in mental hospitals the psychological importance of financial security and social respect, Lasswell projected these categories onto the level of collective psychology. The work of political science therefore demanded a "reorientation of the minds of those who think about society" toward a simple question: "What are the principal factors which modify the tension level of the community?"[47]

For Lasswell, the key to understanding political tensions lay in the social distribution of three "universal" values: "deference, safety, and income." This "values pyramid" stood at the center of Lasswell's emerging system, and when he later eschewed his pessimistic obsession with the irrational, he never relinquished his belief that the values pyramid explained and provided the key to preventable individual and social conflicts and violence. Recognizing that most political conflicts occur over the social distribution of these values should lead social scientists to their therapeutic role, he argued, and because their analytical distance enabled them to see objectively the arrangements of social, economic, and political power that determine the distribution of income, deference, and safety, social scientists should be able to anticipate and ameliorate (through a variety of mechanisms) political frustrations before they result in violence. Thus Lasswell defined his "systematic politics" as "the analysis of the value patterns of society [and] the study of factors affecting the shape and composition of the pyramids of income, deference, and safety."[48]

While the values pyramid emerged as the central concept in Lasswell's framework, the straightforward and simple definition of power he articulated in *Psychopathology and Politics* earned him greater fame. Here he used for the first time the formulation that power is defined by "who gets what, when, how." Distribution of the values pyramid helped explain who had power and how they maintained it, at both the material and the symbolic levels.[49] Understanding politics as the attainment and maintenance of power thus became central to Lasswell's perception of the role of propaganda in international politics. His corollary included the recognition that the capacity to manipulate the symbols of safety, income, and deference was quickly evolving as an efficient way by which new classes of political specialists could obtain power themselves. As Lasswell saw it, political scientists needed to understand more explicitly that the struggle for power defined politics and that in an age of propaganda that struggle would take place in the arena of symbols as much as it would in the arenas of economics and organized violence. For a science of politics interested in preventing violence, understanding the manipulation of symbols and keeping track of those who were most adept at using them was critical.

After *Psychopathology and Politics*, Lasswell continued his travels abroad, making his way into the circles of Alfred Adler, Erich Fromm, and Karen Horney in Europe and further developing his associations with Harry Stack Sullivan and William Alanson White in the United States. Theoretically, he branched out into new areas, turning to Roberto Michels, Karl Mannheim, and, especially, Vilifred Pareto for ideas about political symbolism, ideology, power, myth, and the sociology and psychology of the ruling classes. These new lines of inquiry expanded his developing framework, illustrated by a 1933 article entitled "The Strategy of Revolutionary and War Propaganda" and a 1935 study of power and its maintenance entitled *World Politics and Political Insecurity*. The latter was republished a year later in a simpler, more readable version (with the help of Bruce Lannes Smith), under the title *Politics: Who Gets What, When, How*.

Lasswell's overarching concern with power in the mid-1930s was marked by his increasing focus on political elites and the utility of the social sciences. Focusing on distributions of power (who gets what, when, how) and on what he called the "spread of the rational attitude,"[50] the thread that began to tie many of his writings together was very similar to Lippmann's argument. For both Lippmann and Lasswell, the social sciences offered the keys to getting and keeping power in a world rife with insecurity and profound economic crisis, competing economic and political ideologies, and increasingly powerful mass communications technologies and manipulators.

In his 1935 and 1936 studies, *World Politics and Personal Insecurity* and *Politics: Who Gets What, When, and How*, Lasswell developed his core argument about the role of the symbol carriers or symbol manipulators in the calculus of power, a calculus rapidly changing because of developments in mass communications. Here is an outline of his crystallizing framework: The key to the "spread of the rational attitude" in politics depended on clear analysis of the distribution of the values of deference, safety, and income. Distribution of those values was a function of power, and the science of politics (as the study of power) should be organized around the study of who controls those distributions and the ways in which relations of wealth, respect, and authority are symbolically projected through the different communications channels. Because the achievement and maintenance of power would be fluid in a "world revolutionary" period and because the values of deference and safety (especially) were grounded as much in psychological as in material conditions, the role of those who could manage and manipulate symbols in the struggles for power was going to be especially significant. In these works, Lasswell identified professional opinion makers as belonging among the new "world elite." In *Politics: Who Gets What, When, How*, Lasswell called the study of politics the study of influence and the influential and noted that the "ascendancy of an elite depends in part upon a successful manipulation of its environment."[51] Lasswell's continued fascination with propaganda, especially in the political crises of the 1930s, drew more and more on these frameworks.

In short, Lasswell's vague politics of prevention is best understood as a framework for the management of political ideas and symbols through mass communications rather than as a strategy for actual reform based on the redistribution of power, wealth, respect, and safety. It all takes place in the symbolic arena. And by the eve of WWII, when looking to the U.S. context, Lasswell conceived of information about public attitudes as data for public opinion management and the amelioration of "sore spots," not for enhancing the expression of diverse public frustrations.[52] In 1941 Lasswell published *Democracy Through Public Opinion*, a work his loyalists regard as marking his transition from democratic skeptic to rhetorician of democratic principles. A closer reading suggests, however, that despite the democratic intentions of this work, Lasswell clearly embraced the Lippmann-styled opinion management role for specialists in political communications. He wrote: "Our present task is to utilize the magnificent instruments of modern communication for the purpose of clarifying a common view of the society in which we live. This is the urgent task of all specialists on truth, clarity, vividness—the task of sharing the insight of the few with the many."[53] This was no Dewey-inspired formulation for enhancing the public's awareness of or participation in its own affairs. Indeed, it was an expert-centered prescription for maintaining power in a world in which the propagandist was to play an increasingly significant role.

Propaganda's Utility and Danger

In 1931, recognizing propaganda's importance as a social science subfield, the Social Science Research Council established the Committee on Pressure Groups and Propaganda, comprised of Ralph D. Casey, Merle Curti, Harold Gosnell, Pendleton Herring, Peter Odegard, Schuyler Wallace, Kimball Young, and Harold Lasswell. The council commissioned Lasswell, Bruce Lannes Smith, and Ralph D. Casey to compile an annotated bibliography on the subject of propaganda, and in 1935 they published *Propaganda and Promotional Activities: An Annotated Bibliography*, which contained over forty-five hundred entries and an introductory essay by Lasswell.[54]

Lasswell's essay, "The Study and Practice of Propaganda," elaborated the same cluster of ideas he had been developing about universal values, the capacity of elites to manage conflicts through opinion management, and the emerging role for social scientists as symbol specialists. Two features of this essay stand out, however. One is Lasswell's realist appraisal of propaganda's utility and the significant role played by propaganda specialists throughout history. The other is that the essay was the fullest development of how the psychoanalytic framework could be used to guide propaganda specialists in their work, alerting them to those categories of individual and collective attitudes and expression that any effective propaganda campaign needed to expose.

Rehearsing many of the themes from *Propaganda Technique in the World War*, Lasswell began by noting that the term "propaganda" "fell on evil days during the World War of 1914–1918, when inconvenient news and opinion was stigmatized as 'enemy propaganda.' " The growth of publicity agents, press agents, and public relations firms during the postwar years—what he called "modern promoters of attitudes"—had drawn additional negative attention to propaganda, as had the "fear of Communist propaganda, and . . . the showmanship of Mussolini and Hitler." All these factors had stimulated a negative "propaganda consciousness" explaining why the modern public had developed suspicions about the practices and pejorative associations with the term (pp. 4–5). Propaganda, he acknowledged, "relies on symbols to attain its ends: the manipulation of collective attitudes," and while it might be different in technique from conventional warfare, it shared the same interest in "the management of men by violence, boycott, bribery, and similar means of social control" (p. 3). He recognized the grounds for public consternation.

Unlike most who wrote about propaganda in the mid-1930s, Lasswell viewed the presence of so many agents and organizations intent on transmitting "attitudes that are *controversial* within a given community" simply as evidence that propaganda had become an undeniable but not necessarily negative fact of modern life (p. 3). Its permanence meant that understanding how it works, under what conditions, and for what purposes was a basic requirement for those interested in promoting or transmitting both controversial and accepted attitudes within communities. It made no sense, from Lasswell's perspective, to shy away from the processes and techniques of modern propaganda simply because of the negative connotations. There were more useful ways for the scientifically minded to think about the problem, and the high degree of specialization and success achieved by some "modern promoters of attitudes" meant that it warranted close study, legitimizing the "lively" academic interest in the subject. And such academic attention made it "permissible to give the word an objective meaning," one stripped of its negative connotations. Indeed, Lasswell wrote, it was more useful to suggest that "anybody who uses 'representations' to influence collective responses is a propagandist" (p. 3).

Reiterating his earlier rejection of traditional democratic theory, Lasswell argued once again that profound changes resulting from advances in communications technologies had dramatically reversed the eighteenth-century democratic ideology of "glorifying the will of the people"; now, he said, interests turned to "the objective study of the ways and means of manipulating the common will" (p. 22). As a scientist bound less by normative values and deeply cherished myths than by the pursuit of empirical evidence, Lasswell evinced few anxieties about this diminished role for the public as the driving force behind political practices. He merely reported that "changes in the channels of technical communications have had such diverse effects . . . that it is difficult to appraise their net result" (pp. 17–18). In short, the data were not in. Until they were, he recommended more intensive, value-neutral social scientific observations about individual and collective attitudes and the use of symbols to mobilize or modify those attitudes. Drawing on his own developing specialty, he asserted the necessity of employing psychoanalytic insights and techniques to improve the effectiveness of any given propaganda campaign, whether for commercial or revolutionary purposes. In this framework, Lasswell's notion of preventive politics achieved through a vague public therapy easily translated into preventive politics effected through opinion control: "The high importance of coordinating propaganda with all other means of social control cannot be too insistently repeated," he wrote. And such coordination should be directed by professionals: "Since the distinctive means by which collective reactions are controlled in propaganda involve the use of representations, the principles governing their choice are peculiarly crucial. Some of the most grotesque errors into which propagandists have fallen arise from carelessness in searching for the precise meaning that is attached to words or intonations, pictures or tunes, by those who are presumed to be influenced by them" (p. 10). Psychoanalytic procedures could help avert grotesque errors and should prove very useful in probing and making clear the meanings of the appropriate symbols systems, enabling the propagandist to discern which symbols and which "long chains of association" could be best utilized to produce "concerted action" (pp. 12, 14–15). Detailing the different possibilities, Lasswell struck the scientists' pose.

But the essay was not altogether sanguine. Lasswell ended the piece by noting that revolutionary propaganda seemed to be increasing the public's insecurity, intensifying an overall sense of crisis, and disturbing the established order. As such, it was clear that propaganda was both a tool to be mastered and an increasingly powerful weapon to be controlled. In either case, its techniques and expert practitioners needed careful and continued study. Lasswell's faith in scientific technique commingled in this 1935 essay with growing anxiety about the destabilizing and revolutionary power of propaganda used in Nazi Germany, the Soviet Union, and Fascist Italy and by the Japanese in China. For Lasswell and others, conditions abroad revealed striking examples of how monopoly control over channels of communication had become combined with monopoly control over the instruments of violence, leading to heightened attention to propaganda as an instrument of dictatorial terror and as a threat to international political stability.[55]

Lasswell's case studies of propaganda in the mid- to late 1930s increasingly looked to the present and not the past. His influence was clear among his political science contemporaries, who also turned to more systematic observations about propaganda in the international political sphere, especially with respect to the definitions he used. Some shared his utilitarian perception of the need to study the "ways and means" of "manipulating the common will," as he wrote, but most were not as sure that such studied manipulation would result in democratic outcomes in the domestic sphere.[56] Malcolm Willey, for instance, argued that thirty years of innovations in mass communications had created a "new social environment" in which all spheres of life had become subject to the influence of mass communications, which made it increasingly difficult to distinguish propaganda from nonpropaganda materials and techniques. Propaganda, he said, had created an "enveloping omnipresence," distinguishing the twentieth century from earlier ones. But drawing on the same historical developments as Lasswell, Willey pointed not to the need to reject the "will of the people" but to the incongruities between organized mass persuasion and democracy.[57] He was not Lasswell's only contemporary to wonder whether the term "democratic propaganda" was not, in fact, an oxymoron.

Cornell University political theorist George E. Gordon Catlin raised the same question and then pointed to another problem that would become increasingly salient for Lasswell and his cohort: whether democracies could survive the onslaught of antidemocratic propaganda.[58] As part of a 1936 collection entitled *Propaganda and Dictatorship*, edited by Princeton political scientist Harwood Childs, Catlin's "Propaganda as a Function of Democratic Government" argued that propaganda used under monopoly conditions and in combination with the state's monopoly on the instruments of coercion had become a powerful instrument of force, one that threatened basic distinctions political theorists had heretofore been willing to make between democracies and authoritarian regimes: "The distinction between the functions appropriate to a voluntary society, resting on choice and not armed with coercive powers" and those of the state with its coercive might "is a fundamental one in political theory," he wrote (p. 129). But in a period of growing crisis marked by propaganda's "enveloping omnipresence" (to use Willey's phrase) the relationship between propaganda and democracy required reexamination: Out of the necessity of competition, could democracies themselves resort to state monopolies on propaganda and remain democratic? And could they squelch threatening ideas and insist on acceptance of the government's point of view and remain democratic?

Catlin's answers were couched in traditional liberal distinctions but also acknowledged that antidemocratic propaganda created new dangers that might, in fact, require the democratic state to act in new, not necessarily democratic ways. A democratic government could and should defend and promote its interests through propaganda: it should "meet propaganda by propaganda," but, Catlin warned, "not to terrorize citizens from free discussion." In short, it could not have a monopoly on expression and remain democratic; democracy is based on tolerance and must therefore permit the propaganda of other movements "a free role within the law." For Catlin and for others, a democracy's need to "assure the successful role of its own propaganda" raised the very complicated question of how a democratic state could protect itself from competing propagandas while also tolerating their existence (p. 135). Indeed, the conundrum Catlin raised expressed a central problem for U.S. liberals as they attempted simultaneously to remain tolerant of and to defeat antidemocratic propagandas. To a large extent, this dilemma of tolerating but not being vulnerable to antidemocratic ideas was *the* problem of propaganda for late-1930s liberals.

For Catlin and for Lasswell, the need to accommodate ideological pluralism and assure the triumph of democratic institutions suggested new possibilities for political scientists. As Catlin understood in 1936 (and as Lasswell would soon acknowledge), the enlarged presence of propaganda in modern politics created opportunities for professional political scientists both in the production of democratic propaganda and in the disarming of antidemocratic propaganda. Catlin also thought that political science should be the study of how to use propaganda to achieve consent and generate action among the public: "Political science is a quantitative study, concerned to supply principles for the art of associating predominant masses of men to achieve a given end," he wrote. But he added an important qualifier: "It is not enough merely to agree to the proposition . . . that democratic values are sound and need propagandizing. . . . It is also requisite that we consult political science to discover how that propaganda may be successful against the urge to power of its opponents" (pp. 138–139). For Catlin, the idea that political scientists could offer instruction in defeating the "urge to power" of democracy's opponents also meant that they had a valuable role in ensuring democracy's security.

Catlin argued, in fact, that the liberal state, with its commitment to tolerance, potentially created the conditions for its own demise. Articulating a position that would become routinely expressed in legal circles by the end of the 1930s, Catlin suggested that the danger of propaganda required a rethinking of liberal tolerance: "the peculiar weakness of democracy is disclosed, by scientific analysis, to be that of allocating disproportionate freedom to the individual at the expense of authority and of the security which authority guarantees." At a moment of crisis, he argued, the stress on individual liberty should be subordinated to the need for collective security. Political scientists could be highly useful in this regard because the "demand . . . for security, organization, authority" required expertise at identifying the problems at hand and molding public opinion. There was no room, he suggested as early as 1936, for ethical anxieties about the role of the democratic propagandist: "There is no future for vacillation and genteel doubt," he wrote. "The future is that of fight—probably literally so. In time of war one does not inquire what instruments of propaganda one shall use. One uses all available—press, stage, pulpit, radio, telegraphic lobbying, public platforms." Concluding in terms that Lasswell would soon embrace in extolling his own scientific expertise, Catlin said, "Democracy [need not be] squeamish about the efficient use of propaganda, as emotionalized ideology, in making its views persuasive" (pp. 142–43). Nor should democracy be squeamish about the coercive control of competing propagandas. There were both offensive and defensive ways to fight propaganda wars, and political scientists could play valuable roles in both. Lasswell's career in the late 1930s through the end of WWII illustrates the prescience of Catlin's observation.

By the mid-1930s, Lasswell's technique and process-oriented approach to propaganda, with their academically value-neutral formulations, were out of sync with his generational cohort. They certainly stood out from the consensus among most U.S. intellectuals, who conceived of political propaganda as dishonestly partisan, one-sided, antidemocratic in its techniques and aims, and, Catlin notwithstanding, something that democracies should avoid being contaminated by. Where Lasswell did not find the phrase "democratic propaganda" oxymoronic, most of his contemporaries did, based on their memories of WWI, their retrospective understanding of the propaganda-induced calamities of that war, and the rise in the 1930s of garrison states, with their monopolies over the flow and content of information. Propaganda's critics, ranging from the faculty of Columbia University Teacher's College, who started the Institute for Propaganda Analysis, to semanticists, to anti-Nazi watchdog groups, could not get past propaganda's negative associations. They thought it obstructed debate, abused meaningful language, appealed to emotion instead of rationality, and interfered with the pursuit of truth. As used by totalitarian states (a label being used by the mid-1930s to refer to Italy, Germany, and the USSR), it helped maintain brute power, fueled hatred and violence, and contributed to the destabilization of Europe and Asia. While neither Lasswell nor Catlin denounced propaganda as something inherently antidemocratic, the invidious associations with Fascism (and to a lesser degree Communism) that began to attach to the term by the mid-1930s made it increasingly difficult to employ the value-neutral language of science in connection with an instrument widely seen as immoral and dangerous. Lasswell would soon learn this.

Going to Battle Against the Propaganda Menace

While Lasswell and his political science cohort were offering academically oriented justifications for the study—and practice—of propaganda, U.S. journalists, adult education specialists, editors, publishers, congressmen, and clergy were pointing to an international Fascist movement that made the problem of subversion through propaganda seem perilously immediate.

As before and during WWI, the perception that fifth-column agents were achieving success throughout the world because of their effective uses of propaganda heightened the distrust of foreign nationals in the United States and generated calls for an antipropaganda effort at a variety of levels. By the time the Nazis rolled into Poland in September 1939, starting WWII, the thesis of the highly effective Nazi strategy of using propaganda to bore from within had been confirmed many times over. Thus, while the McCormack-Dickstein Committee formed in 1934 to investigate un-American propaganda activities in the United States focused on both Communists and Fascists (as did its successor, the House Un-American Activities Committee, chaired by Martin Dies), within mainstream and left-liberal thought Fascist propaganda campaigns seemed a far graver threat to U.S. security and domestic unity than did Communist ones, both at home and abroad.[59] Whether the domestic Fascists were foreign nationals explicitly connected to Germany (and to a lesser extent Italy) or old-fashioned anti-Semitic nativists, the forms and channels of communication employed by the extreme right in the United States were identified as instruments of Nazi propaganda, a label that by and large stripped the term of any value-neutrality.

As communications historian J. Michael Sproule has illustrated, by the late 1930s the awareness of and discussion about propaganda was sufficiently extensive and nuanced that there was no dominant school of thought or approach to the problem, and some organizations, such as the Institute for Propaganda Analysis (which published the newsletter *Propaganda Analysis*), tried to remain committed to a value-neutral approach that focused on teaching the public how to discern propaganda techniques, regardless of whether they were part of Nazi, Soviet, corporate public relations, or New Deal legislative campaigns.[60] For the most part, however, all propaganda critics reiterated the WWI-era construction of propaganda as a threat to U.S. democracy, no matter who employed it (including the U.S. government). And most within the Popular Front and interventionist circles of liberal government officials, writers, scholars, and anti-Fascist activists believed that Fascist activities and communication channels in the United States needed surveillance and constant exposure. Nazi propaganda was seen as being too powerful, its conduits in the United States too extensive. The pressing questions were over what exactly should be done and whether efforts to control antidemocratic propaganda would themselves be undemocratic.

Reports by a host of private organizations, together with numerous exposés in well-regarded journals of liberal opinion, confirmed the threat of a not-insignificant, reasonably well-financed, and probably deeply interconnected Fascist movement flourishing in the United States.[61] Expressly anti-Fascist entities that were committed to exposing all varieties of propaganda, such as the Council for Democracy, Friends of Democracy, Inc. (with its journal *Propaganda Battlefront*), the American Council Against Nazi Propaganda (with its newsletter *The Hour*), the B'Nai Brith Anti-Defamation League, and journals including the *Nation*, the *New Republic*, *Harper's*, and the *New Yorker* routinely reported on the far-flung domestic Fascist movement and its communication networks. The reports showed that the movement included several dozen highly active native Fascist publicists who published numerous hate sheets in the form of newsletters and magazines and guided dozens of organizations with overlapping agendas and memberships; this domestic cabal was seen as aiding the cause of the German-American and Italian-American organizations that disseminated Nazi and Fascist propaganda through their newspapers, short-wave radio broadcasts, cultural organizations, political rallies, and other outlets. These efforts were reinforced by the extensive network of native anti-Semites who were also Fascists but were not necessarily connected to the German and Italian political and cultural groups.

The most glaring embodiment of the U.S. Nazi movement was the German-American Nazi Bund, founded by Fritz Kuhn in 1936. Although the Nazis tried to distance themselves from the American Bund (ironically this was partly because of Kuhn's harsh rhetoric and style), anti-Fascist Americans (for good reason) thought that the Bund represented the spearhead of Nazi efforts to penetrate the United States. (Among other reasons for this belief, Kuhn and other fascist sympathizers had a proclivity for publicizing their contacts with Nazi officials in order to enhance their bona fides.) Additionally, specific German organizations, such as the German National Railway, the Tourist Information Bureau, and the Library of Information, were accused of, and eventually successfully prosecuted for, being Nazi propaganda fronts. Likewise, several pro-Nazi intellectuals and their publishing interests were identified (and also eventually successfully prosecuted) as Nazi propaganda agents, including Friedrich E. F. Auhagen, who helped found the American Fellowship Forum, which published two journals, *Today's Challenge* and *Forum's Observer*, and George Sylvester Viereck, who edited these journals and ran Flanders Hall, a New Jersey–based publishing house. More important, perhaps, to the perception of a large, noisy, and interconnected Fascist movement in the United States were those many right-wing groups without formal ties to Germany who were also suspected of serving Nazi ends. Of the right-wing groups devoted to spreading anti-Semitic, antidemocratic, pro-Fascist doctrines through the land who were thought to be supportive of and more than just ideologically connected to the goals of Nazi Germany, the largest U.S. organizations were the Knights of the White Camellia and the American Nationalist Confederation, both led by George W. Christians, and the Silver Shirts, led by William Dudley Pelley. Pelley's publication *Liberation* and Christians's *National American Bulletin* (replete with a swastika in the masthead) were key organs of the domestic far right. Other vehicles for fascist propaganda included Gerald Winrod's *Revealer*, Father Coughlin's *Social Justice*, and the Militant Christian Patriots' *Christian Free Press*. Among other leaders were the high-profile Joe McWilliams of the Christian Front, Robert Edward Edmonson, James True, and dozens more.[62]

Reverend Leon Birkhead's Friends of Democracy, Inc., estimated that by the end of the 1930s over eight hundred organizations made up the Fascist front in the United States.[63] This number was routinely cited in both the mainstream and the anti-Fascist press, and delineating the putative connections among domestic Fascists and foreign nationals and their sponsoring organizations became a central feature of the exposé industry. Several reinforcing theories about propaganda's power dominated the reportage, beginning with the argument that Fascist political control in Italy and Germany was explained by propaganda's effectiveness in both seizing and maintaining power. By the late 1930s, this thesis of propaganda as an especially powerful weapon in the Fascist arsenal explained how fifth columns had succeeded in paving the way for Nazi political and military victories in the Sudetenland, Austria, Czechoslovakia, and Poland. And by the early forties, this framework expanded to include Belgium, Denmark, Holland, Norway, and France. U.S. anti-Fascists needed only to point to the fate of the European nations undermined by fifth columnists to illustrate the threat of pervasive activities in the United States and to argue that some organized response was necessary.[64]

Anti-Fascist propaganda anxieties in the United States were founded on an awareness of Nazi Germany's devotion to creating a "comprehensive state bureaucracy" for the use of propaganda both as a weapon to "gain national goals through the destruction of governments deemed unsympathetic to Nazi policies and through the subversion of populations targeted for attack or annexation."[65] The German propaganda bureaucracy was immense. For those Americans closely observing the rise of Nazism—especially journalists and businessmen reporting from Germany—the "existence of so many agencies allegedly devoted to subversion and propaganda indicated the value attached to psychological warfare by the Nazis and served as confirmation that they intended to use such weapons" (p. 10). Goebbels's Ministry for Popular Enlightenment and Propaganda (RMVP) with its Foreign Press and Broadcasting divisions was the most obvious manifestation; its efforts were duplicated and expanded on by Von Ribbentrop's Foreign Office with its foreign press division and broadcast monitoring stations. Additionally, the Nazi Party had its own agencies for disseminating materials abroad to racial Germans and Nazi sympathizers, including Rosenberg's Foreign Political Office and Bohle's Ausland Organization, which were manifested in the United States in the guise of official German organizations such as the German National Railway, the Tourist Information Bureau, and the Library of Information (all of which were eventually closed down by the U.S. government for being Nazi propaganda fronts). Most obvious was the German-American Bund, which, under the leadership of Fritz Kuhn, boasted over 200,000 members (although U.S. authorities reduced the number by a factor of ten).

Together the Nazi doctrine on the utility of propaganda, the sheer magnitude of the effort to promote Nazism abroad, Nazi boasts about its effectiveness, the apparent effectiveness of it in other European nations, and the existence of substantial Nazi activity in the United States meant that U.S. anti-Fascists could blame "nearly every German organization overseas with spreading Nazi propaganda" (p. 10).[66] Historian Clayton Laurie argues that this was a misperception but also acknowledges that while "most German organizations overseas were not created specifically for propaganda purposes . . . many were used by the Nazis in any capacity deemed useful to the state. Many organizations at home and abroad, although claiming independence and political neutrality, were unknowingly infiltrated and used for subversive purposes." "But," Laurie adds, "never to the degree that anti-Nazis and émigrés alleged" (p. 11). However, the sheer scale of official and clandestine Nazi propaganda activity internationally, combined with the perception that it was a highly successful prelude to and adjunct of armed aggression, made Nazi propaganda seem invincible. Although skeptical about its actual successes, Laurie confirms that "the Nazis succeeded in convincing a gullible world that propaganda was indeed a superweapon" (p. 12). These perceptions were crucial in shaping American perceptions of what the problem of propaganda had come to mean and what needed to be done.

Harold Lasswell would be crucial in helping shape the most important nongovernmental responses. His ideas, influence, and technical solutions to the problem of Fascist propaganda were especially important when he helped set in motion multiple "communications intelligence" projects (to use his phrase) to expose, monitor, analyze, measure, control, punish, and counteract Fascist propaganda activities in the United States and abroad. They were also key when he became an expert witness on the nature of Fascist and Communist propaganda in a handful of federal prosecutions under the authority of the Foreign Agents Registration Act and the various sedition laws. For Lasswell, then, the late 1930s brought new opportunities finally to bring his scientific approaches into the policy realm. He began his shift toward a national security–oriented approach to propaganda at this time, with the impetus coming from several directions, including the growing fear of the antidemocratic propaganda threat at home and the temporary unraveling of his academic career.

Lasswell's promising academic career was interrupted when in 1938 he was denied tenure at the University of Chicago and left the city to join forces with Edward Sapir and Harry Stack Sullivan for "an ambitious program of culture and personality research."[67] They planned to establish a Washington School of Psychiatry, but a series of mishaps befell them: Sapir took ill and never recovered; the monies from the William Alanson White Foundation to set up their institute never materialized; and on a lonely road in Indiana, one of the moving vans carrying Lasswell's possessions crashed, and many of his books and papers were destroyed by fire.[68] Without an academic position, Lasswell turned to the world of government, corporate, and foundation consulting. He consulted with James L. McCamy's survey research division at the U.S. Department of Agriculture, as well as with the Justice Department's Criminal Division. He worked with the General Education Board of the Rockefeller Foundation, wrote and delivered a series of educational broadcasts for NBC radio entitled "Human Nature in Action," and picked up lectureships at Yale Law School and the New School for Social Research, making New York City his home and base of operations after the war years. And, in a move that would set him up for the war years and establish his credentials as an important player in the nation's propaganda defense efforts, Lasswell also helped the Rockefeller Foundation's John Marshall establish an ongoing seminar about the state of the field of mass communications research, a seminar that included the war generation's leading communications scholars. Lasswell proved to be instrumental in guiding the communication seminar's agenda toward war-directed work, methodologically and in practice, as the seminar's formation was coincident with the outbreak of war in Europe. What began as a general discussion about making the inchoate discipline more scientific quickly turned to public opinion control and propaganda-related issues that were inseparable from the European emergency.

Lasswell also took a more furtive route into the world of propaganda control when he was still at the University of Chicago. Against the backdrop of the worldwide economic depression, growing international tensions, and abundant activity by radical and extremist political organizations in the United States, Lasswell saw the need to test his frameworks for the study of propaganda empirically by identifying ideological and strategy shifts, uses of key symbols, and the role of specialists within specific propaganda campaigns in the United States. He developed plans for a series of studies on different propaganda campaigns in the Chicago area as part of the Chicago Community Studies projects at the University of Chicago and received a grant from the university's Social Science Research Council for his research. Working with the city's Unemployed Councils to gain access to those who were the most affected by the Depression and therefore presumably the most susceptible to propaganda influences, he immediately discerned "that the groups most active in manipulating the Unemployed Councils were the Communists and the Socialists."[69] Lasswell therefore focused his first major study of propaganda activity in the United States on Chicago-area Communists and titled the fruits of this research (perhaps a bit disproportionately) *World Revolutionary Propaganda: A Chicago Study*, published in 1939.[70]

Whether or not this was Lasswell's first full recognition that the study of propaganda could be useful from a defensive, national security perspective is not clear, but as he admitted in the 1950s, as the Cold War ironically threatened to derail his ongoing work as a propaganda specialist, he and his coauthor, Dorothy Blumenstock, were not the only parties interested in mapping the influence of the Communists and Socialists on Chicago's unemployed. In fact, he and Blumenstock "were assisted in the study of these elements by the Chicago Police Industrial Squad," better known as the Red Squad. According to Lasswell's explanation, the Red Squad—also nervous about the power of propaganda—had seized so much radical literature that its library was overflowing and was "in a deplorably disorganized state." He helped them organize their library, and, as he later wrote, "a relationship, profitable to both of us, developed, and continued through the course of our study."[71] He and Blumenstock published their book, Lasswell worked out his techniques, and the Red Squad had the contents of its radical literature thoroughly analyzed as Lasswell studied the work of the local propaganda specialists. While this appears to have been his first official, and mutually beneficial, collaborative effort with state agencies as a specialist on propaganda, it was certainly not his last.

By 1940 Rockefeller Foundation officers, security-oriented government officials, and social science propaganda experts like Lasswell began to develop a propaganda prophylaxis based on two main objectives: assessing how the Nazis (and other belligerents) were utilizing all worldwide channels of communication as propaganda instruments and curbing the dissemination of Nazi propaganda in the United States. Both imperatives set in motion extensive efforts among and between institutions, and Lasswell quickly became an energetic figure in bringing the latest techniques of communications research into the government's orbit, including bringing his own content analysis techniques into the federal courts. Lasswell became highly valuable as an organizer and as a sophisticated technician for the state's antipropaganda efforts.

But despite his wishes and efforts, he was never a central figure in the production of democratic propaganda. In fact, as a strategist for shaping the form and content of American wartime propaganda, he had no influence, and those with whom he consulted found his social science jargon nearly incomprehensible as a guide for producing propaganda that might resonate with U.S. audiences.[72] Perhaps, then, his metaphors of mastery and control and his belated acceptance of democratic theory made it too difficult for him ever to internalize and thus articulate the cadences of democratic rhetoric. Even so, his techniques and language were altogether useful in producing a court-accepted strategy for "scientifically" demonstrating the dangers of antidemocratic propagandas.

CHAPTER THREE

Mobilizing for the War on Words: The Rockefeller Foundation, Communication Scholars, and the State

When in August 1938 Rockefeller Foundation officer John Marshall wrote of the "problem of propaganda," he pinpointed tensions and conflicts central to mid-twentieth-century political and intellectual culture in the United States.[1] In a political culture sensitized by World War I to the dangers of propaganda, soaked in foreign-language newspapers and films appealing to millions of European immigrants, and shadowed by the inevitability of a second European war, the debates among social scientists interested in communications research reflected larger tensions within U.S. academic and political liberalism about public capabilities and susceptibilities, about the need for anti-Axis counterpropaganda strategies, and about the public role of social scientists as objective scientists or as social planners. Among the first generation of communications scholars who came together under the aegis of the Rockefeller Foundation's Humanities Division in the late 1930s, the debates were not so much factional as interior, representing commitments to both John Dewey's pragmatic idealism and Walter Lippmann's skeptical realism. Under the pressure of war, these tensions were resolved in favor of Harold Lasswell's so-called scientific instrumentalism: members of Marshall's Rockefeller-funded Communications Group seemed to believe that they, as experts using scientifically verified information about the effects of mass communications, could streamline decision making (a Lippmannite position), facilitate public discussion of complicated problems (a Deweyan position), and take their scientific research methods into the state's emerging surveillance apparatus on behalf of the long-term survival of democracy (a Lasswellian position).

John Marshall (1903–1980) was a Harvard-trained medievalist who taught for a brief time in the Harvard English Department, served as secretary of the Mediaeval Academy of America and editor of publications of the American Council of Learned Societies, and in 1933 joined the Rockefeller Foundation (RF) as a General Education Board officer and as assistant director for the Humanities Division.[2] As an RF humanities officer, Marshall, along with fellow officer David Stevens, directed the foundation's sponsorship of the inchoate field of communications research, a field they considered to be in need of theoretical and methodological coherence and institutional support. Partly their interest came from traditional foundation concerns about public health matters—they hoped that the media could be used to better effect for public education on health issues—and partly it came from their awareness that a research field of potentially great importance was underdeveloped and vitally important in an age of competing propagandas. Marshall took the lead here, writing in January 1936 a memo to Stevens exploring the Rockefeller Foundation's potential role as a funding agency for communications-related activities. He told Stevens that the foundation could play an innovative role in the development of radio and film as tools for public education, and because it was not motivated by profit incentives, it could avoid the commercial barriers that up until then had constrained the uses of film and radio for educational and cultural purposes. "Both radio and motion pictures are recognized as instrumentalities potentially of great importance alike for formal education and for the general diffusion of culture," Marshall wrote, but commercial interests were ill disposed to sponsor academic study and experimentation with these media. The foundation could therefore expand its own vital contributions to social and public health by stepping into the breach. The "most promising way" of expanding the "serious" use of radio and film, Marshall added, was for the foundation to give "a few younger men with talent for these mediums an opportunity for relatively free experimentation . . . men interested primarily in education, literature, criticism, or in disseminating the findings of the social or natural sciences."[3]

Initially Stevens and Marshall channeled Humanities Division resources into educational uses of radio and film on public health matters. But as their interest in the connections between media technologies and education expanded, so did their awareness of the inadequacy of existing theoretical and empirical knowledge about mass communications. After a brief acquaintance with the general field of media production, Marshall and Stevens turned to the familiar world of scholarship and directed foundation monies toward a variety of mass communications research projects ranging from radio and film production to reading behavior, public opinion formation, audience studies, effects studies, and propaganda analysis.

Marshall's central role in the intellectual and institutional history of U.S. mass communications research is a neglected subject. He not only steered financial support to the first university-based communications research projects and mobilized these projects for war but also linked them intellectually. Beginning in 1936, the foundation began funding discrete communications research projects, and Marshall (at Harold Lasswell's urging) saw the need to make the field more scientific and coherent. By 1939 he had drawn together a host of scholars (generally the principals of the various foundation-sponsored communications research projects) into a monthly seminar, interchangeably called the Communications Group or the Communications Seminar, whose primary purposes included achieving consensus on a paradigm for the field. Through his influence on this group, Marshall self-consciously helped create a new discipline, imposing theoretical coherence and a scientific research paradigm on this growing area of interdisciplinary inquiry.

Besides Marshall, other Rockefeller Foundation officers were also involved in the seminar, including Stevens, Stacy May, and R. H. Havighurst. The academic members of the original Communications Group included Lasswell; Columbia University sociologist Robert Lynd; Viennese exile and director of the Columbia Office of Radio Research Paul Lazarsfeld; Hadley Cantril, director of the Public Opinion Research Project at Princeton; Oxford-trained anthropologist Geoffrey Gorer; adult education specialist Lyman Bryson; Donald Slesinger, former dean of social sciences at Chicago and director of the American Film Center; Harvard-based literary theorist and semanticist I. A. Richards; the University of Chicago's Douglas Waples, the leading researcher on print communications and reading behavior; and Charles Siepmann, a communications analyst for the BBC. Their goal, before the war encroached, was to shape a more disciplined research model and agenda for the incipient field. They hoped to address "the problem" of mass communications research as set out by Marshall: mass influence. Marshall explained that

> when millions of people, through the press, the radio, or the motion pictures, are all told the same, or approximately the same thing, at the same time, something relatively new in the history of communication happens. . . . That their responses will be different in large measure can be taken for granted. But it likewise has to be taken for granted that there is enough common to all or to most all of them in the experience to lead to at least some response, *en masse*. . . . Mass communication in reaching millions becomes mass influence, for better or for worse.

Marshall and the others made the critical distinction between imputed effects and actual effects, noting that mass communication "has to be appraised not by what it says, but by what it does."[4]

The seminar defined an empirically oriented, behaviorist research model organized around determining the effects of communications. The model was based on a series of questions—who? said what? to whom? with what effect?—and it assumed a collective research enterprise in which each question would be met by different research strategies capable of address-ing some dimension of the cluster of questions (see table 3.2 at the end of this chapter). Normally attributed solely to Lasswell, the "who said what to whom and with what effect?" paradigm was actually the product of months and months of paper exchanges, meetings, and oral and written dialogue among seminar members. The result was a foundational event in the intellectual history of the field, validating an approach that eschewed unproved and critical assumptions about media effects but also ignored larger issues about social relations and the nature of power in modern, media-dominated societies. If communications research was to be scien-tific, and credible by virtue of its objectivity, it had to employ methods that would produce verifiable results, the scholars reasoned. The so-called founding fathers of mass communications chose to leave philosophical speculation to nonscientists and amateurs.

The threat of war intruded on the Communications Seminar, however, producing another (related) line of inquiry about propaganda, national se-curity, and the role of experts. In the seminar's incipient stages, propaganda research as a national security issue unexpectedly became a central issue; by autumn 1939, with war breaking out in Europe, Rockefeller Foundation of-ficers and the founding fathers of communications research were galvanized by the recognition that the Roosevelt administration, hamstrung politically by isolationist sentiment and bad memories lingering from WWI, could not adequately prepare for war on the propaganda front. Under Marshall's guidance, the Rockefeller Foundation's Humanities Division, whose various communications research projects had more room to experiment with po-tentially controversial activities, took up the slack on matters of public opinion formation and the monitoring of foreign and domestic propagan-da. With Marshall performing a midwife role, Rockefeller-funded research laid the groundwork for a wide range of propaganda studies that were even-tually absorbed by the state when they had proved their value. From its out-set, the Communications Seminar was decidedly interventionist and policy oriented, and its purposes were clearly shaped by Marshall's perception of the Rockefeller Foundation's social responsibilities.[5]

In short, the evolution of the emerging discipline's first research model was ineluctably tied to its historical moment. Its history cannot be sepa-rated—intellectually, institutionally, or epistemologically—from the im-pending crisis of World War II. The Communication Seminar members' collective consciousness of the potential utility for policy of their expert-ise in radio, film, public opinion, and propaganda matters shaped their joint inquiry and the specific work within their individual projects. John Marshall procured monies, and he, along with Harold Lasswell, directed the particular research projects toward what Lasswell called their "communications intelligence"—that is, national security—functions. Seminar members consistently recurred to the question of whether they should engage primarily in the development of a scientific approach to the field (with a focus on methods that could measure effects and ensure reproducible results) or whether they should focus on the state's probable interests in public opinion mobilization and control. Marshall mediated these concerns by averring that the foundation could both serve the development of a scientific approach to communications research and address national security interests. Lasswell's scientific instrumentalism combined the rhetoric of science with opportunity and helped direct the seminar and the research projects toward the creation of what I call the propaganda prophylaxis.

Under Marshall and Lasswell's direction, the Rockefeller Foundation and the interwar generation's foremost social science communications scholars stepped in to fill a critical void during the period from 1939 to 1943, as a handful of interrelated and coordinated research projects quickly shifted from establishing academic standards for the study of mass communications to studying Nazi print, radio, and film propaganda and developing content analysis as an intelligence tool. Illustrating the collaboration among the academy, private foundations, and the state, this chapter suggests that the histories of U.S. communications research and the U.S. defense against Nazi propaganda both need to account for the crucial influences of the Rockefeller Foundation's John Marshall and the handful of projects he subvened and coordinated, including the Princeton Radio Research Project cum Office of Radio Research at Columbia (Paul Lazarsfeld); the Princeton Public Opinion Research Project (Hadley Cantril); the Princeton Shortwave Listening Center (Harold Graves, Harwood Childs, and John Whitton); the Graduate Library Reading Project at the University of Chicago (Douglas Waples); the Film Library of the Museum of Modern Art (John Abbott and Iris Barry, with Siegfried Kracauer); the Library of Congress Film Project; the American Film Center (Donald Slesinger); the Totalitarian Communications Research Project at the New School of Social Research (Ernst Kris and Hans Speier); and the Experimental Division for the Study of Wartime Communications at the Library of Congress (Harold Lasswell).[6] At the end of the 1930s, anxieties in U.S. liberal culture about propaganda, democracy, mass communications, science, expertism, and security linked the emergence of mass communications research as a scholarly field with the growth of communications research as a valuable and multifaceted weapon for the propaganda wars.

The Communications Seminar and the Politics of Expertise

Like Lippmann, Dewey, and Lasswell, John Marshall believed in science and the scientific method as a means of enlightenment and social progress. He saw the foundation as an instrument for making the fruits of science available to society and believed it should be a vehicle for providing vital resources to promising social and political scientists. His concern with propaganda as a "pathology" in American culture and his inchoate ideas about mass society, communications effects, and applied social sciences gave his thought a hybrid quality, embodying the contradictory imperatives of modern liberalism. Debates over the primacy of expert-centered or public-centered decision making created a tension in Marshall's own thinking and suffused the work of the social science scholars whom Marshall brought into the foundation's orbit. A deep intellectual and ideological ambivalence about the democratic and authoritarian implications of their applied social science orientation pervaded the arguments, ideas, and recommendations of foundation officials and research scholars. Their doubts about the public and their faith in experts, science, and a strengthened central government embodied a powerful but fraught movement toward centralization and statism on the eve of WWII.

Indeed, developing a rationale and even a justifying rhetoric for engaging in opinion-control activities produced considerable conflict within the Communications Group, particularly about issues of public capacities versus those of experts. But the tensions reflected larger anxieties about the imperatives (and language) of a democracy mobilizing its intellectual resources for war, especially a total war where the struggle for psychological advantage would potentially be as important as the struggles for military advantage. Group members perceived that opinion control and propaganda were insidious in U.S. civil society but were also necessary instruments of modern warfare, even in a democracy. Their memories and interpretations of WWI propaganda campaigns made them suspicious of both the state and the intellectuals working on its behalf, while they also understood this work needed to be done in preparation for an imminent war. They also knew that anything that could be labeled "propaganda" would be attacked by the public and especially by an isolationist Congress; thus they also recognized that agencies outside the state (and not dependent on congressional monies) would have to embark on propaganda and opinion-control research. In other words, arguments within the Communications Seminar reflected the tensions within modern U.S. liberalism on the eve of WWII: over state-centered administrative liberalism versus civil libertarianism and over the role of intellectuals as independent critics versus intellectuals as servants of power. The capaciousness and variability of prewar liberal intellectual culture become clear when one recognizes that within the Communications Group itself one or another person expressed seemingly contradictory ideas at different moments of the crisis. U.S. intellectuals were not of a single mind nor fixed position about what propaganda represented as problem or which were the most democratic solutions.

To a large extent, Harold Lasswell became the most active and influential seminar member. He clearly adopted the realist position, and his own agenda for communications research on the war's eve dominated the Communications Seminar's debates and applied research. Lasswell's instrumentalism, however, was invariably countered by one or another of his colleagues sensitive to the undemocratic tendencies in Lasswell's rhetoric, if not his agenda. An ongoing dialogue between the Lasswellian rhetoric of opinion control and expertism, on the one hand, and, on the other, a more cautious appraisal of the value of science as an instrument of social reform and of scholars as intermediaries between the state and the public defined the group's political fault lines. Although sensitive to charges of being antidemocratic, Marshall emerged as Lasswell's ally, and under his direction the group became mostly concerned with the public policy applications of verifiable research data. The Communications Seminar thus identified its agenda, almost from the outset, with the state's agenda, in terms of both offensive and defensive propaganda intelligence work.

Although not a social scientist or media student, Marshall was a scholar by training and was interested in imposing academic discipline on the ill-defined field with which he had found himself involved. His importance should be measured by his role as an administrative catalyst and agent for scholars and by the larger vision he had for emergency-period research. Marshall's language for describing mass communications issues seems to derive from his acquaintance with sociologist Robert Lynd, Harold Lasswell, and a Deweyan tradition of social analysis in which he understood propaganda as a significant, inadequately diagnosed factor in the "pathologies" of an increasingly media-driven society. He used the terms "pathology of influence" and "pathology of substitutes" to describe disturbing forces in U.S. political and social life, especially the prevailing commercial ethos that casually and continually substituted what he called "incomplete knowledge" for "genuine knowledge."[7] Like most other critics of propaganda, Marshall drew a sharp distinction between education (the pursuit of truth) and propaganda (never adequate as the truth and usually deceptive).[8] Through public education, he argued to fellow officers, the foundation could provide the missing, and necessary, "genuine knowledge" about public issues.

Given the potential controversy of foundation involvement in anything smacking of politics, Marshall knew he was out on a limb. As historians Mark C. Smith and John M. Jordan show, the theme of democratic engagement and reform versus scientific objectivity was a familiar conflict in the social sciences before WWII, and when foundation monies were involved the politically conservatizing emphasis on "objectivism" (Smith's term) invariably won out.[9] Indeed, during the 1920s and 1930s all the social science disciplines were beset by debates between social reform–oriented liberals or leftists and more conservative service intellectuals subvened by foundation monies, who were committed to demonstrating the legitimacy of the social sciences by proving their objectivity and value-neutrality. Marshall, however, tried to mediate between these competing tendencies, in part by engaging social-planning advocates like Robert Lynd and methodologically driven administrative research types like Paul Lazarsfeld in the same seminar. Marshall hoped to pursue both a democratic strategy and a scientific one. Scientifically produced research results should, he contended, enhance democratic practices. Replacing the pathologies of influence and substitutes with genuine knowledge about complicated social and political problems was, he told fellow officers, "perhaps . . . a constructive approach to the problem of propaganda— seemingly the only approach sufficiently objective to be appropriate for an agency like the Foundation."[10]

In late 1938 Marshall proposed that the foundation pursue four lines of inquiry about the role of mass communications in modern U.S. society: How could film and radio be used to expand public knowledge? How could public desires be discerned, and how could they be changed? Why was the public satisfied with the "pathology of substitutes" instead of genuine knowledge? And how were these issues related to the strengths and weaknesses of democracy? The foundation had a responsibility to safeguard democratic politics in the "society it serves," he argued, and it could best perform its duties by enlisting social science experts to guide this inquiry.[11] Echoing Dewey's position that experts could improve the conditions for public debate and discussion by providing the knowledge that would create a more competent public, Marshall explained that using mass communications technologies to provide the public with the most information "that is at present known" about a given topic would obviate the influence of the pathologies of substitutes, and this would certainly meet the foundation's criteria for scientific and apolitical research. He also embraced Lasswell's faith that democracy and propaganda were not incompatible and that social scientists could facilitate the union: "If their work were well enough done to avoid any serious misdirection, this should supply the last-needed element for a *genuinely democratic propaganda*," he wrote.[12]

Other Rockefeller Foundation officers, aware that mass communication had received "little organized study," were amenable to supporting a series of conferences that might help develop a "general body of theory about mass communications in American culture" that the officers could subsequently use in developing research-support plans and considering proposals. In August 1939 the foundation agreed to fund a series of conferences "to develop a disciplined approach to the study of mass communications, through such media as radio, motion pictures, and print."[13] As with other foundation efforts to avoid associating politically inflected work with the Rockefeller name, Marshall assured his fellow officers that the discussions would be "purely informal and that they should receive no public attention." Similarly, he warned potential seminar members against publicly crediting to the foundation "any materials that grow out of the discussions."[14]

Apart from saying that the seminar's objective was to identify a "general body of theory about mass communications in American culture," Marshall was vague about his overall plans. Columbia University sociologist Robert Lynd pushed Marshall to have the seminar address one primary question: "What work in the field of communication might a foundation usefully do?"[15] Lynd had just completed *Knowledge for What?* (1939), a scathing critique of social scientists' tendency to focus on methodological problems and to divorce their research from social reform and political engagement. The work was a key volume in the attack by Lynd and other "purposivists" (Mark Smith's term) on what they saw as the conservative, status-quo–reproducing scientism of the service intellectuals. By the late 1930s critics like Lynd were arguing that the service intellectuals' penchant for empirical methods was amoral at best and that the crisis produced by the Nazi military and propaganda onslaught precluded any commitment to scientific research simply for the sake of science.[16] Hence Lynd was disposed to push Marshall to move the group's work beyond mere discussion. Lynd was well acquainted with Marshall from his longtime association with the foundation as secretary of the Social Science Research Council, and he deferred to Marshall's authority as administrator, but he wanted Marshall to direct the seminar's work toward engaged social science. As he told Marshall, "I haven't much faith in committee spontaneous combustion. Somebody should have thought thru [*sic*] the field enough to set up a general objective and rough bounds beyond which discussion does not wander. . . . I continue to feel that it is the Foundation staff's job to see the general objective."[17] The Nazi-Soviet Non-Aggression Pact of August

1939 furnished that objective, just as Marshall was pulling together the details for the seminar. It focused Lynd's attention even more intently on the relationship among social research, social planning, and the mobilization of public opinion. Lynd, like most Popular Front partisans, was stunned by the surprise pact, which came just days before the seminar was to convene for the first time; as he told Marshall in a note he sent him on the eve of the group's first meeting, "My God! how are you feeling? I'm just crawling back to my feet. It'll probably be a long war, & we'll have to take it easy. The Soviet move hit me back of the ears like a lead pipe."[18]

Like Lynd, Marshall understood that the crisis produced by the Nazi-Soviet Pact and the immediate German invasion of Poland gave the seminar a quite specific focus. According to the notes compiled by *Public Opinion Quarterly* editor and seminar secretary Lloyd Free, from the Communication Group's first meeting in September 1939 the discussion immediately turned to the problem of predicting and preparing for the "trends likely to result in the United States as a result of the war." Marshall, Free noted, told his colleagues that "in view of the world situation," they should "consider what research studies might be undertaken at once . . . studies that would be of immediate significance."[19]

During the next fifteen months the Communications Group met ten times, always at Rockefeller Plaza in New York.[20] After the first few seminars, regular attendees were Lasswell, Free, Gorer, Slesinger, Lynd, Lazarsfeld, Waples, Cantril, Siepmann, Bryson, Marshall, Stevens, May, and Havighurst. They produced over thirty working papers and a final unpublished report entitled "Needed Research in Mass Communications."[21] This report was widely circulated among academics, communications industry executives, and government officials who were preparing for the emergency. Whether or not Robert Lynd agreed with the focus of the seminar's many working papers and discussions (and he did not), Marshall certainly followed Lynd's injunction to identify work that the foundation "might usefully do."

In its first two meetings, the seminar explored the implications of the war in Europe for communications and public opinion matters in the United States. Predicting an "emergency psychology" with "an increasing degree of [government] control . . . in regard to all phases of communication, such as in the schools, the radio, the films, the press, and even eventually in all public discussion," seminar members tried to arrive at consensus about what part they, as communications experts, should take in the inevitable process of expanding state authority over communications. This was a fraught subject, as the ensuing fifteen months would show. Robert Lynd argued that the emergency called for a certain "realism" about the public and its incompetence and that this realism defined the group's job, which should include actively manufacturing public opinion in order to guide society during the emergency. Lynd also recalled how the hysteria that accompanied WWI did not subside with the armistice and therefore argued that one object should be determining how public opinion could be "demobilized" after the emergency was over. But he did not want to "demobilize" what would undoubtedly be a greater role for experts, arguing that among other things social scientists should identify and make permanent "desirable trends that might otherwise be of short duration," including cementing the place of experts in the policy-making apparatus. According to Free's notes, Lynd suggested that "another related goal would be that of persuading the people that there are many issues too complicated for them to decide, which should be left to experts." Lynd's stance as the seminar's most unabashed democratic skeptic must have recurred throughout the meeting, for Lloyd Free commented in his notes that "Mr. Lynd feels we need a restructuring of democratic action in terms of the capacity of different groups of the population and an abandonment of the American idea of the responsibility and capacity of the man on the street."[22]

Donald Slesinger, former dean of social sciences at the University of Chicago and director of the Rockefeller Foundation–sponsored American Film Center, was just as pessimistic as Lynd about people's susceptibility to propaganda: "The result of most propaganda is to turn people into automatons, reacting blindly and incapable of thought," Free quoted him as saying. But Slesinger rejected Lynd's conclusions; like Marshall, he drew on a Deweyan rhetoric and argued that experts should use social science knowledge to create "more democratic and intelligent citizens in the face of widespread propaganda." He too hoped to use communications technologies to provide the public with the opposite of propaganda—genuine knowledge—and he rejected Lynd's assumptions that government by experts would strengthen democratic processes.[23] (Lynd began the seminar dismissive of Slesinger. In a letter for Marshall's "private eye," he appraised Slesinger as "a bright fellow, but . . . an everlasting promoter. . . . I don't trust his ability to appraise a problem in which he has a potential stake without doing so in the mood of 'What's in it for me?' ")[24]

Lynd's and Slesinger's positions reflect larger debates within the social sciences over the relationship between social knowledge and social action and whether the goals of social sciences should be the creation of a more humane or a more efficient and rational society. In the politics of the era, Lynd's call for aggressive social engineering did not have the reactionary inflections it now seems to carry, and his vanguardist faith in planning was shared by many committed liberals and leftists who thought social knowledge should be utilized on behalf of social democracy. Nevertheless, there were those in the seminar, and outside it, who bridled at what they saw as Lynd's seemingly undemocratic and authoritarian assumptions. Slesinger, for instance, criticized Lynd on these grounds, though he himself frequently claimed that a central film agency (presumably his) should control the content and distribution of both film and projectors during the emergency.

The apparent inconsistencies among the group's members reflect unsettled questions within liberal intellectual culture on the eve of WWII: What should be the relationship between science and social reform? Should social and political considerations direct the kinds of questions social scientists ask? Was undirected public opinion capable of adequately addressing the complex questions of an increasingly unstable world, or should experts direct the public, through persuasion and information control, toward opinions that would permit government authorities and social science experts themselves to act? In the instance of the Communications Seminar, the disagreements about appropriate answers to these questions revolved around whether one thought propaganda and opinion control compatible with democratic processes.

The group's first working paper, produced as a preliminary master plan for its subsequent agenda, embodied the quandary about government manipulation of public opinion and the role of scholars in that process. The title, "The Job to Be Done—Now," suggested the urgency of a manifesto, but the paper itself was an exercise in caution and ambivalence.[25] It highlighted the researchers' concerns that an emergency psychology would induce government propaganda, censorship, and other forms of control, which the seminar did not necessarily desire. It also acknowledged, however, that the government needed to shape opinion in order to meet emergency objectives. Thus, despite an apparent group consensus that propaganda could be used for democratic purposes—especially to mobilize public support for short-term measures—the piece still reflected strong reservations about democratic governments actively manipulating public opinion. The document evinced no ambivalence, however, about these scholars' faith in their own expertise. One of the refrains in "The Job to Be Done—Now" was the central role communications experts could play in the emergency. In a seeming compromise between the objectivists, who assumed that data bore its own truth and would eventually produce reform, and the purposivists, who believed that values must shape the inquiry, the seminar's first collective report was grounded in the assumption that an improved science of mass communications could and should serve national policy purposes.

In its next stages, the seminar moved toward identifying the research strategies that would improve the science. Lasswell's two working papers produced in response to "The Job to Be Done—Now" illuminate his characteristically grandiose policy science obsession with social scientific methods and the application of those methods to public policy matters. For example, Lasswell specified that methodological work had to be integrated among the different foundation-sponsored projects. Like Marshall, he was sensitive to the need for scholars and the foundation to protect their reputation for objectivity and knew that the state would only be interested in their work if it were objective and scientifically reputable; he noted, for example, that "the standards which are used in . . . 'propaganda analysis' are highly subjective and the agency which carries on this function is subject to attack," whereas the "function of encouraging . . . current documentation in the field of communications is much less subjective." He warned therefore that the "success of the program of current documentation would be in danger if it were committed to an agency which also exercises the function of propaganda analysis."[26] (Ironically, at the time he wrote this, Lasswell was serving the Justice Department in Foreign Agent Registration Act [FARA] cases as an expert witness whose credibility depended on the objective and scientific nature of his propaganda analysis techniques).[27] More important, his arguments about improving scientific methods and equipping the state for propaganda warfare reverberated through virtually all the subsequent documents produced by the Communications Group. Lasswell's confidence that he and his fellow social scientists could divide up the world of communications channels and reconnect them through integrated methodological work made him a guiding force in connecting the seminar's work to the policy makers responsible for constructing the nation's propaganda defense.

Lasswell also made it clear that the foundation or some similar agency should play a mediating role between research and policy making. "Specialists in the study of communications" should give direction to "those who have money to support research," and those with the money should strive to serve three primary purposes: "to stimulate and guide research in the field of communications," to maintain the reputation of objectivity for those involved in this research, especially on "controversial public questions," and to push this research toward "the pursuit of truth about important social problems." Lasswell concluded that this combined effort among scholars, foundation officials, and policy makers could "minimize human destructiveness and . . . maximize human constructiveness."[28]

Notwithstanding Lasswell's seemingly benign prescription for combining scientism with social planning, some group members took umbrage at

Lasswell's language and assumptions. Challenging Lasswell as he had Lynd, Donald Slesinger's critical response was representative, especially his concern about his colleagues' willingness to become propagandists themselves in the fight against more nefarious propaganda: "We have used the language of students and practitioners of propaganda, and have tacitly accepted their objectives. . . . We have been willing, without thought, to sacrifice both truth and human individuality in order to bring about given mass responses to war stimuli. We have thought in terms of fighting dictatorship-by-force through the establishment of dictatorship-by-manipulation."[29] The contrast between Slesinger's warning and Lasswell's policy science confidence identifies once again the central dilemmas they faced: could they engage in propaganda-inflected work without becoming propagandists? Alternatively, as Lynd's later attack on Lasswell would ask: could they explore methodological questions about measurement and technique in the effort to make the field more scientific and still produce socially and politically useful work?

Determining how propaganda, or persuasion, works was one place where they could try to answer the second question without immediately having to face the implications of the first. Despite a significant social science literature on propaganda and persuasion from the interwar period, empirical research on communication effects was inadequate. As a second group working paper, "Public Opinion and the Emergency," explained, "There is at present little or no knowledge of the degree to which people or groups of people in the United States . . . are susceptible to persuasion. There is, further, little or no knowledge of what types of persuasion . . . these groups are susceptible to."[30] Holly Cowan Schulman and Allan Winkler, both historians of U.S. propaganda agencies during WWII, argue that on the eve of the war leading social scientists, including seminar member Paul Lazarsfeld, were becoming skeptical of the claims made by social critics that propaganda had "unlimited power."[31] Indeed, "Public Opinion and the Emergency" contended that scientific communications research needed to address at least two empirical problems: How does opinion change? And what factors produce changes in opinions? The emergency, they averred, created a perfect laboratory setting to hone the requisite scientific techniques needed to answer these questions. Reflecting a Lasswellian focus, the working paper suggested they could mesh technocracy and democracy: the experiences provided by the emergency would advance the science, and the science would be applied to the emergency.

Not surprisingly, the seminar's collective research strategy called for discrete, reproducible studies of related aspects of mass communications processes. Drawing on Lasswell's earlier recommendations, the group identified a cluster of related research techniques and problems worthy of applied study, including straw polling and short interviews, panel interviews, content analysis, source analysis (by which it meant studies of the uses and influences of print, film, and radio), and community studies (where these different methods could be employed). Each of the group members was separately engaged in developing one or more of the following techniques: Lasswell and Gorer were content analysis specialists, with Lasswell interested in print communications and Gorer in film. Richards had his own approach to print content analysis, through semantics. Lazarsfeld, who studied both radio and print, and Waples, who specialized in print sources, were both interested in panel interviews. Cantril was a polling specialist who also studied radio. In short, seminar members all had an interest not only in securing ongoing foundation support for their particular projects but also in developing an overarching model to give coherence to the field. Employing the same research strategies in different media to ask the same questions about media messages, audiences, and effects was a practical way of quickly achieving methodological and theoretical coherence.

Between December 1939 and June 1940, the Communications Seminar dedicated the bulk of its individual meetings to developing strategies for perfecting empirical research methods. In terms of the sociology of knowledge of the discipline, these were undoubtedly critically important exchanges among men who were later identified as the founding fathers of communications research in the United States. The more quantitatively oriented members, especially Lazarsfeld, Lasswell, Waples, Cantril, and Gorer, quickly achieved a consensus about the importance of the group's focus on method. Methodological questions dominated the group's agenda, in the process driving away two less scientistic members, Robert Lynd and I. A. Richards. Both Lynd and Richards were frustrated by the obsession with empiricism and data-gathering strategies, but it is clear from Lynd's consistent democratic realism that the methodological humanist/objectivist split in the group was not congruent with the ideological democrat/antidemocratic fissure. Lynd identified the source of his frustration as his colleagues' desire to emulate the natural sciences and their consequent failure to make useful policy-oriented suggestions. He complained to Marshall that they were merely "quantifying the status quo": "Both Lasswell and Gorer are largely content to describe what happens, with the implicit assumption that it will somehow be useful. I think this is a needlessly cumbersome and wasteful way for research to proceed."[32]

By April 1940 Lynd's and Richard's frustrations had not abated. Lynd wrote to Marshall, "I have felt uneasy as hell this winter in my role as committee member for you. I am interested in the field of communication and regard it as very important. But the doggone thing just isn't something in which I have either central interest or special competence."[33] Historians Richard W. Fox and Mark C. Smith are probably right in claiming that during the 1940s Lynd's feeling of being unproductive and methodologically out of date was reinforced by close work with sophisticated quantifiers. Richards, in turn, found the group's work pedestrian and irrelevant. He resigned after his two papers on a semantic theory of communication were snubbed, as he saw it. Marshall tried to mollify both Lynd and Richards, arguing that he too was suspicious of "expertism," but he was unsuccessful convincing the latter to stay on. Despite the loss, Marshall's role as a foundation officer interested in developing a scientifically disciplined approach to the field meant that despite the group's "baffling" "imperviousness" to other perspectives, he was inclined to support the methodologists as experts and reported that he thought their work should be encouraged.[34]

At the conclusion of their first ten meetings, Marshall and the Communications Group put together several documents that laid out their conclusions and recommendations for shaping the field of mass communications. Their July 1940 paper "Research in Mass Communications" identified the problem of measuring "communications effects" as the central problem for the incipient field:

> In brief, that job is to learn what mass communications *do* in our society. . . . What they do became a question of *what effects* do mass communications as a whole, or any single communication, have. What effects they have likewise inescapably involved discovering *to whom was it said*. How these effects occurred necessitated analysis of *what was said*. And that analysis, to be complete and properly illuminating, required answers to a fourth and final question—*who said it and with what intention*. In brief, then, the job of research in mass communications is to determine who, and with what intentions, said what, to whom, and with what effects.

This concise "general theory," as Marshall called it, was one of the vital achievements of the seminar. The model assumed a collective enterprise in which each question would be met by different research strategies. Group members understood that each of the questions was extraordinarily complex and situated deeply within specific social and cultural contexts. Only when the "who?" "said what?" "to whom?" questions were at "least tentatively answered," they wrote, could the key question—"with what effects?"—be asked.[35]

This model bore Lasswell's stamp—it echoes the title and argument of his book *Politics: Who Gets What, When, How* (1936)—and was deeply embedded in the behavioral social sciences. All its key questions were assumed to be answerable with sufficient data. That Lazarsfeld, Waples, Lasswell, Slesinger, Free, Cantril, and Marshall developed a multilayered, multiple-step research model demanding different kinds of empirical data makes sense. They knew that different procedures would produce different kinds of data; they knew that individuals were situated differently in different social and cultural contexts; and they understood that audience and individual responses to mass communications were indelibly influenced by those contexts and that the message of any particular communication was only part of the larger flow of communications. Measuring the effects of any particular communication occurrence or recurrence on individual or group interests, opinions, or behavior would necessarily involve accounting for all these preexisting relationships and contexts. This methodological orientation, on the one hand, reflected the broad interdisciplinarity and empiricism of the interwar social sciences and acknowledged the methodological difficulty of measuring media effects. On the other hand, the "who said what to whom" model indicates a refusal to ask any critical questions about the effects of mass communications on democracy, or public discussion, or epistemology; perhaps Lynd's complaint that they were just "quantifying the status quo" was on the mark. The fact that this model fulfilled Marshall's expectation for a grand theory suggests a rather minimal interest in social theory among these leading interwar social scientists. It also suggests the constraints of a funding agency such as the Rockefeller Foundation that, for public relations and reputation purposes, had to promote objective scientific research and therefore could more easily promote the kind of work Lasswell championed than socially transformative work. The new paradigm bespoke a symbiosis between the social scientists and the foundation: this multidimensional, objectivist research model depended on a coordinating and funding agency like the Rockefeller Foundation, and this type of model also justified the foundation's interests in promoting the incipient field of mass communications within the social sciences.

As I have already suggested, however, the seminar's work had both applied social policy dimensions and serious implications for the foundation because of the negative connotations surrounding anything having to do with propaganda. Thus, while the science was not in itself controversial, the uses of that science were potentially explosive. Marshall understood these dangers and recognized as well that there were important differences between monitoring and countering Nazi propaganda aimed at the United States and actively manufacturing public opinion in the United States. He also knew that wartime imperatives might require unsatisfactory means to achieve desirable ends. As early as May 1940, he expressed this awareness to fellow foundation officer Stacy May: "In a period of emergency such as I believe we now face, the manipulation of public opinion to meet emergency needs has to be taken for granted. In such a period, those in control must shape public opinion to support courses of action which the emergency necessitates. . . . No one, I think, can blame them for that impulse." The "means of molding opinion" had improved so much, he said, that "any real emergency in this country would be characterized by the manipulation of opinion beyond anything we saw during the last war." He acknowledged that it would "simply be easier to shape opinion" than it had been in WWI.[36]

But Marshall hoped that a useful (and operable) distinction could be drawn between means and ends and between short-term and long-term interests, both in the political arena and in the social science realm. Everyone would be "preoccupied with" the problems of the emergency, he told May, but he hoped long-term scientific goals would not be sacrificed: "There is always a danger that if emergency mechanisms are not recognized as such that they become permanent." The foundation therefore had to "keep long-term considerations in view during short-term planning."[37] Despite the pressures of the war and, eventually, his not-inconsiderable contributions to the total U.S. war effort, Marshall tried to maintain the distinction between science and propaganda, between genuine knowledge and pathologies of influence. The fact that he was laying groundwork for a propaganda prophylaxis in anticipation of war against Nazi Germany made the controversial implications of his projects far more acceptable for his fellow foundation officers, some of whom were also at work on readiness matters. Nevertheless, Marshall was frequently reminded he was walking a tightrope between democracy and technocracy.

Marshall's intentions to move the Rockefeller-funded projects in the direction of national security work is very clear in the July 1940 seminar report called "Research in Mass Communications." The report combines the objectivist assumption that the pursuit of fact equaled the pursuit of truth with the social engineering belief that applied knowledge could make the management of public opinion much more rational and efficient. The report is a crucial document in the intellectual history of communications research, in part because it was an ideological manifesto, intended to move scholars into the trenches of propaganda warfare. The assumption that communications research was a new and sure weapon to achieve democratic ends through public opinion control underlay the report. A series of related and supporting assumptions about social scientists and what they could do were implicit: they could help leaders understand the public mind and its prejudices; they could help change troublesome prejudices; they could assuage the public's fears in the crisis; they could effectively mediate between the public and its leaders; and finally, because democracy depends on the consent of the governed, social scientists could contribute to more effective democratic processes because they could help leaders obtain consent more easily. The authors designated this role for themselves in the beginning of the report, where they argued that in the "exacting times which lie ahead . . . public opinion will be a decisive factor":

> If America is to meet the necessity of adapting to a changing world, and at the same time preserve the ways of life that Americans hold dear, that adaptation must be achieved with public consent. In securing that consent, public opinion and the influences affecting it will be crucial. We believe . . . that for leadership to secure that consent will require unprecedented knowledge of the public mind and of the means by which leadership can secure consent. . . . We believe . . . that we have available today methods of research which can reliably inform us about the public mind and how it is being, or can be, influenced in relation to public affairs.

Whatever ambivalence the group had once had about manipulating, or shaping, public opinion had dissolved by July 1940. This document explicitly argued that members should make their consent-manufacturing services available to those in power by making the public mind available to the leadership. Redolent of Lippmann's suggestion that experts could use public opinion to "compose the crisis," the Communications Group wrote: "As in the present crisis, we can anticipate in the future vastly increased responsibilities for government, and a continuing need for education of the public on matters of public policy, *if* leadership is to secure consent. . . . In the race against time which has already begun, we can ill afford to neglect available means of getting data that may be crucial for the solution of our problems." "All that remains to secure the knowledge," it confidently continued, was the application of its research techniques to "the sphere of public policy."

Responses from group members and outside readers once more brought to the surface the tensions raised by the undemocratic and potentially authoritarian assumptions embedded in the report. Group members Charles

Siepmann, Lyman Bryson, and foundation officer Joseph Willits all commented on what they labeled its fascistic tendencies. Perhaps the most horrified response came from Siepmann, whose own language from letters to Marshall had been appropriated in sections of the report. He agreed with most of what he read, especially that researchers could facilitate "two-way" communication between the government and the public. He declared, however, that "research as the essential handmaiden of reform" could easily be mistaken for research as the blunt instrument of authoritarianism: "Public opinion and vested interests are," he said, "violently opposed to such a development which would be labelled as fascist or authoritarian." He implored Marshall and his colleagues to be more specific about the exact role that their proposed agency would have in coordinating and reporting on research and cautioned them against moving their proposed research apparatus within the government. Such activity, although necessary, belonged outside the government, he argued, where it could exert its influence in the same way as any other pressure group in a democratic setting, doing its best to bring about change by intelligent persuasion, not by state-sanctioned coercion.[38]

Lyman Bryson's reaction to the draft was mixed. He felt, on the one hand, that the call to action was neither clear nor literal enough. On the other hand, he thought the memo went too far, treading too close to the slippery slope of fascism, a comparison he explicitly used: "I suppose we are all jittery these days but [one argument] looks to me like something that Herr Goebbels could put out with complete sincerity. . . . I believe that the assertion of the democratic principle should be made without any . . . qualification."[39]

Foundation officer Joseph Willits used the same comparison, blasting Marshall and the seminar for their "semantic evasions" and their antidemocratic prescriptions for public opinion control:

> The preoccupation in this memorandum does not seem to me to be with the critical examination and improvement of what is to be decided upon and put over by government, but with the "putting over" of what has already been decided. . . . Our government may be forced to go in as completely for propaganda as has Mr. Goebbels, especially if it goes to war. But the techniques it needs to employ to make its propaganda effective ought not to be described as a vitalizing of democratic procedure. It too much resembles the methods by which democracy has been destroyed.

At the same time, Willits recognized what he saw as the legitimate and even democracy-enhancing potential of the group's research if differently conceived: "Finding out regularly and completely what the mass of the people feel and believe and think about things and policies is a necessary part of the modern democratic process," he wrote. He went on to say that mass communications technologies had forced a new conception of democratic theory, one that required experts as facilitators or as mediators between the few and the many, but the group had overstepped its bounds by so easily identifying their job as experts in the service of power, not the public.[40]

The Communications Group apparently took these criticisms seriously. In its final report, "Needed Research in Communication," it pulled back considerably from what had been a poorly disguised enthusiasm for social engineering through communications research.[41] The final report reexamined central questions: How could mass communications serve instead of impede or even undermine democracy? How could communications technologies enhance legitimate dialogue between leaders and the public? How could experts promote two-way dialogue, instead of top-down or one-way communication? And could researchers do those things they understood how to do—conduct interviews, take straw polls, and analyze media content—and enhance democratic processes?

"Democracy," the group asserted in its revised final report, "cannot survive without two-way communication." "From democratic government comes a stream of proposal, explanation, and decision. From the people comes an answering stream of counter-proposal, explanation, and consent, which the government takes into account in final decision and administration. If this two-way process of communication does not function, democracy *is* endangered." Communication experts should facilitate this dialogue, the report asserted, but with less attention to what Willits called "putting over" the government's message and more attention to providing better exchanges between the governed and the government. It restated Marshall's case for genuine knowledge as the democratic alternative to propaganda, an antidote to the presumption of the public's incompetence. Research could be used not to predict, shape, and manipulate popular opinion but to generate intelligent discussion and even dissent: "Democracy requires intelligent consent—or dissent—or discussion—for its proposals." Research, it declared, "will both report and weigh what the people themselves have to say when a proposal's costs and gains *to them* have been sufficiently explained to allow for a considered judgment." With the aid of science, an intelligent, rational, engaged citizenry could thus be restored to the center of democratic theory.

Chastened by warnings about their earlier antidemocratic assumptions, committee members acknowledged the danger of authoritarianism but reiterated their good intentions:

> The same research could, to be sure, be used to turn communication into powerful propaganda, if those responsible chose to do so. That, it seems, is a risk which must be taken with all research which has the possibility of application for authoritarian ends. If, however, those responsible, whoever they may be, wish to avoid authoritarian controls, the contributions which research can make can be the means of strengthening one of the essential phases of the democratic process. That process hitherto has been endangered in times of increased tension more by ignorance than by intention.

The next step, they argued, was to mobilize their work. Putting the extant Rockefeller Foundation–sponsored projects into action should be the first step in meeting emergency needs. They identified as key projects Douglas Waples's work on reading behavior and print communications at the Graduate Library School at Chicago, Lazarsfeld's Office of Radio Research at Columbia, Slesinger's American Film Center and Leo Rosten's Motion Picture Research Project in Hollywood, Cantril's Public Opinion Research Project at Princeton, Harwood Child's Shortwave Listening Center at Princeton, and Lasswell's new "World Attention Survey" project on the flow of wartime communications in Great Britain and Canada. These "Needed Research" projects could become training sites for additional communications analysts and points of contact between the government and academic specialists.

Each seminar member sent copies of "Needed Research in Communication" to interested parties, including other communications research scholars, university presidents, other foundation officers, publishers, jurists, and federal government officials. Recipients included, among others, Archibald MacLeish, Adolph Berle, Bronislaw Malinowski, Robert Maynard Hutchins, Louis Wirth, Henry R. Luce, Carl Friedrich, Talcott Parsons, Max Lerner, Jerome Frank, Lowell Mellet, Thurman Arnold, William O. Douglas, and Beardsley Ruml.[42] Marshall, with his chief ally, Lasswell, sought out government officials and quietly made it known foundation monies might be available to facilitate communications research needed by the government.[43]

Marshall believed that the foundation had a responsibility (to the nation and to the European democracies) to enhance the nation's preparation for war. In May 1940 he wrote that the foundation had an obligation to "make available to the country the intellectual resources which its work over the last twenty years has been an important factor in building up."[44] Marshall's logic held sway, as the Rockefeller Foundation generously financed propaganda defense research, supported promising U.S. scholars and European refugee scholars in their collaborative science-and-security efforts, and helped set in motion vitally important exchanges of information and personnel between allied intelligence projects and U.S. ones.

By September 1940, one year after the outbreak of the European war, Marshall reported to his fellow officers the need to continue supporting both scientific and security-geared research projects. Borrowing from Lasswell's explanation of what propaganda does, he announced that the foundation's projects would engage "the three-fold task of maintaining civilian morale at home, of maintaining good relations with friendly countries, and of waging propaganda warfare with countries hostile to us." Knowing that he would encounter objections to the foundation's involvement in morale and propaganda work, he somewhat disingenuously wrote, "Whether or not this is something for the Foundation to consider, I do not know. . . . But the early neglect of this type of study [by others] may mean that it is the only agency as yet ready to recognize its importance and to provide the necessary funds."[45]

Marshall was a determined interventionist and unequivocal about the foundation's responsibility to mobilize intellectual resources. He explained to fellow foundation officers the scope of national security–related projects the Humanities Division should support, projects that would advance both social science methods and security needs. He also pointed to holes in national-security areas and argued that it was the foundation's job to fill them, even if it meant that scientific interests would be temporarily suspended. Relying on the recommendations of the Communications Group, he explained: "It seems to those of us in that group only prudent that preparation should be underway for determining communication policies necessary if world events force this country into war."[46]

The foundation had begun laying such groundwork through the Shortwave Radio Listening Center at Princeton and through Lasswell's analysis of the mobilization of public opinion in England and Canada. However, Marshall said, "these two studies represent only a beginning. Preparation logically ought to include much more comprehensive studies of the flow of German communication at least, and perhaps Italian communication as well." The foundation should begin sponsoring more extensive analysis of the Fascist use of film and radio, he reported, noting that arrangements had already been made to procure "confidential materials which provide a complete record of relevant German and Italian domestic broadcasting since last December, and the Film Library of the Museum of Modern Art has at least some German films of this period."[47] Clearly, Marshall and the seminar members had been preparing the way for extensive propaganda intelligence on several fronts by the time of Marshall's 1940 report to his fellow officers. They had identified work that needed to be done, what the foundation could do, who could do the work, and where it could be done. This represented a significant leap into the potentially politically dangerous domain of propaganda intelligence.

Other foundation officers knew that propaganda-related work would be controversial but entirely necessary, especially given the absence of such preparation in the federal government. Stacy May, who was working with the Office of Emergency Management on scientific preparedness, told Marshall that "the last war left the country suspicious of propaganda," meaning government agencies would be "slow to develop 'morale' activities for fear of being accused of propagandizing. Everyone seems to believe the situation delicate in the extreme. Certainly the isolationist group would be quick to pounce on any known move in the executive branch that could be ticketed with the label 'Propaganda.' "[48] Marshall agreed, remarking that even the label "communications research" was tainted by anxieties about government propaganda activities; despite the "growing recognition of the need for such research," any such activities by the Roosevelt administration "would not be looked on favorably by Congress," he wrote. He and May understood that " 'morale' for the present [would] be left to agencies outside the government" and that it should continue to be the foundation's job to develop those activities.[49] Therefore, despite fears of censure and even congressional retaliation, Marshall and his fellow officers agreed that "until government support is available . . . and that may be some little time yet," the foundation should continue to take responsibility for "the type of work which later may be needed in national defense."[50]

Throughout 1940 the Humanities Division continued mobilizing institutional and intellectual resources for war-related communications research. Much of the work began within the individual research projects, and each of the media projects established before 1940 was tied into at least some security-related research by the end of that year, including those at the Princeton Public Opinion Research Project and the Princeton cum Columbia Office of Radio Research, the Graduate Library at the University of Chicago, the American Film Center, and the Museum of Modern Art. Other ad hoc projects established between late 1939 and early 1941 for the sole purpose of war-related work included Lasswell's Experimental Division at the Library of Congress, the Princeton and Stanford Shortwave Listening Centers, the New School project on totalitarian communications, and Siegfried Kracauer's study of Nazi film at the Museum of Mod-

ern Art's Film Library. Indeed, Marshall's question as to whether this mobilization was something for the "Foundation to consider" was merely
rhetorical. By the time Attorney General Robert Jackson announced the
U.S. Justice Department's program to create a special propaganda defense
unit in spring 1940, the Rockefeller Foundation's Humanities Division
had already erected an extensive, coordinated network of propaganda research projects, and listening posts to monitor, document, and analyze the
international traffic in propaganda, especially the Fascist variety.[51]

The Rockefeller Projects at War

Not all the foundation's projects were oriented toward defensive propaganda work, but they were nevertheless important components of the foundation's wartime communications research network. Donald Slesinger's American Film Center was one such project.

In July 1938 Donald Slesinger proposed to David Stevens and John
Marshall that he establish a central consulting agency for educational and
documentary film production in the United States. His interest, he said,
was not a propagandistic one; rather, it was in "helping furnish the common experience basic to democratic government."[52] A more adequate
adult education film industry could help achieve this Deweyan ideal.
Slesinger explained that his interests in film arose out of educational theory and he had "the strong conviction that, while science is the instrument
of research, art is the instrument of teaching." At the University of Chicago he had found newsreels an "excellent social science teaching instrument," and when he went to New York "it was in pursuit of ways of using
social science material in popular education."[53] On the staff of the Twentieth Century Fund, Slesinger made contacts with people in the motion
picture field and helped establish a motion picture unit called American
Documentary Film, Inc.[54] His experiences made him realize that "what
the field needed was not another producing unit but some central thinking and planning unit . . . an organization that would serve as a connecting link between science . . . and the art of the motion picture."[55]

Slesinger's aspirations comported with Stevens's and Marshall's interests
in expanding the foundation's commitments to film as an educational tool.
Marshall was especially influenced in these matters by the documentary
filmmaker John Grierson of the London Film Centre (also of the BBC and
the Canadian Film Board during the war), who thought the Rockefeller
Foundation should contribute to the development of the documentary
film industry. Marshall and Slesinger thus modeled the American Film
Center (AFC) on Grierson's Film Centre and got it rolling in November

1938 with two small grants.[56] The AFC operated as an "advisory link between public service agencies and educational groups" who could not produce their films without the aid of philanthropy. But it was also expected
to be a filter of sorts, providing background material to the foundation
about the purposes and interests of would-be film producers. Slesinger resigned his other positions, including that of director of education for the
New York World's Fair, and committed himself full time to the center, with
Alice Keliher and Luther Gulick as his primary associates.[57]

The American Film Center's first months were spent making contacts
within a cross-section of private and public filmmaking institutions, including the "March of Time" producers, the film division of the Department of Interior, Nelson Rockefeller's Division of Cultural Relations of
the Department of State, the New York City Department of Health, the
U.S. Public Health Service, the U.S. Film Service, and others. Essentially,
Slesinger established connections with those entities primarily involved in
educational and documentary film production and those in need of films
to serve their constituencies. The AFC created a niche, and by the end of
1938 it was involved with film projects on syphilis, citizenship, and nutrition. It also went right to work for Nelson Rockefeller's State Department
division, organizing an exchange of cultural and educational films between
North and Latin America.[58] Slesinger came to believe fairly early on that
the Film Center would fill the void left by the demise of the U.S. Film Service, which apparently had "antagonized all branches of Government, including the Division of Cultural Relations." As a consequence, Slesinger
and Marshall both expected the AFC to serve a variety of government
agencies.[59] Quite clearly, this was not social science aimed at upsetting the
status quo.

In early 1939 the Humanities Division extended Slesinger a two-year
grant for $60,000.[60] Although the foundation supported other film pro-
duction and distribution organizations at this time, the AFC's agenda was
the most far-reaching. By "keeping its single aim—the promotion of the
production and use of films of educational value—constantly before it,"
Slesinger vowed, the AFC's purposes would always be "education, broadly interpreted."[61] How these educational purposes shifted toward wartime
purposes is an interesting story and illustrates just how broadly John Marshall conceived of the foundation's role within an emerging field of film
intelligence and propaganda.

Under Marshall's guidance, the AFC pursued projects related to both
science and security. Marshall was interested in greater analytical and social scientific understanding of the role of film in modern U.S. society. Besides supporting Leo Rosten's study of Hollywood under AFC auspices,

foundation grants to the American Film Center in 1940 and 1941 included monies for film content analysis studies guided by Lasswell and Leo Rosten and motion picture audience research directed by anthropologist Geoffrey Gorer. Gorer's work on film audiences became a key component of the AFC's overall research agenda, and Marshall compared it in importance to the radio audience research at Columbia under Lazarsfeld.

Marshall, Slesinger, and Gorer (and, to a lesser extent, Lasswell) also expanded the Film Center's work in the international sphere. By May 1940 the AFC and the U.S. Committee on Intellectual Cooperation formed the International Film Center (IFC). Established as the international arm of the AFC, the IFC supplied films abroad for the State and Agriculture Departments, brought foreign films into U.S. schools for the Institute of Pacific Relations (another recipient of foundation monies), brought British films into the United States for the British Library of Information, and continued to work with Nelson Rockefeller's office on North and Latin American cultural relations. Creating common cultural understanding and empathy was the stated educational and political goal of the IFC. It also augmented the flow of personnel and information among governmental, educational, and commercial institutions.[62]

The AFC's work was not without propaganda applications, as Donald Slesinger knew. Slesinger was remarkably candid about the value of social science experts using their skills and knowledge to shape political consensus. In a memorandum to Stacy May in June 1940, for instance, Slesinger outlined the AFC's potential propaganda activities, describing how the AFC should be involved in organizing and controlling the instruments of mass communication in the United States in order to achieve public "unity." Given how Slesinger chastised members of the Communications Seminar for their authoritarian assumptions, it is ironic that he was capable of making the arguments he did about using film as an instrument of opinion control; on the other hand, perhaps he had simply been convinced by his colleagues that they could achieve a democracy-enhancing balance between education and propaganda. Either way, he argued that under emergency conditions generating political unity by controlling the flow of information was worth the slight risk of compromising democracy: "The chief problem in the period immediately ahead is to develop the unity necessary to meet contemporary world conditions at the smallest possible sacrifice of the freedom for which we stand. In preserving that balance, the mass communications have a peculiar responsibility and opportunity." He said that his AFC could help achieve this balance and enthusiastically announced that the "greatest success will arise from an intelligent coordination of all of the means of communication." Caught up in the moment, he continued: "From time to time it may be desirable to reach a public more or less simultaneously with a persuasive communication in film." To do so, "distribution facilities must be organized on an unprecedented scale."[63]

He went on, proposing that the Film Center make an inventory of all the film projectors in the entire country—"projectors should be subject to call by the government . . . as are radio facilities"—and it should coordinate the nationwide distribution of films in order to make possible these moments of "simultaneous" unity. Appropriately, he invoked the analogy of George Creel's choreography of public unity during WWI, describing how the propaganda films could be "exhibited in theatres, concer[t] halls, schools, clubs, union halls, churches, and homes." Anticipating by several years the Office of War Information's controversial Hollywood bureau, Slesinger also suggested that the Film Center and the National Defense Council should exert control over the content of entertainment and documentary films by setting up a scripts department. Apparently the prospect of power was heady stuff for Slesinger. Certainly, his blueprint for manufacturing public unity undermines the credibility of his own umbrage at other seminar members' authoritarian enthusiasms.

As war drew nearer, Slesinger continued to formulate these same media-coordination fantasies in other documents, where he virtually collapsed the distinction between education and propaganda.[64] In an August 1941 letter to Marshall, for instance, he explained in phrases and categories redolent of Lasswell how the AFC's work could contribute to the great battle for the minds of the "masses": "The development of mass education by film depends on (at least) three things: (1) We must learn the proportion of attention getting and teaching material that will win for the maximum audience the maximum effective teaching. (2) We must develop national distribution at all intellectual and economic levels. (3) We must have a coordinated educational or propaganda plan so that the audiences won can have regular exposure to films."[65] Although he never gained the U.S. film ministry he fancied, Slesinger certainly gave voice to the Lippmannesque idea that scientifically trained experts could deliver the masses to the leaders in times of crisis, if given the opportunity.

By the time the United States began fighting the war, Slesinger and his assistant, John Devine, had achieved a considerable constituency for the center within the federal government.[66] By the end of the first year of war, the AFC had achieved, according to Slesinger, "complete direction of the use of film in the Office of Civilian Defense, with eight films in production." It had also contracted with the overseas division of the Office of War Information (OWI) to "catalogue and appraise films which can be advantageously used abroad."[67] As Slesinger had surmised, the war created new possibilities for those involved in film and "educational" work: "To sum up, our work with government and educational institutions has now put us in an extremely strategic position in the domestic and international film field." Alluding to the AFC's putative educational objectives and its long-term economic security, he continued: "I foresee by the end of the war a domestic and international system of distribution and a type of production that will be all any of us hoped for when we started thinking about the place of the medium in mass education."[68]

The foundation continued funding the AFC's wartime work, providing a grant for $50,000 for 1943 and 1944.[69] Apparently Slesinger's self-interested assessment of the AFC's importance within the U.S. wartime filmmaking industry was not without merit. When Marshall went to Washington at the end of 1942 to discuss the center's government work, he learned that it was both reliable and relied on. Leo Rosten, who left the foundation-AFC nexus to become a deputy to Gardiner Cowles in the OWI's film division, told Marshall that the AFC had "exerted a stabilizing influence" in Washington and that "there is no question that Slesinger's advice has been generally sought and respected."[70]

E. A. Sheridan of the Office of Civilian Defense (OCD) confirmed these reports, telling Marshall that before his contact with the AFC, the OCD had made no progress in the use of film. "Now," Marshall reported in his notes, Sheridan "had simply turned all work with film over to AFC. This is proving entirely satisfactory. . . . Its readiness to serve had simply solved a problem which previously seemed insoluble."[71] And Luther Gulick, who was both president of the AFC and director of the Office of Organizational Planning for the War Production Board, told Marshall that the foundation's monies had helped the AFC attain a well-regarded independent status. Gulick said the AFC was free of being associated with any one agency or department and was recognized for being "educational and scientific."[72] The AFC was "generally recognized as representing the truly educational values of work with film," and its "reputation and product has been influential in making the documentary film respectable," Rosten told Marshall, alluding to the political respectability he had helped documentaries achieve by making them instruments for established institutions, not just for partisans of the left.[73]

By July 1943, however, Congress had slashed domestic propaganda filmmaking budgets, eliminating the AFC's main government client, the Office of Civilian Defense.[74] As a result, the AFC began moving out of war work in mid-1943, turning its attention to finding a "strategic" position outside the government.[75] In this respect, the Film Center's trajectory was similar to the other foundation-sponsored media research units: It started with a combined academic and industry-consulting agenda in the late 1930s. It shifted its resources and personnel to defense-related problems well before the United States was officially involved in the war and in so doing laid the groundwork for valuable wartime work. Having done its job, it returned to the world of academic and industry-related work, with valuable experience and a strong reputation earned along the way. Additionally, its personnel had learned a thing or two about the world of opinion formation and the power of technology.

As at the beginning of the war, Slesinger's late-war thoughts about the "place of the medium in mass education" were that mass education and propaganda were not really separable.[76] In a postwar world where competing ideologies would continue to define the terrain on which intellectuals would labor, education and propaganda probably should not be separated, he told the AFC's board of directors. Slesinger restated his formulation that film was a crucial vehicle for mass education and that those interested in maintaining social stability would do well to coordinate its uses. He wrote: "No problem of the postwar world will be solved without an extensive use of adult education. . . . The problem is to reach—and teach—the free, unmotivated citizen. And that will involve an ingenious use and coordination of the mass media of communication." The difference between our propaganda and theirs, he suggested, was the difference between truth and lies, "so, perhaps through no virtue of our own we are forced to fall back on the propaganda of truth as we see it, and that means falling back on education."[77] The problem was not the absence of a message of truth. Rather, the problem toward the end of the war was the same as it had been before the war: how to capture and maintain the interest of the uninterested masses. There was, Slesinger implied, plenty of ideological work for social scientists to do in the postwar world in the cause of disseminating the "truth" against a "lie"-spewing enemy.

Utilizing European Refugees

Slesinger's project was an anomaly in the larger scheme of the foundation's communications projects in that the prominent feature of most was not their propaganda production value but rather their work providing a defense against the "lies" of foreign, especially Nazi, propaganda.

The projects at the Museum of Modern Art's Film Library, the Totalitarian Communications Project at the New School, and the Princeton Listening Center illustrate this pattern and elucidate Marshall's overall agenda: he drew on a range of institutions to carry out this work; he took advantage of the resources of an international community, including émigré scholars; he ensured that all channels of communications would be studied and monitored; and he recognized that setting up research projects as training sites would be a crucial foundation contribution to the allied war effort. The Film Library, New School, and Listening Post projects manifested Marshall's understanding that all propaganda channels would be employed by the enemy, that they should be carefully studied, and that personnel should be trained in the latest social science techniques for emergency work in communications surveillance and analysis.

The Rockefeller Foundation, of course, had had a relationship with the Museum of Modern Art dating from the museum's establishment in 1929. The Rockefeller family was the museum's chief founder and benefactor, and family members and foundation officers were always on the museum's board of trustees. With the coordinator of Inter-American Affairs, Nelson Rockefeller, on its board of directors—along with Archibald MacLeish, the director of the Office of Facts and Figures and Librarian of Congress—the entire Museum of Modern Art (MoMA) was obviously likely to use its various resources for the Allied war effort. By June 1941 those resources were involved at many levels.

For instance, the museum provided office space and service for eighteen members of Nelson Rockefeller's Inter-American Affairs staff. Thirteen members of the museum's own staff devoted "a major portion of their time" working for the coordinator's office as well.[78] MoMA developed art and film exhibits for distribution to ten different Latin American countries and housed several exhibits of Latin American art, architecture, and other cultural forms in 1941.[79] It also circulated fifteen different wartime exhibits to ninety-three U.S. cities, featured a British war documentary film series, held a major exhibit entitled "Britain at War," and much more. In short, MoMA utilized its cultural arsenal as part of the Allied mobilization, even before the United States was at war. A 1941 "Project Memorandum" for the board of directors explained: "In planning the Museum's program through the last year or two, it has seemed essential and advisable to bear in mind the national and international problem." The authors further noted that "consciousness of the need for building American morale and furthering cultural relations" shaped its agenda.[80]

John Marshall's associations with the museum in the prewar period had to do primarily with facilitating the establishment of the Museum's Film Library. The original purposes behind the library were educational in both an Arnoldian sense ("to create discrimination among motion picture goers by giving them a chance to see the best and most significant films that had been produced in earlier years") and in a scholarly sense (to provide "authentic material on the film and its production"). Established as an educational resource for the public, as an archive for film historians and scholars, and as a resource for college and university teachers developing film studies as an academic field, the Film Library became an internationally recognized institution whose holdings were the largest in the world by 1939.[81] By 1941 the foundation had given $270,000 to the Film Library.[82]

As codirectors of the Film Library, John Abbot and Iris Barry put their resources to use for the war effort. Like the other MoMA operations, the Film Library performed extensive film intelligence and cultural relations work for Nelson Rockefeller's office. By June 1942 it had "analyzed and reported upon 3,800,000 feet of film" and made over six hundred prints of different films in Spanish and Portuguese for shipment to Latin America. The Film Library also produced an eleven-reel subject entitled "German Propaganda Films, 1934–1940"; it was prepared and distributed to twenty-five different wartime agencies and departments at Nelson Rockefeller's personal expense. Additionally, the library provided research services, film copies, and in-house studies to the official propaganda production and monitoring agencies, including the Office of Facts and Figures, the Coordinator of Information, the Office of War Information, the Office of Emergency Management, the Departments of Justice, State, and Agriculture, and the Intelligence divisions of the Navy and War departments. And, through the elaborate negotiations of John Grierson of the Canadian Film Board, Marshall, and Archibald MacLeish, it provided copies of captured German films to Army Signal Corps Major Frank Capra.[83]

The library's major study of Nazi propaganda films began in June 1941 with a foundation grant for the German refugee Dr. Siegfried Kracauer. Kracauer, who had been a film critic for the *Frankfurter Zeitung*, came to the United States in 1941. Through the intermediation of Iris Barry, he was funded for several years for a series of studies of German film. Marshall hoped Kracauer's work would be coordinated with the other Nazi propaganda content studies, including Lasswell's Library of Congress project, the Shortwave Listening Centers, and especially the New School project.[84] His 1941 grant expressed the importance of the project's immediate utility: that it would "provide data basic for an understanding of wartime communication while such data can be put to practical use."[85] Marshall told Barry that "he felt that Krakauer [*sic*] ought to be primarily concerned with developing methods for analyzing the German films which could be taken over and more extensively applied by other agencies."[86] Iris Barry's aspirations were similar, although adjusted to accommodate the more theoretical nature of Kracauer's work; she thought Kracauer should "serve as a kind of theorist in the work which the Film Library is now contracting to undertake for government agencies."[87]

In his two-year tenure at the Film Library, Kracauer was highly productive. By June 1942 he completed the first study he was funded to produce, "Propaganda and the Nazi War Film," printed and issued by the Film Library in July 1942 as a confidential document for government agencies. By September of the same year he completed another study of Nazi films, "The Conquest of Europe on the Screen: The Nazi Newsreel, 1939–1940," published the following year in *Social Research*. And, while in residence at the Film Library, Kracauer also began his famous study *From Caligari to Hitler: A Psychological History of the German Film*, published in 1946. His first Film Library study, "Propaganda and the Nazi War Film," was published as the "Supplement" in *Caligari to Hitler*.[88]

"Propaganda and the Nazi War Film" was less concerned with social science methods than were the other propaganda studies conducted elsewhere. Kracauer was interested instead, Marshall noted, with developing a "grammar" of the Nazi propaganda films and drew on film narrative analysis techniques set within a larger psychoanalytic and cultural framework. His "dramaturgical" readings of Nazi newsreels, entertainment films, and full-blown "propaganda epics" staged as documentaries were studies Marshall and Barry found acutely intelligent and valuable for understanding the rhetorical strategies of totalitarian propaganda.[89]

Kracauer developed his study around a cluster of closely related ideas, beginning with the argument that "the natural inclination of Germans" to think in "anti-rational, mythological terms" was seized on and reinforced by the Nazis to create a "new order" mythology.[90] From there he developed the idea that the function of all types of film—entertainment, documentaries, and newsreels—within the totalitarian propaganda strategy was to replace or transform reality with an elaborately orchestrated "pseudo-reality" he called the "Swastika reality." Totalitarianism, he argued, subordinated all values, especially individual ones; the Nazis used film as part of a total strategy to "sterilize the mind" and "counterfeit life" in order to press it into the service of the "Swastika world."[91] All films under Hitler's regime, he argued, were necessarily propagandistic and constructed to produce a reverence for power. Finally, Kracauer said, the Nazi ideology was "sterile at the core" and governed by a "nihilistic lust for domination" that respected "nothing but naked power."[92]

Marshall appreciated what he called the "strictly humanistic outcomes" of Kracauer's work and praised it for its "genuine esthetic criticism" and "solid criticism which is based on careful study and analysis."[93] Moreover, Kracauer had employed the "objective techniques of analysis" proffered by the New School's Ernst Kris and Hans Speier.[94] Mostly Marshall was taken by Kracauer's "unusual maturity," "modesty," and justness. In a December 1942 report Marshall noted that he had "come to regard Kracauer as one of the ablest refugees I've encountered" and that Kracauer had demonstrated "an unusual clarity in his writing," "most unusual" penetration in his thinking, and "painstaking ability in research" and also had "brought to this country an unusual acquaintance with German films." In all, Marshall thought Kracauer provided "something which I think criticism in this country sorely needs": a deep sense of the importance of cultural and historical contexts as explanatory factors in film analysis.[95] Marshall and Barry managed to keep Kracauer supported with foundation monies into 1943, enabling him to get started on his famous historical study. Because of budgetary limits and his status as an enemy alien, they could not give him permanent employment at the Museum of Modern Art. They did, however, help him win grants from the Guggenheim Foundation, with which he was able to complete *From Caligari to Hitler* in 1945.

Marshall and the foundation supported other émigrés as well. As Marshall pointed out on several occasions, Ernst Kris and Hans Speier at the New School influenced Kracauer's work methodologically, and he corroborated the results of their work on Nazi radio propaganda. Kris and Speier came into the foundation's orbit in late 1940, when Marshall began helping the Viennese exile Kris get set up in the United States to monitor German radio broadcasts, work he had begun in England.

Kris was trained as an art historian and was a colleague of Freud in Vienna. Before the Nazi Anschluss in Austria in 1938, he left for London, and he spent 1939–1940 as a senior research officer in the BBC's Monitoring Service, training BBC radio analysts about German propaganda strategies, and producing the BBC's *Daily Digests of Foreign Broadcasts*. Because of his value as an anti-Nazi analyst, he received a temporary visa to go to Canada when it appeared that all enemy aliens in England would be interned. Receiving haven in the United States in late 1940, Kris immediately began serving as a consultant on propaganda matters for a number of agencies, including the National Defense Commission.[96]

Kris came to North America with strong credentials and the recommendations of British colleagues, who described him as a valuable resource for guiding U.S. radio analysis, a development they thought the United States had been laggard in undertaking. Lasswell, Marshall recorded, thought Kris was "a fine speculative thinker, but someone whose speculation must be kept in touch with evidence" (Kris, in turn, thought Lasswell a "first-class technician" who was nevertheless "bound by his techniques").

Like Marshall, Kris believed the United States drastically needed to expand its radio intelligence work, in part because Nazi communications could be profitably studied for understanding the "instructions that underlie [them]," Kris told Marshall.[97] Marshall was impressed with Kris from their first meeting in December 1940 and immediately arranged for him to get together with Lasswell and other foundation officers. "Kris," Marshall noted, "has a line of talk that is well worth hearing," further observing that his "unusual insight into the actual conduct of propaganda in Britain" might make him "the man to undertake a study of the whole complex Nazi *gleichshaltung*."[98] Kris told Marshall he was much interested in this kind of work but that he would not "associate with anyone who is not interested in seeing Germany defeated."[99]

Kris's future partner, Hans Speier, came to the New School when the Hochschule für Politik in Berlin was closed down with Hitler's rise to power. New School president Alvin Johnson provided a position for him at the "University in Exile," and while there he studied militarism and the fascist inclinations of German white-collar culture, taught courses on the sociology of war, and began writing about "morale" issues.[100] Like other German Social Democrats, Speier was appalled by the brutality of Hitler's ascent; he referred to it as "the last fatal step in a decivilization of life."[101] And in 1940 he completed Emil Lederer's study of National Socialism, *State of the Masses: The Threat of the Classless Society* (1940), which Lederer had not finished before his unexpected death.[102]

Speier became acquainted with Kris when the latter took a temporary position at the New School.[103] The two approached Marshall in early 1941 with a proposal for a jointly directed project. When Marshall inquired about Speier, Lasswell told him that Speier was "one of the most distinguished sociologists of his generation" and belonged "to that small group of men capable of balancing rich theoretical perspectives with rigorous technical work on detail."[104] Lasswell appreciated this technical virtuosity, as did New School dean Max Ascoli, who chimed in telling Marshall that Speier was "one of the most valuable" members of the New School faculty and "one of the most skillful and gifted specialists you can find anywhere" for work in the field of propaganda analysis.[105]

When Kris and Speier established the Totalitarian Communications Project at the New School for Social Research, they set it up as a coordinated enterprise with Lasswell's Wartime Communications project at the Library of Congress. As part of the incipient Anglo-American cooperation on propaganda intelligence, the BBC agreed to provide Kris and Speier with its *Daily Digests of Foreign Broadcasts*, each issue of which contained around 30,000 words of German broadcasts related to the war. With this source material, the New School project could employ Lasswellian content analysis techniques to "assemble the evidence these materials afford on the trends and purposes of totalitarian communication, both within Germany and in programs which the Germans have directed toward other countries." But Kris and Speier wanted to go beyond content analysis. They also proposed to develop a history and theory of the "totalitarian theory of propaganda—its formulation in the writings of the totalitarian propagandists . . . the origin and development of this theory . . . and the functions of totalitarian propaganda in wartime, at home and abroad."[106]

One projected outcome was the publication of a book about "one phase of the war waged by Germany—the war of words over the air." The other main goal was that the project would train U.S. personnel for ongoing work of this nature: "A need for American personnel with such training is already evident," noted the Rockefeller grant report.[107] As Speier later noted, this personnel training function became a central and highly valuable feature of the foundation's interest in many of the communications projects: "The Rockefeller Foundation realized that such a project [as his] would give young social scientists an opportunity to be trained in propaganda analysis. These specialists would have useful skills and experiences in the event the United States entered the war. For this reason, Kris and I received the means to employ some assistants and students." But for Speier, the importance of the project was greater than just training personnel. The foundation had provided scholars in exile with a unique opportunity to study the Nazi mind and to develop scientific techniques: "There was at that time no better opportunity in the United States for closely examining the Nazi mentality while trying out new methods of content analysis," Speier recalled.[108]

The foundation provided $15,960 for the initial grant to Kris and Speier in March 1941. Their work was successful enough in its first year that the foundation renewed with $19,000 for another year, despite major changes resulting from the outbreak of war. In the first year the Totalitarian Communications Project yielded three research papers that were circulated among the Communications Group and several government agencies. In addition, it produced five articles. In connection with the project, Speier and Kris also offered at the New School a seminar on wartime propaganda that drew considerable interest to the work they were doing and attracted many well-qualified volunteers who produced an additional eighteen related research papers during the first year of work.[109]

More important, the work attracted the notice of federal officials responsible for communications intelligence. In early 1942 the Federal Communications Commission (FCC) appointed Speier as senior analyst of the

German section in the FCC's Foreign Broadcast Monitoring Service (FBMS). Speier's commitment to this government post drew him away from the Totalitarian Communications project in its second year, but it provided the project's personnel with a direct line to the government orbit. This in turn exposed a much larger group of social scientists to training in its methods. Speier's influence meant that the project's work became closely articulated with the work carried out in different government agencies, especially the FCC and Colonel William B. Donovan's Office of the Coordinator of Information, precursor to the Office of Strategic Services.[110]

Because Ernst Kris had enemy alien status, he could not take on any government employment except through contract work. Despite this, the foundation kept the New School project going through early 1943. True to Marshall's announcement in 1940 that short-term emergency needs should not overwhelm the longer-term goals of quality research and scholarship, the foundation continued funding Kris's work because of its contributions to modern media scholarship. The grant report said: "The recommendation [to renew the grant] rests on the officers' belief in the long-term value of such studies, quite apart from what immediate utility their results may have during the war. Methods of analysis developed by these studies will undoubtedly have more general application in the study of mass communication after the war. The project is making a fundamental contribution toward a better knowledge of the part of mass communication in modern life."[111] The project was terminated at the end of June 1943, with a final grant for $350 for publication of Kris and Speier's *German Radio Propaganda*, published in 1944.[112]

Under Marshall's guidance, the foundation made two other groundbreaking contributions to prewar radio intelligence and training: the establishment of the Shortwave Listening Centers at Princeton and Stanford. The Princeton project, in particular, paralleled the trajectory of the other propaganda-analysis projects. Set up by John B. Whitton in 1939 under the auspices of the Princeton School of Public and International Affairs, this shortwave listening post was the prototype for the FCC's FBMS. With a two-year grant of $39,820, beginning in January 1939, Whitton and political scientist Harwood Childs established the Listening Center to analyze shortwave propaganda beamed from Europe. (They made recordings of the broadcasts on wax cylinders from which they compiled transcriptions and translations.) Their aim was to determine how these broadcasts influenced the war reporting of domestic foreign-language newspapers, in particular. Lasswell certainly recognized the value of the Princeton Listening Center's work, noting that it had "built up a body of basic records of great importance for the study of mass communication, for nowhere else on the American continent is there such a comprehensive collection of shortwave broadcasts."[113] In early 1941 the federal government established the Foreign Broadcast Monitoring Service and absorbed the Princeton Listening Center into its fold, with Princeton's Harold Graves appointed as director. By March 1941 the FBMS had a staff of 350, monitoring shortwave broadcasts twenty-four hours a day.[114]

The similar project at Stanford University was set up in connection with the Hoover Library on War, Revolution, and Peace, under the direction of Stanford president Dr. Ray Lyman Wilbur. The foundation provided a grant for $8,250, from November 1940 to May 1941, to fund the recording and transcription of shortwave broadcasts from Tokyo, Chungking, and Saigon and to "furnish an historical tracing of developments in the Pacific Area related to international affairs." This project was discontinued in June 1941, when the FBMS set up its own facilities for monitoring Far Eastern broadcasting. In August 1942, however, the FCC turned to the Stanford site again, and thereafter it functioned, under foundation subvention, as an FCC substation and an Office of War Information broadcasting station to beam U.S. propaganda to Thailand.[115]

While these projects were innovative, vital, and intellectually and ideologically committed to the same goals, the most important of the war-era projects for the purposes of defeating Nazi propaganda efforts in the United States may well have been Lasswell's project at the Library of Congress.

Finding a Home for Lasswell

Because Lasswell did not have a full-time university base of operations on the eve of WWII, Marshall championed his cause within the foundation. In late 1939 and again in early 1940, Lasswell solicited Rockefeller Foundation support for several research grants to study wartime communication trends in Canada, Asia, and Europe. He and Marshall both appealed to foundation officials' concerns about national security, arguing that U.S. scholars needed to prepare the nation for the communications warfare that would accompany military and economic warfare. Lasswell couched his proposals in scholarly terms, suggesting that he would update his 1927 study, *Propaganda Technique in the World War*, developing more specific and better-tested content analysis categories and providing a history of propaganda technique developments since World War I. He made no real distinctions, however, between scholarship and politics or among his science of content analysis, his expertise about propaganda, and the uses of his work in the policy arena. His proposals were filled with technical descriptions of research problems, couched in the terminology of social scientific rigor, but he was after bigger game than mere science.

Lasswell's May 1940 proposal, "A Study of Public Communication in Wartime," posed a series of problems confronting liberal states. First, how did liberal democracies resolve the conflict between their commitments to open channels of communication and the simultaneous need to control those channels? For Lasswell, the value of this line of inquiry was obvious, and he was sure that the experiences of Britain and France early in war could "be at once a guide and a warning to America." He did not dwell for long on the civil liberties dilemma but instead quickly moved on to other intelligence-oriented questions. He was more interested in analyzing how the totalitarian states handled their "channels of public intelligence" in wartime. Like Kris and Speier, he argued that "one problem of democracies is to guess right about their antagonists." Research on the garrison states' uses of communications channels should help to predict their military and political behaviors, he argued. Additionally, Lasswell wanted to address the matter of developing a U.S. propaganda strategy: on the basis of studying other nations' communications trends, how could the democracies develop strategies to influence the attitudes and behavior of their allies and enemies? Repeating themes from his 1927 study, he said: "We may need to know how to contribute to the preserving of morale in Britain and France, and how to disintegrate the morale of Germany."

To develop these issues, Lasswell proposed a menu of research problems, including the development of better coding techniques for content analysis; monitoring the press and radio of virtually every major country; providing historical background studies; and suggesting possible strategies for a U.S. propaganda policy. This ambitious agenda envisioned a major research facility with access to vast amounts of continually updated information. It would require assistants. And it would depend on acquiring raw data from other intelligence-gathering operations.

The scope of his proposal and his obvious desire to affect policy matters left Lasswell open to criticism from foundation personnel. But Marshall fended off those criticisms. For Marshall, the methodological and policy values of Lasswell's work were both obvious and worthy of support. He told one skeptic, Joseph Willits, that the risk entailed in enabling Lasswell to refine his content analysis method writ large was worth it, particularly given Lasswell's scholarly integrity: "I think it has to be assumed then that the method cannot be finally defined except in some such work as Lasswell wishes to undertake. . . . I should think we might expect systematic analysis of a pretty high order of objectivity."[116] Besides, Marshall argued, the ideological weapons of modern warfare needed further study, and Lasswell could offer vital historical background on the evolution of propaganda as a strategy as well as specific documentation on the expanding European war.

For Marshall, the emergency determined the value of this work, and Lasswell's communications intelligence orientation should not necessarily be subordinated to the foundation's interest in science per se: "In ordinary times the content and effect of current mass communication is as yet a matter of only academic interest; but, when in periods of emergency the state of public opinion becomes a matter of national interest, the need rises to have as a basis for executive decisions some reliable indices of the content and effect of mass communication." Lasswell's techniques promised "reliable and useful findings," and foundation support would have a "two-fold utility." First, it would inform policy making in the United States, and, second, even if the results were not useful for policy makers, the foundation would have advanced the scientific development of the field by enabling Lasswell to develop "reliable methods of analysing the content of current mass communication."[117]

After providing Lasswell the small first grant to get his wartime communications study under way, in autumn 1940 Marshall also approached Archibald MacLeish about housing Lasswell's project at the Library of Congress. As chair of an informal interdepartmental committee on war information, MacLeish was also concerned with getting the nation's communications intelligence apparatus in place, and he "evinced immediate interest in the proposal," Marshall noted.[118] Days later MacLeish confirmed his interest in setting Lasswell up at the library: "Such a project would, in my opinion, be extremely useful to the various departments of this government at the present time and I expect shortly to be able to report to you the attitude of two of those departments [State and Justice]. Meantime, may I say that the Library would be glad to sponsor the project and that a reasonable space can be found for Mr. Lasswell and his assistants."[119]

As one of the men most actively engaged in the capitol's discussions about communications and intelligence needs, Archibald MacLeish recognized the potential utility of Lasswell's work.[120] After confirming his Library's commitment to house Lasswell's project, MacLeish informed Under Secretary of State Welles about Lasswell's work and the foundation's support. Welles replied enthusiastically: "From the standpoint of the Department of State the work which is proposed would be of very great value. I sincerely trust that the Rockefeller Foundation may in fact determine to make the grant so that this important project can be carried through."[121] Solicitor General Francis Biddle gave his support as well: "I sincerely hope that this can be done, and done promptly." He complained there had been "no authoritative information" about the extent of the "foreign propaganda going on in America in the foreign language newspapers, over the radio, or otherwise. No one knows the pattern it is taking." The whole subject was, he said "of vital interest to national defense." And although the Justice Department had collected extensive materials in its files, it was neither authorized nor staffed "to do the kind of careful analytical work which is necessary." Thus the Justice Department was "anxious to cooperate" with MacLeish, Marshall, and Lasswell "in every possible way."[122]

This "quite confidential" exchange of letters among Marshall, MacLeish, Sumner Welles of the State Department, and the Justice Department's Solicitor General Francis Biddle (the latter two were also on the Committee on War Information) verifies that for government planners, the time for developing a coherent propaganda prophylaxis had arrived.[123] Indeed, Marshall, MacLeish, Lasswell, and Biddle's subordinates at the U.S. Department of Justice strove in the fourteen months before the U.S. declaration of war to shape a coherent propaganda defense strategy. Marshall's vision and resources, MacLeish's governmental connections and flexibility, Lasswell's energies, and the Justice Department's need for an effective propaganda defense strategy made it desirable to mobilize available social science personnel in order to enhance U.S. total war capabilities. But the confidentiality of the exchange and subsequent arrangements for Lasswell's project also confirm May's and Marshall's perception about just how delicately the Roosevelt administration—and the Rockefeller Foundation—needed to tread in engaging in any activities that could be labeled as propaganda. The principals involved in the decision to house Lasswell's project in the Library of Congress agreed to keep it quiet, independent of any government agency, and wholly funded by the foundation. While liberal U.S. scholars, administrators, and federal officials considered preparing for war against Nazi propaganda to be a vital national security precaution, such work also produced real skittishness about the dilemmas that such work raised for a liberal democracy.

Long before it was clear that the United States would be a belligerent in WWII, John Marshall recognized that communications research was essential for national security purposes and that the Roosevelt administration was unequipped and politically indisposed to carry out that work. Marshall combined the Rockefeller Foundation's concerns about science and public obligation to give direction to the incipient field of mass communications. He secured monies for promising scholars and their projects and, after a year of meetings and working papers, helped define a role for communication scholars in the emergency and brought their projects into the interstices of the emerging national security state. For Marshall and his fellow foundation officers, the commingling of science and security seemed well justified by the emergency.

Two tables graphically illustrate Marshall's breadth of vision and the importance of the foundation's work in moving these projects into the state. Table 3.1 is my modification of a chart and memorandum prepared for the attorney general by Lawrence M. C. Smith of the Justice Department's Special Defense Unit (SDU), explaining the extant "Public Opinion and Propaganda Intelligence" network in place by April 1941.[124] Three things are striking about table 3.1: First, the SDU, whose operations are centrally presented in the chart, was attempting to cover an extraordinarily wide range of media, materials, and issues and was very dependent on the cooperation of other research and analysis projects. Second, of the twenty-three governmental and public entities engaged in propaganda intelligence work that Smith identifies, nine were financed wholly or in part by the Rockefeller Foundation. Third, of the five categories Smith listed, the Rockefeller projects played important roles in three: attitude and opinion intelligence, foreign press intelligence, and radio intelligence. In short, the Justice Department's propaganda defense strategies depended in large measure on the materials and expertise generated by the Rockefeller-financed radio, print, and film intelligence projects.

Table 3.2 reproduces part of a report produced by Harold Lasswell for the Justice Department and Archibald MacLeish in April or May 1941.[125] It clearly conveys Marshall's vision for Rockefeller Foundation involvement in prewar communications intelligence. What it does not convey, but other records do, is that the project directors consulted frequently on questions of method and technique, shared raw data and finished reports, and exchanged personnel among projects. All were working to develop scientific methods (based on the "who hears what, from whom, and with what effect" model), and most were simultaneously directing their work to the Justice Department and other federal agencies. Lasswell's chart organized the projects according to the geographical origin of the materials analyzed (Europe, Asia, South America, United States); according to medium (print, radio, film); and according to method (content analysis, audience analysis, effects analysis). In short, table 3.2 illustrates how the seminar's new methodological paradigm was worked out in the different Rockefeller projects, and it aptly summarizes the remarkable effort by the Rockefeller Foundation's John Marshall, in collaboration with Lasswell and the others, in putting in place the backbone of the U.S. propaganda defense.

Table 3.1

PUBLIC OPINION AND PROPAGANDA INTELLIGENCE
U.S. and England

ATTITUDE AND OPINION INTELLIGENCE: U.S. AND ABROAD

Department of Agriculture
Gallup
Roper
British Government Morale Reports
*Office of Radio Research
  (Columbia University)
*Reading Research Project
  (University of Chicago)
*Motion Picture Research Project
  (American Film Center)
Public Opinion Quarterly

FOREIGN PRESS INTELLIGENCE

Departments of State, War, Navy
*Library of Congress,
  Experimental Division
Post Office Department
  in Cooperation with
  Department of Justice
*Coordinator of Commercial
  and Cultural Relations
  (Department of State)

DOMESTIC FOREIGN LANGUAGE PRESS INTELLIGENCE

Organizations and Propaganda
Analysis Section
(Department of Justice)

DOMESTIC AND FOREIGN RADIO INTELLIGENCE

*Princeton University Listening Center
*Stanford Universisty Listening Center
*New School for Social Research
CBS, NBC, BBC
Foreign Broadcast Monitoring Service (FCC)

DOMESTIC ENGLISH LANGUAGE PRESS INTELLIGENCE

Office of Government Reports

Based on documents from Special War Policies Unit Records; Folder: Surveillance of Press and Radio; Propaganda
Analysis, Domestic; Box: 75; Record Group 60, National Archives.

*denotes Rockefeller Foundation financial support

Table 3.2   STUDIES OF WARTIME COMMUNICATION

GENERAL	CONTENT			AUDIENCE			RESPONSE
	Print	**Radio**	**Film**	**Print**	**Radio**	**Film**	
	Study of wartime communication H.D. Lasswell, Library of Congress						Princeton Public Opinion Research Project, Hadley Cantril
BY MEDIUM	D of J	FCC	D of J	Graduate Library School, University of Chicago, Douglas Waples	Columbia University Office of Radio Research, Paul Lazarsfeld	American Film Center, Donald Slesinger	
BY AREA							
From Europe		[Princeton Listening Center]	D of J		Princeton School of Public &		
From Far East		[Stanford Listening Center]			International Affairs Harwood S.Childs		
From totalitarian countries		New School for Social Research, Ernst Kris, Hans Speier					
To South America		Coordinator's Office - American Social Surveys					Coordinator's Office - American Social Surveys
From South America	Coordinator's Office - American Social Surveys						
American Domestic			American Film Center, Dorothy B. Jones				
Foreign Language			Columbia Office of Radio Research		Harvard University, C.J. Friedrich		
For abroad		FCC					

( ) = Qualified agency   [ ] = Work terminating

The contemporaneous development of an effects-based research model, honing of measurement techniques, and provision of reliable data to federal authorities suggest that John Marshall's role in the history of U.S. mass communications research needs recognition, and our understanding of the development of the national security state needs to account for the role of the Rockefeller-sponsored communications research. Preparing for war against Nazi propaganda became a vital national security precaution for liberal U.S. scholars, administrators, and federal officials, and it also produced deep dilemmas for those who were sensitive to the dangers of such propaganda intelligence work for a liberal democracy. Perhaps no one understood this better than Archibald MacLeish, and few spoke as eloquently about the tensions and contradictory imperatives involved in protecting national security and ensuring Americans' civil liberties. The next chapter explores those tensions by examining MacLeish's rhetorical call to arms and his remarkable mobilization of the Library of Congress as a weapon in the war of words and ideas.

CHAPTER FOUR

Mobilizing the Intellectual Arsenal of Democracy: Archibald MacLeish and the Library of Congress

Appointed Librarian of Congress in 1939 by President Franklin D. Roosevelt, the lawyer-turned-Pulitzer Prize–winning-poet Archibald MacLeish (1892–1982) produced a voluminous public record as an antifascist, noncommunist liberal. Horrified by what he saw as Western civilization's failure to resist European fascism, MacLeish used his many platforms as poet, essayist, journalist, radio playwright, and establishment insider to combat intellectual and spiritual torpor and rally U.S. intellectuals for the impending war. By 1941 he held two positions within the federal government from which he could speak and act. Concurrently the Librarian of Congress and the director of the Office of Facts and Figures (OFF) (and then briefly deputy director of the OWI during the war's first months), MacLeish helped shape and articulate the nation's pro-Allies, antifascist propaganda line.[1] Just as important but neither as visible or well-known as his role directing U.S. propaganda, MacLeish used these positions to help coordinate the federal government's various communications' surveillance and intelligence activities against fascist propaganda. Between these two roles—democratic rhetorician and architect of the emerging national security state—one can identify the contradictory imperatives of MacLeish's own war-era work and within U.S. liberalism in general.

The central tension in MacLeish's work concerned the highly fraught matter of information management in a democratic society. As a former constitutional law professor, practicing poet, and government official responsible for implementing information control policies and shaping public opinion, MacLeish understood as well as any one the combustible implications of the question, How should a democracy mobilize for war in an age when official lies, half-truths, censorship, and hate campaigns would be employed by all belligerents? Within his two jobs MacLeish confronted the competing imperatives between the free flow of information necessary to democratic practices and the control of information necessary to the wartime state. As Librarian of Congress, he saw himself as the guardian of public information and, more important, Western culture's democratic traditions, especially the Enlightenment-inspired scholarly pursuit of truth. As OFF director he was both an official spokesperson for U.S. war and peace aims and an important behind-the-scenes coordinator of opinion-control and intelligence activities.

This chapter shows how MacLeish worked out both these roles within the Library of Congress by making the library itself a key site for information, intelligence, and publicity activities. For MacLeish, the Library of Congress served as a resonant symbol of U.S. democracy's commitment to openness and unfettered inquiry; as head of the nation's premier information repository he made the library function as an intellectual appendage (literally as an annex) to the expanding security state. Indeed, his work in the library provides a window into the conflicts within U.S. liberalism at this moment of crisis, especially between prodemocracy, affirmative liberalism, on the one hand, and antifascist, security-oriented liberalism, on the other. His work also shows how emergency-period anxieties challenged the commitments of public-centered affirmative liberals. Whether the issue was securing intelligence-related materials for library-based research, keeping unwanted foreign propaganda materials from the public, or pursuing what he described as the "strategy of truth" in the propaganda his OFF produced, MacLeish's civil libertarian–inspired liberalism continually ran up against the powerful information control requirements emerging from his and others' ardently antifascist brand of liberalism.

Interwar U.S. liberalism was not monolithic but rather, as MacLeish's work illustrates, riven by competing ideas about how a democracy should defend itself and how it should prepare for war.[2] He, like many others, perceived that opinion control and propaganda were insidious in U.S. civil society but were also necessary instruments of modern warfare even in a democracy. These antinomies pointed to a central paradox that MacLeish repeatedly addressed. In a 1939 essay, "Freedom to End Freedom," MacLeish assayed the deep conflicts within modern liberalism and took to task those whom he called the "nervous liberals" who were so frightened by the specters of Fascism and Communism and public susceptibility to extremist ideas that they would make certain party affiliations and extreme political speech illegal.

To MacLeish, this was the paradox of strangling democracy in order to save it. In an "age of political paradox," he said, the greatest danger to democratic ideals issued not from the reactionaries but from liberals: "Hitler frees provinces by conquering them. Chamberlain keeps peace by losing wars. Franco saves Spain for the Italians. But it is the liberals who declare that the only way to preserve the gentle heifer of liberalism from the fascists is to shoot her through the head."[3] In the debates between those suspicious about expanding the state's repressive capacities versus those suspicious about the public's susceptibilities to demagoguery, antidemocratic propaganda, and organized violence, MacLeish repeatedly extolled the democratic virtues of public debate and railed against restrictions of what he saw as fundamental and natural rights of speech and association. At the same time, he recognized the need for the authority of experts and the crucial role that information and ideas would play in a war where mass communications would be mobilized as never before. Consequently, he involved Library of Congress facilities and personnel in many of the activities necessary for fighting a total war, including the detection and analysis of Axis propaganda, international and domestic intelligence research, and the production and distribution of democratic propaganda.

Because he was extensively involved in prewar policy discussions about intelligence needs and chaired the informal Committee on War Information that included a host of New Deal officials, MacLeish immediately recognized the potential usefulness of the communications intelligence research begun by the projects sponsored by the Rockefeller Foundation. He encouraged this work and provided a home base within the Library of Congress for one of the most ambitious: Harold Lasswell's Experimental Division for the Study of Wartime Communications.

Lasswell's Experimental Division fit neatly within the Library of Congress, whose many resources were being utilized for the intellectuals' war against fascism, and Lasswell helped further MacLeish's agenda. His project trained numerous federal personnel in the latest techniques of propaganda analysis; he helped the Library of Congress accumulate an unparalleled body of foreign propaganda materials; and, as a consultant to MacLeish, he surveyed the prewar intelligence landscape so that MacLeish might better utilize the library and work effectively with other federal agencies. Lasswell's project also worked closely with the Department of Justice in its war-era prosecutions of foreign propagandists under the Foreign Agent Registration Act. In addition to Lasswell's project, the library also established a Division of Special Information, which was the embryo of the Research and Analysis Branch of the Office of Strategic Services.

In a war for the spirit of the West, as MacLeish saw it, the task of celebrating and continually extolling the rhetoric and ideals of democracy was an equally important role for the Library of Congress, as well as for librarians in general. Yet at the same time MacLeish's Manichaean rhetoric defining the war as a struggle for the spirit of the West and his enlistment of the library as part of democracy's arsenal had unintended consequences. In a revealing episode where he took on the post office book burners out of both principle and necessity, MacLeish's solutions show the extent to which national security logic came to rule his own thinking and how he compromised his own democratic rhetoric by severely restricting the flow of foreign propaganda materials to the public. In the context of the emergency, however, MacLeish's efforts to retrieve doomed materials from postal authorities represented a progressive wielding of First Amendment rhetoric, a heightened attention to the symbolic dimensions of censorship and book burning, and a willingness to intervene against unthinking administrators. Simply stated, MacLeish did better than most of his liberal cohorts in maintaining the important distinction between liberty and security, but anxieties about fascist propaganda and public susceptibility made even this most eloquent critic of nervous liberalism a nervous liberal himself.

MacLeish's Antifascist Commitments

Born in 1892 to a wealthy Chicago merchant, Andrew MacLeish (a founder of the University of Chicago), and Martha Hillard (former president of Rockford College), Archibald was raised in patrician comfort on the shores of Lake Michigan in Glencoe, Illinois, a Chicago suburb.[4] Introduced to the world of literature and the public service ideal at home, he prepped at Hotchkiss and then matriculated at Yale, where he captained the water polo team, played football, became the class poet, edited the class literary magazine, and was admitted to Skull and Bones (the most prestigious of Yale's secret societies). MacLeish made the *Law Review* after his first year at Harvard Law School, married his high school sweetheart (Ada Hitchcock, a concert singer), and after his second year in law school went to France to fight in the Great War, eventually attaining the rank of artillery captain in the army. After the war MacLeish completed his law degree in 1919, earning the prestigious Fay Diploma from the Harvard law faculty, which selected him as the top student in his class for ranking highest "in scholarship, conduct, and character" and for showing "evidence of the greatest promise."[5]

They must have seen something, as MacLeish went on to live a quite extraordinary life as law professor, lawyer, poet, journalist, and experimental radio playwright, all before his government duties as Librarian of Congress, OFF director, assistant director of the OWI, and assistant secretary of state. At war's end he became chairman of the U.S. delegation to the first general conference of UNESCO, was coauthor of the Universal Declaration of Human Rights of the United Nations Charter, and then returned to the academy when appointed Boylston Professor of Rhetoric and Oratory at Harvard in 1949, a position he held until 1962. During his long career he won two Pulitzer Prizes for his poetry and one for his verse play *J.B.* (for which he also won a Tony award) and was also awarded the Medal of Freedom in 1977.

MacLeish was best known to the U.S. public for his poetry, and early on he knew he wanted to be a poet. On graduating from law school he briefly taught constitutional law at Harvard and then worked for one of Boston's most prestigious firms. He was offered a partnership but turned down that position in order to write poetry full-time. He and his wife, Ada, sailed to Europe in 1923, where they lived for the next five years among the literary and artistic expatriates of their generation. When they returned to the United States, MacLeish was unable to support his growing family on a poet's income, so he arranged a deal with editor and publisher Henry Luce (a fellow Yale graduate) whereby he would write and edit journalism half a year for *Fortune* magazine and have the rest of his time to write poetry and plays. This flexibility made it possible for him to travel, study, and eventually experiment with radio as a medium for bringing his poems and plays to a larger public. In the course of his employment with Luce—from 1929 to 1938—MacLeish wrote 119 full-length articles and received, he later said, "a course in the history, geography, and general appearance of the Great Republic such as I had never had before."[6] He also won his first Pulitzer Prize, in 1933, for his long narrative poem "Conquistador."

Like many others in his generation, MacLeish was politically radicalized by the conditions of the people and land during the Great Depression, and, willing to experiment with technique and form, his poetry shifted in emphasis during the 1930s from intensely private high-modernist themes and techniques (inspired by—some say imitative of—Eliot and Pound) to more public themes about the Depression, poverty, the exploitation of the land, the shrinking democratic promise, the rising tide of reaction at home, the menace of fascism abroad (at first in Spain and then in Germany), and the obligation of poets to utter what he called "public speech." Ever-interested in working with ambitious and public-minded people and compelled to try out new venues for the expression of his increasingly political ideas, he wrote several antifascist radio plays that were broadcast by NBC—among them, *The Fall of the City* (1937) and *Air Raid* (1938)—and in 1938 quit writing for Luce's publications because of *Time* magazine's coverage of the war in Spain.[7] He then took a job as the first director of the Niemann Fellows program at Harvard University, at President James B. Conant's behest, which he served in for a year, after which he was appointed Librarian of Congress by FDR, in 1939.

MacLeish moved in many different social and intellectual circles by the time of his appointment as librarian. He befriended poets and artists, lawyers and judges, journalists, editors, and government officials. But, according to his most recent biographer, Scott Donaldson, he was most comfortable politically and socially in the company of the interventionist, public service–minded New Deal liberals. Archie, as his friends knew him, counted among his closest friends several with intimate New Deal connections, including Dean Acheson, Felix Frankfurter, Attorney General Robert Jackson, Solicitor General Francis Biddle, Interior Secretary Harold Ickes, and President Roosevelt's aide Thomas Corcoran. A New Deal supporter as a journalist and a true admirer of Roosevelt (he told one interviewer that FDR was "just the most attractive human being who ever lived"), MacLeish was a critic of corporate capitalism and promoter of left-liberal social and cultural causes and became loosely associated with Popular Front writers. He became the Librarian of Congress when his longtime friend and teacher Felix Frankfurter persuaded FDR that MacLeish's considerable versatility would serve him well as librarian. MacLeish first rejected the offer but then changed his mind after Frankfurter reminded him of what biographer Scott Donaldson refers to as MacLeish's "lifelong determination to be of use." As Donaldson notes, MacLeish knew very little about being a librarian but nevertheless "characteristically . . . assigned himself to a task of extraordinarily wide compass."[8]

Confronted with intensely hostile opposition from some professional librarians (because he was not a trained professional), MacLeish nonetheless gained extensive support from other writers, journalists, and librarians and used his considerable social graces to generate enough backing for his nomination from an isolationist Congress suspicious about his leftist political leanings and his very public cries for intervention on behalf of the Spanish Republicans.[9] One of his chief legacies as librarian, and one acknowledged then and now by professional librarians, is that he quickly modernized the Library of Congress in dramatic and manifold ways.[10] More importantly, MacLeish used the Library of Congress "as a platform from which to speak out on behalf of democracy and its preservation in a time of crisis." As Scott Donaldson adds, "No librarian of Congress, before or since, has been so visible to the American public." Because the job gave him what he described as "the maximum of freedom to act" and because he was a committed interventionist, MacLeish quickly prepared the library as a site for emergency-related information and intelligence-gathering activities.[11] And while MacLeish and his associates kept the library's war-related work from public and congressional view, MacLeish was never quiet about the perils posed by the rise of fascism. Indeed, he had been speaking out on this issue as a public poet long before FDR appointed him librarian.

As early as 1935 MacLeish began warning about fascism's threat to the West's cultural, spiritual, and political life. Over time the consistency of this position—along with his critique of Marxism's antispiritualism and antiindividualism, his repudiation of his own earlier antiwar principles and poetry, his skepticism as to whether other leftist writers were sufficiently independent from the Communist Party, and eventually his position as government propagandist—would make him a highly controversial figure in the fractious, contentious world of U.S. Communists, anti-Stalinist leftists, and Popular Front liberal writers and intellectuals. MacLeish occasionally moved in leftist circles and participated in but essentially remained outside left sectarian politics: his early and gut-level response to the threat of fascism led him to chair the Second Writer's Congress in 1937 (earning him the label "Stalin's stooge" from critics on the right), but he steadfastly refused to join the Communist Party or follow its dictates, including its aesthetic prescriptions for proletarian fiction (earning him the appellation "unconscious fascist" from Communist Party critics).

Thus for his critics on the right he was a Stalinist, and for those on the far left he was a fascist. In fact, he was a noncommunist left liberal who called himself a liberal and supported Roosevelt's New Deal, while his accessible protest poetry and verse, his antifascist radio plays, and his high-profile stance on the need for intervention in Spain made him quite well liked as a Popular Front writer. Yet he was continually embattled with Communist intellectuals over key issues, such as his refusal to adopt the Party line on Spain (he thought that liberals should take the lead here and not cede it to the Communists), and believed that the inconsistency of U.S. Communists on the threat of fascism was obvious evidence of their intellectual obedience to Moscow. This was especially the case after the August 1939 Nazi-Soviet Pact, when official Communist Party rhetoric and policy positions were abruptly reversed (as they were again when the Nazis invaded the USSR in 1941). Such fellow-traveling independence, coupled with his left-liberal sentiments and consistent critique of the Depression era failures of U.S. capitalism, earned him long-term enemies on both the left and the right.[12]

MacLeish also managed to earn critical brickbats because of his penchant for experimental, sometimes exceedingly clunky "public verse." By the early 1930s he had rejected high modernism's concerns with matters of aesthetics, which he found too narrow and inward-looking in an era of such obvious economic and political crisis. While his earlier modernist (and award-winning) verse had earned him scorn from some for its derivative qualities, his public verse of the mid- to late thirties earned him even more scorn for its obvious concerns with topicality, protest, and accessibility, as well as for its technical idiosyncrasies and its occasional mawkish sentimentality. His prescriptive critique of high modernism and shift to a more vernacular public poetry produced, then, vituperation among literary critics, who lacerated him on both aesthetic and ideological grounds.[13] Thus by the time he fired his harshest public volleys at writers and scholars for what he saw as their failure to take up the pen against fascism and ardently to endorse intervention in Europe, he was already positioned to be pilloried from many fronts. And he was.

The travails of Spain first induced MacLeish to reconsider the antiwar positions he had developed after WWI, a position rooted in his own experience on the front, the stories he heard then and after, and, most important, the death of his brother Kenneth in the war. As late as 1935, MacLeish announced that he would do everything in his power to oppose any U.S. participation in another war. But his own travels to Japan when he was writing for *Fortune* gave him firsthand knowledge of the rise of a fascist, militaristic state there. Then came the atrocities committed by the Spanish Fascists under Franco and finally Nazi conquests in Austria, Czechoslovakia, and Poland, all of which led him to repudiate—in brazen, unnuanced, and personal terms—his own antiwar literary past as well as the WWI-generation's deeply felt disgust for war and its propagandists. This rejection of his own legacy and that of the finest writers of his generation became for his critics additional evidence of his intellectual and ideological inconsistency and opportunism.

But in the spring of 1940, as the Low Countries fell to the Nazis, MacLeish fueled the invective already aimed at him and made his legacy as a writer enduringly controversial. Two articles, "The Irresponsibles" and "Post-War Writers, Pre-War Readers," took up the same theme: he chastised his fellow intellectuals for abdicating their responsibilities in the spiritual war against fascism and accused the antiwar novelists from WWI of having created an "irresponsible" literary legacy, one that he now believed contributed to a simplistic antiwar sentiment among the current generation of students, a legacy that made the task of preparing for war against the Axis powers far more difficult.[14] As a highly visible writer and government spokesperson with access to both influential journals and radio audiences, MacLeish directed this hyperbolic message at intellectuals but did so with a larger audience in mind. His willingness to offer stern challenges made him attractive to FDR, and, as one of MacLeish's assistants noted, FDR enjoyed MacLeish's "high-sounding rhetoric" and liked to call him his "minister of culture."[15] Another MacLeish biographer suggests, in fact, that it was on the basis of these articles that FDR appointed MacLeish director of OFF.[16] But while the politically hamstrung president may have appreciated the call to intellectual arms, MacLeish's pronouncements did little to endear him to either the uncommitted literary left (especially those still resistant to prowar propaganda) or the conservative isolationists.[17]

Contemporary critics could certainly find inconsistencies in his positions (and one critic, Morton Dauwen Zabel, writing in the *Partisan Review*, fastidiously pointed to all the inconsistencies in MacLeish's public utterance about war in general), but events challenged his earlier positions, and dozens on dozens of MacLeish's writings from the mid-1930s to the time of his government appointments (as librarian in 1939 and at OFF in 1941) showed his overall consistency on the question of intellectuals' responsibilities to the liberal tradition and to the challenge posed by the spiritual cancer of fascism at home and abroad. The essential themes in his many essays beginning in 1935 were constant: poets, writers, and scholars had central roles to play in the much-needed war of words and ideas against fascism. Inaction would make a grasping, demoralized, and angry U.S. public even more susceptible to the fear-based, hate-mongering appeals of the far right, and, most important, there was no time for intellectually distant, scholastic, and relativistic forms of inquiry because Western civilization's liberal values were in immediate peril.[18] As MacLeish said time and again, democratic values needed "affirmation," and Americans needed hope. This was the job of artists and intellectuals. Confronted, he wrote in a characteristic passage, with a "revolution of negatives, a revolution of the defeated, a revolution of the dispossessed . . . a revolution *against*," writers and political leaders needed to defend "the rule of intellectual truth." At stake, he said, was the "whole system of ideas . . . the whole authority of excellence which places law above force, beauty above cruelty, singleness above numbers."[19]

MacLeish called for poets to be connected to the world of politics and action by offering the public both authentic artistic expression and visions of other possibilities. He staked out his preliminary vision of the artist against fascism in a 1935 review of Clifford Odets's "Waiting for Lefty," acknowledging Odets's work as evidence of the potential value of the live arts as a spiritual force. Fascism appealed to the emotions of the disenchanted and economically dislocated masses of Europe and the United States through an "overwhelming" enlistment of "all the forces which fascism can buy—the press, the movies, the commercial theatre." Against the "false and journalistic emotions of fascism," he wrote, U.S. artists should set the "real and human emotions of art": "No power on earth can outpersuade the great and greatly felt work of art when its purpose is clear and its creator confident."[20] For MacLeish, the distinction between false, mass-produced emotion and the authentic emotion produced by "real" art seemed self-explanatory. In other forums, he maintained this distinction and repeated the larger argument about the responsibility of artists.[21]

"In Challenge, Not Defense," a 1938 essay published in *Poetry Magazine*, he asked whether poetry "will permit us to continue to exist."[22] Missing from the public imagination, MacLeish explained, was an image or idea of some other kind of world "that men can wish to live and make true." Only poetry and poets, he argued, had the imagination and the ability to create that missing image: "its absence *is* the crisis" (p. 6; emphasis in the original), he wrote. Drawing on the usual distinction between "fact" and imagination to celebrate the moral authority of poets, he said, "History draws things which have happened: poetry things which are possible to men. In this time in which everything is possible except the spirit to desire and the love to choose, poetry becomes again the deliverer of the people" (p. 7).

In "The Affirmation," originally published in May 1939, MacLeish explained that any economic critique of capitalism's failures needed to be understood in terms of the spiritual exhaustion that the failure produced; against this exhaustion artists had a responsibility to act. Fascism attacks, he wrote in purplish prose, "in the back rooms, in the dark of railroad trestles, in the sand-lots down by the river, in the loudspeaker on the kitchen table where the grating voice of the ambitious priest rattles the pitiful dishes with spite and hate."[23] Against the hate-based solutions offered by the likes of Father Coughlin and other native fascists, artists needed to speak to the desires of the disenfranchised for decent jobs, dignity, and respect. And against the threat of laws that would restrict liberties in order to silence the fascists, the people needed their love of freedom enhanced, not shrunken. "The most ignorant, the most violent, the most brutal and the most unhappy" would not be won over by policies based on fear, he wrote (p. 11).

MacLeish's own artistic production in the mid- to late thirties reflected his belief that poetry and art had something to teach the public: about fascism, despotism, hatred, war, and the horrific rise of dictatorships, along with the positive values associated with Western democratic traditions. His fear of the dictatorships in Spain, Germany, and Italy prompted him to write several experimental radio plays. Ironically, the first of these allegorical plays, *The Fall of the City* (produced in 1937), depicted a susceptible, weak-willed, and easily managed public so paralyzed by fear that it failed to see that the "Strong Man" it had accepted as its "Conqueror" was, in fact, an empty helmet with empty armor.[24] *Air Raid*, produced in 1938 against the backdrop of the Spanish Civil War, depicted in realistic fashion the devastating bombardment of civilian populations and the ruthless slaughter of women and children.[25] It too made inaction based on fear its motif, a motif that ran, in fact, through most of MacLeish's creative work in the late thirties.

The motif showed up again, perhaps most powerfully, in the extended verse poem, or "soundtrack" (as he called it, still in the experimental mode), that accompanied a compilation of Farm Security Administration photographs from the northern plains states, titled *Land of the Free* (1938). In this text, he asked, What should happen to a people whose beliefs—in the land, in a set of Jeffersonian principles, in the fruits of honest hard work, and in justice—were stripped from them by a ruthless economic system and a political system incapable of meeting their economic and spiritual needs? What happens when their myths collapse? "We don't know," he concluded, "we just don't know."[26] While the visual component of the poem ended optimistically with serial images of collective labor action, the poem ended with a haunting question. In the same vein, the book-length poem he completed shortly after his appointment as librarian ended with the same sense of foreboding, a sentiment captured by the past tense used in the title: *America Was Promises*.[27]

His many prose essays from the period, collected and republished in 1940 in the volume *A Time to Speak*, followed shortly thereafter by a companion volume, *A Time to Act* (1943), embodied MacLeish's prolific attempts to persuade U.S. intellectuals to abandon their concerns with political partisanship or narrow questions of aesthetics and scholasticism. They also represented his efforts to defend the tradition of free speech liberalism increasingly under pressure because of fears about the revolutionary and subversive power of foreign and domestic propaganda.

From 1938 to 1941, when war was breaking out in Europe, government officials sought to safeguard the republic from foreign and domestic enemies by investigating communist- and fascist-sponsored activities in the United States and by passing antipropaganda and antisedition legislation in the form of the Foreign Agent Registration Act, the Voorhis Act, and the Smith Act amendment to the Alien Registration Act.[28] During this period MacLeish, the former constitutional law professor, was a frequent champion of traditional democratic theory and civil liberties premises and warned about what would be lost to democracy if the security-oriented liberals were left alone to define the nation's response to the threats of fascist speech at home and aggression abroad. Yet he also recognized the need to act against those threats.

In a 1939 essay titled "Freedom to End Freedom," MacLeish opposed plans by the nervous liberals to increase state control over speech, press, and rights of association by invoking the Deweyan argument, which held that speech was a natural right existing prior to and making possible the existence of the state.[29] To presume otherwise—that the state made possible freedom of speech—was both to ignore natural rights doctrine and misconstrue the legitimate authority of government. MacLeish's version of democratic theory and his perception of the First Amendment as the guarantor of the democratic state went beyond the modern First Amendment doctrine as it had been construed by liberal jurists such as justices Holmes and Brandeis and by scholars such as Roscoe Pound and Zechariah Chafee Jr. In fact, MacLeish's progressive interpretation found the Holmesian "marketplace of ideas" defense of speech rights a weak conception of the a priori nature of the individual's natural rights.

MacLeish also rejected the commonly asserted idea that speech rights could be denied to members of groups whose own organizations restricted speech and association (this was the standard argument used to legitimize proposals to deny First Amendment rights to avowed Communists and Fascists): "By limiting freedom of expression in democratic states to those who believe in freedom of expression and denying it to those who do not," the nervous liberals were entrenching themselves in "the fundamental liberal paradox" that only those who expressed belief in freedom of expression should be granted that freedom (p. 131). This thinking both mistook the origins of the state and the proper policy of the state. As MacLeish explained, "nothing could be farther from the truth than the supposition that [the Bill of Rights] are still mere privileges in a modern liberal democracy. In American constitutional theory the right of freedom of expression was thought of as a 'natural right' and the only effect of the First Amendment was to forbid Congress to abridge it. The implication is very clear that the right antedated the Constitution. Today, when 'natural rights' are no longer in favor, it is still true that freedom of expression antedates the Constitution" (pp. 134–35).

MacLeish argued that instead of restricting the rights of those who were deemed dangerous to the health of the state—U.S. Communists and Fascists—liberals should embrace the principles of legislative and jurisprudential consistency and universally secure rights:

> To set up one political exception is to set up all political exceptions. . . . The one certain and fixed point in the entire discussion is this: that freedom of expression is guaranteed to the citizens of a liberal democracy not for the pleasure of the citizens but for the

health of the state. . . . Unless it exists, and unless it exists in such terms, the kind of state which is built upon its existence can no longer be maintained. (p. 136)

To undermine this fundamental premise of liberal democracy was potentially to bring down the whole structure of democratic government, which he described as "an act of mayhem which might very easily become an act of suicide" (p. 136). The paradox, he said, was that the nervous liberals would try to "protect themselves against the burning of books by starting a fire to which books will almost certainly be fed" (p. 137).

Elsewhere MacLeish contended that too much attention in the United States was being paid to the idea of an active Communist conspiracy and the hope that restrictive legislation would cure the problem: "The theory is that America is all right and the Americans are all right and everything else would be all right if only the communists could be prevented from spreading their insidious propaganda and wrecking the country." Again he rejected the speech- and association-restrictive implications of such anxieties.[30]

At the same time, MacLeish argued that the U.S. public should not be unprotected against subversion and antidemocratic propaganda coming from the treasonous far right, about which he was far more worried. Yet in the effort to protect the public and the state from native fascists, "prodemocracy" liberalism, as he called it, should not yield to "antifascist" liberalism. In "The Affirmation," MacLeish focused on these two liberalisms and asked: "How does American liberalism propose to defend democratic society against the treason of fascism?" Not by losing faith in the capacity of the American citizenry to rule itself, nor by mobilizing fear and hatred, nor by defending a "status quo of which the most noticeable characteristic is ten millions of unemployed." Such a system "cannot be defended against fascism."[31] Therefore, prodemocracy liberalism should protect the dignity of the individual; meanwhile, the state should strengthen rather than undermine democratic processes. This policy had "so far been adopted by no one" (p. 9), he argued. High unemployment, the appeal to order proffered by fascist spokesmen, and lost public faith in democratic practices required urgent attention. For MacLeish, as writer and as rhetorician, the starting point was to convince the American people—especially those classes that had suffered worst during the Depression—that fascism was not an acceptable alternative to liberal democracy.

MacLeish concluded "The Affirmation" by criticizing liberals, especially intellectuals, for their timidity and failure to take risks and act. Accusing them of enjoying "the sterile and rancid pleasures of self-righteousness" and preferring the "safety of a spinsterish and impotent intellectualism to the risks of affirmation and belief" (p. 16), he developed this critique even more strongly in other essays of the period, most resoundingly in his notorious essays, "The Irresponsibles" (May 1940) and "Post-War Writers, Pre-War Readers" (June 1940).

By 1939 MacLeish had become a strong advocate of full-scale preparation for war and U.S. intervention in Spain, and after the fall of France in June 1940 he became a vocal proponent of intervention against Nazi Germany, telling Harold Ickes that he thought FDR should make an immediate declaration of war.[32] In an interview published forty-six years later, MacLeish explained the context for his attacks on his cohorts by saying that his generation misperceived the reality of fascism and of Hitler's intentions because of their ardent desire to avoid being duped into another war, a residual fear of propaganda from WWI:

> "The Irresponsibles" was written with a good deal of feeling to try to make a point which my academic and writing friends, but mostly academic friends, refused to make. They were doing the opposite of what is done by generals who get ready to fight. They were getting ready to have opinions about Hitler in terms of the last war. They were damned if they were going to get sold down the river again; they weren't going to be caught again by anything like Mr. Wilson's rhetoric; they weren't going to wait as we all did three or four years after the First World War to discover we'd been had, and they were simply, totally, against the war against Hitler, not realizing that in this case we had no choice, and that the war, instead of being what the First World War was, a vicious deceit, was a war that had to be fought. That was what my conscious mind was concerned with.

MacLeish also explained his motives in terms of both moral necessity and personal guilt, the former resulting from his prescience, the latter from his poetic contributions to the isolationist, antiwar climate of the late 1930s: "At the time of 'The Irresponsibles' I felt a considerable responsibility myself for the formation of the opinion which the America Firsters held and which a great many college undergraduates held, and held violently, passionately. My concern was my responsibility for the beginnings of that, because a good deal of what I wrote in the thirties was along that line, too. I was so sick about the First World War that I couldn't cleanse my mind of it."[33]

Delivered first as a speech to the American Philosophical Society in April 1940 in his role as librarian and then reprinted in slightly modified form in the *Nation*, "The Irresponsibles" rebutted the ideas of the America Firsters, refuted MacLeish's own early-thirties isolationist ideas, and warned U.S. intellectuals that something profound was at stake, namely, "the scholar's goods." The fascist assault on language, reason, and universal (as opposed to tribal) forms of knowledge threatened the very principles of unfettered intellectual inquiry, he argued. Thus he called on intellectuals to defend their culture, by which he meant Western civilization's common set of assumptions about individual dignity, the rule of law against force, the liberating spirit of the arts, and the search for truth as the raison d'être of intellectual life. The trope he developed here, and in other essays of the period, was that future historians would ask why a generation of scholars and artists sat by, obsessed with questions of beauty but not with the suffering of humanity. Warning about history's judgment, he wrote:

> History—if honest history continues to be written—will have one question to ask of our generation, people like ourselves . . . : Why did the scholars and the writers of our generation in this country, witnesses as they were to the destruction of writing and scholarship in great areas of Europe and to the exile and the imprisonment and murder of men whose crime was scholarship and writing—witnesses also to the rise in their own country of the same destructive forces with the same impulses, the same motives, the same means—why did the scholars and the writers of our generation in America fail to oppose those forces while they could—while there was still time and still place to oppose them with the arms of scholarship and writing?[34]

The time had come to abandon the pretense that scholarship is somehow pure and has nothing to do with the world. Too enchanted by the scientific ideal of the objective scholar as an observer, academics and writers had failed to engage the crisis directly, he argued.[35] The mythology they had absorbed had led scholars to presume that "the misfortunes of our generation are economic and political misfortunes from which the scholar can safely hold himself apart" (p. 105); consequently, his contemporaries had failed to recognize that Europe's crisis was their crisis, that Europe's affairs were theirs (p. 106).

MacLeish well understood that the legacy of propaganda campaigns from WWI had created profound intellectual skepticism and barriers to action, as had abundant commentary in the mid- to late 1930s about the ubiquity of propaganda of all stripes, and that these had produced a perception that everything was tainted by lies and manipulation.[36] Fascist propaganda, however, was different, he explained; it was the battering ram of a more brutal force intent on utter destruction, and its appeal lay in deeper problems: "Behind the black print on the page and the hysterical voice on the air there is something deeper and more dangerous": despair. The real crisis was that men and women in Europe—and at home—beaten about by the indignities of economic collapse and fears of worse to come, had given up their faith in liberty for the idea of order; they had surrendered their freedom for the promise of discipline and wished "passionately and even violently . . . to surrender their wills and their bodies and even their minds to the will of a leader." (That was the central idea in his radio plays.) The chilling aspect of this, MacLeish argued, was "that whole nations of men [had] gladly and willingly released themselves, not only from their rights as individuals, but from their responsibilities as individuals, so that they are no longer compelled to feel or to respect the individual humanity of others—or to feel or to respect the things that individual humanity has, over many centuries, created" (p. 107).

The most controversial part of MacLeish's argument lay in his reasons explaining why U.S. intellectuals failed to recognize that the crisis affected them directly. In part, the problem was the nature of intellectual inquiry in the mid-twentieth century, when specialization of intellectual labor had led to a breakdown of commitment to the Enlightenment ideal. And in part the problem was cultural relativism. While MacLeish pointed to what he perceived as the baleful results of relativism in academic thinking in general, the intrusions of presentism in writing, and antiquarianism in scholarship, he contended that ultimately the most destructive of these forces was the division of intellectual labor:

> I think it is the organization of the intellectual life of our time. Specifically, I think it is the division and therefore the destruction of intellectual responsibility. The men of intellectual duty, those who should have been responsible for action, have divided themselves into two castes, two cults—the scholars and the writers. Neither accepts responsibility for the common culture or for its defense. (p. 113)

While MacLeish acknowledged the existence of a great deal of excellent scholarship and writing, he said that excellence was not the pressing question, because the larger problem was that science and the arts had become parochial, open frontiers of knowledge had been fenced off, and the common Enlightenment-based cultural imperative toward knowledge, truth, and the ideal of scholarly rationality had been replaced by thinking that promoted cultural chauvinism and rationalized the ideology of brute power. "What matters now," MacLeish intoned, "is the defense of culture" (p. 116).

In "Post-War Writers, Pre-War Readers," he focused on the problem of words without meaning. For MacLeish, the post-WWI writers had been so embittered by wartime propaganda they had become utterly cynical about the possibility that any words could be meaningful; the problem was that this idea, expressed over and over by the WWI generation, had produced in their pre-WWII readers a profoundly paralyzing skepticism. Implicating his own work in this cynicism-producing legacy, MacLeish raised hackles by naming others, including John Dos Passos, Ford Madox Ford, Erich Maria Remarque, Ernest Hemingway, and Richard Aldington, as being equally guilty.[37]

He quoted John Chamberlain arguing that the result was "a younger generation which needs none of Mr. Stuart Chase's semantic discipline. The boys and girls tend to distrust all slogans, all tags—even all words." MacLeish added: "The characteristic of the attitude of the young generation which most disturbs their elders is their distrust . . . of all statements of principle and conviction, all declarations of moral purpose." He then suggested that this very distrust of language had produced the moral and intellectual failure of Europeans to respond in time to the fascist threat; he wondered whether the "thing which has strangled the Allies will also strangle us" (p. 789).

To MacLeish, this moral reticence and distrust was "a more sobering fact than our lack of planes, our lack of antiaircraft guns," because if the young were distrustful "of all words, distrustful of all moral judgments of better and worse," then it made it impossible to use "the only weapon with which fascism can be fought—the moral conviction that fascism is evil and that a free society of free men is worth fighting for. If all words are suspect, all judgments phony, all convictions of better and worse fake, then there is nothing real and permanent for which men are willing to fight." The consequence of this unbelief, he argued, was twofold. It would result in an inadequate faith in the idea of freedom, a faith insufficient to defeat the fascistic "negative faith in obedience, in discipline, in brutality, in death." Absent that positive faith in freedom, the freedoms worth believing in— especially the freedom of expression of opinion and belief—would not last long (p. 789). This was "one fact," MacLeish said. The second was that "a large part of the responsibility for this state of mind in the generation of men and women now young belongs to the writers—belongs specifically to the best and most sensitive and most persuasive writers—of my generation who created in many minds this distrust not only of the tags, not only of the slogans, but of the words themselves." Their books, written against "the hatefulness and cruelty and filthiness of war" were "filled with passionate contempt for the statements of conviction, of purpose, and of belief on which the war of 1914–1918 was fought." And here MacLeish repudiated that contempt for conviction and the WWI-born idea that all moral issues "were false—were fraudulent—were intended to deceive." What the war writers had produced, he suggested, was a generation "defenseless before an aggressor ready to force war *upon us.*" Those writers, he added, "must face the fact that the books they wrote in the years just after the war have done more to disarm democracy in the face of fascism than any other single influence." He acknowledged that people like Dos Passos and Hemingway had "devoted themselves to the fight against fascism with all their talents and all their courage," but the fact remained that "what they wrote, however noble it may have been as literature, however true to them as a summary of their personal experience, was disastrous as education for a generation which would be obliged to face the threat of fascism in its adult years" (p. 790; emphasis in original).

For MacLeish, this presented the problem of breathing meaning and life into words like "liberty," "freedom," "democracy." Making them more than slogans and mere propaganda lines would be necessary to mobilize a nation for a necessary war. The other problem, no less formidable, was to confront the idea (regularly uttered and, he thought, no less cynical) that by preparing for war against fascism, the United States must itself become fascist: "Those who wish to see us weak will employ every means of deception, of misrepresentation and of fraud to keep us so. . . . They will tell us that we cannot assert our belief in the institutions of a free society and our intention to defend them, without becoming as nationalistic, as intolerant and as savage as those who attack our institutions." For MacLeish, this line was simply a false declaration of the love of liberty and democracy; it was a line that could only be expressed by those who did not believe strongly enough in those ideas to fight for them, who did not believe strongly enough in the idea of tolerance to defend the idea of tolerance. It was defeatism, plain and simple (p. 790).

MacLeish took a beating in the left-liberal press for these accusations, especially for the seeming intellectual dishonesty and narrowness of repudiating one generation's truthfully told reflections because those reflections did not meet the needs of another moment.[38] His apparent willingness to rewrite the past to justify the present was, in fact, evidence of the very intolerance and nervousness that MacLeish had himself been warning about. The fact that the civil libertarian, public-centered liberal MacLeish could so fully embrace the idea of war—a full year and a half before the United States was attacked—and could so confidently and floridly slander a generation's received wisdom made him suspect among his intellectual cohort. But his true faith made him an excellent propagandist for preparedness. Surely FDR understood this and so seized on MacLeish when the moment availed itself. Meanwhile, MacLeish carried on, assiduously preparing the Library of Congress for a war of words, ideas, and intellectual resources.

Libraries as the Symbolic Repositories of Democracy

In the name of serving democracy in a broad cultural war against fascist values, MacLeish took up a campaign to reinforce the value of libraries in U.S. life, urging librarians to "become active and not passive agents of the democratic process."[39] At the same time that he was preparing the Library of Congress (LC) and challenging the nation's libraries to enlist their institutions in the battle for democratic values, he was also called into increasingly partisan work by President Roosevelt to become a speechwriter and director of the OFF as FDR's "minister of culture."

This work generated a confluence of activities and rhetoric among permanent cultural institutions and ad hoc wartime agencies. MacLeish understood the rich symbolic and practical roles the Library of Congress, and U.S. libraries in general, could play in the war effort. He also recognized that library resources could be utilized on two fronts of the propaganda wars: as part of the antifascist, national security defense and as instruments for promoting a common perception of national aims and a common cultural inheritance, a major thrust of the democratic propaganda MacLeish tried to promote.[40] MacLeish used these platforms as librarian and OFF director to become a national spokesman on the requirements of a speech-tolerant liberal democracy at war at the same time that he energetically prepared the library for a national security-oriented prosecution of the war.[41]

MacLeish made a series of statements about the relationship among libraries, democracy, and the cultural resistance to fascism that reiterated themes he developed in "The Irresponsibles" and other essays of the period. For instance, in a June 1940 *Atlantic Monthly* essay entitled "Of the Librarian's Profession," he celebrated the librarian as the keeper of a common culture who had a more or less spiritual commitment to humanity. In normal times the librarian's job was merely to preserve the records of human creativity and to show "discretion, dignity, and a judicial calm" in so doing.[42] But the fascist impulse toward a primitive nationalism, propaganda's corruption of language, and intellectual chauvinism changed the job requirement and the significance of those treasures: "In the world in which we live it is no longer agreed that the common culture is a common treasure. There are governments abroad, and there are citizens here to whom the common culture which draws the peoples of the West together is a common evil for which each nation must now substitute a private culture, a parochial art, a local poetry, and a tribal worship." MacLeish pinpointed two especially frightening dangers: fascists seemed intent on destroying the creative, inquisitive impulse in Western culture, and propaganda destroyed faith that meaningful, dependable language could be utilized to express larger purposes. He warned that such cynicism about language had created "the essential character of our time": "that the triumph of the lie, the mutilation of culture, and the persecution of the word no longer shock us into anger" (p. 32). He urged librarians therefore to defend language and books as "records of the human spirit—the records of men's watch upon the world and on themselves." Librarians, he said, had an obligation not just to preserve but to display these records because making that intellectual inheritance available to the people would be "itself a kind of warfare" (p. 35).

MacLeish's other essays and speeches from the prewar period frequently enunciated these ideas about librarians' obligations to affirm the democratic legacy in the Western cultural tradition. His understanding of the crisis meant that by late 1939 the United States and its people were faced with an either/or dilemma. In "Libraries in the Contemporary Crisis," he exclaimed to his fellow librarians:

> The "either," as I see it, is the education of the people of this country. The "or" is fascism. We will either educate the people of this Republic to know, and therefore to value and therefore to preserve their own democratic culture, or we will watch the people of this Republic trade their democratic culture for the non-culture, the obscurantism, the superstition, the brutality, the tyranny which is overrunning eastern and central and southern Europe.[43]

Librarians could serve as democratic propagandists by offering the strategy of truth to counter fascism's propaganda of deceit and could offer valuable information to help Americans make informed decisions about the European war.[43]

In arguing that librarians "must themselves become active and not passive agents of the democratic process," MacLeish explicitly justified what was taking place within the Library of Congress itself. In a May 1940 essay titled "Librarians and the Democratic Process," he tacitly suggested that some libraries should go beyond the mere provision of information to the U.S. public, because they could have an intelligence function as well, mainly through the provision of specialized information to the experts working on behalf of that public. Librarians could make their institutions more efficient and therefore more useful by "subject[ing] the record of experience to intelligent control so that all parts of that record shall be somewhere deposited," by bringing "to the servicing of that record the greatest learning and the most responsible intelligence the country can provide," and by "mak[ing] available the relevant parts of that record to those who have need of it at the time they have need of it and in a form responsive to their need." In an injunction to the librarians, he offered praise for their accomplishments and laid down this challenge: "Surely these are not difficulties beyond the competence of the men and women who have constructed in this country one of the greatest library systems the world has seen" (p. 151).

Putting that great library system to work should be recognized as one of MacLeish's chief contributions to the war effort. It illustrates his pragmatic vision of how intellectual and institutional resources could be deployed. It helps explain why FDR would choose him as OFF director. And it also helps us understand how MacLeish's commitment to his own self-identified brand of "pro-democratic liberalism" was put to the test during the war, especially as he built the LC into an institution that served the nervous "antifascist liberalism" of the emerging national security state.[45]

In the prewar years, MacLeish expressed the free speech ideal when all around nervous liberals were constructing a punitive propaganda prophylaxis. But as the emergency deepened, as MacLeish's own fears about the power of dissenting speech and antiwar propaganda surfaced—witness his attacks on writers—and as the LC itself became part of the intelligence state's bureaucracy, his stated commitments were severely challenged by the imperatives of total war. MacLeish's own drift toward the logic of state-centered, security-oriented liberalism reflects larger shifts within U.S. liberalism in general, based on fears of antidemocratic propaganda, suspicions about public susceptibilities, the overarching desire for uniformity of opinion and action, and an uncritical confidence in and reliance on expert management of information and opinion.[46]

The Office of Facts and Figures

Prodded by interventionist cabinet members and advisers to create an agency that would begin to prepare the nation for war psychologically, President Roosevelt established the Office of Facts and Figures within the Office of Emergency Management in October 1941. Having already declared an unlimited emergency, FDR established the OFF "for the purpose of facilitating the dissemination of factual information . . . on the progress of the defense effort and on the defense policies and activities of the Government" and appointed the able rhetorician MacLeish director.[47] Limited by lack of direction from the White House and overly dependent on other agencies for facts and figures, MacLeish remained at the post only briefly, and his short-lived tenure was rife with controversy.

In his acceptance address of October 26, 1941, MacLeish spoke enthusiastically about the opportunity to "render additional service" in the field of providing information "as to the facts and figures of national defense." He acknowledged that his library had been "necessarily concerned" about matters related to national defense and that his two positions would be mutually reinforcing, not contradictory or competing. He also addressed the perception of potential conflicts in his dual roles, especially the difficulty of reconciling the state's control over the dissemination of information with a democratic citizenry's needs to be informed. Invoking democratic theory, he tried to reconcile these competing imperatives:

> The Office of Facts and Figures is established, as I understand it, upon the assumption that the people of a self-governing country are entitled to the fullest possible statement of the facts and figures bearing upon the conditions with which their government is faced. The essential difference between a democracy and a despotic form of government is that a democracy is based upon a complete trust in the people and a democratic service of information must necessarily reflect that trust.[48]

MacLeish labored in his work as OFF director and librarian to reflect this orientation; however, as the state's security and information needs grew, he sometimes proved a better champion of democratic rhetoric than of democratic practice.

Decades later MacLeish expressed his understanding that the goals of managing the state's information and providing the U.S. public with trustworthy information were not as compatible as he had stated publicly. (Whether he felt this at the time of his appointment is not clear.) In his interviews with Drabeck and Ellis he contended that he always found being director of the OFF and assistant director of the OWI distasteful, explaining his resignation from the OWI by saying that "my experience at the Office of War Information was so repulsive to me that I just wanted to get out of everything I was doing and clear out."[49] He added:

> I hated information work. I did it because I was asked to do it, and I always detested it. I suppose in times of peace, so-called, you could probably devote yourself to information, trying to help a self-governing people to govern themselves by seeing that they got the information they had to have. But in war you were always on the verge of propaganda and . . . although some of the propaganda you could

give your whole heart to, some you couldn't. I just detested it. . . .
As soon as I felt that I could honorably get out of it, I did. (p. 155)

But in 1941 MacLeish knew that U.S. opinion and morale would be the
"crucial battleground of [the] war," that the U.S. public needed to be convinced that U.S. intervention was necessary, and that he could be effective
in persuading them of this. Historians of the Office of War Information
suggest that one of MacLeish's distinguishing characteristics was his insistent hope that the OFF would pursue the strategy of truth with its propaganda and that disseminating "facts and figures" would be a democratic
form of persuasion.[50]

For MacLeish, Nazi propaganda techniques and even those employed
by George Creel's Committee on Public Information in WWI embodied
the antithesis of what he hoped to do in the OFF. He announced that the
OFF would "not use bally-hoo methods," for "a democratic government
is more concerned with the provision of information to the people than it
is with the communication of dreams and aspirations." Assuming that an
informed citizenry is competent to make its own judgments, he went on
to say that "the duty of government is to provide a basis for judgment; and
when it goes beyond that, it goes beyond the prime scope of its duty" (p.
23). Along these lines, MacLeish distinguished between different kinds of
propaganda and their legitimacy. He opposed, for instance, the willingness
of Office of Strategic Services director "Wild Bill" Donovan to use false,
or "black," propaganda as an instrument of psychological warfare. Wanting to avoid deception, lies, disinformation, atrocity stories, and the creation of false expectations, MacLeish thought it possible to formulate a
truthful and inspiring democratic justification for the war—and a blueprint for its aftermath—that could be employed for mobilizing public
opinion without deceiving the public or creating false perceptions of what
was actually at stake. He also learned early on that the information the
OFF provided—about the state of military preparedness, for instance—
had to be accurate and not tainted by undue optimism, whereas there was
more leeway when making distinctions between Nazism as a force and
U.S. democracy as an idea.[51]

Despite MacLeish's reassurances that he would provide straightforward
information, Congress and the press met the establishment of the OFF
with deep skepticism, and MacLeish met with a whole host of frustrations.
As he later reflected, the press—also burned by WWI and acutely aware
of the totalitarian state's information monopolies—made him the scape-
goat because of its hostility to the idea of a centralized government information clearinghouse. Congress, increasingly opposed to the emergency-

period power of FDR's administration, loathed the idea of a wartime propaganda agency that might promote Roosevelt and his interventionist ideas exclusively and so provided little money to the new agency. The War Department, along with the individual military branches, was insistent about controlling information about the progress of war preparedness and the war and frequently failed to provide the OFF with information it desired. And FDR, famous for letting his assistants and cabinet officers float controversial ideas and take the blame for them, provided MacLeish with little direction or support during his eight months as director of the OFF. Thus, after a frustrating start, Roosevelt disbanded MacLeish's OFF and created a new agency, the Office of War Information (OWI), appointing at MacLeish's urging the well-respected journalist Elmer Davis as director. MacLeish worked as Davis's deputy director for a short while but soon left to return full-time to the Library of Congress, where he continued to be extensively involved in war-related communications and intelligence work, until he took a State Department public affairs position in 1944.

Long before his appointment at the OFF MacLeish had been pulled into the interstices of the federal government's expanding information control network. As librarian he served on a host of interrelated public-opinion and intelligence-oriented committees or councils, including the National Defense Commission, the interdepartmental Committee on War Information (which he had established as director of the OFF), and the Committee of the Office of Censorship. Even as he left the official propaganda agency, he remained closely connected to many of the people with whom he had worked to set up the wartime information intelligence agencies and was firmly dedicated to securing the victory over fascism on two fronts: through the mobilization of intellectual and informational resources and through the neutralization of the fascist propaganda directed at the U.S. public.

The Library at War: Procuring Intelligence Materials

The Library of Congress performed vital emergency-period service by procuring a wide variety of domestic and foreign materials for its collections. Records from the library's archives illustrate that every conceivable division or branch turned to war-related work. All research divisions—including the Slavic and Asiatic divisions, the Hispanic Foundation, the Legislative Research Service, and the divisions of Maps, Periodicals, Documents, Reference, and Bibliography—compiled bibliographies and worked with other federal agencies to secure information.[52] Experts from each of the library's divisions surveyed key industries and industrial journals—political, economic, chemical, metallurgical, mining, and manufacturing, among others—to make sure that up-to-date research materials from home and abroad were on hand for the National Defense Council and other scientific agencies engaged in war production, planning, and research.[53]

The library staff compiled a volume on the resources available elsewhere in the nation's libraries, entitled *Guide to Library Facilities for National Defense*. It acquired invaluable collections of domestic and foreign propaganda materials, ranging from films, radio transcriptions, newspapers, periodicals, and pamphlets to official foreign gazettes.[54] And library facilities, including the reading room and the newly constructed annex, were turned over to government agencies, with special sections set aside for researchers from different intelligence agencies, including Harold Lasswell's Experimental Division for the Study of Wartime Communications and the coordinator of information's Division of Special Information (the precursor to the Research and Analysis Branch of the Office of Strategic Services). In short, the Library of Congress under MacLeish's leadership did what he told librarians it should do: it became an intellectual instrument of war by gathering, organizing, and subjecting to expert analysis a tremendous amount of scientific, technical, geographical, cartographic, cultural, economic, legal, political, and military information.

Some examples of MacLeish's work are instructive, both as to the obstacles the LC confronted and to MacLeish's skillful management of useful relationships. With the European war widening, MacLeish and his staff were faced with greater than normal impediments to the collection and transportation of materials to the United States: by as early as 1938 some countries had begun prohibiting exports to the United States, and as tensions intensified from 1939 to 1941, the prohibitions became stricter (especially on military and naval publications). Increasing difficulties of communication and the sinking and delaying of ships added to the problems. Likewise, the United States government's own expanding censorship activities made the LC's task more complicated. This heightened the importance of MacLeish's deftness as a bridge builder and mediator among competing agencies, especially because the task of obtaining materials from abroad required special cooperation with the State Department and U.S. embassy personnel.[55]

As far as German materials were concerned, MacLeish had successfully drawn on the library's prestige and his own State Department and White House connections to make the library a central repository of seized German documents.[56] But negotiating these transfers became increasingly problematic as U.S. conflict with Germany neared. MacLeish's main contact in Germany was Jack Wade Dunaway of the Office of the Military Attaché in the U.S. embassy in Berlin, and their correspondence indicates the shrinking number of information-transfer networks available to embassy personnel, along with the increased danger Americans were experiencing when trying to procure materials of any sort from Germany or any of the German-occupied nations. Dunaway told MacLeish that any Axis materials would have to come from whatever sources they could find: the U.S. consulate in Portugal would make sure that anything passing through there would get to the LC, as would the ambassador in Spain; the librarian of the U.S. embassy in Paris was securing fascist propaganda materials and storing them in the embassy preparatory to shipping them out. Meanwhile, diplomatic pouches from Paris to Berlin had been discontinued since late January 1941, and Germany was opening the mail and censoring the telephone in Vichy France. The U.S. embassy staff in Berlin was trying, Dunaway said, to collect relevant periodicals and publications, but "at this time even some of the most normal activities of the Americans here are considered suspicious, and we are not receiving ordinary cooperation in many of our requests."[57]

A month later, in May 1941, Dunaway added:

> The anti-American feeling is being whipped up here daily. It is becoming increasingly obnoxious, and makes living in Berlin for us more and more difficult and unpleasant. There are a number of interesting large posters on bulletin boards along the streets that have unflattering pictures of the Jewish members of our Government. These photographs are captioned with derogatory and effective comments. Unfortunately, the posters are locked by key behind glass doors, and I have so far been unsuccessful in obtaining any of the four or five that I have seen around.[58]

Dunaway's letters testify to difficulty the library had obtaining materials from abroad. And complaints from other agencies speak to the consequent holes in the library's scientific, political, and economic literature. It was in this context that the Library of Congress and other government agencies struggling to obtain international scientific, economic, and political materials learned that U.S. postal officials were routinely destroying literally tons of books, newspapers, pamphlets, journals, and other items deemed "unmailable propaganda" by port-of-entry postal authorities. The effects of this vast destruction of potentially useful intelligence materials are not clear, but as the following account shows, propaganda analysts, scholars, librarians, and others engaged in communications intelligence were horrified by what the post office officials had allowed. And given the number of agencies relying on the Library of Congress and given that cooperation with other federal agencies was critical, the censorship practices of the Post Office Department seem as outrageous as its critics declared. MacLeish's response to those practices show his exasperation as an intelligence officer and civil libertarian; they also show that he was an effective problem solver, information procurer, and institution builder who worked effectively within the information control bureaucracies.

The Battle Over Postal Censorship

In May 1940 FDR requested that all incoming mail serving the aims of enemies of the United States be seized at the borders; under this secret directive, together with authority granted by the Foreign Agents Registration Act of 1938, an attorney general opinion from December 1940, and a 1857 postal statute barring incendiary (i.e., abolitionist) materials from the mails, the Post Office Department began seizing enormous amounts of bulk mail at its twelve different ports of entry. Between December 1940 and November 1941 the Post Office Department's dead letter office burned approximately a hundred tons of materials deemed unmailable by port-of-entry postal inspectors.[59]

Once he learned about this policy from the Library of Congress–housed intelligence researchers, various university-based scholars, and several U.S. booksellers specializing in materials from Europe and Asia, MacLeish engaged in an eight-month-long battle with postal authorities to rectify the problem. But as he worked toward solutions he also made significant security-related concessions to government censors on this issue. In the end, he helped devise a policy whereby almost all the "unmailable" propaganda would continue to be destroyed but with limited copies made available through the Library of Congress to a small number of carefully selected scholars and intelligence personnel. His actions and language illustrate just how skittish federal authorities were about the power of foreign propaganda materials and exemplify how the movement toward war led officials to accept policies based on the assumption that the public had little to gain and much to lose from exposure to the ideas and images disseminated by Axis and Soviet publicists.

The policies resulting in mail burning also reflect the difficulties of coordinating the vast wartime state. Whereas U.S.-based scholars and government researchers specializing in Germany and the USSR needed the books and full runs of the journal and newspaper subscriptions, the port-of-entry postal officials deemed them unmailable propaganda, with only destructive potential. Justice Department officials worried about these materials being too widely available to the public and wanted access limited to those with official authority. And MacLeish, whose strategy-of-truth pronouncements as OFF director promised public access to vital wartime information, was caught in the middle, brokering a compromise that included the public merely as the indirect beneficiary of better government propaganda analysis.

Before MacLeish learned about the postal policy, academic historians and librarians at the New York Public Library, Stanford University, and Princeton University, as well as the LC's own Reference Division director, David Mearns, wrote letters to the post office inquiring about the whereabouts of missing subscriptions and book orders. Mearns, who himself learned about the policy through a post office press release, requested—to no avail—that the LC should at least be furnished some copies of these materials before the bulk were destroyed. In March 1941 Post Office Solicitor General Vincent M. Miles replied to Mearns in the inimitably passive language of bureaucracies, telling him that with the exception of one copy for the post office files and two copies for the Justice Department's Special Defense Unit, the post office found it "not practicable to comply with your request with respect to foreign propaganda prints heretofore excluded from the mails." Explaining that the procedures were in compliance with authority granted by the attorney general's 1940 opinion, the post office solicitor advised Mearns that perhaps the Justice Department would supply the LC with a copy of each item, but only if these materials "would not be made available for examination by the general public until after the eclipse of six months or so following the date of its exclusion."[60] From the library's perspective this was a wholly unsatisfactory response.

Princeton University librarian Julian Boyd learned about the post office policy from a newsreel, and his letter to MacLeish dripped fury. Articulating the position oft stated by MacLeish that a capable people needed all available information in order for democracy to function, Boyd railed against the assumptions behind the policy and its potential consequences: "I have just seen a profoundly shocking thing: a Metro-Goldwyn-Mayer News Reel showing a Federal official in San Francisco in the act of destroying what he, in language that was scarcely literate, described as subversive propaganda. . . . The profoundly shocking part of this act of destruction was in the officially complacent assumption that the act was in itself a good thing, that it was part of this government's effort to protect American institutions." Boyd, recognizing that national security imperatives were at work, recommended as a solution that "a couple tons" be sent to Princeton, where a carefully chosen faculty committee could analyze and report on the materials.[61]

MacLeish's first attempt to solve the problem appropriated Boyd's idea, but only after addressing the grotesque symbolic failure of the policy. Writing to Postmaster General Frank C. Walker, MacLeish began: "The burning of propaganda material at San Francisco seems to be causing quite a stir in academic circles. . . . I think you will probably agree with me that it is unfortunate to have the idea go abroad that we burn the books we don't like just as the Nazis burn the books they don't like. Undoubtedly, the great masses of propaganda material which come in have got to be dealt with somehow, but I wonder if they can't be dealt with to the advantage of American libraries and the information services of the American government."[62] He then recommended that materials be deposited at a handful of select universities for analysis on behalf of federal agencies.

A week later, in April 1941, Postmaster General Walker told MacLeish that under the legal provisions of the Foreign Agents Registration Act of 1938, ports-of-entry offices were indeed engaged in seizing and destroying incoming propaganda, especially the materials coming "via Siberia in Japanese vessels to the ports of San Francisco and San Pedro." He reported that "several tons [were] received via each incoming Japanese ship" and that "many tons of this matter have already been burned at San Francisco."[63] He further informed MacLeish that he did not appreciate the comparison to Nazi tactics and asserted that sending materials to select universities was not feasible. He then tried to mollify MacLeish by explaining that those opposing post office policy were misinformed and "seemed to have gained the impression that nonpolitical matter was being destroyed." Walker assured MacLeish that only "political" propaganda pamphlets—as defined by the postal authorities themselves—were being destroyed.[64] The difference between political and nonpolitical items was an important one for Walker, because the Foreign Agent Registration Act applied to political propaganda and not to scientific, literary, religious, and other kinds of materials, but to those engaged in formal propaganda analysis, such a distinction made little sense.

Despite subsequent post office efforts to conciliate the librarian, delay followed delay in resolving the interagency jurisdictional and administrative disputes. Over the next four months MacLeish became increasingly incensed about a national security policy that allowed potentially valuable intelligence materials to be destroyed without trained experts first having the chance to examine them; likewise, he continued to protest the symbolic dimension of U.S. government officials burning the mails. Responding to inquiries from Senator Guy Gillette, MacLeish noted that he and others were "distressed to see the United States Government apparently engaged, as the Nazis had been engaged sometime before, in burning printed matter offensive to this Government." Pointing to very recent postal destruction of issues of the Soviet newspapers *Pravda* and *Isvestia*, MacLeish argued that the post office had "inflicted a serious injury upon vital materials of American scholarship." "Moreover," he added, "it is not only American scholarship which suffers. Those charged with the administration of this government are vitally concerned to know the state of opinion and the direction of propaganda, both for internal and external consumption, in the totalitarian states. To deprive them of this information seems to me to inflict a serious injury upon the administration of this government." Finally, addressing the postmaster general's assertion that the morale of the American people would be harmed by contact with such material, he said: "Personally, I have far too much faith in the good sense and sanity of the American people to believe that propaganda materials loaded upon them from abroad can have very much effect in any case— least of all if those materials are held in the files of the great scholarly and research libraries of the country."[65]

MacLeish also tried to enlist other members of the communications intelligence community, including Justice Department officials Francis Biddle and Lawrence M. C. Smith, chief of the Special Defense Unit (SDU). But the post office policies put these Justice Department officials in a quandary. Charged with constructing a legal and physical defense against antidemocratic propaganda, they wrote the pertinent laws and drafted the attorney general's opinion and thus argued that the post office had the legal grounds to seize and destroy all unregistered incoming mail. They knew that tons of material were being destroyed, but because their arrangement with the post office ensured that SDU propaganda analysts were getting enough copies of the seized materials to do their work and keep their files complete, some Justice lawyers did not see the grounds of MacLeish's complaints. Their only questions involved how many copies would be preserved and where they would be placed. Some Justice lawyers agreed with MacLeish, however, and argued that a policy should be worked out where multiple copies of all seized materials should be turned over directly to the Library of Congress, but only for the purpose of government research and analysis.

The SDU chief Lawrence M. C. "Sam" Smith proffered what he hoped would be an administratively workable solution. In mid-May 1941 he told MacLeish that he had learned it would be possible to preserve for scholars copies of propaganda material declared unmailable, but only if ultimate control of these materials would still reside with the Justice Department.[66] Several weeks later Smith modified this position, telling MacLeish that he saw no reason why these materials should not be turned over to the LC once the SDU had "made such use of [them] as we deem necessary."[67]

While these adjustments may have served the needs of the Department of Justice and the Library of Congress–based researchers who would then have access to the materials, they certainly did not satisfy the needs of scholars working outside Washington, D.C. Nor did they address the symbolic problem of burning the mails. And neither did they satisfy the interests of booksellers whose shipments from abroad, especially from the Soviet Union, were being seized. Together, booksellers and academic historians led the next stage of a campaign to secure materials necessary to their commerce and research, with MacLeish becoming increasingly active on their behalf. One bookseller in particular led the campaign: C. J. Lambkin, president of the Four Continent Book Corporation (which had already been convicted and fined by the Justice Department in 1940 for failing to register under the Foreign Agent Registration Act). Lambkin primarily sold books and papers published in the Soviet Union, serving, among others, leading scholars at Columbia, the University of Chicago, and elsewhere. He contacted these customers and explained the problem: "The situation at the present time is that all books coming from the USSR are read by special translators and practically all books and pamphlets dealing with history, economics, politics and law are held non-mailable. Even such books as stenographic reports of sessions of the Supreme Soviet . . . have been held non-mailable and the books destroyed." His customers assailed MacLeish with letters, asking him to get the "absurd ruling reversed." Columbia University historian Geroid Robinson (who was subsequently housed at the LC when he worked for the Office of Strategic Services) wrote to MacLeish saying that "from the point of view of those who are working for the development of research work in the Russian field, the situation described in the enclosed letter is really disastrous. There is not a research man in the field who would not be deeply grateful to you if you could make it possible for the libraries of the country to get the Russian materials that they so urgently need."[68] MacLeish agreed that the policy was disastrous from the standpoint of intelligence work, but he did not advocate a total lifting of censorship. He forwarded the letters to the Justice Department and urged further modification of the policy.

MacLeish become increasingly angry about the legality of the post office's destroying materials subscribed to by other government agencies. Writing to Miles and Smith, MacLeish noted that his law librarian found no legal authority for the Post Office Department to destroy materials addressed to any government agency: "I am sorry to burden you further with observations of mine on this head, but I am, as I believe you have gathered, considerably upset over a practice which combines censorship (and not only general censorship but censorship of the sources of cultural information) with destruction of government property without, as far as I can see, any authority whatever in law."[69] He continued to push the matter, writing to Smith a week later about the Justice Department's own insufficient authority to seize these materials and the overall folly of destroying materials necessary to intelligence work: "I cannot refrain from adding that the spectacle is one of the most ridiculous of which I am capable of conceiving. A great country engaged, or about to engage, in a critical struggle for the defense of liberty of the mind and freedom of the spirit practices in effect a policy of self-censorship which not only denies all its allegations of principle, but which cripples its efforts in its own defense." He continued by telling Smith that he wanted the Foreign Agents Registration Act (FARA) "specifically amended to except all materials purchased by the Library of Congress—the National Library. The Librarian of Congress is an officer of this government . . . and he is, I believe, capable of carrying the responsibility imposed on his collections in the future as he has in the past. Certainly he should not be policed by the Post Office Department, nor should agents of that Department be permitted to determine what the collections of the National Library should contain."[70]

By the fall of 1941, MacLeish and the SDU's Smith helped find a solution, with the post office slowly and reluctantly shifting its position. Smith told Post Office Solicitor Vincent Miles in October 1941 that the Justice Department wanted to secure copies of all materials declared unmailable by the post office; then, rather than having the post office destroy anything, the Justice Department would make the decisions about mailability. In addition, it would see to it that the Library of Congress's heavily used facilities would receive forty-five copies, "if available, of all foreign propaganda material," with the caveat that "studies and analysis thereof . . . would be used solely for the benefit of the Government." Finally, addressing a legal issue about agency jurisdiction that MacLeish had been harping on, Smith noted that this solution of making forty-five copies available was "altogether aside from whatever rights the Library may have to secure material to which it has subscribed."[71] The post office continued to destroy unregistered foreign bulk mail, after obtaining key information—including the names of addressees—that might aid the Justice Department in its enforcement of the FARA and Voorhis Act.

Eight months after MacLeish began his letter-writing campaign, he wrote Postmaster General Walker a conciliatory letter, thanking him for his cooperation and making it quite clear that, like Walker, he still had national security concerns very much in mind and by no means did he intend to make the materials at issue available to the public at large. In a concession to the postal authorities, MacLeish told Walker that the forty-five copies housed at the LC would be handled under restrictions defined by the post office itself: "My suggestion would be that they be reserved from public use, that only officers and agents of government and serious scholars engaged in purely scholarly work should have access to them, and that no publication be authorized except by responsible officers of the federal government. . . . We shall gladly execute your request to destroy intercepted materials above the forty-five copies."[72]

This episode shows MacLeish playing a number of roles: outraged defender of democratic symbolism; mediator between the academy and the government; defender of his own institutional prerogatives; and effective administrator for the burgeoning national security state. This was not the only episode where MacLeish would protect multiple domains in his roles as propagandist and intelligence official, and it was certainly not the only episode where his civil libertarian impulses and strategy-of-truth ideal would run up against what he considered the unsavory and undemocratic practices of black propaganda and the failure to define the meaning of the war in terms larger than a victory over fascism.

Intelligence in the Library: The Division of Special Information

While MacLeish and the Library of Congress staff fought other bureaucracies over access to and control of vital wartime information, they also gathered whatever information they could to function as the central information clearinghouse for a host of government planning agencies and to serve the embryonic domestic and foreign intelligence operations housed in the library. Accordingly, aside from housing Lasswell's Experimental Division (originally called the War Communications Unit), the library worked closely with the State Department and "Wild Bill" Donovan's Office of the Coordinator of Information (which later became the Office of Strategic Services, or OSS) to establish a foreign intelligence research and analysis operation out of the library's annex. The Division of Special Information (DSI) set up shop in the library in the summer of 1941, under the LC's budget, and remained officially separate from Donovan's operations until it was absorbed by the OSS's Research and Analysis Branch in 1943.[73]

Assistant Secretary of State Adolf Berle planted the seeds for the Division of Special Information in June 1941 when he suggested to MacLeish that the State Department ought to establish a "Bureau of Analysis and Information," under LC auspices, to provide analysis of communications and information control policies in all European areas under German and Italian control. As he told MacLeish, even though the State Department received "a certain amount of information on these matters, it ha[d] neither the material nor the staff to enable it to follow closely the vast amount of printed material, newspaper, professional and official, which bears upon the subject," and the United States needed to be able to anticipate "the position and policies of the totalitarian governments" and understand "their treatment of the peoples they have conquered. . . . This fuller insight is essential for the satisfactory direction of American policy and for protection of national interest." Berle told MacLeish that "should the Library of Congress be able to undertake this work," MacLeish could be assured of the State Department's "full cooperation."[74]

MacLeish pursued this idea with Donovan, the newly appointed director of the Office of the Coordinator of Information (CoI), telling him, "It has become increasingly clear to me during the past two years that libraries have a much more important role to play" in adding "depth and historical perspective to the intelligence work of the Federal Government." MacLeish initially suggested that if Donovan wanted he could set up an information-collecting and -organizing unit within the LC, but the LC would establish its own foreign intelligence project in any case. With proper financing, MacLeish wrote, "the Library of Congress stands ready to organize a staff of experts and reference assistants to provide detailed information as needed, translations, background studies, research reports, and analyses of policy issues over the whole area to be covered by the intelligence service. This staff . . . would be an integral part of the Library of Congress, and the Library of Congress would assume full responsibility for its management and for the integrity and completeness of its work." Averring that the LC would better serve Donovan's incipient foreign intelligence needs than the State Department could, MacLeish also addressed existing tensions between the State Department and the CoI, proposing that the LC's "services would be made available exclusively to the intelligence agency . . . and all its work would be confidential to that agency."[75]

For several years, MacLeish did in fact have a semi-independent foreign intelligence research unit in the LC. But it was never as free from Donovan's oversight as MacLeish hoped it might be, nor was it as engaged in primary research and analysis as he had planned. Shortly after he conveyed his plans to Donovan, communications intelligence stalwarts held a July 1941 conference in which they worked out plans for the research project housed at the LC. They also clarified this project's relationship to Donovan's growing operations. MacLeish, University of Minnesota president

Guy Stanton Ford, Edward Earle Mead of the Institute for Advanced Study at Princeton, Robert T. Crane, director of the Social Science Research Council, Dr. Solon Buck of the National Archives, Library of Congress Legislative Research Service Director Ernest Griffith, and Assistant Librarian of Congress Luther Evans focused on finding a group of experts who would be housed at the LC and work with Donovan's staff in a unit the conference participants named the Division of Special Information. As MacLeish explained to Donovan in a postconference memo, "The sense of the conference [was] that it would be more useful to you to have the best intelligence the country affords in the general area of History, Economics, the Social Sciences, with special emphasis on military and naval affairs than to have more purely academic figures chosen because of their competence in a particular area."[76]

Apparently those in attendance could not agree on who those best minds were, but they did agree on a few: "The general view was that President Baxter of Williams would be the best man to head up the scholarly and research services of your Office." Harvard's modern European historian William C. Langer was slated to become the research director. The LC's own Ernest Griffith would serve as the administrative head but would also retain his administrative position with the LC's Legislative Research Service.[77] As MacLeish told Donovan, "It was felt that the Division of Special Information should be organized with a very able Director (ideally Langer) known generally to American scholars whose function it would be, first, to direct the research projects of the Division . . . and, secondly, to maintain consistent liaison with scholars in and outside universities who would act as a sort of Reserve Corps of American scholarship." In an August 26 letter to James Baxter of Donovan's office, MacLeish elaborated on the idea of creating this "reserve corps" of U.S. scholars by establishing networks among scholars, international businesspeople, and others, such as foundation officers, whose expertise and connections could serve the inchoate intelligence network.[78]

Legendary for his take-charge bravura, Donovan wanted control over the Division of Special Information, referring to it as the "joint undertaking." He minimized the role of the DSI as a primary research unit and saw it instead as having a compiling, editing, synthesizing, and analyzing function. Edward Griffith explained to MacLeish Donovan's understanding of the DSI's limits and the institutional hierarchies within the intelligence community:

Colonel Donovan has asked the Library of Congress to act as the instrument through which the scholarly resources of the nation can serve the emergency needs of the federal government. . . . This Division will exist solely to serve Colonel Donovan's Office and will at once undertake to assemble and prepare for use the background material relating to foreign affairs. . . . In this fashion, the United States will have an Intelligence Service which would combine the qualities of immediacy and perspective.

Griffith went on to minimize the role of the DSI, noting that "the methods used must be to some extent experimental" but that the office would consist of "a modest staff of historians, economists, political scientists, geographers, and sociologists working in the Library" who would be in contact with "a much larger panel of consultants throughout the nation who are experts in the particular areas concerned," primarily the British empire, Russia, the Near East, the Far East, Latin America, Western Europe, and Middle Europe. Each unit would have a large enough staff to address historical, economic, geographic, cultural, and governmental questions, Griffith said. But he also went on to inform MacLeish that Donovan foresaw the DSI performing rather mundane background research functions, including discovering and indexing relevant research, preparing bibliographies on existing material, identifying special collections in different libraries, compiling a who's who "of men who are, or are likely to become, significant in policies of specified nations," setting up the reserve army of expert consultants inside and outside the government, identifying possible future problems, issues, and developments, and writing memos on specific problems as they became critical.[79]

Although this was not nearly as prominent a research division as MacLeish had imagined, by autumn 1941 the Division of Special Information was up and running as a background research and data-collecting branch for Donovan's ever-expanding foreign intelligence operations. Donovan offered his thanks: "I cannot write such a letter as this without simultaneously expressing my personal appreciation for your willingness to provide the services outlined and the individual cooperative spirit you and your staff have indicated in this joint undertaking."[80] In part, Donovan was thanking MacLeish for his attention to the administration of financial and spatial arrangements and other administrative problems involved in housing the DSI at the library. The DSI was financed out of the Executive Office budget, and in November 1941 the LC received from the Bureau of the Budget $100,000 to establish a working fund for the DSI. In July 1942 the bureau transferred another $176,749 to the LC for the continuation of the Division of Special Information, providing for 208 employees.[81]

By the beginning of 1943, the relationship between the LC's DSI and Donovan's OSS changed, with the OSS absorbing all responsibility for the DSI into its budget and administrative purview. On New Year's Eve, 1942, Donovan offered MacLeish his deep appreciation "for all the efforts you have made to provide space and to supply special service to members of the Division of Special Information. The assistance of the Library has been invaluable to the work of this office," he said. Noting that the "administrative arrangements originally made were not ideal" and that the administration of the "joint undertaking" had been a source of "constant inconvenience," Donovan told MacLeish that he was placing the entire administration of DSI directly under the OSS. All members of the DSI staff would "cease being employed by the Library of Congress and in the future their status will be that of employees of Office of Strategic Services," and all expenses would become the responsibility of the OSS. While Donovan took these steps to solidify his control over OSS functions and personnel, however, he certainly could not afford to break ties with the library and its reading space and information resources: "We still need the facilities of the Library of Congress as badly as ever and . . . I should suppose that we would want to keep in the Library permanently as many as 150 people."[82]

MacLeish agreed to these changes but also made it clear that if the DSI was no longer officially connected to the library then the relationship between the persons connected to the DSI and the library would change, as would the nature of privileges accorded the OSS by the LC. He told Donovan that all former members of the library staff would be treated as any other government employees and all privileges accorded them would terminate; the library would, however, set aside a special reading room for OSS researchers.[83] Eventually this meant setting aside space on the third floor of the newly built library annex for over one hundred OSS researchers, in addition to housing a small, full-time OSS research and analysis staff consisting of several librarians, clerk-stenographers, receptionists, messengers, and guards.[84] By 1943 the DSI's intellectual labors were entirely controlled by Donovan and the Office of Strategic Services, but MacLeish's war-ready Library of Congress remained a valuable part of the government's intelligence operations.

Lasswell's Experimental Division

Neither as large as the DSI nor as well financed, Lasswell's Experimental Division for the Study of Wartime Communications remained technically independent from the LC and from the Justice Department, for which it did the bulk of its work. Primarily funded by the Rockefeller Foundation (and partially remunerated by Justice), it was essentially a domestic policy counterpart to the DSI. While the DSI worked mainly on background research on foreign intelligence matters, Lasswell's communications research project organized and analyzed antidemocratic, pro-Axis propaganda materials both at home and abroad and became integral to the work of the Justice Department's Special Defense Unit in establishing its strategies for analyzing and controlling propaganda materials in the United States.

The political climate in Congress, in the press, and in larger pockets of public opinion opposed the federal government's establishing anything resembling propaganda research (or even antipropaganda research). MacLeish's prewar work gathering information about U.S. communications intelligence capacities disposed him to support an experimental propaganda analysis project at the Library of Congress, so when Marshall approached MacLeish about the possibility of housing Lasswell's project, MacLeish embraced the idea enthusiastically, as did several officials from the departments of State and Justice who understood the need to develop a more comprehensive propaganda surveillance and analysis network.[85] Thus Lasswell's project began in November 1940 with a $20,000 grant from the Rockefeller Foundation to the Library of Congress Gift Fund.

Like the other Rockefeller Foundation projects with wartime applications, foundation officers intended that Lasswell's project be only temporarily dependent on the foundation, after which its work and methods would be absorbed into either the federal government or private industry.[86] Understanding this, Lasswell quickly tied his project to MacLeish's work, and one of his very first tasks once ensconced in the LC involved compiling a survey for MacLeish and Marshall entitled the "Present State of Communications Intelligence." Lasswell reported in great detail something they had an inkling of: that by the beginning of 1941, astonishingly little had been done to prepare the nation's communications intelligence apparatus for the emergency, with the exception of the Rockefeller projects.[87] Equally little had been organized in the way of measuring and manufacturing domestic public opinion, he reported. Key federal agencies were neither prepared to protect the U.S. public from unwanted propaganda materials from abroad nor to generate consent for emergency measures at home.

In the next eight months, Lasswell and R. Keith Kane of the Justice Department wrote MacLeish several more reports about the weaknesses of the government's prewar communications operations. The upshot of their first report was that even by May 1941 no department or agency in the federal government was undertaking "the over-all comparative analysis [of mass communications] so essential to defense against total warfare" and that the government still had extensive intelligence problems, including the need for greater coordination of "existing analytical activities," more "scientific methods of analysis," and centralized "collection of basic data in the United States and abroad which would be useful in the field of public opinion and propaganda analysis." Obviously, this conformed precisely to MacLeish's vision of the Library of Congress as a wartime agency and to Lasswell's hopes for his own project.

Their second report, written in August 1941, confirmed the same fundamental needs and identified the central role Lasswell's project could play in accumulating propaganda materials and training government personnel in "scientific methods of analysis."[88] While MacLeish used these reports to justify the organization of the Library of Congress itself—and later that of the OFF, with R. Keith Kane as chief of its Bureau of Intelligence—he also encouraged the Rockefeller Foundation's continued financial support for this type of work. Six months after Lasswell's project had been set up at the library, MacLeish wrote Marshall: "I should like to add for your private and confidential information that the Lasswell project has already justified its existence several times over in terms of usefulness to other agencies of the government. I believe you are familiar with the situation to which I refer. What use you may care to make of this information in discussions with your Trustees is for you to decide. I should like you personally, however, to know my views on this subject."[89] MacLeish was alluding in particular to Lasswell's work for the Justice Department's Special Defense Unit, work that Justice Department officials found highly valuable.[90] Armed with Lasswell's reports and MacLeish's judgment of the overall value of the project, John Marshall prodded the foundation to stay involved in these controversial areas, and his fellow officers agreed to renew Lasswell's grant for the duration of the war (although this did not come to pass).[91]

From the inception of Lasswell's project in 1940, the Justice Department had been asking the Library of Congress to subscribe to foreign-language newspapers from abroad; procure recordings of German radio broadcasts; collect pamphlets, posters, speeches, films, and other forms of propaganda; and provide personnel to help Lasswell code and analyze this data for Justice Department uses. While the State Department secured many of these materials and sent them through diplomatic pouch to the LC, the library used subscriptions to obtain others (which the Post Office Department took the liberty of destroying). While MacLeish recognized the value of these materials, he also stated his concerns to Solicitor General Francis Biddle about the drain on the Library's budget for items that were essentially "ephemera":

> To my mind there is no question but that the Library of Congress should accumulate . . . propaganda materials of interest to anyone in the government engaging in a study of totalitarian propaganda and other propaganda attacks upon ourselves. At the same time . . . the materials to be collected are not materials which we would add to our collections except for the special use of persons studying propaganda. Funds should therefore be provided, I should suppose, from some other source than the appropriation for the increase of the Library's general collections.[92]

As U.S. involvement in the war drew nearer, the Justice Department continued to increase its demand for LC acquisitions and personnel. SDU chief Lawrence M. C. Smith told MacLeish in October 1941 that the unit needed a closer working relationship with Lasswell's project, and he wanted a full-time SDU liaison on Lasswell's staff.[93] And just days before the Japanese attack on Pearl Harbor, R. Keith Kane (who would join MacLeish at the OFF with the war's outbreak) reiterated that the Justice Department's demands on the LC would only increase when the United States entered the war. To reassure MacLeish, however, he noted that because of the importance of the propaganda "ephemera" and the value of Lasswell's labors analyzing them, the Justice Department would subvene Lasswell's work on its behalf, pay for some of its own staff to work with Lasswell, and help pay for subscriptions to foreign propaganda materials.[94] It began doing so with its 1942 budget.

The elaborate relationships among the Library of Congress, the Justice Department, the Rockefeller Foundation, and Lasswell's Experimental Division project made for rather complicated and not always identifiable lines of institutional authority and financial responsibility. MacLeish, for example, acknowledged his appreciation of Lasswell's work but expressed exasperation at the inadequate record of the flow of money into his project.[95] But however ambiguous the financial arrangements, two things are clear: the Justice Department found Lasswell's Experimental Division highly useful for its propaganda defense work; and the Rockefeller Foundation subsidized that work for the first two years of WWII.[96]

The relationship benefited all parties: Lasswell's division helped the Special Defense Unit develop its own Organizations and Propaganda Analysis Section (OPAS) by assembling a content analysis staff for the unit; training unit personnel; preparing foundational studies on the structure of the Nazi, Fascist, and Communist parties and propaganda organizations; helping the unit analyze the huge domestic foreign-language press; and serving as a key expert witness in a series of federal trials (as I explore in chapter 6). The Library of Congress gained in importance as a national security research site, and its collections grew in kind.[97] And Lasswell was available to develop and demonstrate the scientific credibility of his techniques, enhancing his stature in the larger community of communication scholars. His wartime location in the Library of Congress gave him the opportunity to augment the communications intelligence network, and according to Justice Department intelligence officers, Lasswell contributed in a variety of ways to the successful prosecution of the state's propaganda enemies.[98]

Lasswell's Experimental Division served as a consulting and training operation for virtually every government agency or department with communications intelligence responsibilities; in fact, training government personnel in content and organization analysis techniques may have been the primary niche Lasswell's project filled. In a postwar retrospective, Lasswell described just how extensive this work had been: "The training facilities of the project supplied personnel to the Office of Facts and Figures; the Office of War Information; the Foreign Broadcast Intelligence Service; the Office of Censorship; the Office of Strategic Services; the Psychological Warfare Branch of the Department of the Army; and the Department of State." "At one point," he added, "we trained 50 people for content analysis work in the Justice Department, in six weeks," most of whom worked for the Organizations and Propaganda Analysis Section of the Special Defense Unit.[99] This training component of Lasswell's project parallels Kris and Speier's work at the New School and illustrates once again how Rockefeller Foundation monies were used to prepare the federal government by paying for the propaganda analysis training of hundreds of government employees.[100]

By the time the Rockefeller Foundation renewed his grant for 1942, Lasswell could report that his Experimental Division had performed numerous labor-intensive intellectual tasks. Besides preparing an extensive body of technical papers on content analysis, it completed a "World Attention Survey" of 120 newspapers published in Germany, the USSR, Great Britain, Italy, and France, in which Lasswell and his associates worked out methods for describing, coding, and graphing the ideological uses of key political symbols in newspaper communications. This work also yielded over 2,000 content analysis charts for comparative analysis of various U.S.-based political groups' propaganda materials, charts that proved useful to the Justice Department in the courts and out. According to Marshall's report renewing Lasswell's grant, his work had established a "firm and objective foundation for the history of communication during the present war."[101] For Lasswell, the overall selling point of his work was that his methods of content and symbols analysis could be applied to all channels of communication, including "periodicals, posters, official notices, leaflets, pamphlets, speeches, books," radio, film, and all other propaganda vehicles: exactly those items the Justice Department and other federal agencies needed analyzed.[102]

Despite Lasswell's entreaties and MacLeish's very positive assessments of the Experimental Division, Lasswell's work at the LC expired at the end December 1943. For MacLeish, whose own propaganda-related interests were in developing and describing the postwar policies that might produce a more stable world, Lasswell's project was still viable, so that "counsel on public opinion resources for a just and lasting peace can be of highest quality and continually available."[103] From the Rockefeller Foundation's perspective, however, the foundation had done its part in setting up an important and experimental project, and even though MacLeish's and the library's needs were still pressing, it was time for this work to be taken over by a federal agency.[104] As with the other Rockefeller communication projects, the foundation set aside monies so that Lasswell could publish the findings from his work, which he eventually did with his 1949 volume, coedited with a number of his wartime assistants, *The Language of Politics: Studies in Quantitative Semantics*, which also contained a host of newer studies that showed Lasswell's shifting focus from wartime concerns with Nazi propaganda techniques to postwar concerns with Communist propaganda content and strategies.

Even though MacLeish ceased being an official propagandist by the end of 1942, when he left the OFF and the OWI, he stayed on as the Librarian of Congress until 1944 and in this way remained very much involved in wartime propaganda policy, if only on the national security end of the work. When MacLeish became an assistant secretary of state in 1944, he would revert once more to the public relations side of propaganda work. In either role, MacLeish manifested the extent to which national security anxieties, fear of the totalitarian menace, the desire for a cohesive national effort, and the need for a coherent communications policy dissolved the differences between a Lasswellian "science" of propaganda and opinion control and his own "policy of truth."

MacLeish's complicated legacy as civil libertarian, interventionist, democratic rhetorician, expositor of a dualistic universe, and engineer of the state's propaganda prophylaxis shows how, as war came and the fear of Nazi power generated a profound mobilization of the state's security operations, public-centered free speech liberals found it extremely difficult to hold in abeyance the logic of national security liberalism. As the following chapters illustrate, the tendency toward restricting the marketplace of ideas and demanding ideological uniformity as a weapon in the war of words and ideas was not what legal liberals in the Justice Department had planned on. But they too found the Lasswellian approach to propaganda control a useful expedient, and in lieu of creating a truly democratic propaganda, as MacLeish and others had hoped might be possible, they also took refuge in the idea that in a time of crisis some criticism was simply irresponsible and that the best free speech liberals could do was develop a democratic defense against propaganda, one that would neither embarrass the liberal conscience nor offend public sensibilities about the symbolic dimensions of a democracy at war.

CHAPTER FIVE

The Justice Department and the Problem of Propaganda

By the late 1930s images and sounds of homegrown fascists and foreign-born Nazi imitators suffused U.S. popular and political culture. Newsreel audiences and readers of popular magazines saw footage and photo-essays featuring German-American Bundists flaunting Nazi paraphernalia and marching alongside Italian-American Blackshirts on the grounds of Camp Siegfried, Long Island. They saw images of American Nazi thugs pulverizing Jewish-American World War I veterans and others who interrupted Hitler-worshiping meetings in New York's Madison Square Garden. They saw Bundists polluting icons of Americana by festooning their podiums with swastikas hung alongside American flags and by claiming George Washington as the "first Fascist" in their effort to create a long, respectable lineage for native fascism. They heard and saw the radio priest Father Charles Coughlin increasingly vilify Jews and attack President Roosevelt over the air and in the pages of his popular *Social Justice*, as did dozens of other native-born fascist agitators who echoed Nazi doctrine in their endless newspaper attacks on Jews, Hollywood, President Roosevelt, FDR's cabinet, U.S. military preparedness, and so-called Jewish bolshevism. Meanwhile, those alarmed by Germany's expansionist thrusts knew that Hitler and his chief propaganda minister, Dr. Joseph Goebbels, were using German nationalist groups throughout the world, along with German press services, libraries of information, consulates, and shortwave radio broadcasts beamed directly from Germany, to promote acrimony and disunity abroad and to try to ensure the eventual military and ideological triumph of the Third Reich. Consumers of popular culture and mainstream political reportage were frequently reminded that the noisy and visible Nazis in the American midst were part of a much larger National Socialist propaganda conspiracy.[1]

For U.S. opinion leaders and policy makers at decade's end, the ubiquitous presence of domestic and foreign-born fascists parading around the United States created an urgent need for action, especially after the outbreak of World War II in September 1939. Government officials knew they had to develop a strategy for preventing the spread of odious Nazi doctrine. Yet New Deal liberals, civil libertarians, and even politically centrist publishers such as Henry Luce believed that the U.S. response should be based on a principle of tolerance and a commitment to protecting all peoples' fundamental freedoms of speech, press, and association. Voices across the political spectrum admonished against excessive government control over the flow of information and—against the backdrop of Nazi book burning—hardly needed to point out that official censorship would be bad policy and symbolically counterproductive. Thus the federal officials assigned the task of developing a defensive propaganda strategy needed to satisfy two irreconcilable requirements: they had to prevent the spread of dangerous propaganda, and they had to protect Americans' rights to disseminate, read, and hear that same propaganda.

When Attorney General Robert Jackson created the SDU in April 1940, he believed the unit could accommodate and fuse the two distinctive dimensions of twentieth-century U.S. liberalism: the growth of the modern administrative and regulatory state and the belief that the state must be the primary vehicle for the protection of civil rights and civil liberties, including the protection of unpopular political speech and opinion.[2] But, as this chapter and the next illustrate, these two tendencies within modern liberalism coexisted uneasily, and in this era of national security crisis, the state's coercive and repressive powers subordinated and neutralized its liberty-enhancing powers, especially when confronting "foreign" ideologies and techniques widely perceived as powerful weapons of subversion. These chapters explore how these potentially contradictory obligations were built into the SDU's mandate and what happened when the potential necessity to silence and punish dissenting speech became imperative.

The Special Defense Unit's place in the U.S. defense effort against propaganda was vital, not only because it was set up precisely to do this work but because it was staffed by (and motivated by) progressive advocates of the emerging modern First Amendment doctrine. As speech-protective liberals, they repudiated prior restraint as a technique for the control of publications, promised to protect the rights of the nation's (and President Roosevelt's) most vociferous opponents, swore to trust in the rational judgment of the public, vowed to let the marketplace of ideas determine which ideas would prevail in the public mind, and hoped to make the Department of Justice "a true symbol of Justice."[3] But as state-building liberals in an anxious time, they wrote new laws and amended others for the purposes of controlling propaganda, built an intragovernmental communications surveillance network, developed the legal strategies for the prosecution of those deemed to be enemy propagandists, and crafted a definition of and theoretical argument about the threat of propaganda that facilitated the wartime reemergence (and cold war triumph) of a speech-restrictive theory of language that severely undermined the same modern First Amendment doctrine they had begun the war championing. In the propaganda-propelled collision of speech- and association-protective liberalism and security-oriented liberalism, the latter emerged as the stronger of the two strains. These chapters illustrate the triumph of nervous liberalism within the WWII-era Department of Justice.

When Robert Jackson established the Neutrality Laws Unit (renamed the Special Defense Unit in March 1941 and the Special War Policies Unit in May 1942, though in this chapter and the next I will refer to it consistently as the SDU or the unit), he created something entirely new in U.S. government: a special division whose main task would be the construction of a speech-tolerant defense against antidemocratic propaganda materials in the United States. A progressive on civil liberties issues, Jackson had high hopes for the unit's work, claiming that he wanted it to make the department a "true symbol of Justice." Like others in the larger community of liberal New Dealers, Popular Front writers and academics, and clergy and activists, he believed that Nazi and Fascist propaganda (more so than Communist) seriously threatened public morale and unity. While Congressman Martin Dies's House Un-American Activities Committee was obsessed primarily with Communist activity, Jackson and his Justice Department subordinates in the SDU saw the Nazis as the real threat to world (and domestic) security and directed the bulk of their efforts at controlling fascist channels of information and dissemination in the United States.

Too many credible sources warned of successful Nazi inroads through propaganda to ignore the threat. A host of groups were specifically created or redirected their previous activities to combat far-right subversion and contributed to a "Brown Scare" mentality by highlighting the Fascist threat. As historian Leo Ribuffo points out, "Many of these groups were ephemeral, but several attracted prominent backers and mobilized substantial constituencies." The Non-Sectarian Anti-Nazi League, the Mobilization for Democracy, the Council for Democracy, the American Council Against Nazi Propaganda (led by Raymond Gram Swing and then William E. Dodd, ambassador to Germany from 1933 to 1938), the Council Against Intolerance, and especially Friends of Democracy, Rev. L. M. Birkhead's operation (which included on its advisory board John Dewey, Thomas Mann, Paul Douglas, and Van Wyck Brooks), contributed to an air of anxiety about domestic fascists.[4] Reports from these private organizations, as well as book-length journalistic accounts and numerous exposés in *Life*, the *Nation*, and the *New Republic*, had long been illuminating an active and well-financed Nazi movement flourishing in the United States.[5] Additionally, congressional investigations by the McCormack-Dickstein Committee in the mid-1930s and the Justice Department's own FBI's research corroborated these nongovernmental reports and gave weight to Jackson's concerns.[6] At the same time, however, Attorney General Jackson desperately wanted to avoid the civil liberties fiascoes of World War I and to make sure that his Special Defense Unit, not the FBI, would be the "control tower" for the nation's propaganda defense.[7] As chief of the SDU, he appointed Lawrence M. C. "Sam" Smith, a Justice Department Anti-Trust Division lawyer. Like Jackson, Smith would become an ardent spokesman for the idea that the SDU could develop democratic strategies of propaganda control, frequently stating that his unit could and would serve two masters: the individual and the state.

For emergency-era Justice Department attorneys and the Lasswell-trained social science analysts on the SDU staff, propaganda was defined as an instrument of subversion, and propagandists were subversive agents. As the unit devised programs against individuals, organizations, and publications suspected of endangering domestic security, its officials believed that a constitutive feature of propaganda was that it provided the most conspicuous evidence of an individual's or group's *intention* to commit subversive acts. Based on this definition—a critical one, as it turned out, for their successful prosecutions of individuals and clandestine front organizations labeled "political propagandists"—dangerous propaganda was ubiquitous throughout the United States, in newspapers, books, posters, pamphlets, newsletters, magazines, commercial and shortwave radio broadcasts, films, bookstores, and libraries. For SDU officials, the content of a given propaganda campaign identified a group's ideas and loyalties, its policies, and— presumably—its plans. The localized consumption of propaganda materials also pointed toward so-called sore spots, that is, individuals and groups who might be discontented and therefore receptive to subversive ideas and programs. In all cases, unit officials believed that the disseminators of and audiences for antidemocratic materials needed to be identified, monitored, responded to, and, if necessary, controlled and punished. Thus the unit's primary duties for propaganda control included intercepting and identifying suspect material; determining the material's source, its audiences, and its possible effects; and creating "preventive and protective" barriers—a prophylaxis—between those who espoused antidemocratic ideologies and those who might be susceptible to them.[8] When necessary, it would turn files over to the Criminal Division for prosecution and would assist in organizing the evidence for the prosecutions. (This latter job made Lasswell's work and expertise quite valuable to the SDU.)

By the time Robert Jackson established the SDU in April 1940, the fascist propaganda threat seemed substantial. The Nazis desired, critics reported, " 'to disrupt and disunite the American people' by furthering racial and religious hatred, destroying confidence in democratic forms of government, halting preparedness and isolating the nation physically and psychologically, and by building up pro-Nazi groups that could one day act as a fifth column."[9] A representative memorandum from July 1941 reveals how the SDU came to articulate the problem: "The Nazi organization abroad has for its aim the establishment of a trained and disciplined body comprised of all persons of German descent scattered throughout the world with the purpose of overthrowing existing governments and imposing the totalitarian rule of the German 'master' race." This target population, according to the SDU, numbered roughly twelve million people of German descent in the United States.[10]

The unit quickly developed a standard litany to describe the fascist propaganda threat in the United States. The Lasswell-trained social science analysts who staffed the unit's Organizations and Propaganda Analysis Section—and covered the different foreign-language and ideological subdivisions within the far right movement—estimated there were three million people in the United States who read nothing but foreign newspapers, one million of whom read pro-Axis newspapers exclusively. They also estimated that the German government was spending $200 million per year on worldwide propaganda activities, including financing at least thirty Nazi propaganda distribution centers in the United States. And, they surmised, at least 20,000 people were involved in fifteen Nazi front organizations in the United States that had contributed over $13 million dollars to the German government (a conservative estimate, as the German-American Bundists boasted having over 200,000 members).[11] Besides the specific Nazi problem, the unit's propaganda analysts reported other potential problems. Through its monitoring of the extensive domestic foreign-language press—totaling almost 1,700 different publications in thirty-nine different languages, with a circulation of approximately four million additional readers—it found other populations susceptible to fascist penetration and manipulation, including Italians, White Russians, Croatians, Irish nationalists, some Polish groups, and others. Over 300 different Slavic newspapers, 249 German ones, 178 Italian ones, and 110 Scandinavian papers served the northeastern United States alone, and within these populations there were clear sore spots.[12] But while the unit's organizations and press analysts kept track of the many different language groups and their publications, on the whole the SDU focused especially on the Italian- and German-language presses.

In a July 1941 survey of newspapers, unit analysts identified between 70 and 80 percent of the domestic Italian-language papers as "altogether pro-Fascist" and interpreted approximately 40 percent of the 192 German-language publications they examined as being "consistently pro-Nazi," with another 50 percent becoming increasingly so as Nazi military successes grew. These German-language publications consistently invoked "the Nazi line," unit analysts reported, and urged German-Americans "to stand together in order to present a united front against their 'persecutors' in this country and to exert greater political influence." The report quoted one paper, *Der Sonntagsbote* of Pittsburgh, to illustrate the ways in which the pro-Nazi press framed issues of economic dislocation, national morale, and the salvation that would be offered by a Hitlerian figure:

> If Hitlerism comes, it cannot be fought off with battleships or armies. It will take root in the great mass of our desperate people who have lost all hope. Hitlerism will grasp the youth who sees no future ahead; and those middle-aged people who have lived the best years of their lives and today find themselves no better off than they were at the age of twenty-one. . . . Out of that mass there will rise an American Hitler who understands and speaks the language of these destitutes. He won't have soldiers, but his storm troopers will be Americans; a great army of discontented Americans.

A quote from the Italian-American press showed similar sentiments in its celebration of the dictator cult and the eventual Fascist triumph: "Nobody can deny that in the prodigious destiny of Adolph Hitler, as well as in that no less prodigious one of Il Duce, of Fascism, there is more than a national mission. Its destiny is Europe and the whole world."[13]

For unit analysts, part of the problem was that as extensive as the printed press was, it was by no means the only foreign-language communication channel used by different nationality groups in the United States. The same 1941 report noted, for instance, that there were approximately two hundred licensed radio stations in the United States broadcasting over 1,700 weekly programs in 31 different languages. The Italian-language programs showed the same tendency as the Italian printed press, being "generally . . . strongly pro-Fascist. Popular music and drama prevail today with a strong Fascist cultural tinge," unit analysts wrote. Nearly two hundred theaters in 84 cities showed foreign-language films, with film and newsreel used as both cultural fare and as propaganda.[14] And shortwave broadcasts from abroad were also used extensively between continents and were "widely used for propaganda purposes."[15]

SDU lawyers and analysts feared that the vast domestic foreign-language media could be used to undermine domestic morale and drive
wedges between so-called hyphenated Americans of different nationalities,
religions, ethnicity, and races. Yet unlike during WWI, when xenophobic
attacks on hyphenated Americans stemmed from the Justice Department
itself, this potential security problem required a delicate response from the
federal government. Indeed, unit personnel understood that the domestic
foreign-language press was an extremely important symbol of the U.S.
commitment to pluralism and liberty. Unit officials recognized that the
Justice Department's treatment of the foreign-language press would be an
important test of whether the department could truly be the symbol of
justice Robert Jackson hoped it would. Instead of stifling the dissent or
anger emanating from the different ethnic groups, Sam Smith and his staff
of lawyers and propaganda analysts knew that the complaints and criticisms they found in the domestic foreign-language press should be attended to. Healing sore spots instead of suppressing and exacerbating
them could be a unifying strategy for the nation, one that would send a
clear message to different potentially disaffected groups that the Roosevelt
administration embraced pluralism in principle and in deed and that it
was highly attentive to their needs.[16]

By summer 1941 Francis Biddle had replaced Robert Jackson as attorney
general after President Roosevelt appointed Jackson to the Supreme Court,
but meanwhile anxieties about Axis might and U.S. unpreparedness had
only deepened. Italy had joined the Nazis in common cause. The British
had retreated back across the English Channel, and the German Luftwaffe
was steadily pounding England. And, according to liberal interventionists,
isolationist forces at home (some of whom were seen as being in concert
with Nazi fifth columnists) had made Hitler's job easier by slowing U.S. enlistment, mobilization, rearmament, and aid to the Allies.[17] When Biddle
took over at the Justice Department, pessimism and fear pervaded the department and the SDU. When SDU chief Smith reported on the activities
of the unit's first year to the new attorney general, he did so in terms that
reiterated the threat posed by Nazi Germany's global propaganda strategies.
The European experience showed that Nazi propagandists were highly effective, he warned, and evidence pointed to the fact that they had the same
strategy of conquest in mind for the United States. He echoed the claims
made by his main assistant, R. Keith Kane, who argued that the Nazi propaganda machinery was being used to divide the U.S. people against themselves: "All means of communication are being used for systematic and organized attack on the morale of the American people."[18] Shortly after he

left the SDU and became MacLeish's director of intelligence for the Office of Facts and Figures at war's outbreak[19]—a position from which he continued to work closely with the SDU—Kane made the same argument. So many communications channels were still available to enemy propagandists that they had easy "access to the minds" of domestic sympathizers, he said. A combination of "short wave cultural and news programs" and diverse organizations with varying "degrees of sympathy toward one or more of the enemy nations" meant that the ground was "well prepared" to undermine U.S. unity and morale.[20]

When SDU chief Smith provided Biddle with these details and interpretive frameworks, he warned that even if the intelligence reports were exaggerated and even if sentiments like Kane's were excessively pessimistic, the Justice Department should still prepare its strategy based on worst-case estimates. It would be remiss not to assume the worst: "The view might be taken that the facts here are not as alarming as they might be. It may be that the foothold has not yet been gained here which we are inclined to think has been gained. . . . On the other hand, if we have analyzed the problem correctly but we do not undertake to cope with it on an adequate scale, we may contribute substantially to a fate for our nation similar to that of France." Pointing to the Nazi successes in the nations already subjugated, Smith employed the language of national emergency and called for "an all-out program of internal security." He explained to Biddle all that the SDU had done to prepare the Justice Department—and the nation—for its defense against enemy propaganda.[21] He assured Biddle (a well-regarded civil libertarian who distrusted J. Edgar Hoover and was in turn distrusted by him) that the SDU had worked hard to protect Americans' rights to debate and dissent while also guarding "the national security" and "promot[ing] the national effort."[22] In short, Smith's call for an "all-out" program of national security makes clear the nervousness of the government agents most responsible for propaganda control. Dedicated to protecting individual and group liberties, they were, by war's eve, ready to shift into high gear on the national defense front.

Smith explained to Biddle that the Special Defense Unit had undertaken a huge and sensitive job. Controlling antidemocratic propaganda activities in the United States during the final days of peace meant that the SDU needed to keep track of a tremendous flow of information in all the media, including domestically and internationally produced print, film, and radio channels. This required considerable coordination with other federal agencies (including military intelligence, the Federal Communications Commission, the post office, the Treasury Department's Customs Bureau, and the Justice Department's own FBI); it also meant working with the handful of private communications intelligence projects sponsored by the Rockefeller Foundation (including the projects at Princeton, Columbia, the New School, Stanford, and especially at the Library of Congress). Adequate propaganda intelligence entailed extensive reading, watching, listening, and analyzing, Smith reminded the new attorney general, and he assured him that these extensive surveillance activities would enable Justice Department officials to make important distinctions among groups and individuals when it came to taking punitive actions. This careful preparation would help the Justice Department avoid the kinds of mistakes that it had made during World War I. But it would also put the department in the position to silence the worst offenders.

Smith assured Biddle that building the state's propaganda defense was not incompatible with protecting civil liberties. Cataloging all the SDU's preparatory work, he reported that the unit's activities had resulted in the development of new surveillance techniques, the forging of cooperative relationships with other governmental and extragovernmental entities, and careful study of all available administrative remedies, all laws pertaining to federal information control in emergencies, and all Supreme Court decisions on speech, press, mail, wiretapping, and other communications issues. The unit's work had also included writing new legislation and fine-tuning existing laws to give the department specific authority over and greater flexibility in handling propaganda matters in the courts and out.

To some extent Smith's assurances that increasing the state's surveillance capacities would prevent repression and guard individual and group liberties seems, in retrospect, to be more evidence of the self-justifying language of the national security state (and it might be). At the same time, given the Justice Department's desultory record during WWI and its WWII-era desire to avoid hysteria (it obviously failed in the case of Japanese Americans), the language of "preventive intelligence" employed by Smith needs to be understood as he intended it. Smith, Jackson, Biddle, and Smith's SDU associates believed it possible to use preventive intelligence to protect civil liberties. Although this idea that increased surveillance would somehow protect individuals and groups was belied by J. Edgar Hoover's use of the same argument in his career as FBI director, Smith did hope that his unit would serve as a brake on the inevitable wartime demand for uniformity of opinion and elimination of dissent. Indeed, he and his subordinates duly protested when their intelligence work was not fully utilized and when repressive measures were enacted against their advice or without their consent.

When Robert Jackson created this propaganda defense unit, he noted that balancing the desire for liberty and security would not be an easy matter, especially in a period of heightened anxiety. But achieving security without sacrificing liberty was fundamental. He expressed the same faith as MacLeish in the symbols, principles, and spirit of democracy. To an audience of security-minded nervous liberals, Jackson argued that the defense of democracy required more than a superficial commitment to its symbols:

> Now some persons tell us that at last we are caught in a dilemma; that if we preserve our liberties we leave ourselves vulnerable to those who would take them from us; that we must choose between freedom and safety. Such persons misunderstand the meaning of freedom. . . . They regard liberty as a luxury which they would hang onto as long as possible; but if necessary they would give up some of it to obtain greater safety. . . . Liberty is not a luxury to be enjoyed, or a theory to be defended; it is a weapon to be used.[23]

Making the preservation of liberty a "weapon" as the nation moved toward war would be, Jackson knew, a struggle. Against the imperatives of control and the apparent security found in uniformity of opinion, it would require great diligence to ensure liberty continually. Maintaining this equipoise became more and more difficult, especially as the Justice Department's own emergency-era propaganda prophylaxis increased in size, achieved bureaucratic stability and momentum, and joined forces with other agencies of the state's expanding security apparatus.

The legacy of World War I hung over the unit's head, and its appropriation of the negative and positive lessons from the Justice Department's WWI record shows both an effort to determine a democratic course of action and to prepare effectively for total war. World War I also produced the most important First Amendment cases of the modern era, and for this reason that war was also important to the SDU. The unit's study of those landmark First Amendment cases and their implications for the control of political speech in the impending war suggests, once again, its contradictory commitments. While unit members embraced, rhetorically but at arm's length, a civil libertarian rendering of the landmark First Amendment cases, they also needed administrative and prosecutory tools and looked to those WWI cases for the license the Supreme Court had granted the state to carry out war against unwanted forms of political speech.

Jackson's intentions to avoid the mistakes of WWI came to symbolize the unit's own sense of purpose. As Smith told Biddle, Jackson created the SDU because he wanted to ensure that the department would avoid "ill-considered prosecutions" and that the whole federal government would tolerate greater political dissent the next time around.[24] Each case, Jackson had promised, would be "scrutinized with reference to both adequate

protection of the national interest and the civil rights of individuals involved."[25] Avoiding a siege mentality would require extensive prewar planning, coordination of efforts within the department (especially among the
nation's U.S. attorneys), cooperation among different federal agencies involved in internal security matters, and a commitment to using preventive
and administrative measures rather than prosecutory ones.

World War I as a Cautionary Tale

As Jackson made clear when he formed the SDU, he was highly conscious
that Justice Department failures during World War I had stained the department's reputation among civil libertarians. He insisted that such mistakes would not occur again. At the same time, the unit members' own
studies of the Justice Department's WWI-era successes (they were looking
for positive lessons too) suggested that uniform policies, standardized procedures, and centralized control would guard against the desultory, illiberal, and overzealous actions that defined the department's failures during the
previous war.[26] For Jackson and the SDU, the main lesson from WWI was
that too little departmental coordination resulted in too much repression,
especially, as one unit lawyer wrote, the department's "ill-consideration of
prosecution for sedition and espionage and the 'slacker' raids [and the]
Palmer 'raids' just after that War."[27] Given that experience, Jackson wanted his U.S. attorneys to act only under strict departmental authorization on
any political matters. He wanted to minimize high-profile wartime prosecutions, and he thought clearer lines of authority and a stricter division of
labor would stave off ambitious U.S. attorneys interested in such prosecutions. So he assigned the unit a gatekeeping function, making it responsible for authorizing the Criminal Division's wartime prosecutions.[28]

An internal report on the activities of the WWI-era Justice Department
identified the primary failures as administrative, especially the department's
exacerbating, instead of controlling, the nationwide enforcement of and
prosecutions under the Espionage and Sedition statutes.[29] These were the
main laws used to punish acts of dissenting political speech during WWI,
and they were applied with a vengeance. According to Harvard Law professor Zechariah Chafee Jr., there were nearly two thousand Espionage Act
prosecutions during WWI (about nine hundred of the defendants were
successfully prosecuted out of 1,956 cases commenced). These new laws—
in combination with the fact that prosecutors, juries, and judges were
"swept from their moorings by war passions" (p. 50)—meant that virtually
all criticism of the war was seen as dangerous and either a product of or useful to enemy propagandists.[30] As Chafee argued, "men were punished with-

out overt acts, with only a presumed intention to cause overt acts, merely for the utterance of words which judge and jury thought to have a tendency to injure the state." "Almost all the convictions," he added, "were for the expressions of opinions about the merits and conduct of the war" (p. 51). "The courts treated opinions as statements of fact and then condemned them as false because they differed from the President's speech or the resolution of Congress declaring war," thereby making "all genuine discussion among civilians of the justice and wisdom of continuing a war . . . perilous." Summarizing, Chafee argued that the Espionage and Sedition legislation became laws "under which opinions hostile to the war had practically no protection" (p. 52). Chafee, like others who tried to explain the excesses of WWI, pointed to propaganda as a chief culprit.

For SDU lawyer Ward C. Allen, whose tasks included examining the problems of World War I, Chafee's history was invaluable in helping him understand where the problems lay and whose fault they were. Like Chafee, he argued that the breakdown of civil protections and the right to dissent was not entirely the fault of the Justice Department, for the problem of wartime hysteria and reaction plagued every level of U.S. society. Drawing on the standard post-WWI litany of propaganda's dangers, Allen argued that the U.S. public had been highly vulnerable to wartime propaganda and therefore capitulated to wartime fervor. So had the courts, U.S. attorneys, and the U.S. Department of Justice.

Like Chafee, Allen also blamed the United States' own nationalistic propaganda campaigns for the civil liberties abuses of WWI.[31] Official U.S. propaganda was, he argued, the unintended enemy of Justice Department professionalism: "Grand juries, judges, and, of course, court juries" that could have been "judicial flood-gates in retaining reason" did not do their jobs. In fact, they even "outstripped United States Attorneys in their patriotic zeal to quench all but the most fulsome praise of the war." Propaganda, Allen declared, both catalyzed and multiplied the problems that the department's lack of administrative centralization caused. While Chafee might have argued that "no one anticipated" that the Espionage and Sedition laws would be used so repressively, Allen suggested that their statutory language was easily abused, and, combined with wartime intolerance, these laws were used to create a highly repressive climate.[32]

Echoing Chafee, Allen warned against the possibility of those in authority being "swept from their mooring by war passion" during the next war and averred that the most certain defense against this was greater administrative control at the federal level. This should be the primary lesson learned from World War I, Allen suggested. To make his point, he explained how the department's record had improved with the creation of

John Lord O'Brian's War Emergency Division in 1918, which centralized control over the department's different war activities.[33]

Besides these administrative lessons, the record from WWI was crucial to the Justice Department in another way, for the landmark First Amendment decisions in the modern era were handed down in the waning hours of that war. These decisions would have to provide the guidelines to the Special Defense Unit's legal analysts as they worked to shape their strategy for addressing matters of free speech and national security. Thus clarifying the meaning of the clear and present danger test as it applied to antidemocratic propaganda became a central issue for the unit's legal theorists.

The Modern First Amendment Doctrine and National Security Liberalism

The SDU had to determine what constituted protected and unprotected speech under wartime statutes, and thus its lawyers explored interpretations of the First Amendment that might give them the tools they needed to protect the national security and most forms of political speech. Seeking this balance provoked internal debates between advocates of the more speech-restrictive and traditional "liberty but not license" position embedded in the bad tendency of speech theory used in the WWI-era cases versus advocates of a more speech-protective interpretation of the First Amendment, the position especially championed by Chafee. In large part the debate focused on the meaning of the clear and present danger test as it was enunciated in the WWI-era Supreme Court cases: Was it a speech-restrictive test (as the majority had meant it to be in the *Schenck* and *Abrams* cases), or had it become, especially within liberal legal circles, a speech-protective test (as Holmes and Brandeis had meant it to be in their dissent to the *Abrams* decision)? The lawyers needed to find grounds to protect most speech but legitimization of the state's authority to control what was widely perceived as a dangerous and destabilizing propaganda menace. To do so, they grounded their First Amendment analysis in the a priori principle that the state's primary obligation is its own self-preservation. This assumption was crucial. They found sanction for it in Chafee's own position.

In essence, Chafee sought balance between individual liberty and government self-preservation and in so doing tried to define the limits on government control over speech. He rejected what he called the "extreme view," the idea that the Bill of Rights is a peacetime document and may be ignored in war. But he also rejected the view that all speech is free and that only actions can be restrained and punished. The government's wartime powers and the First Amendment are both part of the Constitution, in other words, and so neither can be used to limit the other. A declaration of war, he said, cannot be used to silence speech. At the same time, Chafee had an Enlightenment view of the idea of free speech, meaning that speech must be responsible and aimed at achieving both the truth and the social good. Therefore speakers also had duties and obligations to control the nature of their utterances, so that those utterances would enhance discussion and the search for public solutions and not inflame emotions.

Like SDU legal theorists, Chafee was interested in finding a balance of interests. But there was no clear marker for where the line could be drawn. This meant the question would be left up to judges and juries, and they needed some guidelines. One guideline was completely clear: speech should not be punished for its presumed bad tendency. The great failure by the courts in WWI was that they had imposed the bad tendency theory of language on dissenting utterances and had thereby "fixed the line at a point which makes all opposition to this or any future war impossible." The line could only be drawn by keeping the two interests of public safety and the search for truth in mind: "Every reasonable attempt should be made to maintain both interests unimpaired," he wrote (p. 28). For Chafee, giving the state license to punish speech with a supposed bad tendency always granted the state far too much power to silence legitimate opposition. "And we can with certitude declare that the First Amendment forbids the punishment of words merely for their injurious tendencies. The history of the Amendment and the political function of free speech corroborate each other and make this conclusion plain" (p. 35).

Chafee was very critical of the use of the Espionage and Sedition statutes in WWI to prosecute political (and relatively or essentially harmless) speech, and unit legal analysts paid close attention to his arguments, as their frequent references to his works indicate. They found that the central WWI-era cases provided ambiguous guidelines.[34] Like Chafee, they discovered that there was no clear, literal doctrinal guidance that could help the unit construct a constitutionally sound, speech-protective, yet entirely reliable internal security arsenal. They wanted to do both.

The WWI era convictions under the wartime Espionage Act in the *Schenck, Frohwerk,* and *Debs* cases and, under the Sedition statute, in the *Abrams* case were landmark decisions in the evolution of the modern First Amendment doctrine and the main cases in which the Supreme Court upheld the government's authority to punish antiwar publications and speech acts that posed a clear and present danger to the government's war effort.[35] However, in the *Abrams* case, the Court filed a split opinion on conviction under the 1918 Sedition statute. This time, Justices Holmes and Brandeis used the phrase "clear and present danger" in dissent. The Court's majority upheld Abrams's conviction and the constitutionality of the Sedition amendment, but the Holmes-Brandeis dissent provided a new framework for arguing for the protection of political speech.

Their dissenting language steadily became part of the rhetorical arsenal of civil libertarians who wanted to identify the precise point at which speech was no longer protected; Holmes and Brandeis placed the burden of proof on the government to show a dangerous proximity between seditious speech and subsequent acts, and this requirement of proximity and degree of danger gave the clear and present danger test a whole new meaning (even if it was from a dissenting opinion). In short, by the time of the *Abrams* decision, the felicitous "clear and present danger" phrase came to represent for Holmes and Brandeis a speech-protective test of imminence (this was the inflection Chafee had been able to convince Justice Holmes it should have), and in the ensuing decades clear and present danger came to represent liberal fair-mindedness.

As legal historian David Rabban has explained, the reformulation of the clear and present danger test as speech-protective rather than speech-preventive is a fascinating moment in First Amendment history and one greatly influenced by Chafee, who, through several conversations and an exchange of letters, apparently was able to convince Holmes of the great value of using the test for the protection of speech when questions of proximity and degree really are at issue.[36] Holmes first articulated the clear and present danger formulation in the *Schenck* case, when the Court affirmed Schenck's conviction under the Espionage Act for counseling evasion of the draft to draft-age men by distributing circulars calling the draft unconstitutional and urging the men to assert their rights. Upholding the conviction, Holmes wrote, famously:

> The question in every case is whether the words are used in such circumstances and are of such a nature as to *create a clear and present danger* that they will bring about the substantive evils that Congress has a right to prevent. It is a question of *proximity and degree.* When a nation is at war many things that might be said in time of peace are such a hindrance to its effort that their utterance will not be endured so long as men fight and that no Court could regard them as protected by any constitutional right [emphasis in Chafee].

According to Chafee, the problem with this decision was not in the famous language used above nor that the defendant was punished for circulating legal materials: Schenck was quite clearly counseling unlawful action. The problem, rather, was that it made it legal for Congress not only to punish overt acts of interference with the war but also to "penaliz[e] un-successful efforts to interfere, whether they are acts or words." For Chafee, this Court-sanctioned "effort to head off actual injury to the government is the basis of all suppression of discussion." By drawing the boundary line very close to the test of incitement, however, Holmes actually made "the punishment of words for their remote bad tendency impossible," Chafee argued, thereby providing an opening for a reinterpretation of the mean-ing of the language of clear and present danger by attaching requirements of proximity and degree to it.[37] By the time Holmes and Brandeis heard the *Abrams* case a year later, the proximity test had become the key issue in defining what was meant by clear and present danger. In the Holmes-Brandeis dissent in the *Abrams* case, the phrase became speech-protective because of the emphasis on the question of imminence of danger posed to the draft by the dissemination of the defendants' anarchist pamphlets, not on the supposed but unproved bad tendencies of those pamphlets.

By the start of WWII, these decisions were still unclear guidelines for knowing where the Supreme Court would stand on matters of protected and unprotected speech. Some unit lawyers were convinced by Professor Chafee's influential readings of those WWI decisions. Others took a more conservative position and relied on the traditional Blackstonian arguments embodied in the majority decisions in the wartime cases, which validated the state's authority to control speech with a bad tendency, particularly war-time speech.[38] Additionally, they turned to political scientist Karl Lowen-stein, who studied the failures of democratic efforts to control political ex-tremism in Europe in the 1920s and 1930s and thus offered clear object lessons for unit legal theorists that free speech could be an opening wedge to political insurrection and that the principle of state security should be their first priority.[39]

These tensions between the protection of liberty and the assurances of security were embodied in a number of different SDU debates related to information control, including issues such as wire-tapping, postal author-ity to destroy incoming mail, and propaganda-control legislation. The tensions are also clear in the debates about the WWI-era First Amend-ment cases. In a June 1940 memorandum, for instance, unit lawyer Forest Black combined a Chafee-influenced reading of free speech principles with the insights of legal realism to argue that the clear and present dan-ger test in the *Abrams* case should be endorsed by the unit as an unequiv-ocal expansion of protected speech rights.[40] For Black, this speech-protec-tive use of the clear and present danger test was the "high-water mark of liberalism," and he argued that the greatest strength of the test's "danger-ous proximity to success" element provided an objective standard in the law and freed judges and juries from the need for more vague and subjective interpretations of the bad tendencies and bad intentions of language. As a legal realist, Black also contended that the main problem with the bad tendency test was that it made it "easy for the administration in power in war time to brand the views of the opposition as criminal." No doctrine, Black wrote, "has ever been devised that places a more irresponsible power in the courts to punish political and economic heresy." The clear and present danger–proximity test was the objective test that would allow the unit to avoid the pitfalls of judicial or public prejudice.

Nevertheless, Black found limitations even in this strengthened protection of dissenting speech. Most troubling, the Court still accepted the idea that words themselves constituted "overt acts" and therefore failed to restrict punishable offenses to actual overt acts only. In *Schenck* the Court had said "when a nation is at war many things that might be said in time of peace are such a hindrance . . . that their utterance will not be endured." In other words, "mere words" could be construed as creating a clear and present danger—especially in time of war—making the utterance of words punishable, even if they were not followed by overt acts. Drawing on Ernst Freund and Chafee, Black noted that "if this fiction is taken literally, it is obvious that it would wipe out the well settled and sound distinction between intentional and negligent acts." Even though the new test was "a great improvement over the bad tendency and bad intent doctrines," Black argued, it was still no bar to judicial bias, particularly in the heat of patriotic frenzy: "induced by popular panic . . . some judges and some juries will be able to see a 'clear and present danger' where none in fact exists." Black thus wanted the department to go even further, because the "high-water mark of liberalism" was still deficient in "safeguarding the citizen in an atmosphere wherein the war psychosis is rampant."

Ward Allen, another SDU legal theorist, offered a more conservative and security-oriented interpretation of the same cases and found in the clear and present danger formulation an argument for the state's a priori right to self-preservation. In two different internal studies, "Constitutional Basis for Restrictive Legislation" and "The Espionage and Sedition Acts of 1917–1918," Allen also turned to Chafee, reiterating his details about the Supreme Court's wartime speech cases and even accepting most of his arguments. But Allen never lost sight of the unit's national defense agenda. Looking to WWI for lessons about what the department could and should do in preparation for war, Allen especially embraced the language the Court had used in the *Schenck* case to endorse congressional authority to wage war. He said that the "decisions upholding the Espionage Act of 1917 and its Sedition Amendment of 1918 are all bottomed upon the power of

Congress to make war and to raise armies." If Congress "has the power to make war," Allen wrote, then it can "punish acts interfering with its exercise of this power and can thus punish words which lead to the acts of interference." Allen's theory was based on a two-tiered assumption about the relationship between the state and individual liberty: "Protection of the people and protection for the existence of the Government appear to be the two ostensible ends toward which statutory restriction of tongue and pen may be directed," he wrote. But for Allen, the protection of the state was the first priority, and this meant that the criteria for controlling speech need not be limited to "a real danger to the existence of our national government which is imminent." Rejecting the proximity standard Chafee and Black embraced and accepting the bad tendency/bad intent construction they rejected, Allen argued that "words may be forbidden which have a judicially supposed bad *tendency* and/or are intended to endanger our national interests."[41]

From Allen's perspective, the Bill of Rights was a brake on but not a barrier to the state's exertion of its a priori right of self-preservation. From Black's perspective, the Bill of Rights was an a priori curb to excessive statism. Allen articulated this hierarchical relationship between the state and the Constitution when he wrote that "although considerations *must first be given* to the existence of available power to surveille, important also is the existence of other provisions of the Constitution which operate as limitations upon affirmative powers granted." "It is agreed," he added, "that the Bill of Rights limits . . . powers of the government."[42] Based on his hierarchical theory of state power and individual liberty, Allen embraced the bad tendency test in conjunction with the "liberty but not license" framework to suggest what the unit's operative guidelines should be: the First Amendment protected the liberty of speech but did not license abusive speech. Black, on the other hand, rejected the "liberty but not license" test as a "legal fiction."

While the WWI-era cases provided no precise guide to the unit's interpretation of the leverage given or the limits imposed by the First Amendment, other WWI cases gave them specific authority on other strategies for propaganda control. Control of the mails, for example, was a matter fundamental to the unit's creation of its propaganda prophylaxis and central to the efficacy of FARA. In his analysis of governmental authority over second-class mailing privileges, Allen once again began with the a priori assertion of the state's right of self-preservation.[43] Allen asserted that "in the present time of national emergency consideration is necessarily given to all possible and proper means of protecting the Government against its enemies both from within and without." Controlling the mails was an obvious and constitutionally defensible means of both self-protection and control, he argued. Although he recognized that freedom of the press is intimately connected to "the privilege of the mails," the keyword here was "privilege." For Allen, the state's right of self-preservation in extremis took priority over the protection of any individual rights or privileges. Emergency conditions justified restrictions on peacetime liberties: "The weight given freedom of the press will vary," he wrote, "in inverse proportion to the seriousness of the national crisis."[44] Like the WWI jurists who feared the cumulative effects of seditious propaganda on the nation's will to fight and therefore punished dissenters and pamphleteers as threats to national and military morale, Allen invoked the degree of the crisis as the final arbiter of how extensively the Justice Department could employ speech-restrictive mechanisms to protect national security.

Over time, Allen's interpretation of individual rights as subordinate to the authority of the state more fully expressed the unit's positions than did Black's. However, unit lawyers also recognized—and embraced—Justice Holmes's powerful metaphorical expression that the marketplace of ideas was a more democratic arbiter of the acceptability of competing doctrines than was state censorship. Allen used this Holmesian language in a March 1941 study entitled "Surveillance and Censorship in Time of War." Recognizing that achieving the consent of the governed is necessary to wage war in a democracy, Allen noted that the threat of war increased leaders' needs to control communications. This impulse, he argued, needed to be balanced against the long-cherished liberal maxim that holds that public morale—and democracy—would be better served by a free flow of ideas and information.[45] Making the same assumptions as the congressional authors of the FARA and Voorhis Acts about the relationship between public information and enlightened public self-interest, Allen wrote: "The individual is a sufficiently rational being," and if "afforded all opportunities to secure as much information and knowledge as possible," then the individual will "decide upon the correct course of action to be taken." "This concept," he said, was based "upon the unconquerable power of truth and the strength of freedom of thought." Faith in democracy, Allen argued, should curb the impulse to employ censorship as a means for achieving consent. With reasoning redolent of Chafee, Allen said censorship would not only hurt the effective conduct of war, because it would eliminate the dissenting voices of those who might have legitimate criticisms, but also damage public morale by keeping information, both good and bad, from a public eager for news.[46] Allen's framework authorized the government's surveillance and monitoring of the channels of communication. But, as those who embraced the principle of disclosure hoped, it was also a framework that recognized the public's capacity to make rational choices based on access to the full range of political discussion and acknowledged that censorship was politically and symbolically undesirable.

The idea of an enlightened public having access to all available information and opinions buttressed the principle of disclosure that undergirded the two main statutory tools the SDU had at its disposal, the Foreign Agents Registration Act and the Voorhis Act. Both acts were products of congressional anxieties about foreign propaganda activities in the United States, and both were premised on the idea that requiring agents of propaganda materials to register with the federal government and disclose the fact of that registration to the U.S. public was a far more democratic strategy for dealing with unwanted propaganda materials than were censorship and other preemptive punitive measures. Registration and disclosure were, on principle, democratic strategies for propaganda control, ones that could be employed without damaging First Amendment protections. In addition, they were in the spirit of the First Amendment but did not produce legal questions that would bring them under First Amendment scrutiny.

The Voorhis and Foreign Agent Registration Acts

The Foreign Agent Registration Act and the Voorhis Act were both products of a legislative strategy for propaganda control first suggested by the McCormack-Dickstein Committee in 1935 when the committee recommended that Nazi and Communist propaganda activities should be controlled through registration and enforced public disclosure of foreign agency. Established in 1934 to undertake an investigation of Communist and Fascist propaganda activities in the United States, the McCormack-Dickstein Committee found a wide range of organized efforts to spread the Nazi philosophy in the United States through newspapers, booksellers, German-American organizations, diplomatic consuls, public relations firms, and labor organizations.

The committee's report complained that "campaigns were conducted, gigantic mass meetings held, literature of the vilest kind was disseminated and the short-wave radio was added to the [Nazi] effort" to "consolidate persons of German birth or descent, if possible, into one group, subject to dictation from abroad." Nazi propaganda activities were, in other words, widespread, diffuse in form, deceptive in practice, and aimed at promoting dangerous hatreds at home and loyalties to foreign causes. The same held for Communist propaganda activities.[47] Although the committee recommended that both parties be made illegal, a new sedition law be enacted, and new deportation and repatriation treaties be established, the legislative legacy of the committee's work resulted in less restrictive and more democratic forms of propaganda control: the Foreign Agents Registration Act (1938) and the Voorhis Act (1940).

When the committee proffered the registration and disclosure-based legislation, it did so on educational grounds: it contended that registration and disclosure laws would educate the American people about those "who are engaged in this country . . . to spread doctrines alien to our democratic form of government, or propaganda for the purpose of influencing American public opinion on a political question." The "surest safeguard for those fundamental principles of American liberty," the committee wrote, "is an aroused and intelligent public opinion," one informed by an open but closely monitored marketplace of ideas.[48] Congressman McCormack insisted that registration and disclosure would not interfere with the marketplace of ideas but would protect the citizenry, enthusiastically declaring that "the spotlight of pitiless publicity will serve as a deterrent to the spread of pernicious propaganda."[49]

The idea that registration and disclosure were democracy-enhancing techniques became part of the logic that led speech-protective liberals to support this form of propaganda control, as opposed to sedition laws, military disaffection laws, and other forms of gag legislation that free speech liberals opposed. The two main propaganda control laws based on this principle, FARA and Voorhis, both gave the state authority to monitor the political activities of any foreign-based entity engaged in influencing U.S. policy and public opinion, and both also provided damning contextual definitions of propaganda that ultimately gave the federal courts the strongest of words by which to punish those who failed to meet the new laws' requirements. FARA (also known as the McCormack Act) required individual "agents" of "foreign principles" to register with the State Department, while the Voorhis Act required organizations engaged in "political activity" to register with the Justice Department. Propaganda was listed as the primary form of "political activity" in which groups or agents might engage, and although it was not explicitly defined in either act, "political activity" was explicitly stated in the language of the Voorhis Act as "seeking to control by force or overthrow the U.S. Government or any subdivision thereof" and being "subject to foreign control."[50] (The standards for being subject to "foreign control" meant "receiving money from, having an affiliation with, or having policies that are shaped by a foreign government . . . or being an agent, agency, or instrumentality of a foreign government, or of a political party in a foreign country, or of an international political organization.")[51] Thus, while the stated goal of the registration and disclosure requirements was educational, the acts were built on the assumption that loyal Americans and democratic foreign governments would not and did not engage in subversive "political activities," including the production and distribution of propaganda. The legacy of the idea that real Americans did not engage in "political activities" became an especially punitive component of the definition of propaganda in the federal courts during WWII.

The Special Defense Unit used these laws to organize its administrative activities and strove to strengthen them by working closely with Congressmen McCormack and Voorhis to pass a series of amendments from 1939 to 1942 that made FARA, in particular, more precisely tuned to the specific needs of the SDU. Congress transferred FARA administration to the Justice Department in early 1942, explicitly recognizing that it belonged in the same Justice Department legal arsenal as the Voorhis Act, which the SDU had administered from the time it was signed into law.[52] Although both acts supposedly applied to agents of the Allied governments, President Roosevelt insisted that FARA be modified to make the registration requirements easier for friendly powers before he would sign the amendment transferring FARA's administrative authority from the State Department to the Justice Department (the changes were made, and FDR signed the act in March 1942). Thus, while putatively applying to all foreign agencies, the real targets of the acts were political parties, agencies, and subdivisions of potential enemy powers, including the German-American Bund, the German-American National Alliance, the German-American Settlement League, the German-American Business League, the Communist Party U.S.A, the Russian National Revolutionary Party, the Dante Alighieri Society, the Italian American War Veterans League, the Black Shirts, and other Fascist and Communist organizations explicitly identified in the language of the Voorhis Act.[53]

From the SDU's perspective, the FARA and Voorhis acts gave the unit the tools it needed for the construction of an internal security arsenal based on democratic principles. In the long run, FARA was a far more effective registration (and prosecutory) tool, primarily because the definition of "political activity" in Voorhis made registration potentially self-incriminatory under the provisions of the Smith Act (passed against SDU wishes, as an amendment to another registration law, the Alien Registration Act of 1940, which required all noncitizens to be fingerprinted).[54]

In fact, during the prewar and wartime period only two organizations registered, and no organizations were prosecuted under the Voorhis Act provisions. However, from the standpoint of enabling the Justice Department to build its administrative apparatus for propaganda control, the Voorhis Act was an extremely valuable and effective piece of legislation. As one unit official noted in 1943, "Much of the energy of the Unit under the Act has been devoted to bringing about proceedings against the responsible members of subversive organizations. . . . The record of achievement under the program as a whole has been very good."[55] And another writer concluded in 1944 that the value of the Voorhis Act up to Pearl Harbor was that it had been a "great help." All told, he wrote in capital letters, the Voorhis Act was "USEFUL AS A DETERRENT," because it provided "AUTHORITY FOR INVESTIGATION BY [THE] DEPARTMENT."[56]

Voorhis was a "great help" to the unit in two fundamental ways. First, in tandem with FARA, it gave the unit two forms of statutory authority and justified the construction of an internal security bureaucracy focused on developing strategies for monitoring, investigating, analyzing, and deterring propaganda activities. Second, because both measures were based on the principle of disclosure, they satisfied the unit's needs to demonstrate the Justice Department's symbolic commitment to public enlightenment, tolerance, and freedom of speech. As Sam Smith told Attorney General Biddle, the unit had embraced disclosure so that "the public will help itself."[57] By embracing disclosure as the means for shining the "pitiless spotlight of publicity" on "pernicious propaganda," Congress and the Justice Department manifested an important symbolic commitment to a supposedly unfettered marketplace of ideas as an instrument of public enlightenment.

One adviser to the unit, Harvard Law professor Milton Katz, explicitly recognized the sleight-of-hand nature of the disclosure-based measures in an off-the-record letter he wrote to Smith about the Voorhis Act: "The effectiveness of this control would rest upon two factors. In the first place, propaganda which is thus identified as alien and hostile in source would presumably be ineffectual" because the public would respond intelligently to that material once it knew the sources. "In the second place," Katz continued, "failure to disclose (which would probably be the usual case) would make possible prosecution on a basis which involved *no embarrassment arising out of constitutional traditions.*" In short, the Justice Department could gain substantial control over the problem of "political" propaganda in the United States without employing censorship or political trials. Punishment would result from failure to satisfy administrative procedures, not from the government's determination that specific materials were inimical. And, as Katz noted, the legislation gave the unit a "substantial basis to warrant investigations" into the activities of suspect groups.[58]

Unit personnel uniformly embraced the disclosure laws and rejected censorship as antithetical to their democratic purposes. In a February 1941 memorandum, for instance, Ward Allen told Sam Smith that any bill featuring censorship would be "unwise since it represents a complete reversal of the fundamental democratic approach of requiring disclosure which, by repeated congressional action, has become the established policy in dealing with those persons in organizations who seek to proselyte the people with anti-democratic doctrines." He added that FARA, Voorhis, and various postal laws and regulations were all aimed at disclosure and at "avoiding any repression or 'crack-down.' " He concluded by saying that the attorney general "is of the opinion that the policy of disclosure should be the one to be followed at the present time."[59]

Several months after the outbreak of war, when Justice Department officials felt pressure from many directions to control all forms of dissent, two other unit staffers, Franklin Pollak and William Cherin, presented Smith with a thorough defense of disclosure. They acknowledged that the country was under attack by antidemocratic propagandists but insisted that a lively and free-wheeling (but closely monitored) marketplace of ideas was the best "democratic offensive against antidemocratic speech." The department should avoid repeating the failed strategies of WWI, they warned, especially reliance on prosecution which would "seriously" interfere "with a desirable exercise of the right to criticize the Government."[60] At the same time, they wanted to expand the department's capacity to thwart the domestic fascists—such as Pelley, Winrod, Christians, Noble, and their organizations—and suggested that disclosure requirements should also be utilized to apply to individuals and groups not expressly covered by FARA and Voorhis, that is, those without direct foreign agency. While immediate action against the native fascist and isolationist groups seemed necessary, Pollak and Cherin argued, they also wanted to avoid censorship or actions based on charges of sedition. They recommended a democratic "counteroffensive": "We propose not prosecution but 'more speech'—the traditional democratic method. We propose that the Government make use of established techniques of disclosure so that organized anti-democratic speech may be disclosed to the public for what it is, and so that its organized backers may be made known." Quoting Justice Brandeis, they invoked the free speech liberals' creed: "The fitting remedy for evil counsels is good ones. . . . If there be time to expose through discussion the falsehoods and fallacies, to avert the evil by the process of education, the remedy to be applied is more speech, not enforced silence."[61]

Although registration and disclosure did reflect a democratic faith in public enlightenment through full information, it would be a mistake to overlook the substantial power to taint the marketplace of ideas by officially labeling some materials as "foreign propaganda," which the amended version of FARA gave the Justice Department the power to do. Voorhis and FARA represented a step in the direction of enforcing consensus by employing a label that denoted foreignness and un-Americanness. Additionally, these laws gave the Justice Department considerable investigative and coercive might, offering effective administrative remedies and providing legal grounds for prosecutions without the federal government having to resort to overt censorship. Yet, while the labeling and disclosure requirements may have reassured those concerned about government censorship, they also provided ways to control undesirable political activities without resorting to the control of speech and press.

The Domestic Foreign-Language Populations and Their Media

In the year and a half before U.S. involvement in the war and through at least the first year of the war, the Special Defense Unit claimed it served as "a control tower in the Government's fight to eliminate subversive activity," especially through "protecting" the public by "preventing" the destructive effects of the "new and sophisticated techniques of propaganda and psychological sabotage." Most of the unit's "preventive and protective" work focused on monitoring, analyzing, and preparing legal strategies for dealing with the domestic foreign-language and English-language fascist presses.[62]

Internally the SDU was divided into various divisions or sections based on the laws it had at its disposal: there was a Voorhis section, a FARA section, a Sedition section, and a "Laws and Special Projects" section. Serving all of them was the Organizations and Propaganda Analysis Section (OPAS), a division composed primarily of social scientists, many of whom were trained by Lasswell's project at the Library of Congress. OPAS was divided into ten different ideological and language areas: Native Left, Native Right, North Slavic, South Slavic, German and Scandinavian (political), German economic, Italian and French, Spanish and Portuguese, Far East, and Near East. The unit also coordinated its work with the different communications research projects at Princeton, Stanford, Columbia, the New School, the Museum of Modern Art, and the Library of Congress, as well as with the different federal projects, including the FCC's Foreign Broadcast Intelligence Service, the OFF and OWI, the Post Office Department, and the Treasury Department.[63]

It also collaborated—fitfully—with J. Edgar Hoover's FBI. To carry out its organizations analysis work (as opposed to its press content analysis work), the unit was dependent on the FBI's investigative powers for much of its internal security intelligence. As historians studying the FBI and

Hoover's directorship have all noted, the FBI's internal security intelligence activities mushroomed in the mid- to late 1930s, as a consequence of President Roosevelt's animus for his domestic enemies and his confidence in Hoover's zeal and loyalties. Hoover used the authority of a private order from Roosevelt in 1936, along with presidential directives in 1939, to expand his own authority and the breadth of his investigations into the affairs of U.S. citizens and resident aliens, with special attention to "subversive activities in the United States."[64] Richard Gid Powers, among others, argues that FDR essentially gave Hoover three years to carry out general political surveillance without oversight from his superiors, including Attorney General Homer Cummings and Robert Jackson. Only in 1939 did Hoover's license for general surveillance become known to other Justice Department officials, with FDR's official directive.[65] Sam Smith, not knowing about the secret directive of 1936, told acting Attorney General Anthony Biddle in July 1941 that the "tremendous expansion" in the bureau's work was "the direct result of the President's directive of September 6, 1939, and the policy of the Attorney General to have all national defense investigations centralized under the Federal Bureau of Investigation."[66] As the Church Committee noted in its 1976 report on U.S. intelligence activities, the growth of Hoover's domestic intelligence activities came by presidential directive, not by statute, and permitted the investigation of vaguely defined subversion and "potential" criminal acts, laying the "foundations . . . for excessive intelligence gathering about Americans."[67] Numerous SDU memoranda indicate jurisdictional and procedural conflicts with the FBI because of the carte blanche FDR gave to Hoover.

These conflicts did not dissipate once Biddle was appointed attorney general, although he tried to impose some control on Hoover. As solicitor general he had been justifiably suspicious of Hoover; likewise, Hoover was suspicious of Biddle, who had a good reputation as a civil libertarian.[68] Sam Smith, noting the jurisdictional and civil libertarian anxieties produced by Hoover's imperious strategies and methods, tried to reassure Biddle that however much Hoover might be expanding his fiefdom by digging up extensive information on fascist, communist, and other subversive groups and individuals, his work was still directed by and subordinate to the Justice Department's collective goals. Hoover's bureau was responsible only for investigative work, Smith said, and it looked "to the Department for guidance in all matters of policy, general procedure, and legal questions and for the efficient handling of the material it develops."[69]

Although his assertions of Hoover's allegiance were overstated, Smith was entirely correct when he said that Hoover's FBI was a voracious "fact-finding agency" that would dig up whatever material it could find and call it "evidence," regardless of whether there was any tangible proof of criminal activity or intent. Others in the unit complained about the excess as well. One unit attorney working on the "Suspect Citizens List" said this about the FBI: "Intelligence data has been collected and recorded as received regardless of whether or not the same is hearsay and without verifying its truth. The effort has been to collect as much intelligence data as possible rather than to confine the materials collected to evidence suitable for prosecutive purposes."[70] For SDU officials nervous about repeating the mistakes of WWI, Hoover's approach to compiling "evidence" made them uneasy and aware of the difficulties of executing a democratic assault on political propaganda.

The FBI cast a wide investigative net in search of individuals and groups engaged in or suspected of being engaged in activities deemed subversive, including FARA and Voorhis violations. Beginning in 1939, it began compiling a "suspect enemies" list, also known as the "Custodial Detention Index" or the "ABC List." While Attorney General Jackson wanted more detailed supervision of Hoover's operations in compiling these lists and proposed that the Special Defense Unit review Hoover's intelligence files, Hoover resisted any oversight, arguing—as usual—that leaks would endanger his informants and therefore he needed to protect the information. Biddle insisted, however, and after five months of negotiation, Hoover was ordered to transmit the dossiers to the unit in April 1941.[71] By May 1941, when the SDU had begun analyzing the vast amounts of material Hoover procured, the "Custodial Detention Index" consisted of over 18,000 persons who, according to Smith, "constitute[d] the greatest menace to our internal security" and might be interned in case of war.[72] The index included alien residents, naturalized citizens, and over 7,000 native-born citizens. It was reduced to 18,000, Smith told Biddle, "from tens of thousands of cases being investigated" by the FBI.[73] (It warrants noting that in 1943 Biddle ordered the Custodial Detention Index destroyed because it was "impractical, unwise, and dangerous"; Hoover ignored the order and simply maintained the files under another of his filing systems.)[74]

The unit analyzed and developed policy decisions based on the material the FBI gathered about suspect citizens and denizens and assumed it would have control over the implementation of those decisions.[75] The OPAS analysts first divided the suspects according to their citizenship status: alien resident, naturalized, or native born. Then they analyzed and cross-indexed the dossiers according to ideological and organizational categories, from leftists, pacifists, and anarchists to individual members of different groups considered suspect, including the Communist Party, the German-American Bund, the Croatian Home Defenders, the Italian War

Veterans League, and many others. Once divided by citizenship and ideology, the individual dossiers were classified according to the "levels of dangerousness" in case of national emergency.[76] Those considered most dangerous were classified in the A group and subject to consideration for internment in case of war. Those considered less potentially dangerous but dangerous enough to be subject to restricted activity were classed in group B. Those who were not considered dangerous enough for either internment or restricted activity but were nonetheless still suspect were classified in group C.[77] These priority lists, one analyst said, "marked out" the unit's "plan of attack upon the Anti-Democratic forces which threaten the internal security of the United States."[78]

Unit chief Sam Smith considered the individual dossiers and priority lists highly valuable departmental resources and told Biddle that the dossier work "approaches the heart of [the] national defense intelligence effort."[79] At the same time, his explanation of the importance of those files fully articulates the contradictory imperatives of war-era liberalism and illustrates how unit personnel tried to justify their surveillance activities in the language of civil liberties. In the logic of national security, Smith explained that the indexes provided both "preventive" and "protective," or "pure," intelligence.[80] Preventive intelligence would offer evidence about the potentially subversive activities of the nation's domestic enemies, and pure intelligence would enhance policy making and protect against hasty and ill-formed actions against groups or individuals. The indexes provided an overview of the whole field of internal security problems faced by the government, he said. They provided timely intelligence to forestall violent acts against the nation. They pointed out the sore spots where government counterpropaganda activities could be directed. And they facilitated development of an overall plan of action that would avoid governmental excess. As a result, this extensive surveillance of suspect individuals and groups would act as a bulwark against civil liberties abuses: "The purpose of this program is to prevent a hysterical mass arrest should a deeper emergency occur, to work out major problems of handling such a list ahead of time, and to be able to direct ahead of time such intelligent action, both from the point of view of immigration laws and the criminal laws, as may be necessary to protect the country."[81]

Despite the democratic assertions, Smith's argument was the same justification used by President Roosevelt, J. Edgar Hoover, and the four attorneys general who served under Roosevelt, all of whom argued that consolidating domestic intelligence "was . . . a means of protecting civil liberties."[82] Special Defense Unit lawyers who began their work committed to protecting civil liberties and preparing the nation for war against its internal enemies wound up mistakenly confusing the language of civil liberties with the logic of national security. And in fact such preventive intelligence work failed to prevent mass hysteria or protect the civil liberties of the 110,000 Japanese Americans interned in the war's first months, although the decisions on this front were ultimately not Biddle's, Smith's, Hoover's—who argued against internment—or anyone else's in the SDU.

While the language of security and liberty might have been conflated, it is important to note, however, that the unit's "pure" intelligence work appears to have worked successfully with the domestic foreign-language press, the most politically sensitive arena of SDU authority. As SDU personnel knew, the federal government's treatment of the domestic foreign-language press would testify to its tolerance toward and appreciation of the United States' foreign-born citizens and residents. Treating them with care—both to ferret out the troublemakers and to ensure the liberties of the rest— would be vital to cementing wartime loyalties of the different nationality groups in the United States, as well as to carrying out precise national security work.[83] (In view of this official wartime line, the racist treatment of Americans of Japanese descent was glaring and even more deplorable because of the distance between the policy and rhetoric of pluralism.) As unit analysts quickly discerned, the different foreign-language immigrant populations in the United States depended on their native-language newspapers and radio broadcasts for community news, cultural fare, news about their homelands, and news of the war. Antidemocratic agitators assiduously targeted German, Italian, Croatian, Polish, Portuguese, Japanese, Irish, and other distinctive ethnic and religious groups through the domestic foreign-language and native fascist media. The primary groups the unit worried about were mainly white ethnics, who represented important wartime labor and manpower resources whose loyalties would be decisive in a prolonged, total war. Demonstrating the Justice Department's commitment to freedom of expression and acknowledging the special contributions of U.S. immigrant populations would, in the long run, be vital to a unified national effort. Unit officials understood this very well.

For unit planners, especially R. Keith Kane, head of its foreign-language press intelligence division, the problem of the domestic foreign-language press therefore presented many complicated issues. From a national security perspective, the unit needed to develop programs for monitoring all radio, film, and print channels to discover antidemocratic materials. It had to take seriously the complaints expressed in the domestic foreign-language press, addressing frustrations, assuaging opinion leaders, and healing the sore spots. It also needed to provide effective counterarguments, through deeds and counterpropaganda, in answer to the divisive claims made by the fascist press.

Thus Kane and his associates were confronted by the central question confronting the liberal state. Asking the rhetorical question whether "the impotence or liberality of a democracy toward antidemocratic propaganda [would] result in demoralization of this country," Kane's reply evinced the unit's concurrent fear of and faith in speech- and association-tolerant liberalism and its faith in and fear of the country's diverse population groups and their presses. Tolerance of dissent threatened order, Kane argued, and the persistent assault on U.S. unity from antidemocratic publicists threatened morale. But intolerance of dissent would be even more damaging to morale and unacceptable to the American people: "In a democracy we cannot for a moment consider even in war time imposing a gag on free speech," Kane wrote. "We cannot apply the rule of suppression against the more subtle forms of enemy attack. This country will never prohibit listening to shortwave radio, which requires the confiscation of radio sets, nor will the country tolerate the control of that which is published in the press and radio."[84] Unobtrusively guiding but not controlling the vast domestic foreign-language media was thus both a principled and a strategic posture from the SDU's perspective. This approach was a mixture of liberal tolerance, shrewd posturing, and preventive intelligence combined with "pure" intelligence.

The unit embraced surveillance and study, not suppression, as the Justice Department's best overall strategy for dealing with the extensive domestic foreign-language media. Working in tandem with the different Rockefeller Foundation–sponsored communications projects enhanced this strategy. In a phrase used repeatedly by Kane and Lasswell, the unit decided on the "formulae of instant reply" as the best approach for responding to and neutralizing the defeatist messages that proliferated in the domestic foreign-language media.[85]

The decision to cooperate with, reply to, and not punish the domestic foreign-language press seemed to have paid off. One year into the war the unit's OPAS analysts estimated that the domestic foreign-language press was by and large supportive of Allied war aims. Even though between 10 and 15 percent of the foreign-language papers still fairly consistently followed the enemy propaganda line and were "antidemocratic, disloyal, and disruptive in their influence," and another 15 percent were described as "not very constructive in attitude, although they [were] not anti-war or engaged in any attempt to create disunity or foment opposition to the war," between 45 to 55 percent were "pro-democratic, anti-Axis, and definitely favor[ing] the cause of the United Nations." The analyst who reported these figures confirmed Kane's and others' prewar judgment, arguing that the prodemocratic domestic foreign-language press had by far the largest circulation and served "very useful purposes as a channel of communication through which the Government can reach the foreign born. This press is, in a sense," he reported, "a symbol of the freedom of speech for which we are fighting."[86] A year and a half into the war, another unit lawyer argued that the domestic foreign-language press was still a vital "weapon to be used in winning the war": "The foreign-language press is a symbol of two of the most important things about the country," he wrote. "One is the diversity of our national origin. The other is the constitutional right of free speech. . . . Not only is it an important means of communication to citizens of the United States but its continuation during wartime will mean to the peoples of foreign countries that we tell our friends from our enemies by what they say and not by the language they use or their race or their color and that in the United States anyone may speak for democracy in any language." He continued by warning his superiors that any controls aimed specifically against the domestic foreign-language press would "cause apprehension and dismay among many supporters of democracy here and abroad and would also serve to confuse the American public opinion as to who the real enemies to democracy are."[87] Clearly, freedom of the press had a huge symbolic presence in the unit's assumptions about what the United States needed to stand for in World War II, and it knew that a commitment to freedom of speech would be of great symbolic value to the public and of practical value to the Department of Justice in ensuring public support.

Unlike the Western Defense Command under General Dewitt and the Justice Department's Alien Enemy Control Unit, which became responsible for the internment of American Japanese, the Special Defense Unit lawyers recognized the importance of not punishing the innocent along with the guilty. In those instances where they would crack down on a particular paper or publisher, they chose the strategy of careful study and used legal and administrative measures that singled out only the worst cases for punishment and suppression. As one staff lawyer, Eugene Roth, explained, the unit used its administrative measures as instruments of "education and persuasion," which entailed a combination of consultation, coercion, and outright intimidation. Roth elaborated: "Our policy should not be to attempt to run a newspaper, but rather to give it an opportunity to clean itself up by putting in decent editors and omitting Axis propaganda." He averred that the combination of coercion and intimidation usually worked and that outright administrative punishment (freezing funds or withholding mailing privileges) or prosecution was used as a last resort against only the most recalcitrant.[88] As distinct from the racist assumptions underlying the War Department's internment of Japanese Americans, for instance, the Special Defense Unit's strategy toward the domestic foreign-language press pursued an individualized response to a population whose diversity demanded scrutiny at the individual and not the group level.[89] In this regard, the unit's work was an understated and underappreciated victory for liberal tolerance.

The Justice Department was not, however, quite so solicitous of the native far-right (English-language) press nor of U.S.-based agents working on behalf of foreign governments and organizations. The English-language Fascist press and the agents of foreign entities represented different kinds of problems for the Justice Department, both symbolically and administratively, and it dealt with them by using "every instrument at the control of the Government," to quote Sam Smith.[90] "Every instrument" meant mail censorship, fund freezing, repatriation, denaturalization, and especially prosecutions under the authority of the Foreign Agent Registration Act and under the various sedition laws the federal government had at its disposal, primarily the Espionage Act, the seditious conspiracy laws, and the Smith Act. The next chapter will look at the application of those remedies, inside the courtroom and out, and the trials and tribulations of free speech liberalism when the Justice Department went to war against Nazi agents and native Fascists echoing the Nazi propaganda line on the home front.

The differences between the Justice Department's treatment of the domestic foreign-language press and the native Fascist press are instructive: Justice Department officials recognized that in waging a democratic war— and one in which U.S. propaganda of pluralism would not ring falsely— the federal government needed the support of its foreign-language and minority populations. A crackdown on their dissenting presses would have worked against maintaining the support of those symbolically important groups. But there was no comparable public relations reason for caution toward the overtly Fascist domestic English-language press; indeed, the true public relations advantage seemed to be in demonstrating government control over the native Fascist press and any Nazi agents operating in the United States. There were only civil libertarian legal reasons for tolerance, and in the heat of the war those reasons received little attention.[91]

CHAPTER SIX

Justice at War: Silencing Foreign Agents and Native Fascists

The numerous prosecutions under FARA embody a very important but virtually ignored episode in U.S. communications, political, and legal history. They enabled the Justice Department to hone its legal arguments and strategies against those disseminating foreign propaganda materials without resorting to high-profile First Amendment cases. Importantly, they also provided Justice Department lawyers with federal court–approved formulae to prove the connections between propaganda and seditious intent, a proof that relied on an elaborate analogical argument about propaganda's invidious effects. In this way, FARA cases were rehearsals for the more difficult and politically controversial wartime mass sedition trials against the domestic far right.

The propaganda-as-seditious-intent construction utilized by U.S. attorneys William Powers Maloney and O. John Rogge was the centerpiece of the federal government's efforts to silence and punish the thirty-plus defendants indicted in the cases *U.S. v. Winrod et al.* and *U.S. v. McWilliams et al.* The defendants were the main disseminators in the United States of defeatist, anti-Semitic, generally pro-Axis materials during the prewar and wartime years, and because they were ideological—but not demonstrably legal or contractual—agents of foreign governments, most were not subject to the FARA or Voorhis acts' requirements. Rather, they were subject to the Espionage Act of 1917 as well as to the broad reach of the 1940 Smith Act's seditious conspiracy provisions. The indictments and, ultimately, failed prosecution of the so-called seditionists in these cases represents the victory of nervous liberalism over free-speech liberalism within Robert Jackson's and then Francis Biddle's Justice Department.

The rationale behind the prosecution of the far-right publicists and organizers was not that their speech had a demonstrated effect on the morale or efficiency of the armed forces; indeed, there was virtually no evidence of this. Rather, the broad and imprecise definition offered by the federal courts that was subsequently reused by the Justice Department stated that, given that Nazi propaganda had had devastatingly powerful effects in Germany and elsewhere in Europe, propaganda in the United States was clearly aimed at establishing "a foreign system of government" in this country and promoting "group action of a nature foreign to our institutions of government." Even broader, the courts also defined propaganda as "influencing American public opinion on a political question."[1] (Such definitions quite obviously made it easy for U.S. government interests to contend that they did not engage in propaganda activities; according to the court-accepted definition, it would have been impossible for them to do so.) Propaganda thus potentially created a clear and present danger to the morale and readiness of U.S. armed forces. This rationale represented a rebirth of the bad-tendency-of-language argument, made conceptually possible through the employment of a theory of propaganda's presumed bad effects, and threatened the emerging First Amendment doctrine.

In brief, this chapter shows that the SDU's goal of maintaining the balance between security and liberty became increasingly tenuous as war passions deepened. The unit's commitment to a speech-protective interpretation of the First Amendment weakened as its theory of propaganda's invidious effects became more legally compelling and efficacious for carrying out its wartime duties, especially as that theory received sanction from the federal courts. At the same time, it is important to recognize that SDU lawyers' articulation of and commitment to civil libertarian values also moderated the recklessness, if not the growth, of the national security state. There were those within the SDU who challenged the wartime retreat from prewar principles and protested the sedition prosecutions. Additionally, the WWII-era Supreme Court was not as willing to accept prosecutors' charges of espionage and sedition as the courts had been during World War I, signaling to federal prosecutors that they would have to meet high standards in proving the seditious conspiracy charges leveled against the *Winrod* and *McWilliams* defendants. While Justice Department lawyers were willing to assert the dangerous effects of words and images, the courts wanted greater evidence than the merely plausible possibility of dangerous effects. Legal liberalism, albeit rife with tensions and profound contradictions (especially with respect to the internment of Japanese Americans), had changed significantly since WWI.

At War Against Foreign Agents

Before the Japanese attack at Pearl Harbor, the Nazi propaganda apparatus was recognized as the greatest external threat to the United States. Tied to this threat was the knowledge—and evidence gained from a variety of investigations by Congress, the FBI, the SDU, and private entities such as the American Council Against Nazi Propaganda and Friends of Democracy, Inc.—that there was a large and well-financed domestic fascist movement whose activities threatened to advance Nazi-inspired subversion at home. When Justice Department officials looked for evidence of subversive activities, propaganda was the first line of such evidence: it was a clue to intentions and therefore a signal that further and more detailed investigation was necessary. Propaganda was viewed as a uniquely powerful weapon of psychological warfare that needed to be combated at many levels. Therefore, as the Special Defense Unit prepared itself for war, investigating the organizations and individuals who were the producers and disseminators of antidemocratic and insurrectionary materials, it had to look to all available remedies.

Constructing an "active defense against psychological warfare" required, according to Attorney General Biddle, the development of a variety of statutory and administrative solutions. As Biddle warned in his attorney general report for fiscal year 1943, the department needed a host of strategies against a duplicitous and treacherous foe. Prosecution alone would not be adequate: "In the general field of psychological warfare it has been found that new and subtle techniques of attack often cannot be met with the relatively slow and cumbersome device of prosecution."[2] The SDU thus developed prosecutory, administrative, and preventive remedies to address the many challenges posed by total war on the home front. In so doing it worked extensively with different Justice Department divisions and units, including the Criminal Division, the Immigration and Naturalization Service, the FBI, and the Alien Enemy Control Unit, and externally with the departments of War, Navy, State, Treasury, Post Office, Federal Communications Commission and the Office of War Information, the Office of Censorship, Naval Intelligence, and other wartime agencies.

The different federal agencies and departments had distinct administrative tools and regulations at their disposal, which the unit readily utilized as the self-identified control tower in the nation's propaganda defense. The Treasury Department, for instance, had broad powers to freeze the funds and seize the records, reports, and accounts of any organization suspected of foreign agency. Using this recourse against recalcitrant publications a handful of times, the unit and Treasury generally tried to work with editors and owners by first employing coercive tactics they described as "education and persuasion." If persuasion failed, funds were frozen, records seized, and the offending paper shut down while its foreign connections were investigated. These intimidating measures must have been persuasive, for as of mid-1942, only one paper, the *Texas Herald*, had had its entire operation shut down by Treasury because of its connections with

Germany. Eight other papers had their funds temporarily frozen while Treasury and Justice Department agents investigated their ties to Germany (as part of the effort to find evidence of foreign agency in the *Winrod* sedition case).[3]

Similarly, the Post Office Department had a variety of weapons at its disposal and worked with the unit to coordinate its attack on propaganda activities. Under the dubious authority provided by an 1857 anti-incendiary mails statute (aimed at blocking the abolitionist press), authority granted by the Foreign Agents Registration Act, and a December 1940 opinion by the attorney general, the post office could seize all incoming, unregistered foreign propaganda materials at all ports of entry. (As chapter 4 explains, by mid-1941 the post office had been using these postal powers with a vengeance, destroying an estimated one hundred tons of incoming foreign mail only months before the United States was at war. After Archibald MacLeish intervened with the Justice Department to ensure that forty-five copies of all documents would be saved for intelligence research purposes, the post office continued destroying the remaining materials.) The post office also had broad powers to control the domestic press because it could deny second-class mailing privileges and threaten extensive investigations against suspect publications (as it had done during WWI). The postmaster general regularly used the threat of official inquiries into press organizations as a form of coercion, particularly against the "objectionable" and "very plainly disloyal sheets."[4] By mid-1942 a handful of native fascist papers (and one Trotskyite paper) had had their second-class privileges revoked, including Father Charles Coughlin's *Social Justice*, based in Royal Oak, Michigan; the *Boise Valley Herald*, from Middletown, Idaho; the *Philadelphia Herald*, Philadelphia, Pennsylvania; E. J. Garner's *Publicity*, out of Wichita, Kansas; Court Asher's *X-Ray*, from Muncie, Indiana; and the Trotskyite *Militant*, based in New York City. As the war progressed and the unit expanded its investigations into the quite extensive native fascist press as part of the *Winrod* sedition indictment, most of the targeted publications had some or many issues denied access to the mails.[5] In addition, many of the forty-odd native fascist publications were eventually included in the Criminal Division's seditious conspiracy indictments.

However, the bulk of the SDU's legal and administrative actions against propaganda activity derived from its FARA authority. FARA offered the unit a range of administrative actions, from demanding extensive and frequent registration requirements to punishment through fines, internment, repatriation, imprisonment, or deportation. And, as unit personnel were well aware, the act was valuable for intimidation purposes prior to the punitive phases. Overall, seventy-six hundred individuals and organizations actually registered under the FARA requirements, providing the entire government with reports detailing vast information about the activities, finances, agency relationships, and purposes of the different foreign entities and their agents in the United States. (Over two thousand propaganda dissemination reports were filed during fiscal year 1944 alone.) These reports included multiple copies of the propaganda items disseminated by the individual registrants, the addresses to which the materials were sent, the number of copies transmitted, and the number of persons receiving more than a hundred copies each. These registration reports pointed federal officials to networks of individuals and groups in different ideological fields and provided extensive materials for press analysis to help the entire government better understand the varieties of propaganda being disseminated in the United States and throughout the world.[6]

FARA in the Federal Courts

While the FARA and Voorhis acts were based on registration and disclosure and not outright suppression, the definitions of propaganda accepted by the federal judges in the FARA cases belied the value-neutral, speech-protective claims that FARA and Voorhis proponents suggested. In the prewar and wartime courts, propaganda and subversion were mutually defining terms, and the idea that a propaganda campaign indicated an intention to carry out subversive activities was vital for the prosecution of individuals and clandestine front organizations identified, under the rubrics of FARA and Voorhis, as engaged in political activity. The perception that political activity was necessarily subversive was explicitly stated in the Voorhis Act and became implicit in the FARA prosecutions of those termed political propagandists. The Justice Department won successful prosecutions in fifty-plus cases from 1939 to 1944, and the federal courts accepted the Justice Department's argument that propaganda activities were essentially alien to and subversive of U.S. political traditions.[7] Such an interpretation greatly enhanced FARA as an administrative and prosecutory weapon. From the federal courts' perspective, to demonstrate the thematic and semantic consistencies between a foreign government's propaganda campaigns and the materials produced or disseminated by their U.S.-based agents was to provide at least partial proof of foreign agency; in the case of the American ideological counterparts of foreign governments, demonstrating such thematic and semantic consistencies was evidence of the bad tendency—and therefore seditious nature—of that propaganda. Both arguments eventually became central to the unit's and the special prosecutors' efforts to create agency relationships between the mass sedition defendants and Nazi Germany.

As a trial consultant and expert witness in key FARA trials, political scientist Harold Lasswell played a crucial role in aiding the Justice Department to work out these positions. His arguments about the nature of propaganda and his systematic demonstration of the ideological connections between unregistered agents and their foreign agencies enabled the department to prove by so-called scientific techniques the subversive threat posed by certain kinds of political (i.e., extremist) propaganda.

In the various FARA prosecutions, the Justice Department primarily targeted the agents and U.S.–based branches of the official (or semiofficial) international information and propaganda agencies of Nazi Germany, the Soviet Union, Spain, and Japan. The defendants included booksellers, journalists, news services, libraries of information, official consuls, and front organizations (such as labor organizations and fraternal groups) with financial connections to those foreign governments. Importantly, FARA prosecutions in the prewar period all but eliminated the most active of the agents and agencies of the Axis powers from American soil by the time the United States was at war.

Prior to, and shortly after, the U.S.-USSR wartime alliance, Communist propaganda activities were also greatly feared, and the first successful courtroom test of FARA was a 1939 prosecution of three booksellers who sold numerous Soviet-published works through their well-known and widely patronized New York city bookstore, Four Continent Books. The case of *U.S. v. Raphael Rush et al.*, also known as *Bookniga*, was tried in federal court in the District of Columbia. The defendants, Raphael Rush, Norman Weinberg, and Morris Liskin were officers of the Bookniga Corporation who were indicted for failure to register as agents of Meshdunarodnaya Kniga, a Moscow-based organization controlled by the People's Commissariat of Foreign Trade, an arm of the Soviet government.[8] (Ironically, Four Continent Books was a highly valued primary source of published books and journals from the Soviet Union for U.S. scholars and libraries, including the Library of Congress, and remained so after the prosecution. Indeed, Four Continent's president C. J. Lambkin initiated the campaign with MacLeish at the Library of Congress to get the Justice Department to modify its FARA provisions so that intelligence analysts, libraries, and scholars could receive their books and journals from the USSR, instead of having those materials destroyed by the post office as "unmailable propaganda." See chapter 4.)

This was also the first case in which Harold Lasswell served as an expert witness. Justice Department prosecutor Benjamin Parker brought him into the case, and his participation in the trial marks the first time a social science propaganda expert was used in a federal prosecution.[9] For the *Bookniga* trial Lasswell and his Library of Congress assistants examined 76 books in English and 132 books in Russian and compiled detailed content analyses of four periodicals, all of which were distributed by Bookniga. Lasswell explained the effectiveness of this technique for courtroom use as providing "simple and understandable charts from which the jury was enabled to visually grasp the type of information contained in the printed matter presented to them." The charts avoided "the difficulty of attempting to have the mass of newspapers and other printed matter relevant to the issue read and subjectively interpreted by the person or jury connected with the matter."[10]

Lasswell described his content analysis technique as involving a series of steps: First, he recorded "favorable and unfavorable presentations [of key] propaganda words, phrases, ideas, and illustrations" and then quantified and charted these "presentations." The next step involved comparing the materials under question with "known foreign controlled or sponsored sources," which in the *Bookniga* case were the Soviet newspapers *Pravda* and *Izvestia*. He then measured and illustrated how closely the suspects' materials paralleled the "official line" on certain key themes. Lasswell's self-described "propaganda detection" technique involved eight "comparison tests": The "avowal test" measured explicit identification with one side of a controversy. The "parallel test" compared the themes prevalent in a known propaganda channel with the materials in question. The others were the "consistency test"; the "presentation test," which measured "the balance of favorable and unfavorable treatment given to a controversial symbol or idea"; the "source test"; the "concealed source test"; the "distinctiveness test" (identifying the use of vocabulary peculiar to one side of a controversy); and the "distortion test."[11] He used all of these in *Bookniga* to show that the materials sold by Rush, Liskin, and Weinberg at Four Continent Books were in fact pro-Soviet "political propaganda" as defined by the FARA. As he put it, "In every case, the periodicals devoted most of their space to the Soviet Union and gave an overwhelmingly favorable presentation of the USSR" and less favorable ones to other countries, including the United States. As Four Continent Books sold materials published in the USSR, Lasswell's conclusions probably surprised no one, but they sufficed to persuade the jury that Rush, Weinberg, and Liskin were unregistered agents of the Soviet Union and should therefore be punished for their failure to register.[12] The defendants paid their fines, registered, and continued selling books to leading scholars and research libraries, among other patrons.

The *Bookniga* case set important precedents in at least three ways. First, the Federal District Court for the District of Columbia upheld the constitutionality of the Foreign Agents Registration Act in its first test. Second, it accepted the admissibility of Lasswell's expert testimony. And, third, Judge Letts, the presiding judge, provided a definition of political propaganda that went beyond FARA's own definition, admonishing the jury that any political propaganda activities were de facto un-American and contrary to U.S. interests. This definition was damning and shows how the judge was able to take a supposedly value-neutral and descriptive definition and turn it into a weapon that made it possible to punish people for the content of their ideas, despite lack of evidence to demonstrate the effects of those ideas. In a straight-ahead equation of propaganda with foreign propaganda, Judge Letts wrote:

> Furthermore, "propaganda" and "foreign propaganda" are implicitly defined as: Spreading doctrines alien to our democratic form of government; Spreading by word of mouth, or by the written word, the ideology, the principle, and the practices of other forms of government and the things for which they stand; Arbitrarily aiming to inculcate persons in the United States with those principles and teachings which seek to foster un-American activities, to influence the external and internal policies of the country, and to violate both the letter and the spirit of international law, as well as the democratic basis of our own American institution of Government.

He left little doubt that it was this federal judge's opinion that loyal Americans simply did not engage in political propaganda activities and that propaganda was necessarily inimical to democratic governments.[13] In later cases, the same essential definition would be expanded to include propaganda's magic bullet effects.

With this precedent in hand and as war drew nearer, the Justice Department turned from Soviet booksellers to Nazi targets for prosecution under the FARA provisions. In 1941 it began prosecuting U.S.-based agents of Nazi Germany, effectively closing down the German government's primary channels of information dissemination in the United States. In several cases the department used Lasswell's testimony (or similar content analysis testimony by others trained by Lasswell) to show that the unregistered agents were trafficking in political propaganda that was by definition un-American and inimical to U.S. interests.

The FARA prosecutions of Nazi propagandists were more than just trials of agents who failed to meet FARA's registration requirements. These cases enabled the federal government to use FARA as an effective legal device to silence the most active Nazi voices. In March 1941, in the case of *United States v. Manfred Zapp et al.*, the Justice Department indicted and successfully prosecuted two notoriously pro-Nazi German newspapermen and shut down a key Nazi resource, the Transocean News Service. Known as the *Transocean* case, the prosecution employed Judge Letts's damning definition of political propaganda along with Lasswell's parallel tests to demonstrate the connections between the defendants and the official German propaganda line.[14]

The Justice Department indicted another Nazi agent in March 1941, in the case of *United States v. Friedrich Ernst Auhagen*.[15] Again, Lasswell was an expert witness for the prosecution. As in the other cases, he showed that Auhagen's statements in two magazines he published, *Today's Challenge* and the *Forum Observer*, were consistent with the pronouncements of the Nazi Party along key propaganda lines. Lasswell noted that he had refined his methods a few degrees in this case, improving the value of the consistency test by adding a further comparative component to it. Not only did he show comparisons between the defendant's publications and known Nazi propaganda, he also demonstrated that Auhagen's treatment of controversial issues was highly inconsistent with the treatment of those same issues in *Reader's Digest* and the *Saturday Evening Post*. (Lasswell found that *Reader's Digest* paralleled the Nazi line somewhat more consistently than did the *Saturday Evening Post*.)[16]

Other prewar FARA convictions included pro-Nazi speaker and pamphleteer Laura Ingalls and longtime German agent George Sylvester Viereck, owner of Flanders Hall, Inc., which published Auhagens's magazines *Today's Challenge* and the *Forum Observer*. In addition, the department also carried out many successful wartime prosecutions under FARA, including *United States v. Ralph Townsend et al.*, a January 1942 case involving unregistered Japanese nationalists and their U.S. agent; *U.S. v. Glicherie Moraru et al.*, a 1943 case against members of the Free Romania Movement; *United States v. John Eoghan Kelly*, a 1943 case against an agent for the Spanish Library of Information; *United States v. Domenico Trombetta*, a 1943 case against the publisher of two explicitly profascist Italian newspapers in New York; and *U.S. v. German-American Vocational League, Inc. et al.*, a 1944 case against twenty-seven members of the German-American Bund and its subsidiary organizations.[17] (Many of the same Bundist defendants were also convicted of interfering with the draft under the Espionage Act in the case of *U.S. v. Keegan*, but that conviction was later overturned.)[18]

FARA gave the Justice Department an effective and low-profile means for eliminating unwanted political ideas from the U.S. scene without drawing critical attention to its work. Further, the tests that emerged from the FARA cases were used to argue that evidence of consistent employment of propaganda themes that paralleled those used by foreign powers was proof of seditious intent, an argument absolutely crucial to reviving the sedition laws for WWII and the cold war. Lasswell's role in this is significant, because his testimony helped the Justice Department shape an argument about propaganda in which proof of its existence became proof of its evil intent, thereby reviving the presumed intent doctrine that Chafee had so worried about.

Propaganda as Proof of Seditious Intent

When the Justice Department moved from punishing foreign agents in the United States to punishing far-right agitators who were U.S. citizens not under the employ of foreign entities, Lasswell's content analysis strategies and proofs were equally valuable to the prosecution. Without FARA provisions at its disposal, the Justice Department had to meet the more legally difficult standards of seditious intent, and Lasswell's expertise helped them do so. In the several wartime sedition trials, Lasswell's analytical framework and organization of evidence provided the Justice Department with a strategy for presenting ideological consistencies as evidence of presumed intent, presumptive intent being a necessary condition for prosecuting a sedition case. The courts' acceptance of Lasswell's form of proof—based on consistencies in content and inferences about implied intent—corresponded with the Justice Department's need to develop a new standard for proving the seditious nature of the extensive nativist, far-right press in the United States.

A key element of the indictments and prosecutory strategy in the wartime sedition trials was providing evidence that the defendants willfully intended to interfere with and obstruct the recruitment of the military and undermine the morale of the U.S. armed forces.[19] The unit and the Criminal Division used Lasswell's techniques in the sedition trials and in the preparation for them to offer at least partial evidence (and compelling evidence, according to the courts) of the morale-destroying intentions of the far right's Nazi-promoting propaganda. Justice Department attorneys preparing sedition indictments regularly consulted with Lasswell, used the Special Defense Unit's content analysis specialists, and based part of their courtroom strategies on Lasswell's court-proven parallel test technique for defining, demonstrating evidence of, and prosecuting sedition based on consistency with fascist ideology.[20]

In the course of the different sedition trials, the Justice Department identified the official Nazi propaganda line as consisting of fourteen main themes:

1. The United States is internally corrupt (e.g., There is war-profiteering, political and economic injustice, plutocratic exploitation, Communist sedition, Jewish conspiracy, and spiritual decay within the United States).

2. The foreign policies of the United States are morally unjustifiable (e.g., They are selfish, bullying, imperialistic, hypocritical and predatory).

3. The President of the United States is reprehensible. (e.g., He is a war-monger and a liar, unscrupulous, responsible for suffering, and a pawn of Jews, Communists or Plutocrats).

4. Great Britain is internally corrupt (e.g., There is war-profiteering, political and economic injustice, plutocratic exploitation, Communist sedition, Jewish conspiracy, and spiritual decay within Great Britain).

5. The foreign policies of Great Britain are morally unjustifiable (e.g., They are selfish, bullying, imperialistic, hypocritical and predatory).

6. Prime Minister Churchill is reprehensible (e.g., He is a war-monger and a liar, unscrupulous, responsible for suffering, and a pawn of Jews, Communists or Plutocrats).

7. Nazi Germany is just and virtuous (e.g., Its aims are justifiable and noble; it is truthful, considerate and benevolent).

8. The foreign policies of Japan are morally justifiable (e.g., Japan has been patient, long suffering, and it is not responsible for the war).

9. Nazi Germany is powerful (e.g., Germany has the support of Europe; it possesses the manpower, armaments, materials, and morale essential for victory).

10. Japan is powerful (e.g., It possesses the manpower, armaments, materials, and morale essential for victory).

11. The United States is weak (e.g., It lacks the materials, manpower, armaments, and morale essential for victory).

12. Great Britain is weak (e.g., It lacks the materials, manpower, armaments, and morale essential for victory).

13. The United Nations are disunited (e.g., They distrust, deceive, envy, and suspect each other).

14. The United States and the world are menaced by: Communists, Jews, and Plutocrats.[21]

Evidence of enough of these themes used by any given defendant was a conspicuous part of the evidence of that defendant's presumed intention to harm the U.S. war effort and to aid its enemies. (According to one unit propaganda analyst who worked closely with Lasswell, regular duplication of a minimum of ten of the themes seemed necessary to demonstrate such intent.)

The federal government first successfully used Lasswell's consistency tests in a sedition case when prosecuting the virulently fascistic Silver Shirt leader William Dudley Pelley. Pelley, codefendant Lawrence A. Brown, and the Fellowship Press (publisher of Pelley's paper, the *Galilean*) were indicted for disseminating and conspiring to disseminate false information with the intent to impair the operations of the U.S. armed forces. They were convicted in federal court in Indianapolis in August 1942, and the conviction was upheld by the Seventh Circuit Court of Appeals in Indianapolis.[22] The prosecution demonstrated that the defendants' actions met at least two conditions of sedition: they intended to harm the morale of the armed forces, and they willingly made false statements. It showed that Pelley published hundreds of knowingly "false" and therefore seditious statements after Pearl Harbor, including contentions that the Axis cause was just: "We have by every act and deed performable aggressively solicited war with the Axis," Pelley wrote. He also said that the Roosevelt administration had baited Japan into the war with "intentionally-bad diplomacy" and suggested that Americans did not support the war effort, announcing that "from North Carolina to Seattle, Washington, you can travel in these Mobilizing Moments, and scarcely hear a word of condemnation of the Nipponese, Germans, or Italians."[23]

Along with these ill-intended and willfully "false" statements, military officials found a copy of the *Galilean* in a soldier's duffel bag, evidence that not only was Pelley willfully promoting defeatism, he was also directly affecting the morale of the armed forces. As historian Leo Ribuffo has pointed out, however, the prosecution "in fact . . . presented no evidence of direct contact—or attempted contact—between the defendants and military personnel."[24] With Lasswell's evidence in tow, they did not need to.

What the prosecution did show evidence of was the connection between Pelley's writings and Axis propaganda doctrine. In its decision to uphold the lower federal court's conviction, the Seventh Circuit Court of Appeals explained that the prosecution had been able to prove, in its language, Pelley's "evil intent" by showing his personal history, his ideological loyalties, his trafficking in Axis propaganda materials, and the consistency of his writings with the fourteen Axis propaganda themes. The court declared:

To prove the existence of evil intent on the part of the defendants, the Government first disclosed the pre-war activities of defendant Pelley . . . first as the creator of a widely publicized nation-wide Silver Shirt organization, then as candidate for President in 1936 on his own ticket, the Christian Party. His pro-Axis bent was overwhelmingly demonstrated in this campaign [as was] his genuine admiration of the Hitler regime. A search of his home uncovered an extensive library of German, Italian, and Japanese originated propaganda.[25]

Having demonstrated Pelley's Axis loyalties, the prosecution then "proved by scientific research and analysis," the court noted, "that the utterances of Pelley in *The Galilean* were consistent and almost identical with the fourteen major themes of German propaganda."[26] Lasswell's demonstration of the conjunction between the Axis line and Pelley's own writings ensured a successful prosecution. Indeed, the brunt of the appellate court's decision rested on the unequivocal intent of Pelley's antiwar and anti-American slurs, unequivocal because they so closely resembled the Axis line, as Lasswell demonstrated. As in the other cases, he applied the parallel test to the fourteen Axis themes, provided a series of charts to illustrate the consistency of the *Galilean* on each of the Axis themes, and depicted the persistence of those themes in the *Galilean* over time.[27] The court reported that "Dr. Lasswell testified that of the total of 1,240 statements in the 157 articles of *The Galilean*, 1,195 statements were consistent with and suggested copying from the German propaganda themes, and only 45 were not in harmony with them."[28]

Although the prosecution did not in fact demonstrate it outright, the court averred that Lasswell's testimony "gave the jury a basis for a verdict that defendants were 'interfering' with the 'operation or success' 'of the military forces' of the United States." This interference was understood as a direct consequence of the intent of Pelley's propaganda: "In time of war, when success depends on unified national effort, abiding loyalty, and unremitting patriotism," the court wrote, it was "hardly conceivable that a writer or speaker would have written such propaganda." Pelley "entertained the hope," the court said, that his propaganda would weaken "the patriotic resolve of his fellow citizens in their assistance in the country's cause" by "retarding" their "patriotic ardor." For both the trial and appellate courts, Pelley's writings provided ample evidence of his seditious intentions.[29] Demonstration of actual effects was not necessary, only proof of consistency with the enemy line.

When Pelley and company appealed their conviction, they challenged the admissibility of Lasswell's testimony. The federal appellate court upheld it without qualm, however, and made exactly the inference the prosecution wished it to make: that intention could be inferred from content. The court held that Lasswell's testimony "shed light on [the] defendant's intentions." Through Lasswell's testimony, the "jury was thus permitted to get a better understanding of the intent which prompted Pelley in distributing what the jury could have found was secondhand Axis propaganda."[30] In a later context, this Lasswellian-engineered testimony was upheld by another court when W. P. Davison, the Special Defense Unit's German specialist, used content analysis in the FARA prosecution of the German-American Vocational League, a subsidiary of the German-American Bund. Overruling the defendant's challenge to Davison's testimony, the district court cited Lasswell's testimony in the Pelley case, ruling that "propaganda is a subject for expert testimony."[31]

Beyond that, Lasswell's analytical framework proved to have important theoretical value in helping the Justice Department develop a theory of propaganda that would enable it to indict and prove a seditious conspiracy among thirty-odd native fascists. His framework proved central to the state's strategy for prosecuting extreme speech as enemy propaganda.

Indicting the Native Fascist Conspirators

U.S. fascists had few defenders within liberal circles and the mainstream media, and President Roosevelt seemed to have suffered virtually no contemporary criticism for the pressure he put on his attorney general to prosecute the domestic far right. When the Justice Department targeted domestic fascist mouthpieces of Nazi doctrine in a handful of individual sedition cases and as co-conspirators in two mass sedition indictments, *U.S. v. Winrod et al.*, and in the ultimately unsuccessful seditious conspiracy trial *U.S. v. McWilliams et al.*, national security liberalism triumphed and civil rights liberalism remained quiescent, setting a pattern that would define U.S. liberalism's capitulation to security imperatives during the subsequent cold war decades.[32]

The decision to silence and punish the native fascists resulted from several factors, chief among them President Roosevelt's demands that the Justice Department investigate and prosecute his harshest domestic critics. As historian Leo Ribuffo argues, a crackdown on the noisy far-right agitators was "virtually inevitable" with the outbreak of war.[33] After all, President Roosevelt had long before authorized J. Edgar Hoover to investigate his domestic enemies and his foreign policy critics, and his intolerance only grew with the far right's unrelenting criticisms of U.S. foreign policies. FBI and Special Defense Unit investigations, together with those by the

Dies House Un-American Activities Committee, the Tenney Committee in California, the Anti-Defamation League, Friends of Democracy, the American Council Against Nazi Propaganda, and others created a groundswell of Brown Scare momentum to eradicate any Nazi-inflected propaganda activities in the United States. Thus President Roosevelt was in sync with other liberal opinion leaders when he demanded Justice Department action, which he did, repeatedly. As wartime attorney general Francis Biddle recalled in his autobiographical account of the war years, Roosevelt asked him the same question at virtually every cabinet meeting: "When are you going to indict the seditionists?" Biddle tells that he invariably replied that the department would move once it had sufficient evidence for an indictment to hold up in court.[34]

The Justice Department decided to silence the native fascists en masse in early 1942, when top-level Justice officials met to reorganize the department for war. They created a war division, renamed other divisions (at which point the Special Defense Unit became the Special War Policies Unit), drew new lines of authority, and authorized targeting far-right agitators for grand jury investigations, including a motley assortment of twenty-eight far-right publicists, German-American Bundists, German agents, Klansmen, Silver Shirters, America Firsters, and former military officials.[35] Most of the defendants in the *U.S. v. Winrod* indictments were reindicted in the case of *U.S. v. McWilliams et al.*, which eventually went to trial in April 1944 but ended in November 1944 when the trial judge, Chief Justice Eicher, died of a sudden heart attack. (The final legal disposition of the case against the thirty *McWilliams* defendants was not decided until June 1947, when the U.S. Court of Appeals for the District of Columbia dismissed the case.)[36]

In both cases, the defendants were indicted under the Espionage Act of 1917 and Title I of the Alien Registration Act, the peacetime sedition act known as the Smith Act. They were charged with conspiring to "interfere with, impair and influence the loyalty, morale and discipline of the military and naval forces" and with conspiring to cause "insubordination, disloyalty, mutiny and refusal of duty in the military and naval forces."[37] Both cases targeted "people with Nazi connection . . . who echoed Nazi propaganda themes" and "had joined an international Fascist conspiracy to destroy democracy here and throughout the world." This conspiracy, *McWilliams* prosecutor O. John Rogge noted in 1946, at the dawn of the cold war, "was as international in scale as Communism."[38] According to historian Leo Ribuffo, the indictment in the *Winrod* case "set in motion the major prosecution of the Brown Scare," but for a variety of reasons all these attempts were unsuccessful. The *Winrod* case, according to Ribuffo, was marred by the self-aggrandizement of Special Prosecutor William

Powers Maloney, along with his ethical indiscretions and bad political judgment. Both cases were marred by poor trial preparation by the state, questionable legal reasoning about the nature of the evidence, and effective defense strategies. And, as contemporary accounts make clear and Ribuffo skillfully depicts, the *McWilliams* trial was a fascinatingly chaotic but ultimately disastrous prosecution, one that ended, for all intents and purposes, with the unfortunate midtrial death of an overwhelmed trial judge. As Ribuffo notes, the *Winrod* case was hampered by ineptitude, and the *McWilliams* trial was marked by farce and tragedy.[39]

Whether the Justice Department ever had sufficient evidence of a seditious conspiracy by the American far right is questionable. Many of the SDU lawyers and social science propaganda analysts doubted that they had sufficient evidence of an active conspiracy, and leading historians of the far right are skeptical, as was, apparently, the chief prosecutor in the *U.S. v. McWilliams* case.[40] Moreover, by the end of the war the Supreme Court had established difficult standards for proving seditious intent by individuals or groups in the *Keegan* and *Hartzel* cases (both of which had to do with Selective Service Act interference), suggesting that even if the *McWilliams* prosecution had been completed and the Justice Department had had the opportunity to present all its evidence, it was still unlikely the defendants would have been found guilty of seditious conspiracy.[41]

In the spring of 1942, however, under pressure from the president and leading voices of liberal opinion, Justice officials believed they could develop a seditious conspiracy case against the native fascists, based on copious evidence that through their various organs (forty or so newspapers and magazines), they repeatedly echoed the main propaganda themes spewed forth by the Nazi propaganda machinery and were therefore part of a vast international Nazi conspiracy. The Justice Department's proof of an active seditious conspiracy was thin at best. Indeed, other than a "dozen instances" or so showing financial connections and agency relationships between several of the U.S. fascists and Nazi Germany, the bulk of the evidence presented by the Justice Department turned on the argument that by individually and collectively replicating Nazi propaganda themes, the native fascists had joined a "worldwide Nazi movement" aimed at undermining democratic governments through propaganda and then toppling them by force. In fact, a Justice Department press release announcing the first *Winrod* indictment made propaganda synonymous with sedition: "The indictment charges a nationwide conspiracy to destroy the morale of our armed forces through systematic dissemination of sedition." The department, trying to milk the case for public relations, pledged "its best efforts to vigorous[ly] prosecute" any propaganda activity that "directly interferes with our war effort."[42]

As the successful sedition prosecution in the *Pelley* case had shown, the federal judiciary would accept evidence of Nazi-inflected propaganda in the United States as proof of seditious intent to destroy U.S. unity and undermine military morale. Special War Policies Unit lawyers preparing groundwork for the first conspiracy indictment made the same argument, explaining to a hesitant attorney general that the Nazis "have been and are now waging propaganda warfare against the United States" through the domestic fascists' "scurrilous publications." Publications such as the *New York Enquirer, Publicity*, the *Defender*, the *Galilean*, the *Octopus*, *X-Ray*, *Weckruf und Beobachter*, the *Broom*, the *Cross and the Flag*, and dozens of others "consistently and persistently served the objectives of the Nazi propaganda attack," unit lawyers argued.[43] Because of their presumable intent to damage the armed forces' morale and manpower, they were seditious; because they shared among them so many common themes, advertisements, articles, and ideological and semantic consistencies, they were presumed to be part of a master conspiracy; and because the Nazi use of the same propaganda themes had been so effective elsewhere, the publications were presumed to be exceedingly dangerous. This was the argument Lasswell helped them develop.

During the *McWilliams* trial and in postwar documents supporting the government's case, special prosecutor O. John Rogge would make precisely these claims. Summarizing his overall contention about these domestic instruments of the Nazi conspiracy, Rogge wrote: "In attempting to bring about their Nazi or fascist revolution in this country, the defendants . . . followed the Nazi blueprint." This is a line he used regularly, and for Rogge "following the Nazi blueprint" meant intending to do in the United States what the Nazis had done in Weimar Germany and elsewhere in Europe: undermining morale through subversion and then destroying legitimate governments through force. Rogge explained that a

> Nazi or Fascist revolution, the way the Nazis brought it about in Germany and the way the members of the movement here hoped to bring it about in this country, was to take place in two phases: a prerevolutionary phase and the actual seizure of power. During the prerevolutionary phase, they hoped to disintegrate and soften the existing social structure so that the ultimate seizure of power would be easy. They hoped to accomplish this by a mass propaganda campaign inciting people to hatred of our democratic, representative form of government and to hatred of various groups and classes.

After the propaganda had done its work, "then they intended, as an organized minority with the support of at least a section of the armed forces, simply to seize power."[44]

Rogge repeatedly illustrated the conspiracy, and reiterated the dangers, by documenting the numerous ways in which the defendants mirrored Nazi doctrine on, among other themes, the international Jewish-Communist conspiracies, the need for extermination of Jews, the decadence of democracies, the need for military discipline, Hitler's unique historical role, the superiority of Aryan blood, and the eventual worldwide triumph of fascism. The U.S. fascists, Rogge wrote, "followed the Nazi texts chapter and verse" (p. 416), proving that "along with destroying our democratic form of government, the defendants intended to impose upon us a Nazi or Fascist brand of totalitarianism. They intended to impose on us a one-party system just as the Nazis had done before them in Germany. They intended to abolish freedom of speech, freedom of the press, freedom of religion, freedom of assembly, freedom from arrest without cause, and all the other civil liberties guaranteed to us by the Constitution" (p. 415). Such an interpretation justified an all-out war against fascist propaganda; no apologies were necessary.

The goal of protecting individual and group liberty was viewed as a noble position but a luxury as well. As Rogge explained, given the war crisis and the effectiveness of Nazi propaganda, the civil libertarian faith that the marketplace of ideas would produce the victory of truth was not sufficient insurance of national survival. Indeed, Rogge (a hero among Popular Front liberals for prosecuting the fascists) repudiated the modern free speech tradition, arguing that the special case of Nazi propaganda made the First Amendment a potential Achilles heel for U.S. democracy. "It is this very freedom of speech and of the press and other freedoms under a democratic form of government which the Nazis abused in order to destroy the Weimar Republic, a German democratic form of government similar to ours. . . . Paul Joseph Goebbels, the Nazi god of propaganda, once chortled that democracy, by its devotion to freedom of speech and other civil liberties, provided its deadly enemies with the weapons with which to destroy it." The *McWilliams* defendants were "the declared enemies of democracy," Rogge said, and were "intent upon the destruction of democracy here and throughout the world" (p. 414).

Rogge and other Justice Department officials knew that pursuing a crackdown on the organs of the far right based on the threat of their propaganda—instead of for specific deeds—ran counter to free speech liberalism's commitments to protecting speech other than that which showed a clear and present danger of carrying out its intended purposes. Yet, while some of Rogge's support staff in the SDU challenged him about the speech-restrictive implications of a conspiracy case based almost entirely on an argument about the power of propaganda and the inferred effects of speech with "bad tendencies," most unit personnel agreed that Nazi propaganda abroad and at home could conceivably undermine both U.S. democracy and the war effort.

SDU lawyers and the Organizations and Propaganda Section analysts preparing background research and legal positions for the mass sedition trials facilitated the retreat from a speech-protective interpretation of the First Amendment. Legal theorists in the unit's Sedition Section, for instance, refurbished the prosecution-friendly bad tendency of speech approach by employing a magic bullet theory of propaganda's effectiveness. The magic bullet idea was explicitly stated in a draft of the first *Winrod* indictment, which asserted that "no one who has been exposed to such a campaign can escape being affected by it, consciously or unconsciously." This premise led to the conclusion that the existence of Nazi propaganda in the United States created a clear and present danger to the United States and that all materials showing a high incidence of thematic and semantic correspondence to "official" Nazi propaganda were therefore seditious both in intent and effect. "If a military weapon such as propaganda is employed, there is clear and present danger to loyalty, morale and discipline," the same document argued.[45] Propaganda's effects were inferred but could certainly be demonstrated by analogy.

From early on in the indictment-seeking stages of *Winrod* and *McWilliams*, the SDU's legal theorists recognized that the speech-protective interpretation of the clear and present danger test articulated in the WWI-era *Abrams* case and embraced by Chafee and other civil libertarians would not countenance this parallel test argument. As unit officials devised what they referred to as a "new standard" of sedition, they sought to reemploy the original speech-restrictive meaning of the clear and present danger test as it was articulated in the *Schenck* decision, not the speech-protective meaning it had acquired for civil libertarians since the *Abrams* case. Additionally, by positing a conspiracy among the U.S. fascists, they argued that the prosecution's standard of proof would be even less onerous because the state could assert a conspiracy ex post facto. Adopting a legal strategy based on the premise of a seditious conspiracy permitted a sweeping and inclusive treatment of the domestic fascist press. As unit lawyers explained to the attorney general early on, the native fascists' "printed utterances bear such a strong resemblance to each other as to indicate clearly the existence of a common plan or scheme."[46]

The unit lawyers employed Lasswellian parallel tests to assert seditious intent but had little evidence to prove direct effects. In the FARA cases, Lasswell's parallel themes tests had provided so-called proof of foreign agency by showing ideological consistencies among published materials.

In the *Pelley* sedition case, Lasswell's testimony provided proof of Pelley's "evil intent" by showing the same consistencies between Pelley's writings and Nazi propaganda themes. In preparation for the seditious conspiracy cases, the Justice Department used the same framework to argue that parallel propaganda lines proved seditious intent and a conspiracy. This assertion of a clear and present danger based on parallel propaganda themes was the mainstay of Rogge's argument about fascist propaganda in the United States, and, as Ribuffo has pointed out, getting the trial judge to accept the introduction of extensive background materials about Nazi propaganda campaigns in Europe would be crucial to making the argument work in court. (As Ribuffo notes, the judge in the *McWilliams* trial, Chief Justice Eicher of the district court of the District of Columbia, was more than patient in allowing Rogge to submit these background materials as evidence.)[47]

Importantly, Justice Department lawyers came to see the modern First Amendment doctrine as an obstacle to successful prosecutions. Their writings about the legal standards that should guide the unit's propaganda analysis revealed how the Holmes-Brandeis test—although rhetorically extolled as the more principled standard to embrace—was considered simply too difficult to meet under the conditions of modern warfare.[48] "It is our intention," they wrote, "to live up to the standards of conduct necessary to preserve the Four Freedoms in the United States and to that end to refrain from employing techniques of suppression which may be in violation of the Bill of Rights."[49] And to this end they would be guided, they said, by the decisions of the Supreme Court on questions of free speech "and by the famous dissents of Mr. Justice Holmes and Mr. Justice Brandeis."[50] Because of the "sly, dishonest character of these mischievous writings," however, and the "careful" way in which the domestic fascists worked, it would be difficult to establish violations if bound by the Holmes-Brandeis standards of dangerous proximity and imminence.[51] Unit lawyers therefore rejected the speech-protective interpretation of the clear and present danger test as having limited value under the circumstances of total warfare. The WWI-era cases that Holmes and Brandeis responded to were not germane because of the nature of modern propaganda. Those cases "appear to be unrealistic as precedent on the facts," one unit lawyer wrote in late 1942, because "recent experience" demonstrated that the nation's domestic enemies had achieved a "clever understanding . . . of the limits which appear from those cases and a cunning use of language to *achieve the result of sedition without actually making direct seditious statements within the meaning of the earlier cases.*"[52] This was the problem as unit lawyers (and later Rogge) saw it: the far-right agitators could not be proved guilty of actual seditious acts under the more speech-tolerant standards laid out in *Abrams*, even though they had in fact committed sedition. Therefore the Justice Department had to adjust its standards of what constituted proof of sedition, so that sedition could be proved. They had to go back to an older, more speech-restrictive standard. Rogge too rejected the Holmes-Brandeis-Chafee standard as unrealistic, especially in a time of national emergency.

The absence of other substantial evidence of conspiracy beyond the *McWilliams* defendants' common use of Nazi propaganda themes did not seem to bother Rogge much. It did, however, weaken his case and made it clear to him at war's end, when the Supreme Court reversed convictions in two similar Espionage Act cases (*U.S. v. Hartzel* and *U.S. v. Keegan*), that his conspiracy-through-propaganda case probably would not pass judicial muster and should therefore be abandoned.[53] Before that, however, Rogge, along with the SDU's Sedition Section and its OPAS analysts, put fascist propaganda in the United States on trial and by so doing took the key agitators out of circulation for the duration of the war.

The SDU and the Seditious Conspiracy Indictments

Besides allowing the first special prosecutor, William Powers Maloney, to bring scattered defendants to trial in the jurisdiction of his choice in the *Winrod* case, "prevailing practice also allowed juries to find a conspiracy among persons who had never met or reached formal agreement. In order to show intent to conspire, prosecutors customarily introduced—and courts customarily admitted—circumstantial evidence. Federal procedure demanded an overt act in furtherance of the conspiracy, but this act," according to Ribuffo, "might be something as trivial as sending letters." Additionally, the great utility of the conspiracy charge for prosecutors was that "if jurors decided that defendants had conspired, each conspirator [could be] held responsible for words and deeds of the others."[54]

Clearly, the conspiracy charge was prosecution friendly, and its use against the far right divided prominent civil libertarians. Chafee called it "indefensible," and the ACLU was divided about it, Ribuffo notes. Executive Director Roger Baldwin called the *Winrod* case "monstrous," and General Counsel Arthur Garfield Hays drafted a letter of protest to Attorney General Biddle against "this sort of attack on free speech, once removed." But the ACLU's general counsel, Morris Ernst, who had earlier actively worked with the SDU on revising the FARA statutes to serve the state's needs better and "had persistently urged President Roosevelt to take action against the far right," supported the prosecution. Like others in the left-liberal community fearful of Nazi propaganda, the ACLU board of di-

rectors chose to "stand aside" and not offer the defendants counsel or support, the majority believing that the accused "were cooperating with or
acting on behalf of the enemy" (p. 194). The left, in general, supported the
indictment and did not challenge the use of the highly speech- and association-restrictive conspiracy charges.

Unit personnel were in fact initially opposed to the decision to move
ahead on the indictment but were eventually actively involved in helping
Maloney and then Rogge put their cases together. Unit chief Sam Smith
was angered by the sedition program and by the way the decisions to pursue the indictments were made. Despite Attorney General Jackson's intentions to make Smith's unit responsible for authorizing the department's sedition prosecutions, Smith's superiors placed responsibility in the
Criminal Division and the solicitor general's office (leaving the unit responsible for FARA administration and propaganda research and analysis). This was the very fox-in-the-henhouse scenario Jackson had hoped to
avoid when he set up the unit and gave it the job of authorizing such prosecutions. Much to Smith's chagrin, the decisions to develop a grand jury
program were even made without consulting him, despite the fact the
unit's Sedition and OPAS sections had long been working on the far
right's "scurrilous sheets." The decision to place responsibility for prosecution decisions in the hands of those most interested in prosecution
(such as Maloney) portended disaster from Smith's perspective. In April
1942 he complained to Attorney General Biddle, telling him that "cases
are being submitted to the grand juries on which there is no evidence of
sedition and with practically no preparation." There was no "coordination
of material" between the department's investigators in the field, the analysts in his unit, and the Criminal Division's prosecutors. The decision to
move ahead on a sedition program was "hastily conceived," he warned,
adding that he was "afraid of its successful execution."[55]

Despite skepticism within the unit about Maloney's uncoordinated
grand jury probe and the lack of compelling evidence, unit lawyers in the
Sedition Section helped develop the legal strategy for the grand jury prosecution, producing an extensive body of documents on the legal questions
related to the sedition prosecutions, ranging from standards of proof necessary to show conspiracy, to whether or not new sedition legislation was
needed, to the need for a new standard of sedition to meet the stratagems
of modern propagandists. OPAS analysts helped compile and coordinate
the evidence about the indictees' interconnections and the content of their
publications, providing, among other materials, a compendium of quotations from the "scurrilous publications" showing the parallels with Nazi
propaganda themes.[56]

Jesse MacKnight, head of the OPAS analysts, coordinated the unit's work with Maloney and Rogge at the evidentiary end. Based on experience with Lasswell in the FARA and Pelley trials, he knew that organizing the evidence into clear, graphic representations of ideological and agency relationships would be the most powerful weapon for the prosecutors. His staff could help draw an "exact picture of the conspiracy" by constructing master charts showing interrelations among the individuals, publications, and organizations, he told Smith. Maloney would need such graphic evidence to be successful before a jury, and any other "means he might adopt would seem to be piece-meal and tend to build up general confusion about the conspiracy. The mere fact that he has twenty-eight individuals using some forty-odd publications and organizations demands that a clear picture be presented before the case goes to trial, and at the trial itself." MacKnight also recommended that OPAS perform content analyses of the publications to discern the patterns of parallelism with Axis radio propaganda and to find any direct uses of official German materials, such as the publications of the Fichte Bund or World Service.[57] By the time Maloney got his first indictment from the grand jury in July 1942, OPAS had set up schedules showing connections such as mutual endorsements, reprinted materials, appeals for funds, advertisements for the other defendants' publications or writings, and other evidence that could be used as a basis for court presentation.[58] As Eugene Roth of the Sedition Section told Smith, "I feel strongly that Mr. Maloney will find this excellent job tremendously helpful at the trial," although Roth worried that Maloney "would not have enough manpower to help him fully utilize the materials."[59] For unit personnel, both manpower and the quality of evidence actually showing a conspiracy were matters of concern.

Despite completing content analyses of nineteen of the defendants' publications and scouring all the German propaganda materials mailed to the defendants and intercepted by the Post Office Department, OPAS analysts had found only five "unacknowledged reprints" from official Nazi propaganda sources by October 1942, results that led them to be cautious about the claims Maloney should make about active agency relationships with Nazi Germany.[60] By February 1943, at which time Maloney had drawn up a second *Winrod* indictment (and was on the verge of being dismissed by Biddle and replaced by Rogge), unit personnel were still bothered by the overall weakness of the evidence. Even though staffers were able to "gather material which indicates a high similarity of intent, and at least the possibility of collaboration among the other defendants," OPAS research still did not show significant evidence of active collaboration among most of the defendants and revealed that some defendants could simply not be connected to one another, with only Garner, Smythe, Broenstrupp, Hudson, Kullgren, Sanctuary, and Jones shown to have extensive connections.[61] By July 1943, a solid eighteen months into excavating connections among the defendants, the unit was still only able to identify fourteen defendants with "pretty well-established Nazi connections." Even then, they still had "to study the publications of these individuals to determine whether their statements have violated the Smith Act," that is, to determine whether there were any direct effects between the defendants' words and diminished military recruitment or morale. The more civil libertarian of the unit lawyers were doubtful they would find such effects and worried that the Smith Act was going to be used to punish speech acts without any proof of direct or demonstrable consequences.[62]

Part of the problem of preparing evidence of interconnections and thoroughly examining all pertinent publications was that the Justice Department did not direct sufficient manpower to the case. By the time Maloney had been fired as special prosecutor and replaced by Rogge in February 1943, unit personnel who hoped for a successful prosecution were plainly frustrated by the amount of work that needed to be done on the case. Thus, as prosecutorial responsibility shifted to Rogge and as the second *Winrod* indictment was dismissed by the U.S. district judge for the District of Columbia (in March 1943), unit personnel began retracting themselves from the case. Rogge immediately extended the life of the grand jury and attempted to strengthen the case, Ribuffo says, but SDU records indicate that he did so with considerably diminished contributions from the unit, except on the matter of conceptualizing and organizing his theoretical arguments about the native fascists' place in the international propaganda conspiracy.[63]

As Rogge took over, unit personnel worried about his poor management of the conspiracy case materials and the department's apparently limited commitment to the case. Even though by February 1943 the Justice Department was seeking a third indictment against virtually the same defendants and even though Biddle was placing considerable pressure on Rogge to bring the case to trial, unit staff were frustrated by that fact that after two failed indictments there were still huge caches of important sources that had only been unsystematically examined, if at all.[64] The upshot was that the SDU felt that it could not and should not overextend itself, especially for a case that seemed to have low departmental priority and uncertain prospects. Sedition Section head Eugene Roth told Sam Smith after the second *Winrod* indictment was dismissed that Rogge was "insufficiently staffed [on] the law questions" and despite OPAS's "considerable" contribution of material on propaganda background and the interconnections among defendants, Rogge's unmethodical handling of the evidence suggested to Roth that the unit should not waste too much manpower on this case. George Roudebush, Roth's replacement in the Sedition Section, warned of the same problems, noting that "Mr. Rogge's system of organizing his material has been in general to prepare a loose leaf notebook containing all the material as to each defendant."[65]

Before the unit deluged Rogge with any new materials, it seemed necessary that Rogge develop a better system of organization; otherwise, unit hours used on his behalf would be poorly spent, given the unit's own scarce manpower. Moreover, unit personnel knew that the attorney general was losing patience with the lack of progress on the case and that even as late as May 1943 Rogge still did not know under what legal theory he was going to prosecute it.[66] Even with these bad portents, unit personnel did not want their labor to go to waste, nor did they want the defendants to continue publishing materials that, even if not seditious in legal terms, were near-seditious and harmful to the war effort. As Roudebush told Smith in June 1943, "It would be difficult to justify the existence of the Section if it merely examined great masses of material and passed it as not being seditious." He went on to say that the unit, and the Sedition Section in particular, could "aid the war effort immeasurably if it can develop a technique for the prevention of the publication of near-seditious matter, having due regard for the preservation of the freedom of speech and press."[67] The last clause spoke to tensions within the SDU.

Here was the problem: Unit analysts were not convinced they had compiled compelling evidence of a seditious conspiracy. They did, however, have an immense amount of potentially seditious and dangerous materials they wished to remove from public circulation during the emergency, and to this end they could serve a useful purpose in helping Rogge construct a case against fascist propaganda in the United States. But doing so would mean that the prosecutions would be based less on proof of guilt than on the desire to silence. From Ribuffo's account of the *McWilliams* trial evidence and from Rogge's own postwar explanation of his evidence, it seems apparent that Rogge actually had quite limited evidence of an active conspiracy marked by financial relationships or direct collaboration among the defendants; the existence of connections among the defendants and between the defendants and official Nazi organizations was more asserted than demonstrated.[68] Ribuffo says that "even circumstantial evidence . . . suggested that no more than three or four of them had received money from Germany. Nor was there sufficient proof to try the thirty individually for the substantive offenses of urging military insubordination or failing to register as foreign agents. Therefore, Rogge the civil libertarian, like Maloney the showman, took advantage of conspiracy laws."[69] What the conspiracy laws permitted him to do was construct an ex post facto account of a massive propaganda conspiracy, and while this strategy utilized the unit's expertise, it also revived the liberty versus security tensions.

Although Rogge claimed that he was actually protecting the speech and association rights of "sincere Americans" by indicting only those "people with Nazi connections . . . who echoed Nazi propaganda themes," the case really rested on making a convincing argument about an invidious relationship between official Nazi propaganda activities and the native fascists' "scurrilous publications."[70] As the experts in the federal government on such propaganda activities, SDU personnel were able to provide Rogge with useful guidance on these matters. Amassing evidence that the U.S. fascists echoed Nazi propaganda themes was not difficult. The defendants were wont to make outrageous statements. They did so regularly and with apparent enthusiasm. Their themes did parallel Nazi ones, especially along anti-Semitic, even exterminationist, lines. And like the Nazis, the U.S. fascists saw Jews, plutocrats, and communists as being interchangeable, if not synonymous, villains in the modern world, those most responsible for its miseries, especially the world war. (The obvious contradictions here apparently were not problematic to the native fascists: finding enemies and scapegoating them was their goal, not sound logic or historical accuracy.) In cataloging the vast compendium of Nazi-tinged propaganda speech by the native fascists, SDU analysts and Rogge proceeded on the ground that the defendants' anti-Semitic, race-baiting, violent polemics were Nazi-inspired and part of the Nazi's two-stage process of propaganda: creating dissension within society and thereby laying the groundwork for a revolution. As Rogge argued, "The weapon which the defendants used as incessantly and malevolently as the Nazis in Germany was incitement of hatred toward minority groups, especially the Jews and the Negroes. With this weapon they hoped to disintegrate and soften our social and governmental structure, to make us lose our respect for law and order, to accustom us to the methods of terror and violence, to soften us for the kill. . . . The defendants talked much about pogroms, of blood baths, and of blood flowing in the streets." He quoted one defendant, William Robert Lyman Jr., as saying, "Our pogroms will make Hitler's look like a Sunday School picnic" (pp. 421–22).

Like the Nazis, the defendants also masked their intentions by claiming that they were working through existing political institutions and processes. Rogge explained the parallels, noting that "Pelley, Deatherage, True, Edmondson, McWilliams, and the others could talk of winning the Presidency in a legal election, as they did talk, but once the legal victory was won, they were prepared to destroy our form of government, substituting a one-party military dictatorship, just as the Nazis destroyed the Weimar Republic." For unit lawyers and for Rogge, the defendants' consistent use of themes strikingly similar to official Nazi propaganda was clearly their best evidence of the defendants' conspiratorial intentions to "follow the Nazi blueprint" (p. 417).

The Justice Department mined the vast slag heaps of fascist screed to show the many ways the defendants mirrored Nazi themes. Their writings extolled the virtues of violence, the need for military discipline, the need to subvert legal processes, the need to identify and eliminate Jewish and communist conspiracies, the need for civil war, and the efficacy of telling the big lie. Some sample quotes from Rogge's 1946 report illustrate both the fascist capacity to unite all these themes in several sentences and the uses that Rogge made of them as evidence. Explaining the fascist use of anti-Semitism as the center of the fascists' domestic propaganda campaign, Rogge noted that they borrowed directly from Hitler, who regarded anti-Semitism as an "indispensable revolutionary expedient" and contended that anti-Semitism had been his most valuable propaganda weapon: "The method which the defendants used to spread anti-Semitism was the one which Hitler and his Nazi confederates perfected in Germany, a mass propaganda campaign of falsehood for the purpose of inciting people to hatred. . . . Hitler further pointed out that the bigger the lie, the more readily it would be accepted." One of the defendants, Rogge said, exclaimed that "Hitler had made hate work in Germany and that he, McWilliams, 'was going to make it work here to accomplish a similar purpose' " (p. 424). William Dudley Pelley wrote that the "tons upon tons of exposé literature, showing Judaism and Communism to be synonymous, which have steadily blanketed the United States throughout the past five years, are at last showing results" (quoted on p. 425). George Deatherage said that "throughout the nation today [anti-Semitism] is a smoldering fire, sullen, deadly, and ten times more powerful than existed in pre-Hitler Germany" (quoted on p. 418), and he intended to help incite the flames of anti-Semitism into a movement. And James True wrote: "The rumblings are already being heard throughout the United States. They have gone too far and the Jewish-Communist menace has spread too far for the issue to be joined without bloodshed. And, anyway, why shouldn't there be bloodshed? America will never be safe until we have wiped the last vestige of Red Jewry from our shores. I've waited too long for that . . . to be satisfied with anything else" (quoted on p. 420).

To accomplish these ends, Rogge noted, the native fascists organized in small, militaristic armies: "The Bund had its Storm Troopers. Pelley had his Silver Shirts. McWilliams had his Christian Mobilizers, and Deatherage has his White Knights" (p. 417). They used the language of civil war, cited the necessity of violence, and provided their followers with stratagems for a revolution that would take place in two stages, first by fomenting sufficient hatred to destroy the Jewish-Communist menace and then overthrowing the Jewish-dominated two-party system: "They wanted to destroy all existing political parties other than the Nazi or Fascist party which they were trying to establish" (p. 414). Pelley, True, Fritz Kuhn, and Deatherage all said essentially the same thing, according to Rogge. And Joe McWilliams summed up all the themes when he stated that Americans wanted the same thing as the fascists: "An America free of Roosevelt, free of kikes, free of Republicans and free of the Democratic party, which are only the stooges of the jews. We want in America the same methods and the same system that Hitler inaugurated in Germany." On another occasion McWilliams said: "Five years from now, wherever the Democratic or Republican party exists, we'll tear down the building. We'll fumigate the place. We'll fertilize the place, we'll plant a stinking hogweed as a memorial to the most stinking political corruption in the history of the country" (quoted on p. 415). Rogge reported that at one time or another most of the defendants made statements like these. By exposing the commonly used language of counterrevolution and compiling quotations from nearly all the defendants, Rogge strove to make these seditious pronouncements usher forth from the collective voice of the U.S. far right. And while he noted the extremity of the defendants' ideas and plans, he also drew dramatic implications from the propaganda parallels: "Remember what happened to Germany," he warned (p. 421).

For unit personnel, there was some disagreement over what they saw as Rogge's potentially illiberal, liberty-restricting tactics. As Sedition Section chief George Roudebush had noted, even if the department could not prove sedition, it needed to silence the near-seditious speech somehow, but only by maintaining the delicate balance between security and liberty. Roudebush, for instance, was bothered that Rogge was willing to use grand jury proceedings to achieve essentially public relations needs, because he was not convinced that the department would even get an indictment the third time around against the same defendants. He protested that he was "reluctant to use a trial involving the liberties of individuals and the right of free speech as a forum for anything but determining the guilt or innocence of the defendants" but noted that Rogge thought bringing defendants to trial might serve other useful purposes besides prosecution, including good public relations for the Justice Department itself and effective counterpropaganda against the far right. As Roudebush explained, "Mr. Rogge is extremely anxious that the Public Relations aspect of the trial shall be properly handled. He conceives of the trial as a means of informing the country of Nazi propaganda methods and objectives." Roudebush did not think such a strategy would be successful, nor did he think it necessarily should be. As he saw it, Rogge was willing to make a compromise with liberties by staging a show trial of sorts, and even though Roudebush did not want all the unit's work to go for naught in the effort to silence the far right, he believed that Rogge was willing to ignore the absence of evidence of an actual conspiracy in order to expose the propagandists for the larger purpose of defeating fascism as an ideology. "Mr. Rogge conceives of the case as a battle against Nazi propaganda warfare in this country," Roudebush complained half a year before Rogge was able to get a third indictment, and the problem with this strategy was that "Mr. Rogge and most of the members of his staff [were] inclined to the view that almost any statements by conspirators who have Nazi connections may violate the Smith Act." Roudebush disagreed with this as both a legal strategy and as a matter of interpreting fascist propaganda's effects. "I have taken the position that the Nazi connections may well establish an intent to undermine the morale of the armed forces but that they do not show that publications of the conspirators presented a clear and present danger of causing disloyalty of the armed forces," he wrote.[71]

The difference between Rogge's willingness to impute bad effects for public relations and ideological purposes and Roudebush's insistence on demonstrating actual effects as standards of evidence became, Roudebush said, a "rather hot debate" between him and Rogge. The victor appears to have been Rogge, given that the department's standard of proof in the sedition trial did not require demonstration of a direct clear and present danger to the armed forces but only imputed dangers based on analogous reasoning about the bad tendencies of Nazi propaganda elsewhere. Rogge, apparently, was not so concerned about the actual effects of the utterances as he was about punishing the native fascists for their utterances. He succeeded in moving the case forward to trial and seems moreover to have succeeded in convincing others that public relations dimension of the case should receive greater attention. After three days of meetings in July 1943—attended by Rogge; Roudebush; OPAS staffers Jesse MacKnight, Irving Janis, and Morris Janowitz; several FBI officers; an Army Intelligence official; and political scientist Harold Lasswell—the consensus, to Roudebush's dissatisfaction, was that the department should move ahead on the public relations front.[72]

Lasswell became involved in the presentation of the materials and in the selection of expert witnesses for the prosecution's case. He worked with

OPAS personnel (many of whom he had trained in content analysis techniques and in presenting materials for courtroom presentation) on mapping out a public relations strategy.[73] OPAS chief Jesse MacKnight, who worked closely with Lasswell, explained to Rogge in a long memorandum in July 1943 that the desired public relations effect from the attack on Nazi propaganda should be greater recognition of the Nazi line by the U.S. public, nullification of the antidemocratic ideas spread by the Nazis, stimulation of greater participation in the war effort through resentment, "disgust[,] and anger" at fascism, and greater confidence in the government because it had been strong and alert enough to block Nazi propaganda efforts at home and abroad.[74]

Thus, in seeking a third indictment against the native fascist publicists in the case of *U.S. v. McWilliams et al.* (handed down by the grand jury in January 1944), Rogge and his associates went to trial against the thirty-odd defendants by constructing a case based on an elaborate theory of propaganda's dangerous effects. While Rogge contended that he and his team prosecuted only those with connections to Germany, the bulk of the evidence purportedly demonstrating conspiracy was based on the published materials the defendants produced and disseminated. Absent real proof of conspiracy, the prosecution had to resort to a proof of conspiracy-through-propaganda themes.

By the time Rogge got the case to trial in April 1944 (two years after the first grand jury proceedings began), unit involvement was negligible, save for a few OPAS analysts who continued looking into possible evidence for conspiratorial connections between the defendants. Unit records show that Sam Smith and the Sedition Section lawyers became hesitant about throwing too many of the unit's scarce personnel resources into the mass sedition prosecution. Despite the legal framework they had worked out, by late 1943 they were well aware of the limited evidence available to Rogge demonstrating conspiracy and had turned the unit's energies back to their own responsibilities for FARA and Voorhis Act administration.

The Native Fascists on Trial

As historian Leo Ribuffo expertly details in *The Old Christian Right*, the major trial of the Brown Scare was a fiasco from the Justice Department's perspective (and from the perspective of the journalists whose attention to the trial quickly diminished). When Rogge finally brought the case to trial in April 1944, he and his prosecuting team were met at every turn by howls of protest from the thirty defendants and their lawyers, protests that succeeded in endlessly delaying the introduction of evidence and the progression of the state's case. And although the trial judge had few qualms about conspiracy cases, allowed the state to begin entering its elaborate background evidence about Nazi Germany's propaganda techniques and strategy (thirty of a hundred planned prosecution witnesses testified before Judge Eicher's untimely death), and even supported the prosecution's assertion that wrongful intent was sufficient proof of sedition, even if the materials did not reach the armed forces, Rogge still was not able to make his case in such a way that warranted the trial's continuance after Judge Eicher's death in November 1944.[75]

As Ribuffo and subsequent legal commentators suggest, this was largely a result of the delay tactics employed by the defense attorneys and the chaotic courtroom atmosphere created by the defendants.[76] Rogge met with objections against every item he wished to introduce. And even though the judge allowed admission of a huge body of materials to prove the existence of a worldwide Nazi movement—replete with Nazi newspapers, transcripts of Hitler's speeches, copies of *Mein Kampf*, and materials seized from fascist booksellers in the United States—and allowed Rogge wide latitude to prove the defendants' putative role in that movement, Rogge was handicapped by time and by his own limited evidence: by time, because he was not able to introduce his entire case before Judge Eicher (a sympathetic if scrupulous jurist) died, which created a long delay that permitted the defense successful legal challenges in 1945 about the right to a speedy trial; by evidence, because it was not strong enough to meet the standards that the Supreme Court came to require in similar wartime cases in the *Hartzel* and *Keegan* cases, essentially meaning that by 1946, when Rogge was writing his recommendations to Attorney General Clark about how the Justice Department should proceed with the case against the *McWilliams* defendants, he knew that the nation's highest court would overturn any conviction the Justice Department might obtain in the lower courts.

Rogge therefore begrudgingly urged the department to abandon its prosecution. In view of the Supreme Court's decisions in the June 1944 case of *Hartzel v. U.S.* (322 U.S. 680) and the June 1945 case of *Keegan v. U.S.* (325 U.S. 478), Rogge had been forced to reexamine *U.S. v. McWilliams et al.* Both of the other two cases were against multiple U.S. fascist defendants, and in both the Court had thrown out lower court verdicts. Therefore in February 1946 he submitted a memo to the attorney general in which he stated that the decisions had led him "to the unpleasant conclusion that the Supreme Court would reverse any verdict which the government obtained in the Sedition case and that, therefore, the government should *nolle prosequi* the case."[77]

The *Hartzel* decision had come first, in June 1944, and although Justice Eicher had ruled at trial that the Court's decision did not warrant a mistrial in the *McWilliams* case, by 1946 Rogge knew that he did not have the evidence to surmount the Court's standards of evidence. When the *Keegan* decision was handed down in June 1945, at a point when the Justice Department was still deciding what to do with the *McWilliams* prosecution, Rogge became convinced "that sedition convictions would be reversed on appeal."[78] In the *Hartzel* case, the Court overturned the sedition indictment of the pamphleteering, sedition-mongering Hartzel (whose conviction had been affirmed at circuit court level), because there had been no evidence of his having been associated in any way "with any foreign or subversive organization," according to Justice Murphey. This decision was instructive to Rogge because of the high standard of both association and intention required to demonstrate guilt. Rogge quoted Justice Murphey at length in explaining why the Court's decision influenced his decision to urge a *nolle prosequi*:

> We are not unmindful of the fact that the United States is now engaged in a total war for national survival and that total war of the modern variety cannot be won by a doubtful, disunited nation in which any appreciable sector is disloyal. For that reason our enemies have developed psychological warfare to a high degree in an effort to cause unrest and disloyalty. Much of this type of warfare takes the form of insidious propaganda in the manner and tenor displayed by petitioner's three pamphlets. . . . But the mere fact that such ideas are enunciated by a citizen is not enough by itself to warrant a finding of a criminal intent to violate [Section] 3 of the Espionage Act. Unless there is sufficient evidence from which a jury could infer beyond a reasonable doubt that he intended to bring about the specific consequences prohibited by the Act, an American citizen has the right to discuss these matters either by temperate reasoning or by immoderate and vicious invective without running afoul of the Espionage Act of 1917. Such evidence was not present in this case.[79]

For Rogge it was fascinating and somewhat disconcerting that the Court simultaneously acknowledged the threat of Nazi propaganda and reversed a well-established propagandist's conviction.

On top of this, the Court's decision in *Keegan* was especially convincing to Rogge, because together with its companion case, *U.S. v Kunze*, it involved several dozen German-American Bundists convicted of urging draft evasion. "These two cases had much in common with *McWilliams*," Ribuffo notes, "including witnesses, defendants, and transcripts filled with data about the Bund. Overturning the convictions, the Supreme Court noted that introduction of copious 'background material' bordered on 'abuse.' Neither 'Bund Commands' nor testimony by the ubiquitous William Luedtke [a former Bundist turned state's witness] showed a 'nationwide conspiracy' against Selective Service. Essentially the government had tried to prove 'sinister and undisclosed intent' by citing 'so-called un-American sentiments.' "[80] Rogge knew that essentially the same evidence of association and conspiratorial intention was being used in the *McWilliams* case. After the Court handed down the *Keegan* decision, he determined that "the Supreme Court [would] reverse any conviction the government obtains in the Sedition case."[81] In June 1947, fifteen months after Rogge urged the department to abandon its prosecution, the United States District Court of Appeals for the District of Columbia dismissed the *McWilliams* prosecution on the grounds that the defendants had been denied a right to speedy trial because of the prosecutor's lack of due diligence.

Despite this legal ending and the state's prosecutorial debacle, Rogge's September 1946 "Recommendations" to the attorney general is a fascinating document for its assessment of the danger of Nazi propaganda to the world and for its statement of the danger that U.S. democracy faced because of decisions like those handed down by the Court in the *Hartzel* and *Keegan* cases. In this regard, Rogge's argument about the threat propaganda posed to U.S. democracy is a remarkable expression of the logic of nervous liberalism at the outset of the cold war, a logic that would become central to the assault on U.S. Communists by 1947.

As Rogge explained, faith that the marketplace of ideas would guarantee the victory of democracy's truth over fascism's evil lies was not a sufficient guarantee of national security. Indeed, Rogge contended that liberal commitment to the modern First Amendment doctrine was wrong; the Supreme Court was quite likely wrong in the *Hartzel* and *Keegan* cases, he suggested, and more to the point, some speech was too dangerous to be accorded the protections offered by the Holmes-Brandeis-Chafee tradition, a tradition that was now offering protections to known fascist propagandists and antidraft agitators. Rogge's great frustration was that he felt he had abundant evidence showing seditious conspiracy but the wartime Court had wrongly adopted the speech-protective assumptions of the free speech liberals. Consequently, the nation faced greater security problems because the Supreme Court had chosen to demand greater proof of interference in the war effort than just the expression of mere words.

The Court, he averred, had given the modern, deceptive propagandist too much legal cover under the First Amendment, "in spite of the grim nature of the picture I have presented." He continued, noting that "it is difficult in this country, under Supreme Court decisions, to be guilty of sedition," because the "Supreme Court is putting into practice the philosophy and opinions of men like Milton, John Stuart Mill, Jefferson, Zachariah [*sic*] Chafee, and Justices Holmes and Brandeis on freedom of speech" (p. 410). While Rogge claimed that he embraced the "time-honored" civil libertarian doctrine that freedom of speech permits the full development of the individual, that it "provides additional assurance of arriving at the truth," and that in a country with a democratic form of government it results in the "best and wisest course to be followed in public matters," he could not accept the insecure defense it presented against the power and duplicity of Nazi propaganda. This was faith, not reason, he argued, and Nazi propaganda eroded these faith-based assurances. In fact, the real problem for U.S. democracy was that the liberal free speech tradition was not a match for Nazi propaganda and could not account for fascism's willingness to abuse democratic practices or its effective use of propaganda as a technique. From Rogge's perspective, the marketplace of ideas that Milton, Mill, Jefferson, Holmes, Brandeis, Chafee, and others valorized had become polluted by fascist lies: "The injection of the great lie and of thousands of lesser lies which characterized the propaganda of the Nazis and the defendants was a far cry from the fair discussion of issues which Milton had in mind." "How," Rogge asked, "is democracy to meet with this problem?" (p. 425).

This was the problem, he said, which he and his Justice Department colleagues faced when they took over the sedition case in February 1943. They began by considering the Holmes-Brandeis-Chafee model and found it wanting: "We began by studying Chafee's *Free Speech in the United States*, and the decisions of the Supreme Court . . . including dissenting ones, of Justice Holmes and Brandeis" but "nowhere . . . did we find any satisfactory treatment of the Fascist threat to democracy." The problem with Chafee and other guardians of the free speech tradition was that they did not account for the vicious effectiveness of fascist propaganda and they could offer no guarantee that democracy would triumph over such machinations: "We were not convinced to have Chafee . . . answer . . . Walter Lippmann's comment that we shall all be dead, and perhaps not peacefully in our beds" by "simply assert[ing] that the main argument of Milton and Mill still stood." Chafee's answers left Rogge and his colleagues "with a feeling of insecurity." By 1943, he argued, they had come "too close to the debacle for comfort." And in February 1946, when he wrote his first report to Attorney General Clark, he noted that "we are still too close to it." By September 1946 they still were, because fascist propaganda was more powerful than mere truth, and the federal government had failed to take countermeasures that would "guarantee freedom of speech" but would first "protect itself" so that, in the long run, freedom of speech would be guaranteed (p. 426). Such countermeasures needed to begin with the prosecution and silencing of enemy propagandists in the United States based on the evidence of the "bad tendencies" of certain kinds of language. As far as Rogge was concerned, however, the liberal free speech tradition had made this a most difficult path to pursue.

For O. John Rogge, expositor of the creed of nervous liberalism circa 1946, Nazi propaganda embodied a new and powerful threat, one that was not adequately defended against by democracies and one not adequately understood and accounted for by liberal free speech champions. It was a special case. Such an argument would soon dominate U.S. political culture in the discussion of Communist propaganda. While the propaganda threat and the enemy might have changed, the fundamental concerns about the conflict between liberty and security did not, and neither did fears of fifth columnists bearing subversive ideas, making possible a military victory by the nation's most powerful external enemy. In the face of these propaganda anxieties, nervous liberalism would continue its evolution into a confident but increasingly ideologically intolerant and suspicious national security liberalism, one that would satisfy Lippmann's concerns more than Chafee's.

The idea that propaganda was too dangerous a poison in the body politic for the state to allow individual bodies to develop their own defenses meant that a propaganda prophylaxis was necessary to protect the body politic from those who would spread "germs of hate" and defeatism, and that prophylaxis continued to increase in size with the onset of the cold war. Try as they might, the progressive Justice Department lawyers charged with protecting both civil liberties and national security could not hold at bay the more powerful impulse toward security. The apparatus they put in place became part of a larger effort to eliminate radical voices (from the right and the left) from within U.S. political culture. Regulating political language by labeling some ideas as seditious and expressly un-American may have been necessary, especially given the nature of the native fascists' creed and the Nazi enemy abroad, but it also had a longer-term effect of making it easier to ignore or vilify speech labeled as propaganda.

In all, the fear of words and ideas that divided U.S. liberalism in the WWII era remained a central feature of the nervous liberalism that dominated postwar U.S. political culture. By the end of WWII, the optimistic faith of Zechariah Chafee Jr.'s tolerant liberalism was defeated by the nervous liberalism of an administration that wanted its enemies silenced, by a culturewide fear of internal subversion through propaganda, by a definition of propaganda as an especially dangerous (and un-American) form of speech, and by the rapid and continuous growth of a national security state mentality that made the protection of security a far greater good than the protection of unpopular ideas. Despite the Supreme Court's high standards of evidence in the *Hartzel* and *Keegan* cases, the postwar federal judiciary, including the Supreme Court, accepted the Roggean logic about propaganda's dangerous effects when the Justice Department mounted its assault on U.S. Communists in the postwar era. The consequences for dissent, debate, and even the exploration of political alternatives in the postwar freeze were profound. So were the ironies.

EPILOGUE

The far-reaching attack on U.S. Communists and Communist propaganda that began in the immediate postwar era is beyond the scope of this study. I suggest, however, that from the end of the 1930s, with the formation of the Justice Department's Special Defense Unit, through the Cold War, concerns about the subversive effects of propaganda remained continuous in U.S. intellectual and political culture and consistently resulted in the triumph of national security liberalism over free speech liberalism. In the academic and literary discussions about propaganda and U.S. democracy, a split between the cultural critics and the social science empiricists produced two divergent, unsatisfactory schools of thought: an aesthetics-based repudiation of mass culture and, by extension, mass democracy and a social scientific defense of postwar democratic culture that failed to examine critically the political intolerance of U.S. culture during the cold war and the limited political debate that intolerance produced.[1]

At the end of World War II, fears of Communist propaganda returned to the center of U.S. politics with a vengeance, resulting in an even more intensive mobilization of a restrictive and punitive propaganda prophylaxis, directed by J. Edgar Hoover's FBI and the Justice Department's Internal Security and Criminal divisions, instead of being under the putative control of a coterie of Chafee-inspired free speech liberals housed in the Special Defense Unit. Overall, the continuities from the prewar era to the postwar period were more pronounced than were the aberrations, and the results of the roughly fifteen-year-long (1939–1954) defense against so-called foreign propaganda in the United States produced, among other things, a deep fissure between civil libertarians and national security liberals; a widespread, multi-institutional assault on civil liberties, especially against freedom of speech and association and freedom from self-incrimination and the right to confront one's accuser; a failure on the part of the federal judiciary to protect extreme speech by making sure that the tests of its dangerousness were based on proximity and degree (and actual effects), as opposed to the state's assertions of probable bad tendencies; and a foreboding among policy makers, opinion leaders, and intellectuals that the psychological dimension of the national security crisis had grown more ominous with the onset of the cold war because, in a war for the minds and souls of men and women everywhere, the modern public—the masses—might not be entirely dependable.[2]

If liberal policy makers and intellectuals were nervous about Nazi propaganda and the potential weaknesses of democratic theory before World War II, they became nearly apoplectic in the postwar era in the face of the combined threats of mass society and communist propaganda. Fears of the great Red Menace stalking the planet renewed calls for an "all-out internal security effort" (to use the words of the SDU's Sam Smith from an earlier era), resulting in a magnification and acceleration of the intellectual patterns and institutional practices forged in the mobilization of the antifascist propaganda prophylaxis: intellectuals became even more convinced of their importance as propagandists of U.S. civilization as a normative concept; the U.S. public was understood as less crucial to the policy-making arena and increasingly replaced by public opinion managers and policy scientists; and public entertainment became even more disparaged by intellectuals as evidence of mass culture's stupefying effects and public incapacity. But, most obvious, the national security state—with its legislative, investigative, and prosecutory functions—grew in size, scope, and urgency as Communism replaced Nazism as the totalitarian enemy.[3]

As mutual distrust, personal recrimination, and sphere-of-interest territorial disputes quickly shattered the wartime alliance between the Soviet Union and the United States (and between U.S. leftists and liberals), the problems of Soviet propaganda (and armies) abroad and at home deepened the divisions between the liberal internationalists and the anticommunist liberals within the Truman administration and the Democratic Party. The Henry Wallace–led internationalists rejected the hardening cold war foreign policy positions, while the administration and Americans for Democratic Action–led liberal centrists were willing to play the anti-Soviet card to win domestic political goals and employed a crackdown on the U.S. left in order to protect President Truman's and the party's right flank. Congressional and journalistic conservatives consistently attacked liberals for being too willing to tolerate communist influence, especially in foreign policy circles and in key industries (including mass communications). Thus assertions of communist influence and liberal susceptibility to that influence pushed the Truman administration to the right, with the result that national security liberals began the calamitous second Red Scare, which quickly spun out of control.[4]

As the second Red Scare accelerated, pressures toward ideological con-formity intensified, and the voices of restraint that had earlier argued for protecting basic rights and cautioned against illiberal actions either became nervous themselves or were so few as to be nearly silenced by the ideologi-cal roar accompanying the purge of leftist thought and activity. Addition-ally, the kind of MacLeishean prewar division of the universe into Manichaean forces (of lie-spreading fascists versus truth-telling democrats) gained momentum as the standard trope for comparing Soviet mendacity with U.S. innocence; the propaganda of innocence that came to be a cen-tral feature of U.S. self-perception and presentation during the war and after was invariably juxtaposed with what was termed totalitarian deceit. One State Department public relations officer invoked what historian Nancy Bernhard calls the "hyperbolic rationale" for cold war mobilization when he wrote that "in the context of the vast and dangerous game which is being played . . . what we are dealing with is . . . a victory or defeat in the most titanic struggle in which this nation has ever found itself in-volved." Such "utterly axiomatic . . . pronouncements," Bernhard writes, left no room for ambivalence or neutrality in the overheated atmosphere.[5]

The central questions about the relationship between propaganda and democracy laid out in the body of this study persisted into the cold war: To what extent were the American people vulnerable to totalitarian prop-aganda? What should be done about it? And how extensively should the United States produce and disseminate democratic propaganda in order to clarify and promulgate its postwar goals and interests? By the end of WWII the answers were abundantly clear: there was no room for foreign propaganda in U.S. life; it was an entering wedge for alien ideals, danger-ously undemocratic beliefs, and potentially revolutionary deeds.

In fact, beginning in 1939 with the first FARA trials, those responsible for the dissemination of foreign propaganda would be punished by a host of propaganda-control laws, including the Voorhis Act, the Foreign Agents Registration Act, the Smith Act (used against the Socialist Workers Party during WWII and extensively against the Communist Party beginning in 1948), the McCarran-Walter Act, and various other strategies for controlling radical ideas and entities through censorship, intimidation, loyalty oaths, blacklisting, deportation, and custodial detention. The federal judiciary consistently upheld the constitutionality and sanctioned the punitive uses of those laws. And a whole roster of federal and congressional entities were em-powered to investigate and expose communist activities, from J. Edgar Hoover's FBI and the Justice Department's Internal Security Division (which subsumed the SDU's Communist Section) to the revived House Un-American Activities Committee, along with a myriad of joint congressional committees and select Senate committees on intelligence, foreign relations, subversive propaganda, Hollywood, labor relations, and any other suspected sources of communist fifth-column activities.

As to the question of how extensively the United States should be involved in producing democratic propaganda, an abbreviated list indicates no shortage of entities receiving congressional monies: the State Department had its own foreign and domestic propaganda divisions under the Assistant Secretary of State for Public Affairs; Voice of America and (later) Radio Martí developed into politically and financially invulnerable institutions; and the CIA, given a carte blanche, became extensively involved in all matters of propaganda activities, ranging from scholarly and cultural activities to covert forms of psychological warfare.[6] The cold war witnessed little squeamishness about producing democratic propaganda, only about the symbolic politics of attaching that label to any U.S. activities.

The second Red Scare, like the first, permitted ambitious attorneys general to step up their attacks on so-called alien influences and communistic propaganda activities through political trials, thereby silencing and incapacitating left-wing leadership and the organizations they used as their main channels of communication and organization. It also permitted the Justice Department, but especially the FBI, to become an endless source of anticommunist propaganda and advertisement for national security consciousness. If the first Red Scare was energized by the ambitious, clever, self-promoting J. Edgar Hoover, the second was often publicized and orchestrated by him. Hoover quickly learned the fine art of public relations as FBI director, and during the cold war he strategically deployed the FBI as the chief federal law enforcement agency responsible for investigating and preparing the evidence against those engaged in subversive activities.[7] In a typical example of Hoover's moralistic justification for rooting out the Red Menace, he rehearsed all the prevailing motifs of communist treachery, imperiled American innocence, and the need for constant vigilance:

> The forces which are most anxious to weaken our internal security are not always easy to identify. Communists have been trained in deceit and secretly work toward the day when they hope to replace our American way of life with a Communist dictatorship. They utilize cleverly camouflaged movements, such as some peace groups and civil rights organizations, to achieve their sinister purposes. While they as individuals are difficult to identify, the Communist Party line is clear. Its first concern is the advancement of Soviet Russia and the

godless Communist cause. It is important to learn to know the enemies of American life.[8]

Such logic animated the endless special congressional committees that
yielded so much opportunity for political grandstanding and career building, especially with the dawn of television.

During both Red Scares the federal courts, including the Supreme
Court, retreated to the national security assumption that the state's duty
of self-preservation took precedence over the speech and association
rights of groups and individuals. In the various political trials during and
following both world wars, the courts almost invariably accepted the
prosecution's arguments that the particular forms of propaganda on trial
were evil, dangerous, and beyond First Amendment protection. Indeed,
even Judge Learned Hand capitulated to Red Scare nervousness in his
appeals court decision in the case of *United States v. Dennis et al.*; the jurist whom Chafee held up, on the eve of World War II, as offering the
most reasonable speech-protective guidance on the matter of determining the point at which speech was truly dangerous essentially ignored his
own WWI-era judgment.

In the anxiety of the cold war, Judge Hand accepted the state's argument
that based on the Communist Party's propaganda a "probable danger" of
its revolutionary teachings coming to fruition was sufficient evidence for
prosecution. He refused to accept the defense's appeal that the clear and
present danger test actually protected their speech (they argued there was
no "present" danger), but Hand said that in this instance a "present danger" need not be immediate, since a "probable danger" clearly existed.
Based on the state's expert witnesses' interpretations of party propaganda,
Hand surmised that there were "thousands of 'rigidly and ruthlessly disciplined' members for whom 'the violent capture of all existing governments
is one article of the creed of that faith.' Either American democracy 'must
meet that faith and that creed on the merits, or it will perish,'" he wrote.
The United States could not afford to wait to see if a present danger actually existed; that is, the imminence test did not apply in this special case,
because based on worldwide events, revolutionary struggles in the previous
thirty years, and party teachings in the United States, he could infer that
the state had sufficient evidence of party danger to warrant the incarcera-
tion of its leadership.[9]

Hand, in other words, retreated to the same speech-restrictive probable
bad tendency test that the Supreme Court had accepted in its landmark
WWI-era espionage and sedition cases and accepted the same kind of proof-
by-analogy evidence of propaganda's power that the Justice Department

lawyers had developed in the WWII propaganda cases. When the defendants appealed to the Supreme Court (in *Dennis et al. v. the United States*), the Court upheld the constitutionality of the Smith Act and affirmed the lower court decisions, buying the Justice Department's argument that the literature disseminated by the American Communists was part of the "worldwide totalitarian political movement which employs freely the methods of military aggression, civil war, espionage, sabotage, and mendacious propaganda to overthrow non-Communist governments."[10]

As historians Peter Steinberg and Michael Belknap have demonstrated, the state's evidence of the Communist conspiracy to foment violent revolution in the United States was based entirely in the party's propaganda; there were no actual evidence of plans, timetables, weapons stockpiles, or paramilitary strategies, and all of evidence came from propaganda texts, which the Justice Department described as "inherently evil . . . utterances" that "are as devoid of the values protected by the First Amendment as obscene and fraudulent utterances."[11] By the height of the cold war, the First Amendment was hardly more useful as a defense for radical propagandists than it had been during WWI.

Clearly, there was something about propaganda that made it unworthy of First Amendment protection. During the cold war, the argument against communists echoed that used against U.S. fascists and their propaganda: both were foreign ideologies, and both employed invidious and powerful weapons that had proven highly effective when used by the Soviets and Nazis as part of their master plans. This effectiveness made those who disseminated those materials in the United States more than just dupes: they were dangerous fifth columnists who intended to breed discontent and anti-Americanism and would destroy the moral fabric of U.S. society. Those who failed to recognize propaganda's real dangers—such as fellow-traveling liberals, or the isolationists just before WWII—were the real dupes. And as for the public, sustained contact would make it susceptible to the virus of foreign ideas.

Within the national security state and mainstream U.S. culture, this viral theory of propaganda took hold. Because propaganda was a virus, and anyone who encountered it might become infected by it, which might result in an epidemic, an extensive and vigorous prophylaxis was necessary. Such a perception in the postwar period resulted in all-out attacks on communists by liberals and conservatives, conservative attacks on liberals in general, liberal purging of fellow-traveling leftists, and overall a paranoia that any kind of association with foreign propaganda materials made one untrustworthy and potentially dangerous.

Harold Lasswell's experience is a case in point and a useful tableaux to illustrate how fears of contamination by propaganda led to a perception that extensive contact with it equaled acceptance of the ideology behind it. In 1951, when Lasswell applied for access to classified matter as part of his consulting work with the Rand Corporation, the Department of the Army-Navy-Air Force Personnel Security Board denied him security clearance. The board wrote: "Based on information now available to it, the Board has tentatively decided that consent for your employment on classified Army, Navy, or Air Force contracts must be denied. This information indicates that for many years you have been a Communist Party member and have closely and sympathetically associated with Communist Party members. You have also openly and actively expressed sympathy with many Communist doctrines and ideologies."[12] What the evidence was, or who the accusers were, the board did not say. On the face of it, the charges were outrageous. Lasswell had worked with the Chicago Police Department's Red Squad helping them organize their materials on communist activity in the area. Moreover, he had testified against Communists in the federal courts (not as a redeemed former member, but as a social science expert). One can infer, then, that two kinds of evidence led the Personnel Security Board to the assumption that Lasswell was a Communist.

First, the viral theory: Lasswell wrote extensively (and in the imperative mood) about propaganda in general, and by studying communist propaganda and knowing it intimately, he became it. Too much knowledge made him dangerous. The second bit of "evidence" may have been something that trailed Lasswell and stayed in his files. In 1939, when Lasswell left Chicago and moved to New York/New Haven, one of the moving vans carrying his papers crashed in a ditch in Indiana, and in the charred remains the local townspeople found all manner of Communist propaganda pamphlets (leftover from his Chicago study), alarming evidence that the Reds had begun their local infiltration. In either case, the irony is the same: by virtue of being an expert on propaganda he had become contaminated by it.

In the end, Lasswell began a campaign of rehabilitation to clear his name and get his security clearance. His papers show that virtually every person with whom he was associated before, during, and after the war who could testify to his patriotism and tireless efforts to defend the country and defeat the causes of Communism and Fascism did so. He also prepared a lengthy *Affidavit* on his intellectual and career trajectory and, together with the many statements on his behalf, sent a letter in which he denied all the accusations. He wrote:

My professional career over the last twenty years has been devoted in great part to the scientific analysis and exposure of communist ideology and method. My expressed opposition to the communist philosophy goes back to a period when such opposition was unfashionable in many circles. I have contributed to the struggle against communism as a scholar, as an educator, as an expert witness, as a government executive, and as a private citizen who has taken the time and energy to identify the communist line, and to expose it in all its manifestations.

Outraged by the specious accusations and the fact that he was not provided the opportunity to examine the evidence used against him, Lasswell asserted that his entire career was "incompatible with any sympathy toward any form of communism." And then he responded to the "shocking" and chilling illiberalism that had become widespread in U.S. culture during the cold war by railing at the "hysteria," as he called it, that permitted the "ignorance, carelessness, or malice" that "inspired" the charges against him.[13] Lasswell wound up convincing the board of his innocence of the unfounded charges, gained his security clearance, and continued his work as a political communications (i.e., propaganda) consultant for the Rand Corporation and as a professor at Yale Law School, where he taught and wrote for the next several decades. And although he wound up not being a long-term victim of the propaganda hysteria that visited U.S. society during the cold war, he certainly encountered the political paranoia of the cold war garrison state, where rumor and innuendo could derail or destroy a reputation and career. The parallels between the social scientists and the atomic scientists such as J. Robert Oppenheimer are compelling.

Finally, the general trajectory of postwar propaganda anxieties raises important questions about perceptions of the public and the consequences of the ongoing influence of a Lippmann-styled critique of democratic theory in postwar culture. I want to suggest that the propaganda anxieties that beset U.S. culture in the postwar era might not have resulted in such undemocratic results had the nation's political and intellectual classes perceived the U.S. public as being capable, rational, and responsible. However, there was a discontinuity here between the content of U.S. propaganda at mid-century—celebrating individualism, the competent everyman, and good old-fashioned apolitical common sense—and the pessimistic mass society assumptions about public incompetence and susceptibility that pervaded intellectual culture in the cold war era.

I believe that fear explains the discontinuities because it shaped the ideas. Anxieties about mass communications, public vulnerability, and totalitarian propaganda shaped an anxious view of the world and a security-seeking response to it, a framework undergirded by a body of ideas about mass society and the inadequacy of democratic theory in an age of totalitarianism. As the threat of totalitarianism grew, the commitment to civil libertarian values diminished, and although I cannot demonstrate a one-to-one correspondence between the reemerging mass culture critique following the war and the retreat from free speech liberalism, Justice Department lawyers, federal jurists, and others consistently posited the idea of mass susceptibility to Nazi and Soviet propagandas. Motivated by fear, nervous liberals curtailed civil liberties and did so against the backdrop of diminished expectations about public-centered democracy. Put another way, if leading liberal thinkers and policy makers had had a higher estimation of public capacity, would they have countenanced the national security state's enormous constriction of the marketplace of ideas and its punitive restrictions of freedom of speech and association? Had they not so thoroughly accepted a modified theory of democratic governance based on public opinion control, expertism, and crisis management, would nervous liberalism have triumphed? Although there is no clear cause-and-effect relationship, the convergence of national security liberalism, opinion-management politics, and the antidemocratic assumptions of the mass culture critique seem to have all been minted by the fear and heat of propaganda anxieties. Their confluence at the outset of World War II profoundly shaped liberal U.S. intellectual and political culture for the next several decades. Examining the consequences for U.S. thought and culture in the cold war era will have to wait for another day.

NOTES

INTRODUCTION

1. A number of scholars have looked to World War I as the starting point for U.S. concern with propaganda. They include Garth Jowett and Victorian O'Donnell, *Propaganda and Persuasion*, 2d ed. (Newbury Park, Calif.: Sage, 1992); Michael Schudson, *Discovering the News: A Social History of American Newspapers* (New York: Basic, 1978); Holly Cowan Schulman, *Voice of America: Propaganda and Democracy, 1941–1945* (Madison: University of Wisconsin Press, 1990); Daniel Czitrom, *Media and the American Mind: From Morse to McLuhan* (Chapel Hill: University of North Carolina Press, 1982); Terence Qualter, *Opinion Control in the Democracies* (New York: St. Martin's, 1985); Peter Buitenhaus, *The Great War of Words: British, American, and Canadian Propaganda and Fiction, 1914–1933* (Vancouver: University of British Columbia Press, 1987); J. Michael Sproule, *Propaganda and Democracy: The American Experience of Media and Mass Persuasion* (Cambridge: Cambridge University Press, 1997); and Stuart Ewen, *PR! A Social History of Spin* (New York: Basic, 1996). In 1933 Ralph Lutz wrote a bibliographic essay on the matter, "Studies of World War Propaganda, 1914–1933," *Journal of Modern History* 5 (December 1933): 496–516.

2. Lutz, "Studies of World War Propaganda." For an excellent treatment of this postwar discovery, see Barry Alan Marks, "The Idea of Propaganda in America" (Ph.D. diss., University of Minnesota, 1957).

3. Lasswell uses the phrase "propaganda consciousness" in "The Study and Practice of Propaganda," the introductory essay to Harold D. Lasswell, Ralph D. Casey, and Bruce Lannes Smith, eds., *Propaganda and Promotional Activities: An Annotated Bibliography* (Minneapolis: University of Minnesota Press, 1935), pp. 1–27.

4. Harold D. Lasswell, "The Function of the Propagandist," *International Journal of Ethics* 38, no. 3 (April 1928): 261.

5. Harold D. Lasswell, *Propaganda Technique in the World War* (1927; rpt., Cambridge, Mass.: MIT Press, 1971), p. 2.

6. Lasswell, Casey, and Smith, *Propaganda and Promotional Activities*. The bibliography was sponsored by the Social Science Research Council. In 1946 Smith, Lasswell, and Casey edited another bibliography, with introductory essays, entitled *Propaganda, Communications, and Public Opinion* (Princeton: Princeton University Press, 1946).

7. Marks, "The Idea of Propaganda in America." Marks refers to "some writers" using the label "Age of Propaganda" on p. 51; all the quotations are also drawn from this page.

8. Modern students of public opinion and propaganda generally begin with Lippmann's *Public Opinion* as the first significant post-WWI study of propaganda.

See, for instance, Terence H. Qualter, *Opinion Control in the Democracies* (New York: St. Martin's, 1985); Jowett and O'Donnell, *Propaganda and Persuasion*; Schudson, *Discovering the News*; James W. Carey, *Communication as Culture: Essays on Media and Society* (Boston: Unwin Hyman, 1989); Ronald Steel, *Walter Lippmann and the American Century* (Boston: Little, Brown, 1980); and Marks, "The Idea of Propaganda."

9. Ewen, *PR!*, lays out the intellectual genealogy of social psychology as a field and outlook when he examines the interplay of ideas and the influence of Gustav Le Bon, Wilfred Trotter, Graham Wallas, Robert E. Park, Everett Dean Martin, Sigmund Freud, and others on U.S. theory; these quotations and tag lines noted in the text are discussed in chapter 7, pp. 131–45. As many have noted, Lippmann was especially indebted to Wallas for his critique of the "intellectualist fallacy."

10. See Ewen, *PR!*, especially chapters 6–8, pp. 102–73, for his discussion of WWI propaganda campaigns, Lippmann's influence during the war and after, and the postwar history of the idea of the public. Sproule, in *Propaganda and Democracy*, offers an encyclopedic account of the same sets of issues as they were examined and developed by a whole host of WWI-era writers.

11. Robert Westbrook, *John Dewey and American Democracy* (Ithaca: Cornell University Press, 1991), refers to Lippmann's "democratic realist" position. See Westbrook's description of Dewey's and Lippmann's competing ideological frameworks, pp. 275–318.

12. Lasswell, *Propaganda Technique in the World War*, p. 4.

13. William Leuchtenburg describes Lippmann's "Promethean urge to reform" in his introduction to Lippmann's *Drift and Mastery: An Attempt to Diagnose the Current Unrest* (1914; rpt., Englewood Cliffs, N.J.: Prentice-Hall, 1961). See also David A. Hollinger, "Science and Anarchy: Walter Lippmann's *Drift and Mastery*," in *In the American Province: Studies in the History and Historiography of Ideas* (Bloomington: University of Indiana Press, 1985), pp. 44–55. For a full discussion of the use of science and engineering-based metaphors, see John M. Jordan, *Machine-Age Ideology: Social Engineering and American Liberalism, 1911–1939* (Chapel Hill: University of North Carolina Press, 1994).

14. Patrick Brantlinger, *Bread and Circuses: Theories of Mass Culture as Social Decay* (Ithaca: Cornell University Press, 1983), p. 18. As Brantlinger suggests, in the electronic age, the conception of the masses as either dangerous hordes or passive audiences for "the 'propaganda' and electronic 'kitsch' of the mass media" (18) is especially prevalent. He adds that " almost without exception, the masses of popular culture criticism are seen as the 'raw material' for the 'industrialization of consciousness' " (110). Eugene Leach and Leon Bramson, however, both have argued that the American version of this predominantly European concern about mass society was distinct. Those working within the U.S. sociological tradition, for instance, rejected the harshest assumptions of the mass society thesis, especially during and after World War II. See Eugene Leach, "Mastering the Crowd: Collective Behavior and Mass Society in American Social Thought, 1917–1939," *American Studies* 27, no. 1 (spring 1986): 99–114. For an overview of post-WWII U.S. debates about the mass society thesis, see Leon Bramson, *The Political Context of Sociology* (Princeton: Princeton University Press, 1961). See also Salvador Giner, *Mass Society* (New York: Academic, 1976), especially chapters 8, 11–12.

15. As Brantlinger, *Bread and Circuses*, p. 23, explains, the "phrase 'mass culture' originated in discussions of mass movements and the effects of propaganda" shortly before the outbreak of WWII, and "kindred terms—'mass art,' 'mass entertainment,' and 'mass communications' " also cropped up at the same time.

16. Gary Gerstle, "The Protean Character of American Liberalism," *American Historical Review* 99, no. 4 (October 1994): 1043–73; Steve Fraser and Gary Gerstle, *The Rise and Fall of the New Deal Order, 1930–1980* (Princeton: Princeton University Press, 1989); Alan Dawley, *Struggles for Justice: Social Responsibility and the Liberal State* (Cambridge: Harvard University Press, Belknap, 1991); Westbrook, *John Dewey and American Democracy*; and Alan Brinkley, *The End of Reform: New Deal Liberalism in Recession and War* (New York: Knopf, 1995).

17. Brinkley, *The End of Reform*, pp. 8–9, 10.

18. Steven M. Gillon, *Politics and Vision: The ADA and American Liberalism, 1947–1985* (New York: Oxford University Press, 1987), shows how ideological centrism and insistent, security-oriented anticommunism became a pillar of postwar liberal thought and thus a barrier against the internationalist, labor-oriented, redistributive, free-speech orientations popular among left liberals in the pre-WWII era. See Arthur Schlesinger Jr., *The Vital Center: The Politics of Freedom* (Boston: Houghton Mifflin, 1949), esp. pp. 201–18, for a discussion of the tribulations of free speech liberalism in an age of totalitarianism.

19. Mark C. Smith, *Social Science in the Crucible: The American Debate Over Objectivity and Purpose, 1918–1941* (Durham, N.C.: Duke University Press, 1994), examines funding matters in the social sciences, especially as they pertained to foundation monies.

20. This study draws extensively on archival materials from the Rockefeller Archive Center, particularly the records of the different Rockefeller-sponsored communications research projects; the National Archives and Records Administration, especially the records of the Justice Department's Special War Policies Unit; the Archives of the Library of Congress, where I examined records from Harold Lasswell's Experimental Division for the Study of Wartime Communication and Archibald MacLeish's official papers as Librarian of Congress; and Harold Lasswell's papers at Yale University.

21. The phrase comes from MacLeish's essay, "Freedom to End Freedom," first published in *Survey Graphic* (February 1939) and reprinted in Archibald MacLeish, *A Time to Speak: The Selected Prose of Archibald MacLeish* (Boston: Houghton Mifflin, 1940), p. 131.

22. Brantlinger, *Bread and Circuses*, p. 23, suggests this linkage when he writes, "Closely linked to the emergence of 'the masses' as a revolutionary threat in the last century, and then also to the reactionary and fascist threat in this century, mass culture as a theoretical category is viewed as the special product of 'mass society,' which in turn is either totalitarianism or a stage between democracy and totalitarianism, as the former collapses into the latter." He goes on to suggest that because the term "mass culture" is framed by the totalitarian movements, it is fraught with negative connotations, and seen from either the right or the left, the idea of mass society is conceptually inextricable from fears about totalitarian propaganda.

23. Jacques Ellul, *Propaganda: The Formation of Men's Attitudes* (New York: Knopf, 1965; rpt., New York: Vintage, 1973), pp. xvii–xviii.

24. Jowett and O'Donnell, *Propaganda and Persuasion*, pp. 2–7.

25. I borrow a crucial part of my definition from Lasswell, whose standard definition included the idea that propaganda was the use of words or symbols for the "transmission of attitudes that are recognized as *controversial* within a given community"; he said the goal of the propagandist was always "the manipulation of collective attitudes" ("The Study and Practice of Propaganda," in Lasswell, Casey, and Smith, *Propaganda and Promotional Activities*, p. 3).

26. See, for instance, Edward Barrett's cold war study of Soviet propaganda stratagems in *Truth Is Our Weapon* (New York: Funk and Wagnalls, 1953).

27. Quotations from "Investigation of Nazi and Other Propaganda," *House Report No. 153*, 74th Cong., 1st sess., February 15, 1935. The committee noted that most of the unassimilated denizens who were most susceptible were of European origins and weren't acquainted with a long history of republican forms of government and constitutional traditions. Although the committee did not believe that the Communist movement in the United States was "sufficiently strong numerically" to constitute a "danger to American institutions at the present time," it did warn that "unless checked, such activity will increase in scope and . . . will inevitably constitute a definite menace."

28. Ibid. The committee recommended that Congress "enact a statute requiring all publicity, propaganda, or public-relations agents or other agents or agencies, who represent in this country any foreign government or a foreign political party or foreign industrial or commercial organization, to register with the Secretary of State of the United States." It also recommended new deportation and repatriation treaties.

29. It bears noting that President Roosevelt would not pass an amended version of the Foreign Agent Registration Act in 1940 until registration provisions for the Allies were simplified and made less onerous.

30. Michael Sproule details the varieties of ways that late-thirties propaganda critics tried to use more value-neutral, less ideologically driven definitions. But as the war approached, this became less tenable, as the case of the Institute of Propaganda Analysis (IPA) shows: the IPA was essentially closed down with the beginning of U.S. involvement in WWII because of the belief that the time had passed for value-neutral, scientific studies of propaganda techniques. See Sproule's excellent chapter on the IPA, "Propaganda Analysis, Incorporated," in *Propaganda and Democracy*, pp. 129–77.

31. For the most influential libertarian discussion of sedition and state control in the interwar period, see Zechariah Chafee Jr., *Free Speech in the United States* (Cambridge: Harvard University Press, 1941; rpt., New York: Atheneum, 1969). For alternative and equally influential points of view, see Karl Lowenstein, "Legislative Control of Political Extremism in European Democracies," *Columbia Law Review* 38, nos. 4–5 (April–May 1938): 591–622, 725–74; and David Riesman, "Democracy and Defamation: Control of Group Libel," *Columbia Law Review* 42, no. 5 (May 1942).

32. Among the chroniclers of the idea of propaganda who point to Lasswell's central place in the field of propaganda studies are Ellul, *Propaganda*; Jowett and O'Donnell, *Propaganda and Persuasion*; and Everett Rogers, *A History of Communications Study* (New York: Free Press, 1994).

33. Standard histories of communications studies recognize the relationship between propaganda and organized media research but tend to focus less on the ideo-

logical commitments of early scholars and more on the development of methodologies and standardized research for the field. See, for instance, Shearon Lowery and Melvin L. DeFleur, *Milestones in Mass Communications Research: Media Effects*, 2d ed. (New York: Longman, 1988); and Daniel Czitrom, "The Rise of Empirical Media Study: Communications Research as Behavioral Science, 1930–1960," in *Media and the American Mind*, pp. 122–46. See, in general, James W. Carey, ed.-in-chief, "Remembering Our Past: Early Communication Studies in the United States and Germany," *Communication* (special issue) 10, no. 2 (1988); Elihu Katz, "Communication Research Since Lazarsfeld," *Public Opinion Quarterly* 51 (1989): 525–45; Wilbur Schramm, "The Beginnings of Communication Study in the United States," in Everett Rogers and Francis Balle, eds., *The Media Revolution in America and in Western Europe* (Norwood, N.J.: Ablex, 1985), pp. 200–211; and Steven H. Chaffee and John L. Hochheimer, "The Beginnings of Political Communication Research in the United States: Origins of the 'Limited Effects' Model," in Rogers and Balle, *The Media Revolution*, pp. 267–96.

ONE Dangerous Words and Images

1. Les K. Adler and Thomas G. Paterson delineate the history of the idea of totalitarianism and connect it to propaganda activities in "Red Fascism: The Merger of Nazi Germany and Soviet Russia in the American Image of Totalitarianism, 1930s–1950s," *American Historical Review*, no 4 (April 1970): 1046–64; see also Thomas R. Maddux, "Red Fascism, Brown Bolshevism: The American Image of Totalitarianism in the 1930s," *The Historian* 40, no. 1 (November 1977): 85–103.

2. Zechariah Chafee Jr., *Free Speech in the United States* (Cambridge: Harvard University Press, 1941; rpt., New York: Atheneum, 1969).

3. A number of scholars have looked to WWI as the starting point for U.S. concern with propaganda. See n. 1 of the introduction.

4. David M. Kennedy, *Over Here: The First World War and American Society* (New York: Oxford University Press, 1980), p. 46.

5. As David Kennedy explains, the confusion about the purposes of the war "persisted in the minds of many for the duration of the conflict, and would endure even after the guns had fallen silent" (*Over Here*, p. 20).

6. For the most thorough—and forgiving—recent history of the Creel Committee, see Steven Vaughn, *Holding Fast the Inner Lines: Democracy, Nationalism, and the Committee on Public Information* (Chapel Hill: University of North Carolina Press, 1982).

7. For a further discussion, see Kennedy, *Over Here*, pp. 51, 22, 24. See also Michael J. Sproule, *Propaganda and Democracy: The American Experience of Media and Mass Persuasion* (Cambridge: Cambridge University Press, 1997), especially pp. 1–6.

8. Kennedy, *Over Here*, p. 62.

9. Creel wrote that the CPI's work had been a "plain publicity proposition, a vast enterprise in salesmanship, the world's greatest adventure in advertising," in *How We Advertised America* (New York: Harper, 1920), p. 3. James Mock and Frederick Larson's 1939 study of the Creel Committee's efforts, *Words That Won the War*, stressed the effectiveness of George Creel's frequent distinctions between the "information" and "publicity" he provided and the "insidious and all but irresistible" propaganda used by

the German enemy abroad and by its agents in the United States (quoted in Barry Alan Marks, "The Idea of Propaganda in America" [Ph.D. diss., University of Minnesota, 1957], p. 16).

10. Marks, "Idea of Propaganda," p. 22.

11. See Robert K. Murray, *Red Scare: A Study in National Hysteria, 1919–1920* (Minneapolis: University of Minnesota Press, 1955); and Howard Zinn, *A People's History of the United States* (New York: Harper and Row, 1980). Stuart Ewen makes the same argument about U.S. propaganda, intolerance, and vigilantism in *PR! A Social History of Spin* (New York: Basic, 1996); see pp. 102–27.

12. John Morton Blum, "Nativism, Anti-Radicalism, and the Foreign Scare, 1917–1920," *The Midwest Journal* 2, no. 1 (winter 1950–51): 46–53; rpt., as "The Foreign and the Radical: The Red Scare of 1919–1920," in *Liberty, Justice, Order: Essays on Past Politics* (New York: Norton, 1993), p. 112.

13. Kennedy, *Over Here*, p. 24.

14. See, for instance, Francis MacDonnell, *Insidious Foes: The Axis Fifth Column and the American Home Front* (New York: Oxford University Press, 1995), for a discussion of German espionage and propaganda activity in the United States during WWI. Clayton D. Laurie, *The Propaganda Warriors: America's Crusade Against Nazi Germany* (Lawrence: University Press of Kansas , 1996), discusses German subversive activities during WWI as well.

15. Quoted in Kennedy, *Over Here*, p. 24.

16. Marks, "Idea of Propaganda," p. 8. Marks explains on pp. 1–5 the pervasive tendency to connect propaganda with things German. Sproule, *Propaganda and Democracy*, also discusses how German propaganda in the United States created an identification between propaganda as a construct and things German; see pp. 9–10.

17. It was this connotation and understanding, as I will argue later in this chapter, that underlay the decision making in the major First Amendment cases of the same period.

18. Marks, "Idea of Propaganda," pp. 11, 15. As Marks explains, these views were reinforced in the years following the war when the wartime German ambassador to the United States, Count Bernstorff, wrote of U.S. susceptibility to German propaganda in his 1920 book *My Three Years in America* (New York: Scribner's, 1920; cited in Marks, "Idea of Propaganda," p. 14).

19. Wilson quoted in Kennedy, *Over Here*, pp. 14, 25–26.

20. See Zechariah Chafee Jr., *Freedom of Speech* (New York: Harcourt, Brace, and Howe, 1920); and Kennedy, *Over Here*, pp. 75–80. For an excellent discussion of the conflation of words with acts, see Richard Polenberg's discussion of the wartime sedition trials in *Fighting Faiths: The Abrams Case, the Supreme Court, and Free Speech* (New York: Viking, 1987).

21. Chafee, *Freedom of Speech*, p. 36.

22. Quoted in Chafee, *Free Speech*, p. 40, from the third section of Title I of the Espionage Act, enacted on June 15, 1917. The act stated that those convicted "shall be punished by a fine of not more than $10,000 or imprisonment for not more than twenty years, or both."

23. The federal sedition statute of May 16, 1918, which was modeled on a sweeping Montana sedition statute, was repealed in March 1921.

24. Chafee draws on John Lord O'Brian, "Civil Liberty in War Time," *Reports of the New York Bar Association*, 275, 291 (1919), vol. 42, to explain official policy on controlling propagandistic speech.

25. Kennedy, *Over Here*, p. 26.

26. Chafee, *Free Speech*, p. 41. For a more recent account of the Court's concerns about seditious materials in the context of the antiradical hysteria, see Polenberg, *Fighting Faiths*.

The Justice Department reviewed its wartime indictments at the end of the war and, as proof of its mistakes, ordered a dismissal of over three-fourths of the indictments brought under the Espionage Act on grounds that the evidence was too weak to go to a jury. After the war, the president handed out individual pardons or commutations, as recommended to him by the department, and by January 15, 1921, some 199 persons had received pardons. See the attorney general circular quoted in Ward P. Allen, "The Espionage and Sedition Acts of 1917–1918—Activities of the Department of Justice," November 4, 1940, National Archives and Records Administration, Main Branch, Washington, D.C., Department of Justice Records, Record Group 60, Special War Policies Unit, box 5, folder: Espionage and Sedition (DOJ 1917 Activities).

27. R. G. Brown et al., "Report Upon the Illegal Practices of the United States Department of Justice," pamphlet (Washington, D.C.: National Popular Government League, 1920), p. 3. This was reprinted in 1969 as part of the *Mass Violence in America* series, published jointly in New York by the Arno Press and the New York Times.

28. An extensive body of literature describes the civil liberties violations during World War I, including Chafee's *Freedom of Speech* (1920) and his updated version written and published on the eve of World War II, *Free Speech in the United States* (1941). In 1933 former attorney general Homer S. Cummings wrote a history of the Justice Department, *Federal Justice* (New York: Macmillan, 1933) in which he added to the catalog of wartime abuses by Justice Department officials. He listed excessive violence against suspects, drunkenness by departmental agents, cases "indiscriminately brought on" with "unsupportable evidence," and the frequent use of indictments as a strategy for silencing dissent. Justice officials drew insupportable indictments to block the spread of strikes and labor protests, Cummings noted. Moreover "newspapers who made statements in articles or editorials untrue or unfair to the Department of Justice were 'jerked before a Grand Jury' and thoroughly examined" as a strategy of intimidation. According to Cummings and other subsequent Justice Department officials, the postwar Palmer Raids were simply a continuation of the "unfortunate episode" of wartime repression. See Cummings, *Federal Justice*, quoted by Justice Department lawyer Ward P. Allen in "The Espionage and Sedition Acts of 1917–1918—Activities of the Department of Justice," November 4, 1940, National Archives and Records Administration, Main Branch, Washington, D.C., Department of Justice Records, Record Group 60, Special War Policies Unit, box 5, folder: Espionage and Sedition (DOJ 1917 Activities). Allen wrote: "It appeared to be the custom, without orders from the Department, to indict persons for statements which the Attorneys realized constituted no crime, and for which they were certain convictions could not be secured, returning the indictments for the hopeful salutary effect in silencing such statements and because public opinion called for action" (p. 21).

For an excellent discussion of activities of bureau investigators and departmental lawyers in pursuit of anarchists, see Polenberg's *Fighting Faiths.* Any of the biographies of J. Edgar Hoover treat the WWI period, but all tend to focus on Hoover's activities in the Anti-Radical Division; see, e.g., Richard Gid Powers, *Secrecy and Power: The Life of J. Edgar Hoover* (London: Collier Macmillan, 1987); and Athan Theoharis and John Stuart Cox, *Boss: J. Edgar Hoover and the Great American Inquisition* (Philadelphia: Temple University Press, 1988). For an overview of the antiradical activities of the era, see Murray's *Red Scare.*

29. Marks, "Idea of Propaganda," p. 24.

30. Ibid., p. 32. Drawing on works pursuing this line, Marks cites Lewis Gannett, "They All Lied," *Nation,* October 11, 1922, pp. 353–57; C. J. Rolphe, "A Record of Propaganda," *The Freeman* 7 (September 5, 1923): 610; and H. C. Englebrecht, "How War Propaganda Won," *The World Tomorrow* 10 (April 1927): 159–162 ("Idea of Propaganda," pp. 32–33).

31. For a discussion of Sir Gilbert Parker's 1918 article, "The United States and the War," see Marks, "Idea of Propaganda," pp. 29–30.

32. Marks, "Idea of Propaganda," p. 44. Sir Campbell Stuart's *Secrets of Crewe House: The Story of a Famous Campaign* (New York: Hodder and Stoughton, 1920) gave firsthand testimony about British propaganda efforts against enemy countries; eight years later, the pacifist Arthur Ponsoby used Stuart's book as one of the texts for his antiwar, antipropaganda work *Falsehood in Wartime, Containing an Assortment of Lies Circulated Throughout the Nations During the Great War* (New York: Dutton, 1928). Marks says Ponsoby's work was widely quoted, went through five editions, and sold approximately six thousand copies (p. 39).

33. Walter Millis, *The Road to War: America, 1914–1917* (Boston: Houghton-Mifflin, 1935).

34. Quoted in Marks, "Idea of Propaganda," p. 47. In 1927 U.S. journalists probed this theme when the *American Mercury* published a series of three articles about the role of intellectuals in the war: Hartley Grattan, "The Historians Cut Loose," vol. 11 (1927): 414–430; Charles Angoff, "The Higher Learning Goes to War," vol. 11 (1927): 177–91; and Granville Hicks, "The Parsons and the War," vol. 10 (1927): 129—142; all cited in Marks, "Idea of Propaganda," pp. 47–49.

35. Marks, "Idea of Propaganda," pp. 49–50. For an excellent overview of the role of U.S. intellectuals in WWI, see Carol Gruber, *Mars and Minerva: World War I and the Uses of Higher Learning in America* (Baton Rouge: Louisiana State University Press, 1975). See also Peter Novick, *That Noble Dream: The "Objectivity Question" and the American Historical Profession* (Cambridge: Cambridge University Press, 1988), and Kennedy, *Over Here.*

36. Kennedy, *Over Here,* pp. 56–59; Kennedy quotes Gruber.

37. For Europeanist versions of the mass culture and mass society critiques, see Patrick Brantlinger, *Bread and Circuses: Theories of Mass Culture as Social Decay* (Ithaca: Cornell University Press, 1983); Raymond Williams, *Culture and Society: 1780–1950* (1958; rpt., New York: Columbia University Press, 1983); and Michael Gurevitch, Tony Bennett, James Curran, and Janet Woollacott, eds., *Culture, Society, and the Media* (London: Methuen, 1982). See also Salvador Giner, *Mass Society* (New York: Academic, 1967).

38. Tony Bennett, "Theories of the Media, Theories of Society," in Gurevitch et al., *Culture, Society, and the Media*, p. 32; see, in general, pp. 30–55.

39. James Curran, Michael Gurevitch, and Janet Woollacott, "The Study of the Media: Theoretical Approaches," in Gurevitch et al., *Culture, Society, and the Media*, pp. 11–12; see, in general, pp. 11–29.

40. See J. Michael Sproule's piece on the magic bullet thesis, "Progressive Propaganda Critics and the Magic Bullet Myth," *Critical Studies in Mass Communication* 6 (1989): 225–46; see also Ewen, *PR! A Social History of Spin*, especially the first eight chapters. J. Michael Sproule, in *Propaganda and Democracy*, offers a less focused but more encyclopedic account of the same sets of issues as they were examined and developed by a whole host of WWI-era writers.

41. Marks argues that "unquestionably what had the largest impact on the idea of propaganda was Freud's emphasis on the extent to which the unconscious provided the real springs of action, his emphasis on the controlling influence of the unconscious 'even for those acts which are thought to be most conscious and intentional' " ("Idea of Propaganda," p. 129). Among the popular commentators on propaganda specifically, Edward Bernays was undoubtedly the most keenly and directly aware of the theoretical backgrounds of anti-intellectualist theory. During the 1920s he referred to and quoted freely from Le Bon, Trotter, Martin, Wallas, McDougall, and Freud, and he made effective use of their views (Marks, ibid., pp. 150–51).

42. Walter Lippmann, *Public Opinion* (1922; rpt., New York: Free, 1960); idem, *The Phantom Public* (New York: Harcourt, Brace, 1925); John Dewey, *The Public and Its Problems: An Essay in Political Inquiry* (1927; rpt. [with a new introduction by Dewey], Chicago: Gateway, 1946).

43. See Graham Wallas, *The Great Society: A Psychological Analysis* (New York: Macmillan, 1914). Lippmann studied under Wallas as an undergraduate, and *Public Opinion* was a response to and continuation of a dialogue with him.

44. Dewey, *The Public and Its Problems*, p. 138. "Adrift" paraphrases one of the terms in the title of Lippmann's *Drift and Mastery: An Attempt to Diagnose the Current Unrest* (1914; rpt., Englewood Cliffs, N.J.: Prentice-Hall, 1961) with an introduction by William E. Leuchtenburg; my later uses of both "drift" and "mastery" are inspired by the same work. In *The Public and Its Problems*, Dewey provided a useful definition of what he and Lippmann meant by cultural lag: "Mental and moral beliefs and ideals change more slowly than outward conditions. If the ideas associated with the high life of our cultural past have been impaired, the fault is primarily with them. . . . For the older symbols of ideal life still engage thought and command loyalty. Conditions have changed, but every aspect of life, from religion and education to property and trade, shows that nothing approaching a transformation as taken place in ideas and ideals" (pp. 141–42).

45. Dewey, *The Public and Its Problems*, p. 110.

46. For a detailed discussion of the crisis, see Edward A. Purcell Jr., *The Crisis of Democratic Theory: Scientific Naturalism and the Problem of Value* (Lexington: University Press of Kentucky, 1973). Purcell mainly explores the vigorously contested debates about democratic theory in the U.S. academy in the 1930s and 1940s. The strength of Purcell's brilliant work is that he illustrates how the advent of philosophical relativism in different academic disciplines led to skepticism about the philosophical basis of tra-

ditional democratic theory. He shows how the same general philosophical concerns reached across disciplines and engendered similar crises of democratic faith in different fields.

47. In his 1946 introduction to *The Public and Its Problems*, Dewey restated his longtime faith in scientific inquiry as a vehicle for progressive reform.

48. For a discussion of Lippmann's reformist impulse, see William E. Leuchtenburg's introduction to Lippmann's *Drift and Mastery*.

49. See Robert Westbrook, *John Dewey and American Democracy* (Ithaca: Cornell University Press, 1991), for a discussion of the Dewey-Lippmann debate, especially pp. 275–318. Westbrook uses the term "democratic realism" to describe Lippmann's position and the position Dewey understood Lippmann as representing. His exhaustive and carefully reasoned intellectual biography of John Dewey argues that Dewey's commitment to participatory democracy was his central objective.

50. In *The Crisis of Democratic Theory*, Purcell does not account for the influence of the mass society critique and a concern with mass communications to explain the roots of the crisis of faith in democratic theory among interwar intellectuals. Any discussion, however, of a failure of democratic faith in the interwar period needs to address this propaganda–mass society nexus.

51. In general, modern students of public opinion and propaganda generally begin with Lippmann's *Public Opinion* as the first and most influential postwar study. See, for instance, Garth Jowett and Victorian O'Donnell, *Propaganda and Persuasion*, 2d ed. (Newbury Park, Calif.: Sage, 1992); Terence H. Qualter, *Opinion Control in the Democracies* (New York: St. Martin's, 1985); and Michael Schudson, *Discovering the News: A Social History of American Newspapers* (New York: Basic, 1978); Ronald Steel, *Walter Lippmann and the American Century* (Boston: Little, Brown, 1980). Others frame the history of the discipline of communications in terms of Lippmann's and Dewey's respective positions. See, especially James W. Carey, *Communication as Culture: Essays on Media and Society* (Boston: Unwin Hyman, 1989); Everett Rogers, *A History of Communication Study* (New York: Free Press, 1994); and Daniel Czitrom, *Media and the American Mind: From Morse to McLuhan* (Chapel Hill: University of North Carolina Press, 1982).

52. Communications historian James W. Carey persuasively argues that Lippmann's work (and John Dewey's response to it) comprised the beginnings of the two most important traditions in U.S. communications theory and scholarship: the administrative and the critical research traditions (see "Reconceiving 'Mass' and 'Media,'" in *Communication as Culture*, pp. 69–88, 75). He suggests that Lippmann's *Public Opinion* is "the founding book in American media studies [because] it was the first serious work to be philosophical and analytical in confronting the mass media" (ibid., p. 83).

53. According to John M. Jordan, these rhetorics were grounded in the language of the natural sciences and "engineering modes of reason," reflecting a top-down realignment of politics in the early and mid-twentieth century (*Machine-Age Ideology: Social Engineering and American Liberalism, 1911–1939* [Chapel Hill: University of North Carolina Press, 1994], p. 1).

54. Mark C. Smith, *Social Science in the Crucible: The American Debate Over Objectivity and Purpose, 1918–1941* (Durham, N.C.: Duke University Press, 1994). See my

"Dueling Deweys: Moralism, Scientism, and American Social Science History," a review of the positions laid out by Jordan and Smith, in *Reviews in American History* 23 (1995): 623–30. Smith offers an interpretation of the differences between the Deweyan framework and the Lippmann-styled framework that is much more compatible with my interpretation.

55. Lippmann, *Public Opinion*, pp. 14–15, 31.

56. Lippmann, *The Phantom Public*, pp. 9, 14. Carey notes this consistency of vision metaphor in Lippmann's argument and sets it in opposition to Dewey's hearing metaphor.

57. Lippmann, *Public Opinion*, pp. 20–21.

58. Lippmann, *The Phantom Public*, p. 24.

59. Lippmann, *Public Opinion*, pp. 89–90.

60. Lippmann's understanding of the gap between perception of the world and action in the world was remarkably similar to the semantic model devised by the British-language theorists C. K. Ogden and I. A. Richards. See their *The Meaning of Meaning: A Study of the Influence of Language Upon Thought and of the Science of Symbolism* (1923), 5th ed. (New York: Harcourt, Brace, 1935). Like the imputed relationship between words and their referents in the semanticists' schema, Lippmann posits only an imputed relationship among thoughts about the world, action in the world, and the actual world. Lippmann said the way in which the world is imagined "does not determine what [people] will achieve. It determines their effort . . . not their accomplishments" (*Public Opinion*, pp. 25–26).

61. Steel, *Walter Lippmann*, p. 172.

62. For a discussion of *Liberty and the News* (New York: Harcourt, Brace, and Howe: 1920), see Steel, *Walter Lippmann*, pp. 170–72.

63. See also Schudson, *Discovering the News*, for a discussion of Lippmann's arguments about objectivity and journalistic standards.

64. In 1920 Lippmann and Charles Merz undertook a study of three years of the *New York Times's* coverage of the Bolshevik revolution. Their study, called "A Test of the News" (originally published as a supplement to the *New Republic*, 4 August 1920, pp. 1–42), discovered that the coverage was not based on facts: it reported atrocities that never occurred, relied on hearsay, and was infected with prejudice. Lippmann and Merz charged that the paper's stories were "dominated by the hopes of the men who composed the news organization," men who hoped the revolution would fail. "The chief censor and the chief propagandist," they wrote, "were hope and fear in the minds of reporters and editors" (quoted in Steel, *Walter Lippmann*, pp. 172–73).

65. Lippmann, *Public Opinion*, p. 365.

66. Steel describes Lippmann's work with the Inquiry, in *Walter Lippmann*, pp. 128–41.

67. John Dewey, "Public Opinion," *New Republic*, May 3, 1922, pp. 286–88.

68. John Dewey, "Practical Democracy," *New Republic*, December 2, 1925, pp. 52–54, esp. p. 54.

69. Dewey, *The Public and Its Problems*, p. 208.

70. According to Westbrook, *The Public and Its Problems* was Dewey's only attempt at formal political philosophy. See Westbrook, *John Dewey and American Democracy*, p. 300. Both James Kloppenberg, in *Uncertain Victory: Social Democracy and*

Progressivism in European and American Thought, 1870–1920 (New York: Oxford University Press, 1986), and James W. Carey, in *Communication as Culture*, claim that Dewey's chief concern in this work was to address Lippmann's arguments. Neither offers any evidence for this, however, and nowhere in the text of *The Public and Its Problems* does Dewey explicitly state that he has set out to respond to Lippmann. At the same time, the license granted by Kloppenberg and Carey is useful. Although Dewey and Lippmann were not engaged in direct dialogue, Dewey took up many of the same issues addressed by Lippmann, and therefore a comparative reading is both possible and helpful. Robert Westbrook takes the same license, arguing in *John Dewey* that Dewey was responding to Lippmann and other democratic realists.

71. See *The Public and Its Problems*, p. 116n, where Dewey wrote: "See Walter Lippmann's *The Phantom Public*. To this as well as to his *Public Opinion* I wish to acknowledge my indebtedness, not only as to this particular point, but for ideas involved in my entire discussion even when it reaches conclusions diverging from his."

72. Dewey, *The Public and Its Problems*, p. 141. Kloppenberg *Uncertain Victory*, Casey Nelson Blake, *Beloved Community: The Cultural Criticism of Randolph Bourne, Van Wyck Brooks, Waldo Frank, and Lewis Mumford* (Chapel Hill: University of North Carolina Press, 1990), and Daniel J. Wilson, *Science, Community, and the Transformation of American Philosophy, 1860–1930* (Chicago: University of Chicago Press, 1990), all develop how Dewey's contemporaries were vexed by the same gemeinschaft/gesselschaft problem.

73. James W. Carey, *Communication as Culture*, p. 275

74. Dewey, *The Public and Its Problems*, p. 206.

75. Jordan, *Machine-Age Ideology*, pp. 8, 3.

76. Ernest Hemingway, *A Farewell to Arms* (New York: Scribners, 1929), pp. 184–85.

77. Archibald MacLeish, "The End of the World," *Collected Poems, 1917–1952* (1926; rpt., Boston: Houghton Mifflin, 1952), p. 23.

78. Wilfred Owen, "Dulce Et Decorum Est," *The Collected Poems of Wilfred Owen*, ed. C. Day Lewis (1920; London: Chatto and Windus, 1966), p. 55, lines 21–28. For a full study of WWI poetry, see Paul Fussell, *The Great War and Modern Memory* (New York: Oxford University Press, 1975).

79. Richard H. Pells, *The Liberal Mind in a Conservative Age: American Intellectuals in the 1940s and 1950s* (New York: Harper and Row, 1985), p. 2.

80. H. I. Hayakawa, *Language in Action: A Guide to Accurate Thinking, Reading, and Writing* (New York: Harcourt, Brace, 1941); Stuart Chase, *The Tyranny of Words* (New York: Harcourt, Brace, 1938); Alfred Korzybski, *Science and Sanity: An Introduction to Non-Aristotelian Systems and General Semantics* (1933; rpt., Lancaster, Pa.: International Non-Artistotelian Library Publishing Co., 1941); Paul W. Bridgman, *The Logic of Modern Physics* (New York: Macmillan, 1927).

81. Chase, for instance, cited among his main inspirations P. W. Bridgman, Thurman Arnold, Eric T. Bell, Lancelot Hogben, Edward S. Robinson, Bronislaw Malinowski, Ludwig Wittgenstein, Vilfredo Pareto, Charles Beard, and F. C. S. Schiller, along with Ogden and Richards and Korzybski. Hayakawa named many influences, Chase's *Tyranny of Words*, Bridgman's *Logic of Modern Physics*, and Korzybski's *Science and Sanity*, as noted, but also Thurman Arnold, A. J. Ayer, Eric Temple Bell, Leonard Bloomfield, Karl Britton, Rudolf Carnap, Felix S. Cohen, John Dewey, William Emp-

son, Jerome Frank, Wendell Johnson, Lucien Levy-Bruhl, Kurt Lewin, I. A. Richards, and James Harvey Robinson.

82. Ogden and Richards, *The Meaning of Meaning*, pp. 12, 17.

83. Hayakawa, *Language in Action*, pp. 8–9.

84. Chase, *The Tyranny of Words*, p. 27.

85. Hayakawa, *Language in Action*, p. 27.

86. Chase, *The Tyranny of Words*, p. 9.

87. Hayakawa, *Language in Action*, p. 121.

TWO Harold D. Lasswell and the Scientific Study of Propaganda

1. See Mark C. Smith, *Social Science in the Crucible: The American Debate Over Objectivity and Purpose, 1918–1941* (Durham, N.C.: Duke University Press, 1994), ch. 6, "Harold D. Lasswell and the Lost Opportunity of the Purposive School," pp. 212–52. Probably Lasswell's clearest expression of this idea is in *Democracy Through Public Opinion* (Menasha, Wis.: Banta, 1941), which is, to my mind, his most pedestrian work and a not very convincing effort at reconciling expert-centered politics with democratic theory.

2. Notes from a conversation with Professor Ronald D. Brunner, Center for Policy Research, University of Colorado, June 26, 1996, in my possession. Brunner was a student of Lasswell's and has worked to develop Lasswell's integrative, context-oriented approach to the policy sciences. See Brunner's various essays and tributes to Lasswell and his legacy, including his biographical profile of Lasswell in Seymour Martin Lipset, ed., *The Encyclopedia of Democracy* (Washington, D.C.: Congressional Quarterly, 1995), 3:723–25; and "A Milestone in the Policy Sciences," *Policy Sciences* 29 (1996): 45–68, a review of Harold D. Lasswell and Myres S. McDougal, *Jurisprudence for a Free Society* (New Haven: New Haven Press; Dordrecht, The Netherlands: Martinus Nijhoff, 1992).

3. For general commentary on Lasswell's intellectual history, see Arnold Rogow, ed., *Politics, Personality, and Social Science in the Twentieth Century: Essays in Honor of Harold D. Lasswell* (Chicago: University of Chicago Press, 1969); Dwaine Marvick, introduction to Dwaine Marvick, ed., *Harold Lasswell on Political Sociology* (Chicago: University of Chicago Press, 1977), pp. 1–72; Rodney Muth, Mary M. Finley, and Marcia F. Muth, eds., *Harold D. Lasswell: An Annotated Bibliography* (New Haven: Yale University Press, 1990); Bernard Crick, *The American Science of Politics: Its Origins and Conditions* (1959; rpt., Berkeley: University of California Press, 1967), especially ch. 10, "The Conceptual Behaviour of Harold Lasswell," pp. 176–209; and Smith, *Social Science in the Crucible*, pp. 212–52.

4. Leo Rosten, "Harold Lasswell: A Memoir," in Rogow, *Politics, Personality, and Social Science*, pp. 1–14, esp. p. 2.

5. Gabriel A. Almond, "Harold Dwight Lasswell (1902–1978)," Guide to Harold Dwight Lasswell Papers, Manuscript Record Group 1043, Yale University Manuscripts and Archives, Sterling Memorial Library, Yale University, 1985.

6. Crick, *The American Science of Politics*, pp. 176–77.

7. This was a theme Lasswell repeated in many of his writings in the late 1930s; see, for instance, "The Propagandist Bids for Power," *American Scholar* 8 (1939): 350–57.

8. Harold D. Lasswell, "The Garrison State," *American Journal of Sociology* 46 (1941): 455–68.

9. Harold D Lasswell, "The Person: Subject and Object of Propaganda," in Harwood Childs, ed., *Pressure Groups and Propaganda, Annals of the American Academy of Political and Social Science* 179 (1935): 187–93. Hereafter cited as *Annals* 179.

10. Bernard Crick, in *The American Science of Politics*, writes scathingly of Lasswell's conflation of science with technology and even suggests that there were fascistic implications to his technocratic urges. Mark Smith notes the complicated legacy, critiquing Lasswell for his failure to question the "cost of access to policymaking roles" but also acknowledging more reformist-oriented aspects to his work (*Social Science in the Crucible*, p. 215). For more critical appraisals, see also Raymond Seidelman, *Disenchanted Realists: Political Science and the American Crisis, 1884–1994* (Albany: State University of New York Press, 1984); and Christopher Simpson, *The Science of Coercion: Communication Research and Psychological Warfare, 1945–1960* (New York: Oxford University Press, 1994).

11. Smith, *Social Science in the Crucible*, pp. 212–14. Although not an adherent of the policy sciences, Smith resuscitates Lasswell's legacy on similar grounds as Brunner and others involved in the policy sciences.

12. Smith discusses the "career reversals" in *Social Science in the Crucible*, pp. 215 and 243–50.

13. See Dwaine Marvick, introduction, pp. 1–72; see also Lasswell's own *Affidavit*, October 23, 1951, Yale University, Sterling Memorial Library, Yale University Manuscripts and Archives, Manuscript Record Group 1043, Harold Dwight Lasswell Papers, box 213, folder 14.

14. Lasswell, *Affidavit*.

15. For the standard work on Merriam, see Barry D. Karl, *Charles E. Merriam and the Study of Politics* (Chicago: University of Chicago Press, 1974).

16. Almond, "Harold Dwight Lasswell."

17. Lasswell, *Affidavit*.

18. Crick, *The American Science of Politics*, p. 177.

19. Harold D. Lasswell, *Propaganda Technique in the World War* (London: K. Paul, Trench, Trubner, and Co.; New York: Knopf, 1927); reprinted as *Propaganda Technique in World War I* (Cambridge, Mass.: MIT Press, 1971).

20. For the best account and bibliography on the post-WWI intellectual response to wartime propaganda, see Barry Alan Marks, "The Idea of Propaganda in America" (Ph.D. diss., University of Minnesota, 1957). Carol Gruber's *Mars and Minerva: World War I and the Uses of Higher Learning in America* (Baton Rouge: Louisiana State University Press, 1975) is an excellent account of the role of academics in the WWI propaganda trenches and the postwar fallout. Peter Novick takes up the same issues in *That Noble Dream: The "Objectivity Question" and the American Historical Profession* (Cambridge: Cambridge University Press, 1988). George Creel's own account of the U.S. activities is *How We Advertised America* (New York: Harper, 1920).

21. Harold D. Lasswell, review of *The Phantom Public*, in *American Journal of Sociology* 31, no. 4 (January 1926): 534, 535.

22. Harold D. Lasswell, "The Theory of Political Propaganda," *American Political Science Review* 21, no. 3 (August 1927): 629.

23. See, for instance, Marks, "The Idea of Propaganda"; Garth Jowett takes the same position in "Propaganda and Communication: The Re-emergence of a Research Tradition," *Journal of Communication* (winter 1987): 97–114.

24. Almond, "Harold Dwight Lasswell."

25. Lasswell, *Propaganda Technique*, p. 12.

26. Morris Janowitz, "Content Analysis and the Study of 'Symbolic Environment,' " in Rogow, *Politics, Personality, and Social Science*, p. 167.

27. Ibid. Lasswell's dissertation included a companion content analysis study entitled "Prussian Schoolbooks and International Amity," in which he focused on and counted references to national superiority, military glory, foreign inferiority, and military heroes as the key political symbols in those textbooks.

28. Lasswell, *Propaganda Technique*, pp. 2–3.

29. Harold D. Lasswell, "The Study and Practice of Propaganda," in Harold D. Lasswell, Ralph D. Casey, and Bruce Lannes Smith, eds., *Propaganda and Promotional Activities: An Annotated Bibliography* (Minneapolis: University of Minnesota Press, 1935), p. 3.

30. Lasswell, *Propaganda Technique*, p. 12.

31. See E. L. Bernays, *Propaganda* (New York: Horace Liveright, 1928), and his earlier work, *Crystallizing Public Opinion* (New York: Boni Liveright, 1923). Stuart Ewen's *PR! A Social History of Spin* (New York: Basic, 1996) is a first-rate account of Bernays's ideas, intellectual development, and his influence. See especially chapters 1–8.

32. E. L. Bernays, "Molding Public Opinion," *Annals* 179: 87.

33. This is language he approvingly used (p. 534) in remarking on the picture of the public painted by Lippmann in his review of *The Phantom Public*.

34. Lasswell, *Affidavit*.

35. Bruce Lannes Smith, "The Mystifying Intellectual History of Harold D. Lasswell," in Rogow, *Politics, Personality, and Social Science*, p. 61.

36. Lasswell, *Affidavit*.

37. Mark Smith, *Social Science in the Crucible*, pp. 223–29, provides an excellent treatment of Lasswell's relationship with Mayo.

38. Almond, "Harold Dwight Lasswell."

39. Smith, "The Mystifying Intellectual History of Lasswell," p. 58.

40. Lasswell, *Affidavit*.

41. For complete bibliography of Lasswell's published and unpublished works, see Muth, Finley, and Muth, *Harold D. Lasswell*.

42. Almond, "Harold Dwight Lasswell."

43. Smith, "The Mystifying Intellectual History of Lasswell," p. 62.

44. Harold D. Lasswell, *Psychopathology and Politics* (Chicago: University of Chicago Press, 1930), reprinted in *The Political Writings of Harold D. Lasswell* (Glencoe, Ill.: Free, 1951), pp. 202–3.

45. Almond, "Harold Dwight Lasswell."

46. Lasswell first used the term "preventive mental hygiene" in *Psychopathology and Politics*.

47. Lasswell, *Psychopathology and Politics*, pp. 197–98.

48. Harold D. Lasswell, "The Strategy of Revolutionary and War Propaganda," in

Quincy Wright, ed., *Public Opinion and World Politics* (1933; rpt., New York: Arno, 1971), p. 188; see, in general, pp. 187–224.

49. Lasswell first articulated this formulation of power in *Psychopathology and Politics*, and it became the central organizational construct in both *World Politics and Personal Insecurity* (New York: McGraw-Hill; London: Whittlesey House, 1935) and *Politics: Who Gets What, When, How* (New York: McGraw-Hill; London: Whittlesey House, 1936);

50. Lasswell, "The Strategy of Revolutionary and War Propaganda," p. 195.

51. Lasswell, *Politics: Who Gets What, When, How,* reprinted in *The Political Writings of Harold Lasswell,* p. 444.

52. "Sore spots" is a phrase Lasswell used repeatedly when he worked as a consultant for the Justice Department and one that became central to Justice Department perceptions of how they should address the problem of propaganda, especially among immigrant groups.

53. Lasswell, *Democracy Through Public Opinion,* p. 79. David Easton, in "Harold Lasswell: Policy Scientist for a Democratic Society," *Journal of Politics* 12, no. 3 (August 1950): 450–77, describes this work as a transitional work, one that marked the end of Lasswell's elitist phase and the beginning of his democratic phase.

54. Lasswell, *Affidavit.*

55. See *Annals* 179.

56. Lasswell, "The Study and Practice of Propaganda," pp. 3–4.

57. Malcolm M. Willey, "Communication Agencies and the Volume of Propaganda," in *Annals* 179, p. 197.

58. George E. Gordon Catlin, "Propaganda as a Function of Democratic Government," in Harwood Childs, ed., *Propaganda and Dictatorship: A Collection of Papers* (Princeton: Princeton University Press, 1936).

59. For the work of the McCormack-Dickstein Committee, see "Investigation of Nazi and Other Propaganda," February 15, 1935, 74th Cong., 1st sess., *House Report No. 153,* U.S. House of Representatives. For additional discussion of the committee's work, see chapter 5.

60. For an encyclopedic treatment of the idea of propaganda in the interwar period, see J. Michael Sproule, *Propaganda and Democracy: The American Experience of Media and Mass Persuasion* (Cambridge: Cambridge University Press, 1997). Sproule has an especially good chapter on the Institute for Propaganda Analysis; see pp. 129–77.

61. Among the many articles in mainstream journals, see, for instance, Johan J. Smertenko, "Hitlerism Comes to America," *Harper's Magazine,* November 1933, pp. 660–70; Ludwig Lore, "Nazi Politics in America," *Nation,* November 29, 1933, pp. 615–17; Raymond Gram Swing, "Patriotism Dons the Black Shirt," *Nation,* April 10, 1935, pp. 409–11; Charles Angoff, "Nazi Jew-Baiting in America," parts 1 and 2, *Nation,* May 1, 1935, pp. 501–3; May 8, 1935, pp. 531–35; Harry F. Ward, "The Development of Fascism in the United States," *Annals of the American Academy of Political and Social Science* 180 (July 1935): 55–61; Robert Lewis Taylor, "The Kampf of Joe McWilliams," *New Yorker,* August 24, 1940, pp. 32–39; Dale Kramer, "The American Fascists," *Harper's Magazine,* September 1940, pp. 380–93; Albert Grzenski, with Charles Hewitt Jr., "Hitler's Branch Offices, U.S.A.," *Current History and Forum* 26 (November 1940): 11–13.

62. See, for example, the coverage of the far right in "Fascism in America," *Life*, March 6, 1939, pp. 58–59. This issue identifies many of the people listed here as being the leading voices of hate in the United States. Leo Ribuffo's *The Old Christian Right: The Protestant Far Right from the Great Depression to the Cold War* (Philadelphia: Temple University Press, 1983) provides an excellent account of the leaders of the domestic Fascists and the anxieties they produced.

63. One of the most respected and energetic anti-Fascist investigators during the Brown Scare era, Reverend L. M. Birkhead, founder of Friends of Democracy, Inc., and publisher of the journal *Propaganda Battlefront*, used the phrase "publicity spotlight" to explain his purposes in exposing the propaganda strategies, financial linkages, political connections, and ideological profiles of domestic right-wing groups and individuals. For evidence of Birkhead's handiwork, see *Propaganda Battlefront*. For a biographical sketch of Birkhead, see E. J. Kahn Jr.'s series "Democracy's Friend," parts 1–3, *New Yorker*, July 26, 1947, pp. 28–36; August 2, 1947, pp. 28–39; and August 9, 1947), pp. 28–38. Historian Leo Ribuffo attests to Birkhead's importance among anti-Fascist investigators in *The Old Christian Right*, especially in the chapter on the Brown Scare.

64. For a useful overview of the way each nation was reported on by the U.S. press, particularly by Edmund Taylor, see Clayton D. Laurie, *Propaganda Warriors: America's Crusade Against Nazi Germany* (Lawrence: University Press of Kansas, 1996), pp. 8–23.

65. Laurie, *Propaganda Warriors*, p. 8.

66. Among these, the Ausland Organization was seen as being the most aggressive of all, claiming three million members in forty-five foreign countries, with a budget of over $100 million by 1937 and including 25,000 agents, 2,000 of whom were supposedly members of the Gestapo.

67. Almond, "Harold Dwight Lasswell."

68. Lasswell, *Affidavit*.

69. Ibid.

70. Harold D. Lasswell and Dorothy Blumenstock, *World Revolutionary Propaganda: A Chicago Study* (New York: Knopf, 1939).

71. Lasswell, *Affidavit*.

72. John Morton Blum, *V Was for Victory: Politics and American Culture During World War II* (New York: Harcourt, Brace, 1976), for a discussion of Archibald MacLeish's purported inability to comprehend Lasswell; Smith repeats these claims in *Social Science in the Crucible*. Based on my own reading of Lasswell's documents where he proposed to MacLeish specific content for U.S. propaganda campaigns, I can understand Blum's and Smith's assertions. At the same time, however, they fail to take into account the fairly active relationship Lasswell had with MacLeish with respect to propaganda defense work. See chapter 4.

THREE Mobilizing for the War on Words

1. John Marshall used the terms "pathology of influence" and "pathology of substitutes" to describe what he called the "problem of propaganda." See "Next Jobs in Radio and Film," August 31, 1938, and the updated version, "Next Jobs in Radio and Film," September 13, 1938. Both memoranda are in RAC, Series 911, Program and Pol-

icy Files, Radio and Motion Pictures, box 5, folder 60. The records of the Rockefeller Foundation's Communications Projects are extensive. They are housed at the Rockefeller Archive Center, Pocantico Hills, hereafter referred to as RAC.

2. Marshall stayed with the Rockefeller Foundation until 1970. From 1959 to 1970 he was the resident director of the foundation's Study Conference Center in Bellagio, Italy, where he and his wife, Charlotte Trowbridge Marshall, coordinated the Bellagio conferences.

3. John Marshall, memorandum to David Stevens, January 22, 1936, in RAC, Series 911, Program and Policy Files, Radio and Motion Pictures, 1914–1940, box 5, folder 5. Official foundation rationales for different programs and policies are contained in the Program and Policy Files, Series 911, Radio and Motion Pictures, 1914–1940, box 5. The notes for the Program and Policy Files include all the grant documentation for Rockefeller Foundation programs in radio and motion pictures.

4. John Marshall, "Introduction" (draft), June 1940, in RAC, Record Group 1.1, Series 200, 200R, box 224, folder 2677. All further citations in this chapter will be from RAC, Record Group 1.1, Series 200, 200R, unless otherwise designated.

5. With the exception of several essays in James W. Carey, ed., "Remembering Our Past: Early Communications Studies in the United States and Germany," *Communication*, special issue, 10, no. 2 (1988), in which the foundation's support of Lazarsfeld is mentioned and specific documents from the Communications Group referred to, little has been written about the Rockefeller Foundation's central role in the history of the field. See Brett Gary, "American Liberalism and the Problem of Propaganda: Scholars, Lawyers, and the War on Words, 1919–1945" (Ph.D. diss., University of Pennsylvania, 1992); see also David Morrison, "The Transference of Experience and the Impact of Ideas: Paul Lazarsfeld and Mass Communications Research," in Carey, "Remembering Our Past," pp. 185–210, which correctly suggests that this history needs further study. Other writers in this same volume rely on Morrison's 1978 article "The Beginning of Modern Mass Communication Research," *European Journal of Sociology* 29: 327–59, as their source on foundation influences. Historian Daniel Czitrom in *Media and the American Mind: From Morse to McLuhan* (Chapel Hill: University of North Carolina Press, 1982), pp. 130–33, discusses one of the group's documents and suggests the foundation had some undefined central role in the emergence of communications research. His discussion is suggestive but undeveloped. See also Everett Rogers, *A History of Communication Study* (New York: Free, 1994).

6. Files for these individual research projects are available at the Rockefeller Archive Center in Record Group 1.1, Series 200 and 200R.

7. See note 1.

8. Marshall, "Next Jobs in Radio and Film," September 13, 1938. This dichotomy between propaganda and education was the most standard way of defining propaganda. See, for instance, Frederick Lumley, *The Propaganda Menace* (New York: Century, 1933); the publications of the Institute for Propaganda Analysis, Inc., especially the four volumes of its newsletter edited by Harold Lavine and Violet Edwards, *Propaganda Analysis: A Bulletin to Help the Intelligent Citizen Detect and Analyze Propaganda*, vols. 1–4 (New York: Institute for Propaganda Analysis, 1938–1941); and Elmer Ellis, ed., *Education Against Propaganda* (Washington, D.C.: National Council for Social Studies, 1937), the seventh yearbook of the National Council for the Social Studies.

9. See John M. Jordan, *Machine-Age Ideology: Social Engineering and American Liberalism, 1911–1939* (Chapel Hill: University of North Carolina Press, 1994), Mark C. Smith, *Social Science in the Crucible: The American Debate Over Objectivity and Purpose, 1918–1941* (Durham, N.C.: Duke University Press, 1994).

10. Marshall, "Next Jobs in Radio and Film," September 13, 1938.

11. Marshall explored these four organizing questions in the second draft of the memorandum, "Next Jobs in Radio and Film," September 13, 1938.

12. Marshall, "Next Jobs in Radio and Film," September 13, 1938.

13. Grant action form, "Studies and Surveys and Conferences," August 12, 1939, box 223, folder 2672.

14. Marshall, letters to Robert Lynd, August 17, 1939, and to Lyman Bryson, August 14, 1939, both in box 233, folder 2672. Marshall's imposed elision of this important detail of foundation history might explain why the central role of the Rockefeller Foundation in the history of mass communications has been largely excluded from the standard histories of the discipline.

15. Lynd, letter to Marshall, August 23, 1939, box 223, folder 2672.

16. See Edward A. Purcell Jr., *The Crisis of Democratic Theory: Scientific Naturalism and the Problem of Value* (Lexington: University Press of Kentucky, 1973), for an extended discussion of the crisis of democratic theory in the U.S. academy between the wars.

17. Lynd to Marshall.

18. Lynd, letter to Marshall, September 13, 1939, box 223, folder 2672.

19. Seminar memorandum No. 1, box 224, folder 2677. Seminar Memorandum No. 1 was actually a record of the first two seminar meetings, both held in September 1939. *Public Opinion Quarterly*, also funded by the Rockefeller Foundation, proved to be an important vehicle of communication between the different seminar members and government officials on the eve of and during the war. Officials from the Justice Department, Office of Facts and Figures, and others published numerous articles on their wartime communications policies and research, as did members of the Communications Group.

20. The Communications Group held its first ten meetings from September 1939 to June 1940. Free's records of those meetings and the supporting materials, consisting primarily of working papers that different seminar members presented for discussion at the meetings, are available in box 224, folder 2677, under cover of "Communications Research Report 1938 [*sic*]" (Section 1) and "Communications Research Report 1939" (Section 2).

21. Group report, "Needed Research in Mass Communication," October 1940, box 224, folder 2677.

22. All quotations from seminar memorandum No. 1.

23. Quotations in ibid. Slesinger left his job as a social science dean at the University of Chicago to take a job as director of education at the 1939 New York World's Fair and subsequently left that job to become the director of the American Film Center.

24. Lynd, letter to Marshall, August 23, 1939.

25. Group memorandum, "The Job to Be Done—Now," September 25, 1939, box 244, folder 2677.

26. Harold D. Lasswell, Communications Seminar documents nos. 3 and 4, September 29, 1939, box 224, folder 2677; emphasis in original.

27. The FARA trials also set a legal seal on the scientific validity of Lasswell's methods and confirmed the expert status of communications researchers, whose content analysis techniques were upheld by the courts as "admissible scientific evidence" in *U.S. v. German-American Vocational League*, 153 F.2d 860, 865.

28. Harold D. Lasswell, Communications Seminar documents nos. 3 and 4. Lasswell's agenda for the development and employment of specific research-oriented methods included (1) propaganda analysis; (2) current documentation in the field; (3) public opinion measurement, using straw ballots and interviews; (4) reporting who promotes what; (5) representation analysis (analyzing the symbols shot through the total flow of communication); and (6) studies of authoritative standards regarding communication, including legal standards for regulating the flow of communications.

29. Donald Slesinger, Communications Seminar document no. 5, September 29, 1939, box 224, folder 2677.

30. Group document, "Public Opinion and the Emergency," December 1, 1939, box 224, folder 2677.

31. Predating the war years, the Communications Group scholars stated their skepticism about the unlimited power thesis. Holly Cowan Shulman argues in *Voice of America: Propaganda and Democracy, 1941–1945* (Madison: University of Wisconsin, 1990) that on the eve of the war, the thesis of propaganda's unlimited power began to crumble when it was submitted to empirical tests. Allan Winkler, *The Politics of Propaganda: The Office of War Information, 1942–1945* (New Haven: Yale University Press, 1978), makes the same argument about government propagandist's growing awareness of the "limited effects" demonstrated by empirical testing.

32. Lynd, letter to Marshall, December 9, 1939. Marshall responded in a letter of December 11, 1939, saying: "Of course, I find it hard to agree with you that Lasswell and Gorer take utility as a tacit assumption. Certainly it doesn't seem to me that Lasswell does. I think you and he ought to have all this pretty thoroughly thrashed out sometime. I may have the layman's knack of missing essential distinctions, but it does seem that you are much closer together than either of you realize." Both letters in box 223, folder 2672.

33. Lynd, letter to Marshall, April 17, 1940, box 223, folder 2673. See Richard W. Fox, "Epitaph for Middletown: Robert S. Lynd and the Analysis of Consumer Culture," in Richard W. Fox and T. J. Jackson Lears, *The Culture of Consumption: Critical Essays in American History, 1880–1980* (New York: Pantheon, 1983). Fox argues that Lynd felt that he had become rather unproductive in the 1940s largely because he did not consider himself to be methodologically up-to-date, especially with respect to the use of statistical techniques. See also Smith, *Social Science in the Crucible*.

34. Marshall, letter to I. A. Richards, April 25, 1940, box 223, folder 2673, responding to Richards's resignation, communicated in a letter to Marshall dated April 23, 1940, located in box 223, folder 2673. The quotations in the text appear in the following passage: "I am sorry that I didn't say to you after the last meeting what I felt, namely, that there had been a degree of imperviousness on the part of some members of the group to the point you were making that I found rather baffling. . . . As I told [Lynd], we could have taken the easy way and turned the group over to the supposed

'experts' in research. But I have just enough suspicion of 'expertism' to make me reluctant to do that, at least in the earlier phases. Possibly the time has come for them to take responsibility in formulating the results of the year's work. But I hope we may at the very least have your criticism of whatever they do put in form." In an April 22, 1940, letter to Lynd (box 223, folder 2673), however, Marshall suggested that perhaps the group should be relying more on experts. He said: "The meeting [at which Lazarsfeld's work] was discussed was certainly the most profitable we have had since last autumn. Is that an indication that we ought to depend more on the experts?" He then added, "At any rate, the whole business has been an interesting experience in intellectual procedure. I hope, of course, it will be something more."

35. Communications Group report, "Research in Mass Communication," July 1940, box 224, folder 2677; emphasis in original.

36. Marshall, interoffice correspondence to Stacy May, re "JHW's Memorandum on Lasswell's Proposal," May 29, 1940, box 274, folder 3271: Public Opinion Study— Harold Lasswell, 1940.

37. Ibid.

38. Charles Siepmann, letter to Marshall, September 13, 1940, box 224, folder 2674.

39. Lyman Bryson, letter to Marshall, September 23, 1940, box 224, folder 2674.

40. Joseph Willits, memo to Marshall, September 30, 1940, box 224, folder 2674.

41. Group report, "Needed Research in Communication," October 1940, box 224, folder 2677.

42. "Persons to Whom the Communications Memorandum was Sent," box 224, folder 2675. Copies were sent out under each seminar member's name, not under the foundation's name.

43. Marshall, interoffice memorandum to Raymond Fosdick, re communication research projects for foundation aid, September 26, 1940, box 224, folder 2674.

44. Marshall, interoffice correspondence to Stacy May, re JHW's memorandum on Lasswell's proposal, May 29, 1940, box 274, folder 3271.

45. Marshall, interoffice correspondence to Stevens, "Communication Research Projects which should be considered before the end of 1940," September 13, 1940, box 224, folder 2674: Communications Research, Aug–Dec 1940. Marshall proposed expanding research based on the Communications Group's blueprint, especially focusing on film audience research "comparable to what the Columbia Office of Radio Research is doing in that field and the Graduate Library School of the University of Chicago is doing for reading." One thing he wanted was for these projects to become self-sustaining so that they could eventually be weaned from the foundation dollar. Marshall's concern in linking film-oriented market research to national security concerns supports my argument that the real focus of communications research during this period was its role in building the national security state, not in commerce building.

46. Ibid.

47. Ibid.

48. Quoted in Marshall, interoffice memorandum to Stevens, January 17, 1941, box 224, folder 2675.

49. Marshall, interview with Stacy May, January 29, 1941, box 224, folder 2675.

50. Marshall, interoffice memorandum to Stevens, January 17, 1941. The few fed-

eral projects Marshall mentioned that were already functioning, including work in Nelson Rockefeller's Office of Inter-American Affairs and FCC surveillance through the listening posts at Princeton and Stanford, were Rockefeller Foundation–financed activities. Marshall found this paucity of research unacceptable and knew that FCC personnel were frustrated at the lack of U.S. commitment to communications intelligence. The necessity of this work was impressed on Marshall by Gerald Cock, U.S. representative of the BBC, who told him that U.S. monitoring of broadcasts was entirely inadequate.

51. For some background on these projects and the wartime consulting work they did, see Jean Converse, *Survey Research in the United States: Roots and Emergence, 1890–1960* (Berkeley: University of California Press, 1987). Lazarsfeld's work was less explicitly involved in war-related research as its primary agenda than other project leaders would have wished. At one point, Lasswell told Marshall in a letter that he wished Lazarsfeld would "integrate his future researches more closely in the emergency program" (December 23, 1940, box 260, folder 3098).

52. Donald Slesinger, letter to Marshall, July 9, 1938; for a fuller statement, see "Draft of American Film Center Plan," June 9, 1938, both in box 199, folder 2383: American Film Center (AFC). Henceforward, the label "American Film Center (AFC)" will be abbreviated "AFC."

53. Slesinger, letter to Stevens, December 28, 1938, box 199, folder 2383.

54. Slesinger's many jobs in New York included director of the Education Division of the New York World's Fair, consultant to the New York Board of Health, and staff member of Raymond Rich Associates.

55. Slesinger to Stevens, December 28, 1938.

56. "Draft of American Film Center Plan," June 9, 1938, box 199, folder 2383.

57. Grant-in-Aid form, November 28, 1938, box 199, folder 2383.

58. See Luther Gulick, letter to David Stevens, November 3, 1938 (box 199, folder 2383), and the November 28, 1938, Grant-in-Aid form for a discussion of the Latin American cultural exchange project.

59. Slesinger, letter to Marshall, February 18, 1939, box 199, folder 2384: AFC. In this letter, Slesinger noted that the U.S. Film Service's problems were "highly confidential and should not be made part of the [foundation's] general memoranda."

60. The AFC also received $19,500 for incidental expenditures in the period from January 20, 1939, to December 31, 1940. See Draft of Grant request, January 14, 1939, box 199, folder 2383.

61. American Film Center Report, November 2, 1939, box 200, folder 2393: AFC.

62. American Film Center Report, May 7, 1940, box 199, folder 2385: AFC.

63. Slesinger, letter to May, June 1940 proposal, box 199, folder 2385.

64. See, for instance, Slesinger's interim report, December 4, 1941, box 200, folder 2393.

65. "Extract from personnel letter from DS of AFC to JM, dated 8/23/41," box 199, folder 2387: AFC.

66. "Excerpt from Trustees' Confidential Bulletin," November 1941 issue, box 199, folder 2387. The excerpt notes that the Film Center consulted with a host of different agencies and departments, including the Tennessee Valley Authority on its visual aid program, the Civil Service Commission on in-house training films, the Economic De-

fense Board and the War Department on content analysis and film use, the Federal Security Administration on the production of nutrition and national security films, and mainly with Paul McNutt of the Office of Coordinator of Defense "to extend on a national scale all the things that we have been doing a smaller way through American Film Center."

67. Grant-in-Aid, December 2, 1942, box 199, folder 2388: AFC 1942.

68. Slesinger, memorandum to Marshall, October 27, 1942, box 199, folder 2388.

69. From the period January to November 1940, the AFC had a total income of $113,000, $76,840 of which came from the foundation. By December 1942 the foundation had spent a total of $158,000 on the AFC. (These figures are from Slesinger, memorandum to Marshall, October 27, 1942.)

70. Quoted in "JM Interview," November 5, 1942, box 199, folder 2388.

71. Ibid.

72. Luther Gulick, letter to Marshall, November 10, 1942, box 199, folder 2388. Slesinger, on the other hand, told Marshall he thought that the AFC's association with the OCD "meant that it had less influence with other government agencies" ("JM Interview," July 13, 1943, box 199, folder 2389: AFC).

73. "JM Interview," November 5, 1942.

74. For a history of wartime film activities, see Clayton R. Koppes and Gregory D. Black, *Hollywood Goes to War: How Politics, Profits, and Propaganda Shaped World War II Movies* (New York: Free, 1987).

75. "JM Interview," July 13, 1943. In late 1943 the AFC had already negotiated film production contracts with Swift Co., Standard Oil, and the Federal Council of Churches.

76. Slesinger, memorandum to Marshall, October 27, 1942, box 199, folder 2388.

77. Slesinger, memorandum to AFC board of directors, October 26, 1943, box 200, folder 2394: AFC.

78. RF grant 41067 (June 30, 1941–June 30, 1942), box 250, folder 2983: MoMA–Film Library.

79. These were the Latin American Arts Project (to distribute exhibitions of North American art to ten Latin American countries) and the Latin America Film Project (to distribute nontheatrical film to the U.S. embassies in Latin America).

80. "Project Memorandum," June 4, 1941, box 250, folder 2989: Museum of Modern Art–Film Library. See also "Project Memorandum: The Museum of Modern Art," December 31, 1942, Record Group 2, series III 2E, box 22, folder 219: Rockefeller Family Cultural Interests.

81. "Museum of Modern Art—Film Library," 1939, box 250, folder 2986, MoMA–Film Library, 1938.

82. RF grant 41067.

83. Materials the Film Library provided to Capra included all twenty-six reels of *Triumph of the Will*, along with forty-two other reels of propaganda films. For details, see the minutes of a meeting of the Film Library Advisory Committee, June 19, 1942, box 251, folder 2990: Museum of Modern Art–Film Library, 1942. The correspondence is in box 250, folders 2983, and 2989.

84. A letter from Barry to Marshall shows her interest in housing Kracauer (May 14, 1941, box 250, folder 2989: Museum of Modern Art–Film Library, 1941. The li-

brary's 1941 grant (for $5,000) explained Kracauer's project as a "study of the part which films, particularly films from totalitarian countries, are playing in wartime communications."

85. RF grant 41067.

86. "JM Interviews," Miss Iris Barry and Mr. Krakauer [*sic*], July 1, 1941, box 250, folder 2983.

87. "JM Interviews," January 28, 1942, box 251, folder 2990.

88. Siegfried Kracauer, *From Caligari to Hitler: A Psychological History of the German Film* (Princeton: Princeton University Press, 1946).

89. All drafts, along with Marshall's brief comments on them, are in box 251, folder 2990.

90. Kracauer, "Screen Dramaturgy," box 251, folder 2990.

91. Kracauer, "Conflict with Reality," box 251, folder 2990.

92. Kracauer, "Summary," box 251, folder 2990.

93. Marshall note, March 3, 1942, box 251, folder 2990. A letter from Hadley Cantril to Marshall in 1945 points to the gulf between the "qualitative" "humanistic" approach to media studies and the quantitative approach that Cantril championed. Cantril told Marshall he had had lunch with Kracauer, because, as Cantril said, "he was apparently eager to talk to me to see if I had any suggestions as to how his intuitive, observational approach might be supplemented with some more rigorous scientific approach which would more conclusively demonstrate the validity of his interpretations" (June 12, 1945, box 251, folder 2992: MoMA–Film Library).

94. Marshall to Kracauer, May 22, 1942, box 251, folder 2990.

95. Marshall, "Inter-Office Correspondence," December 1942, box 251, folder 2990.

96. Rumors were that Kris had been killed by the Nazis and that an impostor was masquerading as him in the United States, but those who knew him from the BBC were able to identify him positively. See Marshall, interview notes on Kris, December 1940, box 260, folder 3098: Totalitarian Communication Studies.

97. Marshall noted these opinions in his interview notes on Kris. Kris was not the only one who was put off by the quantitative fetish of the Lasswell-Lazarsfeld school of communications studies. In his memoirs, Speier wrote: "Studies of propaganda had been conducted in the United States since the end of World War I, especially under the influence of Harold D. Lasswell. . . . Not very much later Paul Lazarsfeld's market research attracted wide attention, as did many studies on methods and techniques of opinion polls. The growth of this literature was not an unmixed blessing for the social sciences. Certain analytical methods were refined, but the substantive questions that were being asked became shallower. Interest in the structure of modern society faded along with interest in the fate of man in that society" (Hans Speier, "Autobiographical Notes," in *The Truth in Hell and Other Essays on Politics and Culture, 1935–1987* [New York: Oxford University Press, 1989], p. 14).

98. Although he thought the Princeton Listening Center was off to a good start, Marshall believed they were not getting "to the root of things" ("Interview" notes).

99. "Interview" notes. Kris's comment referred to the Institute for Propaganda Analysis, whose neutrality Kris took to be defeatist. The Institute for Propaganda Analysis actually closed down its operations when its value-neutral approach to propaganda became untenable in the crisis.

100. "Morale and Propaganda" was the title of the introductory essay of Hans Speier and Alfred Kahler, *War in Our Time* (New York: Norton,1939).

101. Speier, "Autobiographical Notes," p. 11.

102. For details, see ibid., pp. 3–32.

103. For a history of émigré scholars at the New School, see Peter M. Rutkoff and William B. Scott, *New School: A History of the New School for Social Research* (London: Collier Macmillan, 1986).

104. Lasswell to Marshall, February 7, 1941, box 260, folder 3099: Totalitarian Communication Studies, 1940.

105. Max Ascoli to Marshall, February 6, 1941, box 260, folder 3099.

106. New School Project Grant in Aid, RF 41014, March 21, 1941, box 260, folder 3098.

107. Ibid.

108. Speier, "Autobiographical Notes," in *The Truth in Hell and Other Essays on Politics and Culture, 1935–1987* (New York, 1989), pp. 14.

109. New School Project Grant in Aid, RF 42030, April 1942, box 260, folder 3098.

110. Ibid.

111. Ibid.

112. Ernst Kris and Hans Speier, *German Radio Propaganda* (London: Oxford University Press, 1944).

113. Lasswell, proposal, "A Study of Public Communication in Wartime," n.d. [before May 30, 1940], box 274, folder 3271. As a result of the first two years of analysis, Childs and Whitton edited a collection of reports titled *Propaganda by Shortwave* (Princeton: Princeton University Press, 1942).

114. Graves was succeeded at this post by Robert Leigh, president of Bennington College, who subsequently became the project director of the Commission on Freedom of the Press.

115. See *Radio: 10 RF Projects*, a 1949 internal history of the foundation's projects, box 275, folder 3277: Radio.

116. Marshall, interoffice correspondence, re JHW's Memorandum on Lasswell's Proposal, May 29, 1940.

117. Grant-in-Aid, June 21, 1940, box 274, folder 3271.

118. "JM Interview," October 23, 1940, box 239, folder 2852: Library of Congress, Communication Trends, 1940. For the exchange of letters surrounding this development, see also Lasswell's memorandum to Marshall, re communication research, October 27, 1940, box 239, folder 2852.

119. Archibald MacLeish, letter to Marshall, October 30, 1940, box 239, folder 2852. Lasswell's chief assistants included, among others, Nathan Leites, Ithiel deSola Pool, Raymond Fadner, Irving Janis, and Joseph Goldsen. Lasswell, Leites, and associates published a collection of papers reporting on their wartime work at the library, entitled *The Language of Politics: Studies in Quantitative Semantics* (1949; rpt., Cambridge, Mass.: MIT Press, 1965).

120. For background on MacLeish's wartime work as director of the Office of Facts and Figures and assistant director of the Office of War Information, see Allan Winkler, *The Politics of Propaganda: The Office of War Information, 1942–1945* (New Haven: Yale University Press,1978).

121. Marshall to MacLeish, November 7, 1940; MacLeish to Welles, October 31, 1940; and Welles to MacLeish, October 31, 1940, all in box 239, folder 2852.

122. Francis Biddle to MacLeish, November 1, 1940, box 239, folder 2852.

123. Welles to MacLeish, October 31, 1940.

124. Lawrence M. C. Smith, April 29, 1941, memorandum, National Archives and Records Administration, Department of Justice Records, Record Group 60, Special War Policies Unit Papers, box 10, folder: RKK, #2.

125. Lasswell, memorandum to the Justice Department and Archibald MacLeish, n.d, National Archives and Records Administration, Department of Justice Records, Record Group 60, Special War Policies Unit Papers, box 75, folder: Surveillance of Press and Radio.

FOUR Mobilizing the Intellectual Arsenal of Democracy

1. Roosevelt appointed MacLeish Librarian of Congress in 1939 and then appointed him director of the Office of Facts and Figures in mid-1941, a position MacLeish held until that office was absorbed into the Office of War Information in mid-1942, when he was made deputy director. He resigned from that post by the end of 1942 and returned full-time to the Library of Congress. MacLeish stayed at the library until November 1944, when he was appointed Undersecretary of State for Cultural and Public Affairs. He resigned from the State Department after FDR's death in 1945 to return to private life. In 1949 he resumed teaching, taking a position as the Boylston Professor at Harvard University. The most recent and authoritative biography of MacLeish is Scott L. Donaldson, *Archibald MacLeish: An American Life* (Boston: Houghton Mifflin, 1992). For a warm reminiscence of MacLeish's life as poet, government official, and man of liberal conscience, see John M. Blum, "Archibald MacLeish: Art for Action," originally published in *Yale Review* 81, no. 2 (April 1993), and reprinted in *Liberty, Justice, Order: Essays on Past Politics* (New York: Norton, 1993), pp. 227–60.

2. For a useful treatment of the various strains within twentieth-century U.S. liberalism, see Gary Gerstle, "The Protean Character of American Liberalism," *American Historical Review* 99, no. 4 (October 1994): 1043–73. See also Alan Brinkley, *The End of Reform: New Deal Liberalism in Recession and War* (New York: Knopf, 1995), especially pp. 8–10, for his discussion of different tendencies within liberalism.

3. Archibald MacLeish, "Freedom to End Freedom," *Survey Graphic* (February 1939); rpt., Archibald MacLeish, *A Time to Speak: The Selected Prose of Archibald MacLeish* (Boston: Houghton Mifflin, 1940), p. 131.

4. These details are available in any standard biographical work on MacLeish. See R. H. Winnick, introduction to *The Letters of Archibald MacLeish, 1907–1982* (Boston: Houghton Mifflin, 1983), pp. xi–xviii; see also Robert Cowley, "America Was Promises: An Interview with Archibald MacLeish," *American Heritage* 33, no. 5 (August/September 1982): 22–32.

5. MacLeish quotes the Fay Diploma citation in his interview with Cowley, "America Was Promises," p. 26.

6. Quoted in Cowley, "America Was Promises," p. 28.

7. For these biographical details, see Winnick, *Letters*, p. xiv. For some contemporary reviews of MacLeish's radio plays, see Merrill Denison's positive review of *The*

Fall of the City in "Radio and the Writer," *Theatre Arts* 22 (May 1938): 366–69; Hermine Rich Isaacs's criticism of *Air Raid* in "The Fall of Another City," *Theatre Arts* 23 (February 1939): 147–49; Randall Jarrell's denunciation of MacLeish's first radio play, especially its presentation of a passive, overwhelmed public, in "The Fall of the City," *Sewanee Review* 51 (April 1943): 267–80.

8. Donaldson, *Archibald MacLeish*, pp. 293, 309. For Donaldson's discussion of this episode, see pp. 292–310. For other discussions of MacLeish's appointment and the controversy about his appointment, see Frederick J. Stiewlow, "Librarian Warriors and Rapprochement: Carl Milam, Archibald MacLeish, and World War II," *Libraries and Culture* 25 (1990): 513–33.

9. In support of his nomination, see John Chamberlain, "Archibald MacLeish," *Saturday Review of Literature*, June 24, 1939, pp. 10–11; H. S. Canby, "Archibald MacLeish and the Library of Congress," *Saturday Review of Literature*, June 17, 1939, p. 8; Freda Kirchway, "Some Personalities of the Week," *Nation*, June 17, 1939, p. 689; Llewellyn M. Raney, "MacLeish's Case," *Library Journal* (July 1939): 522; "The Roving Eye," *Wilson Library Bulletin* 14 (September 1939): 57.

10. For a piece recognizing MacLeish's work as librarian, see Harry C. Shriver and Cedric Larson, "Archibald MacLeish's Two Years as Librarian," *Saturday Review of Literature*, October 18, 1941, pp. 10–11; for an early retrospective of his accomplishments as librarian, see Keyes D. Metcalf, "Editorial Forum: Merits Respect and Gratitude," *Library Journal* (March 1945): 213.

11. The quotations are from Donaldson, *Archibald MacLeish*, p. 310.

12. Several of the standard works on leftist intellectuals in the 1930s through the beginning of WWII speak to the controversies swirling around MacLeish. See Daniel Aaron, *Writers on the Left: Literary Communism* (New York: Harcourt, Brace, and World, 1961); James Gilbert, *Writers and Partisans: A History of Literary Radicalism in America* (New York: Wiley, 1968); and Richard Pells, *Radical Visions and American Dreams: Culture and Social Thought in the Depression Years* (Middletown, Conn.: Wesleyan University Press, 1973).

13. MacLeish was most famously and savagely attacked by Edmund Wilson in "The Omelet of A. MacLeish," *New Yorker*, January 14, 1939, pp. 23–24. Some supported his efforts to develop his public speech but found him wanting as a poet; see, e.g., John Malcolm Brinnon, "For a Wider Audience," *Poetry* 56 (April 1940): 43–46. Others supported his efforts to develop a nonmodernist public speech, including Dayton Kohler, "MacLeish and the Modern Temper," *South Atlantic Quarterly* 38 (October 1939): 416–26; and John Peale Bishop, "The Muse at the Microphone," *Nation*, February 3, 1940, pp. 132–33. The disdain of highbrows was especially acute in the postwar era. Dwight MacDonald used MacLeish as his primary example of the edgeless quality of middlebrow art in his famous critique of middlebrow culture, "Mass Cult and Mid-Cult," in *Against the American Grain* (New York: Random House, 1962). A more recent treatment of MacLeish's public speech is John Timberman Newcomb, "Archibald MacLeish and the Poetics of Public Speech: A Critique of High Modernism," *Journal of the Midwest Modern Language Association* 23 (spring 1990): 9–26.

14. Archibald MacLeish's "The Irresponsibles" was first delivered as a speech, reprinted in part in the *Nation*, which gave it its title: "The Irresponsibles," *Nation*, May

18, 1940, pp. 618–23; it was shortly thereafter published in book form under the title *The Irresponsibles* (New York: Duell, Sloan, and Pearce, 1940) and reprinted in *A Time to Speak*, pp. 103–21. MacLeish's "Post-War Writers, Pre-War Readers" was also first delivered as a speech and shortly thereafter published in the *New Republic*, June 10, 1940, pp. 789–90.

15. For a discussion of this episode, see Donaldson, *Archibald MacLeish*, pp. 333–40.

16. Winnick, *Letters*, p. xv, suggests the connection between MacLeish's attacks and FDR's appointment.

17. One volley of attacks appeared in the "Letters" column in the June 10, 1940, issue of the *New Republic*, which *Life* magazine reprinted in a brief section entitled "War Writers on Democracy" (*Life*, June 24, 1940, pp. 8, 12, 15), containing responses from those MacLeish named, including Ernest Hemingway, Maxwell Anderson, Robert E. Sherwood, Walter Millis, e. e. cummings, G. Hartley Grattan, Dalton Trumbo, and Richard Aldington. Full-scale attacks on MacLeish came next, e.g., in Burton Rascoe's "The Tough-Muscle Boys of Literature," *American Mercury* 51 (November 1940): 369–74; especially hard-hitting was Morton Dauwen Zabel's two-part piece, "The Poet on Capitol Hill," parts 1 and 2, *Partisan Review* 8 (January–February 1941): 1–19; and (March–April 1941): 128–45.

18. In this respect, MacLeish echoed, but did not mimic, claims made by other interventionists who accused intellectual relativists of making the triumph of fascism possible. For a full discussion of this vituperative debate, see Edward A. Purcell Jr., *The Crisis of Democratic Theory: Scientific Naturalism and the Problem of Value* (Lexington: University Press of Kentucky, 1973), especially chs. 7–12.

19. The quotations are from "The Irresponsibles" as reprinted in slightly modified form in *A Time to Speak*, pp. 110–11, 104–5.

20. Archibald MacLeish, "A Question of Audience," first published in *New Theatre*, 1935, and reprinted in *A Time to Speak*, pp. 72–73. The full text appears on pp. 70–73.

21. Other essays addressing the same themes include "In Challenge, Not Defense," first published in 1938 in *Poetry Magazine*, and "Poetry and the Public World," first published in June 1939 in the *Atlantic Monthly*. Both are republished in *A Time to Speak*, pp. 1–7, 81–96.

22. Archibald MacLeish, "In Challenge, Not Defense," p. 2.

23. Archibald MacLeish, "The Affirmation," originally published in *Survey Graphic* (May 1939) and reprinted in *A Time to Speak*, p. 10.

24. Archibald MacLeish, *The Fall of the City* (New York: Farrar and Rinehart, 1937).

25. Archibald MacLeish, *Air Raid* (New York: Harcourt Brace, 1938).

26. Archibald MacLeish, *The Land of the Free* (New York: Harcourt Brace, 1938).

27. MacLeish, *America Was Promises* (New York: Duell, Sloan, and Pearce, 1940).

28. The Foreign Agents Registration Act (1938; amended 1940), the Voorhis Act (1940), the Alien Registration Act and the Smith Act amendment to the Alien Registration Act (1941) were all efforts to shore up the State and Justice Department's administrative tools for the control of propaganda and subversive organizations.

29. "Freedom to End Freedom," first published in *Survey Graphic*, February 1939, and reprinted in *A Time to Speak*, pp. 131–39.

30. Archibald MacLeish, "Libraries in the Contemporary Crisis," dated October 19, 1939, and reprinted in *A Time to Speak*, p. 123.

31. MacLeish, "The Affirmation," p. 10.

32. For a discussion of MacLeish's interventionist ideas, see Donaldson, *Archibald MacLeish*, pp. 261–93.

33. All the quotations are from an interview with MacLeish conducted by Bernard A. Drabeck and Helen E. Ellis and published as *Archibald MacLeish: Reflections*, ed. Bernard A. Drabeck and Helen E. Ellis, with a foreword by Richard Wilbur (Amherst: University of Massachusetts Press, 1986), pp. 144–45.

34. MacLeish, "The Irresponsibles," p. 103.

35. For the larger currents of this debate in U.S. intellectual culture in the 1930s, see Edward Purcell, *The Crisis of Democratic Theory*; for the debate in the history profession, see Peter Novick, *That Noble Dream: The "Objectivity Question" and the American Historical Profession* (Cambridge: Cambridge University Press, 1988); for the debate in the social sciences, see Mark C. Smith, *Social Science in the Crucible: The American Debate Over Objectivity and Purpose, 1918–1941* (Durham, N.C.: Duke University Press, 1994).

36. Sproule's articles and book do an excellent job discussing the ways in which propaganda criticism produced skepticism. See *Propaganda and Democracy: The American Experience of Media and Mass Persuasion* (Cambridge: Cambridge University Press, 1997); "Progressive Propaganda Critics and the Magic Bullet Myth," *Critical Studies in Mass Communications* 6 (1989): 225–46; and "Propaganda Studies in American Social Science: The Rise and Fall of a Critical Paradigm," *Quarterly Journal of Speech* 73 (1987): 60–78. Kenneth Cmiel's article "On Cynicism, Evil, and the Discovery of Mass Communication in the 1940s," *Journal of Communication* 46, no. 3 (1996): 88–107, does so as well.

37. MacLeish, "Post-War Writers, Pre-War Readers," pp. 789–90.

38. See note 17.

39. Archibald MacLeish, "The Librarian And the Democratic Process," May 31, 1940, reprinted in *A Time to Speak*, p. 150.

40. The American Library Association, under the leadership of its president, Carl Milam, worked closely with MacLeish to put the nation's libraries on a war footing. On January 25, 1941, Milam wrote MacLeish about the range of activities that should be undertaken, including aiding foreign libraries devastated by war, providing books to war prisoners (something which had not been adequately addressed at all, he argued), providing materials for U.S. military training-camp libraries, providing materials for technical education, and working with government agencies to help secure specialized materials. See Milam, letter to MacLeish, January 25, 1941. For a fuller discussion of Milam's and the ALA's perception of the range of its useful prewar activities, see Milam's memo to the executive board of the ALA, November 15, 1940. See also MacLeish, letter to Milam, February 1, 1941. All sources located in LC Archives, Central Files, MacLeish-Evans Papers, box 901, folder: National Defense, 2-2. For Milam and MacLeish's wartime work in general, see Frederick J. Stiewlow, "Librarian Warriors and Rapprochement: Carl Milam, Archibald MacLeish, and World War II," *Libraries and Culture* 25 (1990): 513–33

41. Donaldson, *Archibald MacLeish*, pp. 323, 329. MacLeish is well regarded for enhancing the relationship between the LC and U.S. belle lettres by providing fel-

lowships to poets and writers; importantly, he also enhanced the relationships among the LC and various government departments and agencies such as the departments of State and Justice, private philanthropies like the Rockefeller and Carnegie foundations, research universities, social scientists, historians, and displaced émigré scholars. Establishing collaborative relationships among these different institutions proved vitally important to the state's emerging intelligence capabilities and should be understood as an integral part of building the incipient national security state.

42. Archibald MacLeish, "Of the Librarian's Profession," first published in the *Atlantic Monthly*, June 1940, and reprinted in *A Time to Speak*, p. 32.

43. Archibald MacLeish, "Libraries in the Contemporary Crisis," October 19, 1939, reprinted in *A Time to Speak*, pp. 122–23.

44. Archibald MacLeish, "The Librarian and the Democratic Process," May 1940, reprinted in *A Time to Speak*, p. 149.

45. MacLeish, "The Affirmation," p. 8.

46. The triumph of national security liberalism is illustrated by the fact that when I went to the Library of Congress in June 1993 to research MacLeish's official papers as Librarian of Congress (forty-eight years after the conclusion of WWII), numerous documents related to the library's wartime work had been pulled for what were termed national security reasons, some of them as recently as the spring of 1993. The irony would not have been lost on MacLeish.

47. FDR, Executive Order, October 24, 1941, LC Archives, Central Files Unit, Putnam-MacLeish Papers, box 327, folder: Office of Facts and Figures, 1941. MacLeish's contemplation of this appointment is captured in a letter he wrote to Harold Smith, Bureau of the Budget, October 22, 1941, in the same location.

48. Statement by Archibald MacLeish, October 26, 1941. LC Archives, Central Files Unit, Putnam-MacLeish Papers, box 327, folder: Office of Facts and Figures, 1941.

49. Drabeck and Ellis, *Archibald MacLeish*, p. 143.

50. For MacLeish's experience at the OFF and the OWI, see Donaldson, *Archibald MacLeish*, pp. 350–65; see also Allan Winkler, *The Politics of Propaganda: The Office of War Information, 1942–1945* (New Haven: Yale University Press, 1978). The quotations in the text are from Donaldson, p. 351, and Winkler, p. 13.

51. In his interviews with Drabeck and Ellis, MacLeish explained that as director he was the press's main target, and he understood why he would be. He also noted that on the occasions when the OFF's portrayal of the war mobilization was too rosy, the office did get its legitimate comeuppance. He observed: "We had to state the American cause; the American cause was our cause, and by God we weren't ashamed. Fortunately . . . Harry Truman burned our fingers very early. If he'd done it later, I don't think it would have been as effective, but he did it early enough so that we could begin to see that taking a factual matter like the state of American preparedness, which was pretty precarious . . . and printing the good facts and not the bad ones was not a good idea. So we became a great deal more even-handed about that sort of thing. But when it came to the question of what fascism was and what democracy should mean, what the Republic was, what it had been, we never hesitated to take a very strong position—*the* position" (pp. 150–51).

52. LC Archives, Central Files Unit, MacLeish-Evans papers, box 1082, folder: War 7-4, 1942–43. Unless otherwise noted, the remainder of this chapter draws on ma-

terials from two archival sources in the Library of Congress. The first is the MacLeish-Evans Papers, in the Manuscripts Division of the Central Files Unit of the Library of Congress Archives, which will hereafter be designated as M-E Papers in citations, which will also include box and folder references. The other main source is the Library of Congress Gift Funds Files in the Office Systems Services section of the Central Files Unit. These papers will be referred to as the LC Gift Fund Files.

53. See, for instance, Richard Heindel, memorandum to David Mearns, November 29, 1940, M-E Papers, box 399, folder: Acquisitions Foreign—Propaganda, 5-9, 1939–45.

54. See, for instance, a memorandum from Stacy May, director, Bureau of Research and Statistics, to the Advisory Commission to the National Council of Defense, July 6, 1940, M-E Papers, box 1082, folder: WAR 8, 1940–41. See also, in the same folder, May to MacLeish, July 3, 1940. Commission member Stacy May thanked MacLeish for the range of services the LC would make available and said: "I am still rubbing my eyes a bit in wonder at the generosity of your offer."

55. Memorandum from the Documents Division to David Mearns, Reference Department, June 21, 1941, M-E Papers, box 1083, folder: WR HS DOC 3.

56. See, for instance, a memorandum from MacLeish to the Secretary of State, March 7, 1941, requesting copies of all leaflets dropped over Axis countries by the RAF (M-E Papers, box 399, folder: Acquisitions Foreign—Propaganda, 5-9, 1939–45).

57. Jack Wade Dunaway, American Embassy, Office of the Military Attaché, Berlin, letter to MacLeish, April 26, 1941, M-E Papers, box 399, folder: Acquisitions Foreign—Propaganda, 5-9, 1939–45

58. Jack Wade Dunaway, American Embassy, Office of the Military Attaché, Berlin, letter to MacLeish, May 27, 1941, M-E Papers, box 399, folder: Acquisitions Foreign—Propaganda, 5-9, 1939–45

59. Along with materials related to this controversy in the MacLeish-Evans papers, the Justice Department's approach to the problem of unmailable materials can be found in the files of the Special War Policies Unit, RG 60, National Archives and Records Administration, Washington, D.C.

60. Vincent Miles, post office solicitor, to David Mearns, LC Reference Division, March 12, 1941, M-E Papers, box 400, folder: Acquisitions, 5-9-3-2.

61. Julian Boyd to MacLeish, March 29, 1941, M-E Papers, box 400, folder: Acquisitions, 5-9-3-2.

62. MacLeish to Postmaster General Walker, April 1, 1941, M-E Papers, box 400, folder: Acquisitions, 5-9-3-3.

63. Postmaster General Walker to MacLeish, April 7, 1941, M-E Papers, box 400, folder: Acquisitions, 5-9-3-3.

64. Postmaster General Walker to MacLeish, April 16, 1941, M-E Papers, box 400, folder: Acquisitions, 5-9-3-3.

65. MacLeish to Senator Gillette, May 8, 1941, M-E Papers, box 399, folder: Acquisitions Foreign—Propaganda, 5-9, 1941–53.

66. Lawrence M. C. Smith (hereafter L. M. C. Smith) to MacLeish, May 17, 1941, M-E Papers, box 400, folder: Acquisitions, 5-9-3-2.

67. L. M. C. Smith to MacLeish, June 3, 1941, M-E Papers, box 400, folder: Acquisitions, 5-9-3-2.

68. C. J. Lambkin, president of Four Continent Book Corporation, letter to Professor Geroid Tanquary Robinson, Columbia University, July 25, 1941, M-E Papers, box 400, folder: Acquisitions, 5-9-3-2. University of Chicago historian S. N. Harper and Robinson both sent along copies of Lambkin's letter to MacLeish; see, e.g., Geroid Robinson to MacLeish, August 14, 1941, in the same location.

69. MacLeish to L. M. C. Smith, October 9, 1941, National Archives and Records Administration, Main Branch, Washington, D.C., Department of Justice Records, Record Group 60, Special War Policies Unit (hereafter referred to as SWPU Files), box 73, folder: 148-302-2, sec 4, #1. See also MacLeish to Solicitor Miles, October 10, 1941, M-E Papers, box 400, folder: Acquisitions, 5-9-3-3.

70. MacLeish to L. M. C. Smith, October 18, 1941, M-E Papers, box 400, folder: Acquisitions, 5-9-3-3. In similar letters to Attorney General Biddle and Secretary of the Treasury Morgenthau in the same folder, MacLeish continued to rail about the "spectacle" of the government censoring itself; see, e.g., MacLeish to Biddle, October 16, 1941. For the whole chronology from the post office's point of view, see Postmaster General Walker to Biddle, n.d. (between October 10 and 17, 1941), in the same folder.

71. L. M. C. Smith to Solicitor Vincent M. Miles, October 7, 1941, M-E Papers, box 400. folder: Acquisitions, 5-9-3-2.

72. MacLeish to Postmaster General Walker. November 1, 1941, M-E Papers, box 400, folder: Acquisitions, 5-9-3-3.

73. Although he is a bit cloudy on specific details, MacLeish discusses the overall genesis of the Division of Special Information in Drabeck and Ellis, *Archibald MacLeish*, especially pp. 145–55.

74. Berle to MacLeish, June 18, 1941, LC Archives, Central Files Unit, Putnam-MacLeish Papers, box 327, folder: Coordinator of Information, 1941.

75. MacLeish to Donovan, June 29, 1941, M-E Papers, box 748, folder: Division of Special Information, General, 1939–47.

76. MacLeish to Donovan, July 29, 1941, M-E Papers, box 748, folder: Division of Special Information, General, 1941–45.

77. Langer, in fact, headed up the Research and Analysis Branch of the OSS, not the DSI. For an intellectual history of the Research and Analysis Branch, see Barry M. Katz, *Foreign Intelligence: Research and Analysis in the Office of Strategic Services, 1942–1945* (Cambridge: Harvard University Press, 1989); see also Robin Winks, *Cloak and Gown: Scholars in the Secret War, 1939–1961* (New York: Morrow, 1987).

78. MacLeish to Donovan, July 29, 1941, M-E Papers, box 748, folder: Division of Special Information, General, 1941–45; MacLeish to Baxter, August 26, 1941, LC Archives, Central Files Unit, Putnam-MacLeish Papers, box 327, folder: Coordinator of Information, 1941.

79. "Suggested Memorandum Explaining the Part Which the Library of Congress Will Play in Connection with the Office of Coordinator of Defense Information," submitted by Ernest S. Griffith, August 1, 1941, M-E Papers, box 748, folder: Division of Special Information, General, 1939–47.

80. Donovan to MacLeish, July 30, 1941, M-E Papers, box 748, folder: Division of Special Information, General, 1939–47. By October 14, 1941, a partial list of personnel shows that the DSI formed the backbone of the OSS's future Research and Analysis Branch, including the Administrative Section (Ernest Griffith, chief) the British Em-

pire Section (Reed Conyers, chief; Ralph Bunche, James Green, and Kermit Roosevelt Jr. as analysts; Norman Brown as consultant); the Latin American Section (Preston James, chief); the Mediterranean Section (Sherman Kent, chief); the Far Eastern Section (John K. Fairbanks, chief); the Near Eastern Section (Walter Wright, chief); the Central European Section (Walter L. Dorn, chief); the Eastern European Section (Geroid T. Robinson, chief); and the Western European Section (Robert K. Gooch, chief). See Division of Special Information, Staff by Sections, M-E Papers, box 748, folder: Division of Special Information, 5 1941–43.

81. Schedule of Collections, Library of Congress, November 1941, and Coy to Donovan, July 16, 1942, M-E Papers, box 748, folder: Division of Special Information, 6 1941–43.

82. Donovan to MacLeish, December 31, 1942, M-E Papers, box 2009, folder: REF 18-1, 1943–47.

83. MacLeish to Donovan, January 13, 1943, M-E Papers, box 2009, folder: REF 18-1, 1943–47.

84. MacLeish to Donovan, March 3, 1943, M-E Papers, box 2009, folder: REF 18-1, 1943–47. See also the memorandum from William Applebaum, OSS, to Philip O. Keeney, Librarian, OSS, May 8, 1943, in the same location.

85. For several exchanges in which MacLeish was seeking State Department input on Lasswell's project (and materials for the project), see MacLeish to Sumner Welles, October 31, 1940, LC Gift Fund Files, and MacLeish to Welles, November 12, 1940, M-E Papers, box 392, folder: Acquisitions—Foreign Publications—Cooperation with Government-State Department, 5-3-2.

86. Although putatively organized for the purpose of advancing social science methodologies, such as content analysis, Lasswell's original statements about his project's value indicated that he fully intended to merge his work with the nation's war preparation efforts; see Library of Congress Studies of Communication Trends grant report, November 15, 1940, Rockefeller Archive Center (hereafter, RAC), box 239, folder 2852: Library of Congress, Communication Trends, 1940. The findings were also to be published in the *Public Opinion Quarterly*, and it was assumed that a book would result as well, which eventually occurred. Lasswell, Ithiel deSola Pool, Nathan Leites, Raymond Fadner, Joseph Goldsen, and other associates in Lasswell's project produced a series of highly technical papers on their work, some of which were published in Lasswell, et al., *The Language of Politics: Studies in Quantitative Semantics* (1949; rpt., Cambridge, Mass.: MIT Press, 1965).

87. Memorandum by Harold Lasswell, "The Present State of Communications Intelligence," n.d. [1/41], RAC, box 224, folder 2675.

88. Lasswell, memorandum to MacLeish, re Public Opinion and Propaganda Intelligence (prepared in consultation with R. Keith Kane), May 2, 1941. The August 25 memorandum was another version of this same report for MacLeish, in which Lasswell and Kane showed the same structures in place but provided greater details about the materials analyzed within each research project. See memorandum from Lasswell to MacLeish, re Report, August 25, 1941. Both are in Yale University Manuscripts and Archives, Sterling Memorial Library, Harold Dwight Lasswell Papers, Group 1043, box 62, folder 842 (hereafter cited as HDL Papers).

89. MacLeish to Marshall, May 17, 1941, LC Gift Fund Files.

90. As Lasswell noted in a memorandum to MacLeish, "The Department of Justice found that the methods of content and organizational analysis developed in this research were closely related to their own needs" (Lasswell, memorandum to MacLeish, re Report, August 25, 1941, HDL Papers).

91. See John Marshall, interoffice memorandum to David Stevens, January 17, 1941, RAC, box 224, folder 2675. From the foundation officers' perspective, Lasswell's project was so useful that they agreed the foundation should "continue to recommend grants for the work of this project for the duration of the war . . . and for the formulation of its findings after the war" (Grant Report, Library of Congress Studies of Communication Trends, August 1941, RAC, box 239, folder 2852).

92. MacLeish, letter to Biddle, April 2, 1941, M-E Papers, box 404, folder: Acquisitions 6-3-2-2, 1941–50.

93. Smith reminded MacLeish that much of Lasswell's work had been "undertaken as much for the benefit of the Department of Justice as for the special purposes of the project [itself]" (L. M. C. Smith, letter to MacLeish, October 6, 1941, LC Gift Fund Files).

94. Kane, memorandum to T. D. Quinn, Administrative Assistant to the Attorney General, April 14, 1941, re Administration of the Voorhis Act, LC Gift Fund Files. Later, to mollify MacLeish's concerns about the LC's budget, Kane told MacLeish that the Justice Department would try to get the Bureau of the Budget and Congress to provide money for additional personnel (Kane, letter to MacLeish, December 5, 1941, M-E Papers, box 404, folder: Acquisitions 6-3-2, 1941–52).

95. See, e.g., MacLeish to Lasswell, August 8, 1941, LC Gift Fund Files.

96. See Kane to MacLeish, December 5, 1941, M-E Papers, box 404, folder: Acquisitions 6-3-2, 1941–52; see also Kane, memorandum to T. D. Quinn, Administrative Assistant to the Attorney General, April 14, 1941, re Administration of the Voorhis Act, LC Gift Fund Files.

97. See Kane, memorandum to T. D. Quinn, April 14, 1941. Lasswell told MacLeish, "It has been necessary to spend a great deal of time in stimulating the collection of this material," but he was able to do so through the Library of Congress's "cooperative arrangements" with "several official and unofficial agencies" (Lasswell, memorandum to MacLeish, re Report, August 25, 1941, HDL Papers).

98. MacLeish's erstwhile assistant, who left the Special Defense Unit to join him at the OFF, acknowledged Lasswell's valuable work well before the war began. Kane acknowledged Solicitor General Anthony Biddle's part in "accelerating" the unit's intelligence program by "bringing it to the attention of . . . the leading authority in the field . . . Dr. Lasswell," who had put the Nationalities section in contact with other communications specialists. Lasswell, Kane noted, had "generously favored the Section with his advice and encouragement." Likewise, Kane recognized the "enlightened" and critical role MacLeish was playing at the Library of Congress by transforming it "into an instrument of national policy" and noted the "foresight of the Rockefeller Foundation in encouraging investigation in this field before the present crisis began to be acute." Kane even stroked FDR a little for having the "sound judgment" to appoint the "enlightened" MacLeish as Librarian of Congress. See Kane to Biddle, memorandum for the Solicitor General, February 3, 1941, SWPU Files, box 10, folder: Kane, RKK, #1.

99. Lasswell, *Affidavit*, October 23, 1951, HDL Papers.

100. For example, Lasswell's August 1941 memorandum to MacLeish lists the different people who were trained by Lasswell's division for work at the Department of Justice under the "Library of Congress Gift Fund." The list includes over sixty people trained between December 1940 and July 1941. Additionally, in an April 1942 memorandum to Luther Evans, Lasswell noted that his project had hired and trained an entire staff of thirty-nine people taken over by the Justice Department, as well as nine people trained for special research on cases arising under the Voorhis Act Administration; three trained and transferred to the FBMS; thirteen trained for the OFF, and others were trained for the CoI, Office of Price Management, War (both G2 and Military Intelligence), State, Naval Intelligence, Public Health, and the British Information Service. See Lasswell to Evans, April 23, 1942, "Report and Proposal," LC Gift Fund Files.

101. The "Library of Congress Gift Fund" received another $28,000 to carry the project until the following September. Implicitly acknowledging the potential outcry this kind of propaganda-based project would evoke if discovered by an isolationist Congress, Lasswell's grant for 1942 noted: "This study, by its nature, calls for private rather than governmental support." "Consultation with governmental agencies interested in its methods" should continue, but the foundation and the project would not "assume responsibility" for the applications of the project's methods and data (Grant Report, Library of Congress Studies of Communication Trends, August 1941, RAC, box 239, folder 2852).

102. Lasswell, memorandum to MacLeish, re Report, August 25, 1941, HDL Papers; and Lasswell to Evans, "Report and Proposal," April 23, 1942, LC Gift Fund Files. Lasswell develops this theme in Lasswell et al., *The Language of Politics*. Many of the working papers the Experimental Division produced are in Lasswell's papers at Yale University Archives.

103. Evans to David Stevens, June 17, 1943, LC Gift Fund Files.

104. "The grant recommended last May was understood here to be the final grant for the project. At that time we recorded our expectations that by the end of the year it covered, the work of the project would have reached the point where its full absorption by government agencies would be favorable and desirable. This was in accordance with our general practice of making final grants for all projects in the field of research in mass communication, and that practice is still in force" (Marshall to Evans, June 22, 1943, LC Gift Fund Files). The final statement on the RF gift for the Experimental Study of Trends of War Time Communications for September 1, 1941, through August 31, 1942, shows that RF41069 provided $28,800; from September 15, 1942, through December 31, 1943, RF42057 provided $33,000. See memorandum of May 10, 1944, Trust Funds: Gifts, LC Gift Fund Files. In July 1943 Lasswell wrote to MacLeish and Evans to thank them for their support of his work: "I should like first of all to emphasize for the record my vivid appreciation of the whole-hearted cooperation that I have received from the Librarian and from all Library officials and humbler members of the staff. A research project of this character presented a great many administrative problems for which there was no adequate precedent, but matters have been handled with so much good will that routines have functioned with a minimum of vexation" (July 28, 1943, LC Gift Fund Files).

FIVE The Justice Department and the Problem of Propaganda

1. The images suggested here are drawn from *Life* magazine's coverage of the far right in the prewar years. *Life* produced quite a few pieces on the domestic fascists, including "The 'American Nazis' Claim 200,000 Members," March 27, 1937, pp. 20–21; "Headlines Proclaim the Rise of Fascism and Communism in America," July 27, 1937, pp. 19–27; "German-Americans and Italian-Americans Hold a Fascist Rally at Yaphank," September 13, 1937, p. 31; "Nazis Hail George Washington as First Fascist," March 17, 1938, p. 17; "U.S. Veterans Lose Battle With Germans in Manhattan," May 2, 1938, pp. 18–19; "It Can Happen Here," March 6, 1939, pp. 22–23; and "Fascism in America," March 6, 1939, pp. 57–63. For a discussion of *Life*'s treatment, see Brett Gary, " 'The Pitiless Spotlight of Publicity': *Life* Magazine and the WWII-Era Exposure of American Extremists," in Erika Doss, ed., *Looking at LIFE: Framing the American Century in the Pages of LIFE Magazine, 1936–1972* (Washington, D.C.: Smithsonian Institution Press; forthcoming).

2. The bulk of this chapter is drawn from the records of the National Archives and Records Administration, Main Branch, Washington, D.C., Department of Justice Records, Record Group 60, Special War Policies Unit (hereafter referred to as SWPU Files).

3. Quoting Jackson's desire to make the department a "true symbol of Justice," see Lawrence M. C. Smith (hereafter L. M. C. Smith at first citation of a reference; Smith thereafter), "Memorandum for the Attorney General," October 21, 1941, SWPU Files, box 1, folder: Francis Biddle.

4. Historian Leo P. Ribuffo looks at these different groups and attests to Birkhead's importance among antifascist investigators in *The Old Christian Right: The Protestant Far Right from the Great Depression to the Cold War* (Philadelphia: Temple University Press, 1983), where he lays out in general the antifascist organizations and investigations in his "Brown Scare" chapter. See also Clayton Laurie's strong account of the "Brown Scare" anxieties in *Propaganda Warriors: America's Crusade Against Nazi Germany* (Lawrence: University Press of Kansas, 1996), especially the first chapter; and Morris Schonbach, *Native Fascism During the 1930s and 1940s: A Study of Its Roots, Its Growth, and Its Decline* (Ph.D. diss., University of California, 1958; rpt., Los Angeles: University of California Press, 1985).

5. For a sampling of articles from liberal journals of opinion, see note 67 of chapter 2.

6. See "Investigation of Nazi and Other Propaganda," *House Report No. 153*, 74th Cong., 1st sess., February 15, 1935. See also "Foreign Propaganda," *House Report No. 1381*, 75th Cong., 1st sess., July 28, 1937, referring H.R. 1591 to the whole House, 81 *Congressional Record*, 75th Cong., 1st sess., 1937, pts. 1–2, 7774.

7. "Annual Report, Special War Policies Unit," November 30, 1942, SWPU files, box 16, folder: Reports—Annual and Quarterly. SDU personnel were self-consciously aware of the problems in the Justice Department during World War I and repeatedly cited the most influential criticisms, including R. G. Brown et al., "Report Upon the Illegal Practices of the United States Department of Justice," National Popular Government League pamphlet (Washington, D.C.: National Popular Government League, 1920; reprint, New York: Arno, 1969); and especially Zechariah Chafee Jr., *Freedom of Speech* (Cambridge: Harvard University Press, 1920).

8. "Annual Report, Special War Policies Unit."

9. Laurie, *Propaganda Warriors*, pp. 20–21. Numerous memoranda from the records of the Special War Policies Unit provide this interpretation. For a useful overview of the fifth-column thesis abroad and at home, see ibid., pp. 8–23, and Lawrence C. Soley, *Radio Warfare: OSS and CIA Subversive Propaganda* (New York: Praeger, 1989).

10. L. M. C. Smith to Francis Biddle, July 2, 1941, "Report of the Special Defense Unit with Recommendations Concerning the Future Handling of Civil Defense Matters in the Department of Justice," under cover with L. M. C. Smith to Francis Biddle, "Memorandum for the Acting Attorney General," July 2, 1941, SWPU Files, box 15, folder: Policy of Department and Neutrality Unit.

11. Ibid.

12. Memorandum, "Foreign Language Groups in the United States," from the Foreign Language Press section of the Nationalities section, July 1941, SWPU Files, box 14, folder: Nationalities Section—General, #3. By April 1942 that circulation number had shrunk by half, but the unit estimated there were still 1,513 foreign language papers published in the United States, in 39 different languages.

13. Quoted in ibid.

14. Ibid. Twenty-eight of the theaters showed films from Germany; twenty-nine from Hungary; twenty-nine from Spain; thirteen from Russia; and eleven from Italy.

15. Kane, memorandum to L. M. C. Smith, "Radio," November 15, 1940, SWPU Files, box 77, folder: Analysis of Foreign Language Broadcasts.

16. For different statements on the government's efforts to recognize wartime diversity and mollify different groups' grievances, see Patrick Washburn, *A Question of Sedition: The Federal Government's Investigation of the Black Press During World War II* (New York: Oxford University Press, 1986); John Morton Blum, *V Was for Victory: Politics and American Culture During World War II* (New York: Harcourt Brace Jovanovich, 1976); Clayton R. Koppes and Gregory D. Black, *Hollywood Goes to War: How Politics, Profits, and Propaganda Shaped World War II Movies* (New York: Free, 1987); Allan Winkler, *The Politics of Propaganda: The Office of War Information, 1942–1945*, (New Haven: Yale University Press, 1978).

17. See Wayne S. Cole, *America First: The Battle Against Intervention, 1940–41* (1953; reprint, New York: Octagon, 1971), for his discussions of the isolationists.

18. R. Keith Kane, memorandum, "Notes on Propaganda and Freedom of Expression," December 26, 1940, SWPU Files, box 10, folder: RKK, #1.

19. Converse states that Kane was chosen for the position at the recommendation of Lasswell. See Jean Converse, *Survey Research in the United States: Roots and Emergence, 1890–1960* (Berkeley: University of California Press, 1987), p. 172.

20. Kane, memorandum to William Cherin and Lasswell, "Statements for use before Appropriations Committee," June 19, 1942, SWPU Files, box 2, folder: Budget Hearings—WB Cherin.

21. Smith said: "That this is the program for the United States just as it was for the 13 countries already subjucated [*sic*] is indicated by . . . items . . . which have come to our attention during the past year" (Smith to Biddle, "Report of the Special Defense Unit").

22. Smith, "Memorandum for the Attorney General."

23. Jackson's speech was quoted by SDU staff lawyer Joseph Prendergast in a letter to Attorney General Biddle, December 17, 1941, SWPU Files, box 33, folder: 148-106-2 (Prendergast file). Prendergast so admired Jackson's speech that he obtained an autographed copy.

24. L. M. C. Smith, memorandum to Acting Attorney General Biddle, Re: "Dossiers," June 13, 1941, SWPU files, box 16, folder: Reports to the Attorney General on the Work of the Unit.

25. "Neutrality Laws Unit," Department of Justice press release, April 29, 1940, SWPU files, box 26, folder: Press Releases.

26. Unit memoranda indicate that perceptions of civil libertarians' criticisms of WWI were derived primarily from Zechariah Chafee Jr.'s *Freedom of Speech*. See also Abraham Glasser's department memorandum on WWI and the Justice Department (memorandum to L. M. C. Smith, December 6, 1940, "World War Materials," box 10, folder: Kane, RKK, #3). Along with Chafee's studies, the most damning immediate postwar analysis of the Justice Department's failures was R. G. Brown et al., "Report Upon the Illegal Practices of the United States Department of Justice," pamphlet (Washington, D.C.: National Popular Government League, 1920). See also "Charges of Illegal Practices of the Department of Justice," Hearings Before a Subcommittee of the Committee of the Judiciary of the United States Senate, January 19 to March 3, 1921, 66th Cong., 3d sess. [Printed for the use of the Committee on the Judiciary] (Washington, D.C.: U.S. Government Printing Office, 1921).

For an excellent discussion in the recent literature of activities of bureau investigators and departmental lawyers, see Richard Polenberg's *Fighting Faiths: The Abrams Case, The Supreme Court, and Free Speech* (New York: Viking, 1987). Any of the biographies of J. Edgar Hoover treat the WWI period but tend to focus on Hoover's activities in the Anti-Radical Division; see Richard Gid Powers, *Secrecy and Power: The Life of J. Edgar Hoover* (London: Collier Macmillan, 1987); Athan Theoharis and John Stuart Cox, *Boss: J. Edgar Hoover and the Great American Inquisition* (Philadelphia: Temple University Press, 1988). For an overview of the antiradical activities of the era, see Robert K. Murray's *Red Scare* (Minneapolis: University of Minnesota Press, 1955).

27. This is L. M. C. Smith's explanation to acting Attorney General Biddle of Jackson's reasons for creating the unit (Smith to Biddle, Re: "Dossiers").

28. This agenda is described by Jackson in "Neutrality Laws Unit."

29. Ward P. Allen, memorandum to L. M. C. Smith, "The Espionage and Sedition Acts of 1917–1918—Activities of the Department of Justice," November 4, 1940, SWPU Files, box 5, folder: Espionage and Sedition (DoJ 1917 Activities). Congress passed the Espionage Act on June 15, 1917; the 1918 Sedition Act amended the Espionage Act and was in effect from May 1918 until it was repealed in March 1921.

30. Zechariah Chafee Jr., *Free Speech in the United States* (Cambridge: Harvard University Press, 1941; rpt., New York: Atheneum, 1969), p. 50.

31. Ward P. Allen, memorandum to LMCS [L. M. C. Smith], "The Espionage and Sedition Acts of 1917–1918—Activities of the Department of Justice," November 4, 1940, SWPU Files, box 5, folder: Espionage and Sedition (1917 DoJ Activities). Allen argued elsewhere that the department should refuse to sanction the creation of private vigilante organizations, such as the American Protective League, and should attempt to prevent, so far as possible, private individuals and groups from engaging in the detection or extra-

legal suppression of so-called seditious activities (Allen, memorandum to L. M. C. Smith, "Steps to be Taken by the Department with Respect to Seditious Utterances," April 22, 1941, SWPU Files, box 5, folder: Espionage and Sedition).

32. Allen to LMCS, "The Espionage and Sedition Acts of 1917–1918." Allen was also ambivalent about the Espionage and Sedition statutes themselves. The problem was mostly in their use, he argued. He favorably quoted John Lord O'Brian, who said that the problem with the sedition statute was that it "covered all degrees of conduct and speech, serious and trifling alike, and, in the popular mind gave the dignity of treason to what were often neighborhood quarrels or barroom brawls." Chafee's chief complaint, which Allen adopted, was that the Supreme Court handed down too few decisions on these statutes during the war itself and therefore provided too little interpretive guidance for lower courts on their limits.

33. O'Brian, Allen said, "finally came around to the policy of prohibiting the institution of further cases without its prior approval' (ibid.). At least one contemporary analyst of the growth of the state's repressive capacity points to the Justice Department's highly coordinated and centrally organized wartime crackdown and prosecution of the Industrial Workers of the World (I.W.W.) as evidence for the emergence of the modern state. See John Noakes, "Enforcing the Domestic Tranquillity: State Building and the (Federal) Bureau of Investigation, 1908–1924" (Ph.D. diss., University of Pennsylvania, 1993).

34. For a history of the emergence of the modern First Amendment doctrine, see David Rabban, "The Emergence of Modern First Amendment Doctrine," *University of Chicago Law Review* 50, no. 4 (fall 1983): 1207–1351. For other treatments of the emergence of the modern First Amendment doctrine, see Anthony Lewis, *Make No Law: The Sullivan Case and the First Amendment* (New York: Random House, 1991); and Richard Polenberg, *Fighting Faiths*.

35. *Charles T. Schenck v. U.S.*, 249 U.S. 47, 63 Law Ed. 470 (1919), unanimous opinion on conviction under 1917 Espionage Act. This opinion is where the clear and present danger test was first enunciated by Holmes, writing for the majority upholding the conviction. Here the idea of clear and present danger is punitive.

Frohwerk v. U.S., 249 U.S. 204 (1919), unanimous opinion on conviction under 1917 Espionage Act. Again, the clear and present danger language is used in support of conviction.

Debs v. U.S., 249 U.S. 211 (1919), unanimous opinion on conviction under 1918 Sedition statute. Once again the felicitous phrased is used as a "test" by the majority in support of conviction.

Abrams v. U.S., 250 U.S. 616 (1919), split opinion on conviction under 1918 Sedition statute.

36. Rabban, "The Emergence of Modern First Amendment Doctrine," pp. 1283–1303, does an excellent job of showing Chafee's relevance here. Polenberg, *Fighting Faiths*, treats the same episode.

37. See Chafee's critique in *Free Speech in the United States*, pp. 80–82.

38. The literature on the history of the First Amendment is voluminous. I have relied on Zechariah Chafee Jr.'s classic *Free Speech in the United States*; David Rabban, "The Emergence of Modern First Amendment Doctrine"; Paul L. Murphy, *The Meaning of Freedom of Speech: First Amendment Freedoms from Wilson to F.D.R.* (Westport,

Conn.: Greenwood, 1972); and Anthony Lewis, *Make No Law: The Sullivan Case and the First Amendment* (New York: Random House, 1991).

39. Karl Lowenstein, "Legislative Control of Political Extremism in European Democracies," *Columbia Law Review* 38, nos. 4–5 (April–May 1938): 591–622, 725–74. The internal unit debates between Chafee's libertarian interpretation and the "liberty versus license" conception of speech rights is attested to by Morris Schonbach in *Native Fascism During the 1930s and 1940s*; Schonbach interviewed several unit employees in the mid-1950s, and they told him that Chafee's work was extremely influential but that an equally influential argument for a contrary point of view was provided by Karl Lowenstein, who thought the speech-protective version of the clear and present danger test was "conceived under the inspiration of postwar democracy" and was the "residue of a by-gone mentality." The libertarian test was clearly inadequate, he argued, to meet the "superior knowledge of mass psychology possessed by the totalitarians" (quoted on p. 374). My own research found that Lowenstein was cited in virtually every bibliography SDU lawyers compiled.

40. Forest Black, memorandum to Smith, "The 'Clear and Present Danger' Test," June 13, 1940, SWPU Files, box 3, folder: Compiled Memoranda of Law—SWPU—vol. 2.

41. Ward P. Allen, memorandum to R. Keith Kane, "Constitutional Basis for Restrictive Legislation," November 18, 1940, SWPU Files, box 72, folder: 148-302-2, sec. 1, #1; and Ward P. Allen, memorandum to Smith, "The Espionage and Sedition Acts of 1917–1918." Allen noted in the former that although there was significant controversy about how many of the post-Schenck wartime cases relied on the same formulation of clear and present danger, he believed that at least *Frohwerk* and *Debs* reaffirmed the doctrine in its fullest, including the power of Congress to wage war successfully.

42. Allen, "Constitutional limitations upon governmental power of surveillance of mails," January 15, 1941, SWPU Files, box 20, folder: Surveillance and Censorship—Constitutional Limits On; my emphasis.

43. In his earlier memorandum, "Constitutional Basis for Restrictive Legislation," Allen turned to the problem of the postal power and the extent to which congressional authority over the post office and the mails permitted restrictions on the press through denial of access to the mails. In *U.S. ex rel. Milwaukee Social Democratic Publishing Co. v. Burleson*, 255 U.S. 407 (1919), the Court gave the postmaster general authority to revoke second-class mailing privileges. Because this did not entail complete exclusion from the mails, it did not entail censorship, the Court (and Allen) argued. Holmes and Brandeis dissented, calling the decision the "low ebb of defeat" of freedom of the press, but Allen found the opinion consistent with other "liberty v. license" cases that were reinforced by the argument that the government can refuse to "assist in the dissemination of matter condemned by its judgment through Governmental agencies which it controls."

44. Allen, "Constitutional limitations upon governmental power of surveillance of mails."

45. Ward P. Allen, memorandum, "Surveillance and Censorship in Time of War," March 29, 1941, SWPU Files, box 20, folder: Surveillance and Censorship—Constitutional Limits On.

46. Allen, "Constitutional limitations upon governmental power of sur of mails."

47. "Investigation of Nazi and Other Propaganda." Although the committee not believe that the Communist movement in the United States was "sufficient strong numerically" to constitute a "danger to American institutions at the present time," it did warn that "unless checked, such activity will increase in scope and . . . will inevitably constitute a definite menace."

48. Ibid. The committee recommended that Congress "enact a statute requiring all publicity, propaganda, or public-relations agents or other agents or agencies, who represent in this country any foreign government or a foreign political party or foreign industrial or commercial organization, to register with the Secretary of State of the United States."

49. "Foreign Propaganda."

50. The Voorhis Act also required other organizations to register, including those "engaged in 'political activity' and . . . 'civilian military activity' and 'subject to foreign control'; and those whose aim is the establishment, control, conduct, seizure, or overthrow of a government or subdivision thereof by force, violence, military measures, or threat thereof."

51. Black, memoranda to Smith, "Compiled Memoranda of Laws," "The Voorhis Bill," January 24, 1941, SWPU Files, box 3, folder: Compiled Memoranda of Law—SWPU—vol. 2.

52. The unit wanted all authority for the act to be transferred from the State Department to the Justice Department and authored the appropriate amendment. It also wanted labeling requirements applied to all registered propaganda materials. See Smith's testimony in "Hearings before Subcommittee No. 4 of the Committee on the Judiciary, House of Representatives," *House Report No. 24*, 77th Cong., 1st sess., November 28 and December 1, 1941.

53. These entities were expressly identified in the language of the Voorhis Act.

54. As one unit analyst said, Voorhis was "a dead letter" law because it was "so narrowly drawn that membership in practically any organization subject to registration is unlawful and subject to prosecution under the Smith Act. . . . Therefore, the officers of such organizations which are subject to registration under Voorhis Act can lawfully claim privilege against self incrimination and thus refuse to register the organization" (Nesbitt Elmore, memorandum to Norman Altman, "Voorhis Act Revision," February 1, 1943, SWPU Files, box 21, folder: The Voorhis Act).

55. "Special War Policies Unit: Justification of Estimate. Budget Proposal for FY 1943–1944," SWPU Files, box 2, folder: Budget Material.

56. Jesse MacKnight, "Administration of the Voorhis Act," October 1944, SWPU Files, box 21, folder: The Voorhis Act.

57. Smith, "Memorandum for the Attorney General."

58. Milton Katz to Smith, June 17, 1940, SWPU Files, box 16, folder: Propaganda—Legislative; emphasis in original.

59. Allen, memorandum to Smith, "Proposed bill to prevent propaganda which would interfere with the national defense program," February 20, 1941, SWPU Files, box 16, folder: Propaganda—Legislative.

60. F. Pollak and W. Cherin, memorandum to Frank W. Crocker, "A Procedure

outbreak of war. Section 21 of Title 50 provided that "whenever there is a decℓ between the United States and any foreign nation or government, or any invasℓ predatory incursion is perpetrated, attempted, or threatened against the territorℓ the United States by any foreign nation or government, and the President makes puℓ lic proclamation of the event, all natives, citizens, denizens, or subjects of the hostile nation or government, being of the age of 14 years and upward, who shall be within the United States and not actually naturalized, shall be liable to be apprehended, restrained, secured, and removed as alien enemies" ("Master Memorandum," re: "Potential Alien Enemies," July 16, 1941, SWPU Files, box 1, folder: Alien Enemies [Before AECU was organized]).

73. Dewey Balch corroborates these figures in his July 1941 memorandum, noting 18,000 suspects on the list; see "Master Memorandum," re: "Potential Alien Enemies."

74. Church Committee Report, pp. 34–35.

75. Smith said: "Thus, the matter of the treatment of data developed . . . largely is the responsibility of the Department as is also the matter of long-range planning and directives toward the end of making the most effective inroads possible upon organized subversive activities" (Smith to Biddle, "Memorandum for the Acting Attorney General").

76. Ibid.

77. Smith, "Master Memorandum," re: "Potential Alien Enemies."

78. R. M. J. Fellner, memorandum to Ward Allen, "re: Description of the Functions of the Section," January 21, 1942, SWPU Files, box 1, folder: Francis Biddle. Additionally, the department had a variety of areas under surveillance, including military and industrial mobilization centers (where different populations and organizations were analyzed). Areas surrounding military installations were monitored, with regard to assimilation of labor groups, housing, labor, transportation, health, welfare, and recreational opportunities. "Disadvantaged Populations" also were monitored, with concentration on "Negroes" and alien enemies, especially Germans, Italians, and Japanese. In a Lasswellian phrase, department analysts also looked for "conjunctures of insecurity factors," such as the exclusion of particular nationality groups from jobs and the treatment of that exclusion. All manner of propaganda activities, including channels, themes, senders, and recipients were also closely monitored (ibid.).

79. Smith, "Memorandum for the Acting Attorney General."

80. For a discussion of two forms of intelligence, "preventive" and "pure," see Church Committee Report, pp. 21–38.

81. Smith to Biddle, Re: "Dossiers."

82. Church Committee Report, p. 33.

83. Frances MacDonnell discusses the need to attend to the sensibilities of different foreign national groups while rooting out fifth columnists in *Insidious Foes: The Axis Fifth Column and the American Home Front* (New York: Oxford University Press, 1995), especially in ch. 4, "Other Fifth Columns," pp. 73–90.

84. Kane to Cherin and Lasswell, June 19, 1942.

85. Kane, Memorandum for the solicitor general, "On Program for Nationalities Section," December 18, 1940, SWPU Files, box 14, folder: Nationalities Section—Program and Reports. See also Kane memorandum, "Notes on Propaganda and Freedom of Expression."

86. R. M. J. Fellner, memorandum, "Activities of the Organizations and Propaganda Analysis Section, December 7, 1941–December 7, 1942," SWPU Files, box 32, folder: 148-103-6, sec. 1.

87. Franklin S. Pollak, memorandum, "Control of the Foreign Language Press," June 23, 1942, SWPU Files, box 74, folder: 148-303-0, sec. 1, #2.

88. Eugene Roth, memorandum for Mr. Chester T. Lane, "Foreign Language Publications Program," November 24, 1942, SWPU Files, box 7, folder: Foreign Language Press Program—Chester T. Lane.

89. Several scholars make clear the racist basis of the exclusion and internment decisions. See especially Peter Irons, *Justice at War: The Story of the Japanese Internment Cases* (New York: Oxford University Press, 1983); and Roger Daniels, ed., *Concentration Camps: North American Japanese in the United States and Canada During World War II* (Malabar, Calif.: Krieger, 1981). Patrick Washburn, on the other hand, in *A Question of Sedition*, provides a detailed examination of the tactics the Justice Department and other government agencies used to investigate and pressure but not suppress the African-American press during the war.

90. L. M. C. Smith, memorandum to Charles Fahy, Director, War Division, "Status of Sedition Cases—December 7, 1941 to September 30, 1942," October 8, 1942, SWPU Files, box 17, folder: Reports on Sedition.

91. Patrick Washburn, in *A Question of Sedition*, credits Biddle's restraint and his recognition that the symbolic importance of enlisting the black press in the war effort overrode any value that would come from punishing its most ardent critics of the administration and its policies. He argues that Biddle had to win this battle against pressures from the White House, the post office, and the FBI. In *The Old Christian Right*, historian Leo Ribuffo gives Biddle generally high marks for his civil libertarian intentions, basically arguing that Roosevelt forced Biddle into unleashing his department on the seditionists. Two unit officials, L. M. C. Smith and Joseph Prendergast, however, had different estimations of Biddle's leadership on civil liberties issues, especially in the early months of the war; see L. M. C. Smith, memorandum to the attorney general, draft of April 25, 1942, SWPU Files, box 33, folder: 148-106-3, #2; and Joseph Prendergast, letter (of resignation) to the attorney general, December 17, 1941, SWPU Files, box 33, folder 148-106-2, Prendergast file. Similarly, Peter Irons, in *Justice at War*, shows how Biddle capitulated to military and political pressures on the Japanese-American internment questions. Geoffrey Perret too is highly critical of Biddle. See *Days of Sadness, Years of Triumph: The American People, 1939–1945* (1973; reprint, Madison: University of Wisconsin Press, 1985).

SIX Justice at War

1. 7. Definition used by the federal court in *U.S. v. Rush et al.*, "Transcript of Proceedings," vol. 1, *U.S. v. Rush, Weinberg, Liskin*, Criminal Action No. 65,043, SWPU Files, box 15, folder: Post Office Department—Dissemination of Political Propaganda.

2. Francis Biddle, "Report of the Attorney General, War Division," Fiscal Year ending June 1943, Department of Justice Library Files.

3. Lawrence M. C. "Sam" Smith (hereafter L. M. C. Smith at first citation of a reference; Smith thereafter), memorandum for the attorney general, "Plan of Proce-

dure on Newspapers," May 14, 1942, National Archives and Records Administration, Main Branch, Washington, D.C., Department of Justice Records, Record Group 60, Special War Policies Unit (hereafter referred to as SWPU Files), box 33: folder: 148-106-3, #2.

4. Eugene Roth, memorandum for Mr. Chester T. Lane, "Foreign Language Publications Program," November 24, 1942, SWPU Files, box 7: folder: Foreign Language Press Program—Chester T. Lane.

5. Smith, "Plan of Procedure on Newspapers."

6. Roth, "Foreign Language Publications Program." FARA requirements were burdensome. Besides having to label all documents, registration was frequent and lengthy, but only for agents of enemy or neutral countries. (By contrast, registration requirements for agents of the allied governments involved a simplified form of registration, an exemption Roosevelt had demanded before he would sign the amended FARA in 1942.) The average number of people covered by the statements filed by one agent increased from ten in 1943 to sixteen in 1944 ("Annual Report of the War Division," fiscal year 1944, Department of Justice Library files).

7. For a complete roster of the prosecutions under FARA and the Notification Act, see *Report of the Attorney General to the Congress . . . on the Administration of the Foreign Agents Registration Act . . . for the Period from June 28, 1942 to December 31, 1944* (Washington, D.C.: U.S. Government Printing Office, 1945), hereafter cited as *FARA Report.*

8. *FARA Report.*

9. H. D. Lasswell, "Propaganda Detection and the Courts," in H. D. Lasswell, Nathan Leites, and associates *Language of Politics: Studies in Quantitative Semantics* (1949; rpt., Cambridge, Mass.: MIT Press, 1965). Lasswell credits Harold Elsten with making the original connections between social scientists and the Justice Department.

10. Quoted in "Work Performed by the Special Defense Unit in the Foreign Language Press Field in the Administration of the Voorhis Act," January 17, 1942, SWPU Files, box 7, folder: Foreign Language Press—FCC and Radio.

11. Lasswell reproduced the charts and described the tests in "Propaganda Detection and the Courts," pp. 177–208. He also described them in "Communications Research and Politics," in Douglas Waples, ed., *Print, Radio, and Film in a Democracy* (Chicago: University of Chicago Press, 1942), pp. 101–17.

12. Lasswell, "Propaganda Detection and the Courts," pp. 199–208.

13. "Transcript of Proceedings."

14. *FARA Report.* Lasswell provides a brief description in "Propaganda Detection and the Courts," pp. 192–98.

15. *FARA Report.*

16. Lasswell, "Propaganda Detection and the Courts," pp. 192–98.

17. See *FARA Report.*

18. See *Keegan v. U.S.,* 325 U.S. 478.

19. Congress passed the Espionage Act on June 15, 1917, establishing three new offenses when the United States is at war: (1) willfully making false statements with intent to interfere with the operation of the military forces or to promote the success of the enemies of the United States; (2) willfully causing or attempting to cause insubordination, disloyalty, mutiny, or refusal of duty in the military forces; and (3) will-

fully obstructing the recruiting or enlistment service to the injury of the service of the United States. The 1918 Sedition Act amended the Espionage Act, making presumption of intention more adequate as proof, by inserting "attempting to obstruct" into the Espionage provisions.

20. For discussions of the value of Lasswell's strategy, see, for instance, R. Keith Kane, memorandum to Samuel Bisgyer, Frank Crocker, and Raymond Whearty, "Preparation of cases for possible grand jury proceedings and trial," September 16, 1941, SWPU Files, box 21, folder: Voorhis Act—Misc. Correspondence, #2; and Raymond P. Whearty, memorandum to Mr. Franklin S. Pollak, December 2, 1941, in the same locations.

21. The FCC's Foreign Broadcast Intelligence Service and the unit's OPAS section had long identified the predominant themes of the official "Enemy Propaganda Line," and the fourteen themes show up repeatedly in the unit's memoranda. See "Appendix D, Memorandum for the Organization and Propaganda Analysis Section," June 9, 1942, SWPU Files, box 25, folder: Priority Lists—Procedures.

22. The full names of the cases are *United States v. Pelley*, *United States v. Brown*, and *United States v. Fellowship Press, Inc.* My discussion is based on the decision of the Seventh Circuit Court of Appeals, Indianapolis, December 17, 1942, 132 *Fed. 2d* 170. Conviction affirmed. Pelley was sentenced to fifteen years.

23. The quotations are from Pelley's *Galilean*, cited in the decision of the Seventh Circuit Court of Appeals, p. 175.

24. Leo P. Ribuffo, *The Old Christian Right: The Protestant Far Right from the Great Depression to the Cold War* (Philadelphia: Temple University Press, 1983). Ribuffo provides a detailed account of Pelley's career, his ideology, and the sedition trial in ch. 2, pp. 25–79.

25. *United States v. Pelley*, 177.

26. Ibid.

27. The charts are reproduced in Lasswell, "Propaganda Detection and the Courts," pp. 188–93.

28. *United States v. Pelley*, 176.

29. Ibid., p. 177.

30. Ibid., p. 178.

31. *United States v. German-American Vocational League*, 153 F.2d 860, 865 (Circuit Court of Appeals, Third Circuit, decided January 31, 1946).

32. Among the newspapers, pamphlets, and books targeted in the *Winrod* indictments were the *New York Enquirer*, the *Defender*, the *Galilean*, the *Octopus*, *X-Ray*, *Weckruf und Beobachter*, the *Broom*, *The Cross and the Flag*, and many more. The *Winrod* defendants included Gerald B. Winrod, Herman Schwinn, George Sylvester Viereck, William Griffin, Hans Diebel, Howard Victor Broenstrupp, William Dudley Pelley, Prescott Freese Dennett, Elizabeth Dilling, Charles B. Hudson, Elmer J. Garner, James F. Garner, David J. Baxter, Hudson de Priest, William Kulgren, C. Leon de Aryan, Court Asher, Colonel Eugene Nelson Sanctuary, Robert Edward Edmondson, Ellis O. Jones, Robert Noble, James C. True, Edward James Smythe, Oscar Brumback, Ralph Townsend, William Robert Lyman Jr., Donald McDaniel, and Otto Brennerman.

The *McWilliams* defendants included Gerald B. Winrod, Howard Victor Broenstrupp, Joseph E. McWilliams, George E. Deatherage, Edward James Smythe, Ellis O.

Jones, Robert Nobel, Franz K. Ferenz, Lois de Lafayette Washburn, Frank W. Clark, E. J. Parker Sage, William R. Lyman Jr., Garland L. Alderman, Elmer Frederik Elmhurst, Robert E. Edmondson, James True, Charles B. Hudson, Elmer J. Garner, David Baxter, Peter Stahrenberg, Elizabeth Dilling, Lawrence Dennis, Colonel Eugene Nelson Sanctuary, George Sylvester Viereck, Prescott Freese Dennett, Gerhard Wilhelm Kunze, August Klapprott, Herman Max Schwinn, and Hans Diebel.

33. Ribuffo, *The Old Christian Right*, p. 188. Ribuffo discusses the *United States v. Winrod et al.* and the subsequent *United States v. McWilliams* sedition conspiracy trials at length in chapter 5 of *The Old Christian Right*, pp. 178–224. Francis Biddle provides an account as well in *In Brief Authority* (Garden City, N.Y.: Doubleday, 1962), pp. 233–51.

34. Biddle, *In Brief Authority*, p. 238.

35. Memorandum, March 21, 1942, Re: Conference in office of Attorney General, SWPU Files, box 16: folder: Subversives Administration—SWPU.

36. See *United States v. McWilliams et al.*, 163 F.2d 695 (June 30, 1947).

37. Copy of indictment, *United States of America v. Gerald B. Winrod et al.*, in SWPU Files, box 72, folder: 148-301-4, #4.

38. O. John Rogge, "Recommendations and Conclusions from the Report to the Attorney General, September 1946," reprinted in O. John Rogge, *The Official German Report: Nazi Penetration, 1924–1942, Pan-Arabism, 1939–Today* (New York: Thomas Yoseloff, 1961), p. 430. This study relies mainly on Rogge's "Recommendations" for its analysis of his framing of the propaganda-as-sedition argument and is supplemented by Leo Ribuffo's more detailed study of the *McWilliams* trial in *The Old Christian Right*.

39. Ribuffo, *The Old Christian Right*, pp. 188–89.

40. Ribuffo notes that thirty-six years after the trial, Rogge admitted to Ribuffo in an interview that he probably should not have proceeded with an indictment, for lack of evidence (*The Old Christian Right*, p. 195).

41. For a persuasive discussion of the legal obstacles to a successful prosecution, see Rogge's September 1946 "Recommendations." For a solid historical assessment of various factors that made a guilty verdict difficult to achieve, see Ribuffo, *The Old Christian Right*, esp. pp. 214–15.

42. Draft indictment, "United States v. John Doe (Grand Jury)," June 17, 1942, SWPU Files, box 33, folder: 148-106-3; Rogge, "Recommendations," p. 415; Wendell Berge, press release, July 23, 1942, SWPU Files, box 72, folder 148–301-4, #1.

43. Sedition Section memorandum, "In Combat Against Enemy Propaganda," June 9, 1942, SWPU Files, box 25, folder: Priority Lists—Procedures. Those named in this document as the producers of the "scurrilous publications" included, among others, Gerald B. Winrod, George Sylvester Viereck, William Dudley Pelley, Elizabeth Dilling, Charles B. Hudson, Court Asher, Eugene Nelson Sanctuary, Robert Edward Edmondson, Ellis O. Jones, Robert Noble, and James C. True. Most were defendants in both the *Winrod* and the *McWilliams* cases (some were also prosecuted in individual sedition cases).

44. Rogge, "Recommendations," pp. 407–48, esp. pp. 417–18.

45. Memorandum to the attorney general, "United States v. John Doe (Grand Jury)," June 17, 1942, SWPU Files, box 33, folder: 148-106-3, #2.

46. Memorandum to the attorney general, "United States v. John Doe (Grand Jury)."

47. To prove the existence of the worldwide Nazi movement, Rogge submitted histories of Germany, Nazi newspapers, speeches by Hitler and his subordinates, copies of *Mein Kampf,* and a swastika-bearing flag. Defense attorneys "objected to everything" as prejudicial, but Judge Eicher admitted the evidence "provisionally," expecting Rogge to "connect [it] up" (Ribuffo, *The Old Christian Right*, p. 202).

48. The memoranda outlining the "new standard" of sedition included L. M. C. Smith, memorandum to Alexander Holtzoff, "H.R. 6340, the proposed re-enactment of the so-called Sedition Amendment to the Espionage Act of June 15, 1917," March 19, 1942; and Eugene Roth, memorandum to L. M. C. Smith, "Sedition," September 9, 1942, both in SWPU Files, box 17, folder: Reports—LMCS—(Sedition Section). Three memoranda from the unit's lawyers to the OPAS analysts included "Procedural Instructions for the Preparation of Priorities Lists Under Subversive Activities Administration"; "In Combat Against Enemy Propaganda"; and "Appendix D, Memorandum for the Organization and Propaganda Analysis Section," all dated June 9, 1942, and found under cover of "Memorandum for Attorneys and Analysts, Special War Policies Unit, War Division," October 15, 1942, SWPU Files, box 25, folder: Priority Lists—Procedures.

49. Sedition Section memorandum, "In Combat Against Enemy Propaganda."

50. Ibid.

51. "Appendix D."

52. Roth, memorandum to Smith, "Sedition"; my emphasis.

53. Besides providing the full theoretical justification and evidentiary support for the indictment and trial in the *McWilliams* case, Rogge's September 1946 report also recommended to the attorney general that, despite the fact that the defendants had been and still were dangerous members of the international Nazi conspiracy, recent Supreme Court decisions led him to the conclusion that the state should abandon its case against the defendants.

54. Ribuffo, *The Old Christian Right*, p. 194.

55. L. M. C. Smith, memorandum to the attorney general, draft of April 25, 1942, SWPU Files, box 33, folder: 148-106-3, #2.

56. See, for instance, the work of the Organizations and Propaganda Analysis Section in the report "Nazi Propaganda Warfare," prepared by Wm. B. Cherin, OPAS/SWPU, February 25, 1943, SWPU Files, box 25, folder: Nazi Propaganda Warfare.

57. Jesse MacKnight, memorandum to LMCS [Smith], "Assistance to William Powers Maloney on the conspiracy indictment," August 22, 1942, SWPU Files, box 26, folder: U.S. v. Winrod.

58. Eugene Roth, Memorandum for LMCS, "U.S. Against Winrod et al. (D.C. Blanket Indictment)," November 24, 1942, SWPU Files, box 26, folder: U.S. v. Winrod.

59. Roth, memorandum to LMCS, December 15, 1942, SWPU Files, box 26, folder: U.S. v. Winrod.

60. Morris Janowitz, memorandum to Jesse MacKnight, "Status of Work Done on Publications Named in the District of Columbia Grand Jury Conspiracy Indictment," October 29, 1942, SWPU Files, box 26, folder: U.S. v. Winrod.

61. Morris Janowitz and Homer Caulkin, memorandum, "Interpretation of the

Propaganda Inter-connection of Individuals Named in the U.S. v. Winrod et al.,"
February 10, 1943, SWPU Files, box 26, folder: U.S. v. Winrod. Smythe, Broenstrupp,
Hudson, Kullgren, Sanctuary, and Jones published frequently in E. J. Garner's *Publicity*, reprinted one another's pieces in their own publications, mutually endorsed
each other, and provided advertising space to one another. Collaboration was less
probable but some evidence existed to connect Brennerman, Winrod, Dilling, Pelley,
Baxter, DeAryan, Griffin, Edmondson, and True. Connections were only indirect and
did not indicate collaboration with Asher, Brumback, Townsend, Dennett, Noble,
and DePriest. And no interconnections could be found to connect Deibel, Lyman,
McDaniel, Schwinn, and Viereck to the rest of the defendants.

Janowitz and Caulkin reported that data pointing to interconnections fell into
seven major types, listed according to decreasing significance: reports of joint meetings, plans, or activities; appeals for funds for one another; endorsements for one another; citing each other or one another's publications as propaganda outlets; printing
news of one another's publications or other activities; advertisements of one another's
publications, etc.; and reprints from one another's writings.

62. George Roudebush, interoffice memorandum to LMCS, July 17, 1943, SWPU
Files, box 26, folder: U.S. v. Winrod.

63. Ribuffo, *The Old Christian Right*, p. 196.

64. See, for instance, David Ogle and Morris Janowitz, memorandum to Chester T.
Lane, Asst. Chief SWPU, "Work Completed on U.S. v. Winrod et al. indictment. Outline of Additional sources," April 17, 1943, SWPU Files, box 26, folder: U.S. v. Winrod.

65. George Roudebush, interoffice memorandum for Chester T. Lane, May 26,
1943, SWPU Files, box 26, folder: U.S. v. Winrod.

66. George Roudebush, memorandum to LMCS, May 28, 1943, SWPU Files, box
26, folder: U.S. v. Winrod.

67. George Roudebush, chief, Sedition Section, memorandum to LMCS, "Program for Sedition Section for Six Month Period Beginning April 1, 1943," June 9, 1943,
SWPU Files, box 37, folder: 148-103-9.

68. Some of the defendants' agency and financial relationships were stipulated in
close detail. George Sylvester Viereck, for example, had connections with many of the
official Nazi agencies, according to Rogge, and "from the fall of 1939 until the summer of 1941, Viereck received from the Nazis for propaganda purposes approximately
$350,000." Others, such as Pelley, Deatherage, Smythe, Noble, Dilling, True, and
Dennis were said to "have connections," which were identified but not stipulated in
close detail. Rogge basically listed the Nazi organizations and individuals with whom
the defendants might be involved if engaged in seditious activity and then asserted
that a handful of the defendants "had connections" with the following: Hitler, Goebbels, Alfred Rosenberg, Ernest Wilhelm Bohle (head of the Foreign Organization of
the Nazi Party), Julius Streicher (editor of *Der Stuermer*), Hans Heinrich Dieckhoff
(formerly German ambassador to the United States), Heribert von Strempel (a secretary at the German embassy), Ulrich von Gienanth (also a secretary at German embassy and head of Gestapo in the United States), Manfred Zapp (head of the Transocean News Service), and such entities as the Nazi Party, the Foreign Organization of
the Nazi Party, the Nazi Propaganda Ministry, the Foreign Office of the German
Reich, World Service, the Transocean News Service, the Amerika Institut, the German

embassy in Washington, D.C., German consulates in the United States, and the German Library of Information. See Rogge, "Recommendations," p. 428.

69. Ribuffo, *The Old Christian Right*, p. 196.

70. Rogge elaborated on this claim of protecting speech rights: "In order to make certain that we protected the right of freedom of speech to the fullest extent possible; in order to be on the safe side in seeing to it that sincere Americans received their full measure of freedom of speech; in order to be sure that anyone accused had the evil intent which the statute required, we devised a safeguard of our own; we considered evidence only on those persons who had Nazi connections. This safeguard is not to be found in the statute. We employed it in order to give as wide a scope as possible to freedom of speech. We employed it in order to avoid even the slightest risk of proceeding against sincere Americans" ("Recommendations," p. 430).

71. Roudebush, interoffice memorandum to LMCS, July 17, 1943.

72. Ibid.

73. Jesse MacKnight, interoffice memorandum to Chester T. Lane and George Roudebush, July 19, 1943, SWPU Files, box 26, folder: U.S. v. Winrod.

74. MacKnight, memorandum to Rogge, "Propaganda and public relations aspects of U.S. vs. Winrod et al. case," July 20, 1943, SWPU Files, box 26, folder: U.S. v. Winrod.

75. Ribuffo, *The Old Christian Right*, pp. 198–212.

76. See, for instance, unsigned "Notes" to "The Sedition Trial: A Study in Delay and Obstruction," *University of Chicago Law Review* 15 (spring 1948): pp. 691–715.

77. Rogge, "Recommendations," p. 408. Rogge's "Recommendations" reproduce the text of his February 1946 memorandum outlining why the government should *nolle prosequi* the case. The memorandum goes on, however, to outline in great detail the extant nature of the Nazi propaganda threat.

78. Ribuffo, *The Old Christian Right*, p. 212.

79. Justice Murphey, at p. 689, *Hartzel v. U.S.*, 322, quoted in Rogge, "Recommendations," p. 431.

80. Ribuffo, *The Old Christian Right*, p. 212.

81. Rogge, "Recommendations," p. 432.

EPILOGUE

1. For representative U.S. versions of the mass culture critique, see Dwight MacDonald's essays, including "A Theory of Popular Culture," first published in *Politics* (1944), and "MassCult and Midcult," a revised version of "A Theory of Popular Culture," (1962), in *Against the American Grain* (New York: Random House, 1963), pp. 3–78; and Bernard Rosenberg, "Mass Culture in America," in Bernard Rosenberg and David Manning White, eds., *Mass Culture: The Popular Arts in America* (New York: Free, 1957), pp. 3–12. Also in *Mass Culture*, see Leo Lowenthal, "Historical Perspectives of Popular Culture," pp. 46–58; and Gilbert Seldes, "The People and the Arts," pp. 74–97. Social scientists defended the U.S. public against the mass culture critique in the "End of Ideology" thesis. See Daniel Bell, *The End of Ideology: On the Exhaustion of Political Ideas in the Fifties* (New York: Free, 1960); and Edward Shils, "The End of Ideology?" (1955), in Chaim Waxman, ed., *The End of Ideology Debate* (New York: Simon and Schuster, 1968), pp. 49–63. For an excellent overview of the social scientist posi-

tion, see Leon Bramson, *The Political Context of Sociology* (Princeton: Princeton University Press, 1961). Recently, communications historians have revisited this terrain, criticizing the social scientists for their theoretical weaknesses and ideological certainties. See James Curran, Michael Gurevitch, and Janet Woollacott, "The Study of the Media: Theoretical Approaches," in Michael Gurevitch et al., eds., *Culture, Society, and the Media* (London: Methuen, 1982), pp. 11–29; Stuart Hall, "The Rediscovery of 'Ideology': Return of the Repressed in Media Studies," in Gurevitch et al., *Culture, Society, and the Media*, pp. 56–90; and Elihu Katz, "Communication Research since Lazarsfeld," *Public Opinion Quarterly* 51 (1989): 525–45. Christopher Simpson provides a compelling critique of social scientists as cold warriors in *The Science of Coercion: Communication Research and Psychological Warfare, 1945–1960* (New York: Oxford University Press, 1994).

2. For a full discussion of postwar psychological warfare, see Nancy E. Bernhard, *U.S. Television News and Cold War Propaganda, 1947–1960* (New York: Cambridge University Press, 1999); see also Nancy E. Bernhard, "Clearer than Truth: Public Affairs Television and the State Department's Domestic Information Campaigns, 1947–1952," *Diplomatic History* 21, no. 4 (fall 1997): 545–67.

3. See Richard Pells, *The Liberal Mind in a Conservative Age* (New York: Harper and Row, 1985), especially chs. 3–4, on the idea of intellectuals promoting the United States as a normative concept and feeling the need to promote the cold war as a moral battle; see also Arthur Schlesinger Jr., "National Interests and Moral Absolutes," in *The Cycles of American History* (Boston: Houghton Mifflin, 1986), pp. 69–86.

4. Steven M. Gillon, *Politics and Vision: The ADA and American Liberalism, 1947–1985* (New York: Oxford University Press, 1987); Thomas Paterson, *Meeting the Communist Threat: From Truman to Reagan* (New York: Oxford University Press, 1988).

5. C. D. Jackson, quoted in Bernhard, "Clearer than Truth," p. 566.

6. See Simpson, *The Science of Coercion*.

7. The literature on J. Edgar Hoover's FBI is extensive. See Richard Gid Powers, *Secrecy and Power: The Life of J. Edgar Hoover* (London: Collier Macmillan, 1987); Athan Theoharis and John Stuart Cox, *Boss: J. Edgar Hoover and the Great American Inquisition* (Philadelphia: Temple University Press, 1988).

8. Quoted in Peter L. Steinberg, *The Great "Red Menace": United States Prosecution of American Communists, 1947–1952* (Westport, Conn.: Greenwood, 1984), p. 197.

9. Hand's "Opinion for the Court of Appeals for the Second Circuit" in the case of *United States v. Dennis et al.* (August 1, 1950), quoted in Peter L. Steinberg, *The Great "Red Menace,"* p. 198.

10. "Brief for the United States" in the Supreme Court of the United States (October Term, 1950) in the case of *Dennis et al. v. United States*, 342 U.S. 494 (1951), p. 160, quoted in Steinberg, *The Great "Red Menace,"* p. 207.

11. Ibid.

12. Colonel M. J. Fitzgerald, Office of the Provost Marshal General, to Lasswell, August 29, 1951, Yale University, Sterling Memorial Library, Yale University Manuscripts and Archives, Manuscript Record Group 1043, Harold Lasswell Papers, box 213, folder 14.

13. Lasswell, letter to Army-Navy-Air Force Personnel Security Board, October 23, 1951, Harold Lasswell Papers, box 213, folder 14.

SELECTED BIBLIOGRAPHY

Bell, Daniel. *The End of Ideology: On the Exhaustion of Political Ideas in the Fifties*. New York: Free Press, 1960.

Bernays, E. L. *Crystallizing Public Opinion*. New York: Boni Liveright, 1923.

Bernays, E. L. *Propaganda*. New York: Horace Liveright, 1928.

Bernhard, Nancy E. *U.S. Television News and Cold War Propaganda, 1947–1960*. New York: Cambridge University Press, 1999.

Blum, John Morton. *V was for Victory: Politics and American Culture During World War II*. New York: Harcourt, Brace, 1976.

Blum, John Morton. *Liberty, Justice, Order: Essays on Past Politics*. New York: Norton, 1993.

Bramson, Leon. *The Political Context of Sociology*. Princeton: Princeton University Press, 1961.

Brantlinger, Patrick. *Bread and Circuses: Theories of Mass Culture as Social Decay*. Ithaca: Cornell University Press, 1983.

Brinkley, Alan. *The End of Reform: New Deal Liberalism in Recession and War*. New York: Knopf, 1995.

Brinkley, Alan. *Voices of Protest: Huey Long, Father Coughlin, and the Great Depression*. New York: Vintage, 1983.

Buitenhaus, Peter. *The Great War of Words: British, American, and Canadian Propaganda and Fiction, 1914–1933*. Vancouver: University of British Columbia Press, 1987.

Carey, James W. *Communication as Culture: Essays on Media and Society*. Boston: Unwin Hyman, 1989.

Chafee, Zechariah Jr. *Free Speech in the United States*. Cambridge: Harvard University Press, 1941; rpt. New York: Atheneum, 1969.

Chase, Stuart. *The Tyranny of Words*. New York: Harcourt, Brace, 1938.

Childs, Harwood, ed. *Propaganda and Dictatorship: A Collection of Papers*. Princeton: Princeton University Press, 1936.

Converse, Jean. *Survey Research in the United States: Roots and Emergence 1890–1960*. Berkeley: University of California Press, 1987.

Creel, George. *How We Advertised America*. New York: Harper, 1920.

Crick, Bernard. *The American Science of Politics: Its Origins and Conditions*. 1959; rpt., Berkeley: University of California Press, 1967.

Czitrom, Daniel. *Media and the American Mind: From Morse to McLuhan*. Chapel Hill: University of North Carolina Press, 1982.

Dawley, Alan. *Struggles for Justice: Social Responsibility and the Liberal State*. Cambridge: Harvard University Press, Belknap, 1991)

Dewey, John. *The Public and Its Problems: An Essay in Political Inquiry.* 1927; rpt. Chicago: Gateway, 1946 edition.

Donaldson, Scott L. *Archibald MacLeish: An American Life.* Boston: Houghton Mifflin, 1992.

Drabeck, Bernard A. and Helen E. Ellis, eds. *Archibald MacLeish: Reflections.* Amherst, Mass.: University of Massachusetts Press,1986.

Ellul, Jacques. *Propaganda: The Formation of Men's Attitudes.* New York: Knopf, 1965; rpt., Vintage: 1973.

Ewen, Stuart. *PR! A Social History of Spin.* New York: Basic, 1996.

Fraser, Steve and Gary Gerstle. *The Rise and Fall of the New Deal Order, 1930–1980.* Princeton: Princeton University Press, 1989.

Gillon, Steven M. *Politics and Vision: The ADA and American Liberalism, 1947–1985.* New York: Oxford University Press, 1987.

Giner, Salvador. *Mass Society.* New York: Academic, 1967.

Gruber, Carol. *Mars and Minerva: World War I and the Uses of Higher Learning in America.* Baton Rouge: Louisiana State University Press, 1975.

Gurevitch, Michael, Tony Bennett, James Curran, and Janet Woollacott, eds. *Culture, Society, and the Media.* London: Methuen, 1982.

Hayakawa, H. I. *Language in Action: A Guide to Acccurate Thinking, Reading, and Writing.* New York: Harcourt, Brace, 1941.

Herman, Ellen. *The Romance of American Psychology: Political Culture in the Age of Experts.* Berkeley: University of California Press, 1996.

Irons, Peter. *Justice at War: The Story of the Japanese Internment Cases.* New York: Oxford University Press, 1983.

Jordan, John M. *Machine-Age Ideology: Social Engineering and American Liberalism, 1911–1939.* Chapel Hill: University of North Carolina Press, 1994.

Jowett, Garth and Victorian O'Donnell. *Propaganda and Persuasion,* 2d ed. Newbury Park, Calif: Sage, 1992.

Katz, Barry M. *Foreign Intelligence: Research and Analysis in the Office of Strategic Services, 1942–1945.* Cambridge: Harvard University Press, 1989.

Kennedy, David M. *Over Here: The First World War and American Society.* New York: Oxford University Press, 1980.

Koppes, Clayton R. and Gregory D. Black. *Hollywood Goes to War: How Politics, Profits & Propaganda Shaped World War II Movies.* New York: Free, 1987.

Kracauer, Siegfried. *From Caligari to Hitler: A Psychological History of the German Film.* Princeton: Princeton University Press, 1946.

Kris, Ernst and Hans Speier. *German Radio Propaganda.* London: Oxford University Press, 1944.

Lasswell, Harold D. *Propaganda Technique in the World War.* 1927; rpt., Cambridge, Mass.: MIT Press, 1971.

Lasswell, Harold D. *Psychopathology and Politics.* Chicago: University of Chicago Press, 1930., reprinted in *The Political Writings of Harold D. Lasswell.* Glencoe, Ill.: Free Press, 1951.

Lasswell, Harold D. *World Politics and Personal Insecurity.* New York: McGraw-Hill; London: Whittlesey House, 1935.

Lasswell, Harold D. *Politics: Who Gets What, When, How*. New York: McGraw-Hill; London: Whittlesey House, 1936; reprinted in *The Political Writings of Harold D. Lasswell*. Glencoe, Ill.: Free Press, 1951.

Lasswell, Harold D. *Democracy Through Public Opinion,*. Menasha, Wisc: Banta, 1941.

Lasswell, Harold D. and Dorothy Blumenstock. *World Revolutionary Propaganda: A Chicago Study*. New York: Knopf, 1939.

Lasswell, Harold D., Ralph Casey, and Bruce Lannes Smith, eds. *Propaganda and Promotional Activities: An Annotated Bibliography*. Minneapolis: University of Minnesota Press, 1935.

Lasswell, Harold D., Nathan Leites, Ithiel deSola Pool, et al. *The Language of Politics: Studies in Quantitative Semantics*. 1949; rpt., Cambridge, Mass.: MIT Press, 1965.

Laurie, Clayton D. *The Propaganda Warriors: America's Crusade Against Nazi Germany*. Lawrence: University of Kansas Press, 1996.

Lavine, Harold and Violet Edwards. *Propaganda Analysis: A Bulletin to Help the Intelligent Citizen Detect and Analyze Propaganda*, vols. 1–4. New York: Institute for Propaganda Analysis, 1938–1941.

Lewis, Anthony. *Make No Law: The Sullivan Case and the First Amendment*. New York: Random House, 1991.

Lippmann, Walter. *Public Opinion*. 1922; rpt., New York: Free Press, 1960.

Lippmann, Walter. *The Phantom Public*. New York: Harcourt, Brace, 1925.

Lippmann, Walter. *Drift and Mastery: An Attempt to Diagnose the Current Unrest*. 1914; rpt., Englewood Cliffs, N.J.: Prentice-Hall, 1961.

Lowery, Shearon and Melvin L. DeFleur. *Milestones in Mass Communications Research: Media Effects*, 2d ed.. New York: Longman, 1988.

Lumley, Frederick. *The Propaganda Menace*. New York: Century, 1933.

MacDonald, Dwight. *Against the American Grain*. New York: Random House, 1963.

MacDonnell, Frances. *Insidious Foes: The Axis Fifth Column and the American Home Front*. New York: Oxford University Press, 1995.

MacLeish, Archibald. *The Fall of the City*. New York: Farrar and Rinehart, 1937.

MacLeish, Archibald. *Air Raid*. New York: Harcourt Brace, 1938.

MacLeish, Archibald. *The Land of the Free*. Harcourt Brace, 1938.

MacLeish, Archibald. *A Time to Speak: The Selected Prose of Archibald MacLeish*. Boston: Houghton Mifflin, 1940.

MacLeish, Archibald. *The Irresponsibles*. New York: Duell, Sloan, and Pearce, 1940.

Marks, Barry Alan. "The Idea of Propaganda in America." Ph.D. dissertation, University of Minnesota, 1957.

Marvick, Dwaine. *Harold Lasswell on Political Sociology*. Chicago: University of Chicago Press, 1977.

Murray, Robert K. *Red Scare: A Study in National Hysteria, 1919–1920*. Minneapolis: University of Minnesota Press, 1955.

Muth, Rodney, Mary M. Finley, and Marcia F. Muth, eds. *Harold D. Lasswell: An Annotated Bibliography* . New Haven: Yale University Press, 1990.

Novick, Peter. *That Noble Dream: The 'Objectivity Question' and the American Historical Profession*. Cambridge: Cambridge University Press, 1988.

Ogden, C. K. and I. A. Richards. *The Meaning of Meaning: A Study of the Influence of*

Language Upon Thought and of the Science of Symbolism. 1923; 5th ed. New York: Harcourt, Brace, 1935.

Pells, Richard H. *Radical Visions and American Dreams: Culture and Social Thought in the Depression Years.* Middletown, Conn.: Wesleyan University Press, 1973.

Pells, Richard H. *The Liberal Mind in a Conservative Age: American Intellectuals in the 1940s and 1950s.* New York: Harper and Row, 1985.

Polenberg, Richard. *Fighting Faiths: The Abrams Case, the Supreme Court, and Free Speech.* New York: Viking, 1987.

Powers, Richard Gid. *Secrecy and Power: The Life of J. Edgar Hoover.* London: Collier Macmillan, 1987.

Purcell, Edward A. Jr. *The Crisis in Democratic Theory: Scientific Naturalism and the Problem of Value.* Lexington: University of Kentucky Press, 1973.

Qualter, Terence. *Opinion Control in the Democracies.* New York: St. Martin's, 1985.

Ribuffo, Leo. *The Old Christian Right: The Protestant Far Right from the Great Depression to the Cold War.* Philadelphia: Temple University Press, 1983.

Rogers, Everett. *A History of Communications Study.* New York: Free Press, 1994.

Rogers, Everett and Francis Balle, eds. *The Media Revolution in America and in Western Europe,.* Norwood, N.J.: Ablex, 1985.

Rogge, O. John. *The Official German Report: Nazi Penetration, 1924–1942, Pan-Arabism 1939-Today.* New York: Thomas Yoseloff, 1961.

Rogow, Arnold, ed. *Politics, Personality, and Social Science in the Twentieth Century: Essays in Honor of Harold D. Lasswell.* Chicago: University of Chicago Press, 1969.

Rosenberg, Bernard and David Manning White, eds. *Mass Culture: The Popular Arts in America.* New York: Free Press, 1957.

Rutkoff, Peter M. and William B. Scott. *New School: A History of the New School for Social Research.* London: Collier Macmillan, 1986.

Schlesinger, Arthur Jr. *The Vital Center: The Politics of Freedom.* Boston: Houghton Mifflin, 1949.

Schudson, Michael. *Discovering the News: A Social History of American Newspapers.* New York: Basic, 1978.

Schulman, Holly Cowan. *Voice of America: Propaganda and Democracy, 1941–1945.* Madison: University of Wisconsin Press, 1990.

Schonbach, Morris. *Native Fascism During the 1930s and 1940s: A Study of Its Roots, Its Growth, and Its Decline.* Ph.D. diss., University of California, 1958; rpt., Los Angeles: University of California Press, 1985.

Simpson, Christopher. *Science of Coercion: Communication Research and Psychological Warfare, 1945–1960.* New York: Oxford University Press, 1994.

Smith, Bruce Lannes, Harold D. Lasswell, and Ralph Casey, eds. *Propaganda, Communications, and Public Opinion.* Princeton: Princeton University Press, 1946.

Smith, Mark C. *Social Science in the Crucible: The American Debate Over Objectivity and Purpose, 1918–1941.* Durham: Duke University Press, 1994.

Speier, Hans. *The Truth in Hell and Other Essays on Politics and Culture, 1935–1987.* New York: Oxford University Press, 1989.

Sproule, J. Michael. *Propaganda and Democracy: The American Experience of Media and Mass Persuasion.* Cambridge: Cambridge University Press, 1997.

Steel, Ronald. *Walter Lippmann and the American Century.* Boston: Little, Brown, 1980.

Steinberg, Peter L. *The Great "Red Menace": United States Prosecution of American Communists, 1947–1952.* Westport, Conn.: Greenwood, 1984.

Theoharis, Athan and John Stuart Cox. *Boss: J.Edgar Hoover and the Great American Inquisition.* Philadelphia: Temple University Press, 1988.

Vaughn, Steven. *Holding Fast the Inner Lines: Democracy, Nationalism, and the Committee on Public Information.* Chapel Hill: University of North Carolina Press, 1982.

Washburn, Patrick. *A Question of Sedition: The Federal Government's Investigation of the Black Press During World War II.* New York: Oxford University Press, 1986.

Waxman, Chaim, ed. *The End of Ideology Debate.* New York: Simon and Schuster, 1968.

Westbrook, Robert B. *John Dewey and American Democracy.* Ithaca: Cornell University Press, 1991.

Winkler, Allan. *The Politics of Propaganda: The Office of War Information, 1942–1945.* New Haven: Yale University Press, 1978.

Winks, Robin. *Cloak and Gown: Scholars in the Secret War, 1939–1961.* New York: Morrow, 1987.

Zinn, Howard. *A People's History of the United States.* New York: Harper and Row, 1980.

INDEX

Holmes-Brandeis "clear and present danger" test, 13, 47–48, 142, 187, 188–90, 226; marketplace of ideas metaphor, 193, 197–99; Modern doctrine (Rabban), 176, 189; propaganda as evidence of clear and present danger, 208; usefulness of bad tendency test, 208, 240–41, 247; weakening of clear and present danger test's protective features, 225–26; WWI cases, 50–53, 184, 188–89; *see also Abrams v. U.S.; Schenck v. U.S.; Debs v. U.S.; Frowerk v. U.S.; U.S. v. Dennis*
Ford, Ford Madox, 147
Ford, Guy Stanton, 165
Foreign Agents Registration Act (FARA), 9–10, 13, 48, 82, 141, 157–58, 192–94, 201, 206–7, 210–11, 245; criticism of, 162; definitions accepted in federal courts, 214; definition of propaganda under, 208; Lasswell's testimony in trials, 82, 171, 212–15, 297*n*; organizations targeted by, 194–96, 212–15; origins of, 194–96; registrations under, 210–11; scope of, 215–16; trials 161, 211–16, 297*n*; uses of, by Special Defense Unit, 196–99
Foreign Broadcast Monitoring Service (FBMS), 120–22
Foreign Language Press, extent of, 179–80; symbolic importance of for Special Defense Unit, 181
Four Continent Books, *see Bookniga*
Fox, Richard W., 100, 272*n*
Frankfurter, Felix, 22, 136
Free, Lloyd, 94, 101
Freund, Ernst, 22
Friends of Democracy, Inc., 79–80, 221; *see also* Antifascist organizations
Fromm, Erich, 70
Frowerk v. U.S., 23, 188, 291*n*

G
Garner, E. J., 210
German-American organizations, 79, 179–80; German-American Bundists,

79–81; German-American Vocational League, 220; images of, 175; targetted by FARA, 194–96, 214–15; *see also U.S. v. Hartzel; U.S. v. Keegan*
German (Nazi) Propaganda Organizations, international, 79–81; Nazi doctrine on propaganda, 78, 81; U.S. fears of Nazi uses, 4–6, 40, 76–82, 181, 207; worldwide organization, 175, 207–8; German National Railway, 79; German Tourist Information Bureau, 79; German Library of Information, Inc., 79; *see also* FARA, organizations targeted by; FARA trials
Gerstle, Gary, 5, 255*n*
Gilbert, James, 279*n*
Gillette, Guy, 159
Gillon, Steven M., 255*n*, 303*n*
Giner, Salvador, 254*n*
Goebbels, Joseph, 42, 104, 224; *see also* German (Nazi) Propaganda Organizations, international
Gorer, Geoffrey, 87, 94, 99, 101, 111; *see also* Rockefeller Foundation Communication Group
Gosnell, Harold, 72
Grattan, Harley, 22
Graves, Harold, 89, 122
Gregory, Thomas, 21–22
Grierson, John, 109, 116
Griffith, Ernest, 165–66
Gruber, Carol, 260*n*
Gulick, Luther, 110, 113

H
Hall, Stuart, 303*n*
Hand, Learned, 47, 247, 303*n*; Chafee on Hand's *Masses* decision, 47–49, 51–53
Hartzel v. U.S., 221–22, 227, 237–38, 242
Hatch Act, 16
Havighurst, R. G., 87, 94; *see also* Rockefeller Foundation Communication Group
Hayakawa, S. I., 16, 40–46; on propaganda, 41–45; *Language in Action*, 40–41, 264*n*

Columbia Studies in Contemporary American History Series

William E. Leuchtenburg and
Alan Brinkley, General Editors

David L. Anderson, *Trapped By Success: The Eisenhower Administration and Vietnam, 1953–1961* 1991

Steven M. Gillon, *The Democrats' Dilemma: Walter F. Mondale and the Liberal Legacy* 1992

Wyatt C. Wells, *Economist in an Uncertain World: Arthur F. Burns and the Federal Reserve, 1970–1978* 1994

Stuart Svonkin, *Jews Against Prejudice: American Jews and the Fight for Civil Liberties* 1997

Doug Rossinow, *The Politics of Authenticity: Liberalism, Christianity, and the New Left in America* 1998

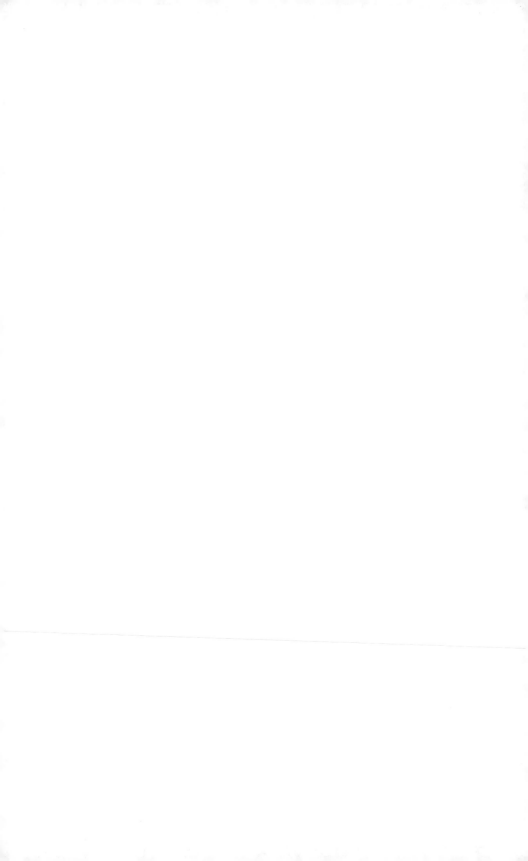